161204

THE COMPLETE ENCYCLOPEDIA OF AUTOMATIC

ARMY RIFLES

THE COMPLETE
ENCYCLOPEDIA OF
AUTOMATIC
ARMY RIFLES

**A comprehensive guide to automatic army rifles
from around the world**

A. E. HARTINK

REBO
PUBLISHERS

© 1999 Rebo International b.v., Lisse, The Netherlands

This 3rd edition reprinted in 2004

Text and photos: A. E. Hartink
Editing, production, and coordination: TextCase, The Netherlands
Design/layout: Signia, The Netherlands
Cover design: Minkowsky Graphics, Enkhuizen, The Netherlands
Typesetting: de Zrij, The Netherlands

ISBN 90 366 1489 9

Contents

Swat team with FN-P90 sub-machine-gun

Introduction

Armed conflicts are as old as mankind. One of the earliest known disputes was that between Cain and Abel, in which an ass's jawbone was used as a weapon. After their nomadic existence as hunters, our forefathers began to concentrate more on animal husbandry, fishing and agriculture. This gave rise to territories, which were at times the cause of clashes with neighboring tribes. At that time, such conflicts were still fought out with clubs and stone axes. Until roughly halfway through the Middle Ages, weaponry consisted of bow and arrow, spear, sling, battle-axe, sword, dagger and halberd.

In the fifteenth century gunpowder was introduced to the West from China. Various theories exist about how this came about. The formula is said to have been brought from China by the famous Venetian merchant Marco Polo. Another theory is that gunpowder was invented by the Franciscan monk Berthold Schwarz from Freiburg. In any event he lent his name to the infernal substance known as black powder ("schwarz" means "black" in German).

Black powder consists of some 75% saltpeter, 15% sulfur and 10% charcoal. When someone discovered in the fourteenth century that it was possible with this powder not only to make beautiful fireworks, but also to shoot heavy projectiles, the seed of firearms development was

A number of swords made by the Czech cutler Pavel Skryja

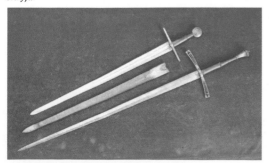

The wheel lock, here combined with a matchlock and flintlock

sown. It was in this century that the various types of hand cannon appeared: a short iron tube, closed at one end and connected to a long wooden pole that served as the stock.

Soon afterwards, the carriage-borne cannon was introduced. After this, technology did not stand still, but the old principles still applies: an iron tube, closed at one end, with a small port left open for the match.

The gunpowder and projectile were loaded into the bottom of the tube through the open end. The gunpowder charge was then ignited, whereupon the projectile, usually in the form of a stone, lead or iron ball, was shot out of the tube. Initially, the gunpowder was ignited by glowing wood chips, but these were later replaced by the slow match.

Good ignition with a match was to a large extent dependent on the weather conditions. When it was raining it was not possible to shoot and the battling armies simply took a break. Furthermore, the glowing end of the match betrayed the shooter's position. Sometimes that could cost him dear, as even in those days there were sharpshooters. A marked improvement was the invention of the wheel-lock. The wheel-lock was a metal wheel with a spiral spring. The spring was wound up with a key and then locked. When the lock was released by pulling a trigger, the metal wheel rotated at high speed under the spring's tension and scraped against a flint. This produced a shower of sparks that was more than sufficient to ignite the fine gunpowder in the flashhole. This technique is also commonly used today – in our cigarette lighters.

As the wheel-lock system was complex and expensive to produce, a simpler, more economical solution was sought. This was the flintlock firing system. A flint was held in the jaws of a kind of hammer. This hammer, called a cock, was fitted to the side of the gun and could be drawn back against the pressure of a spring (cocked) and held in this position (locked). When the trigger was pulled, the flint struck an iron plate located above the flashhole. Beneath the flashhole was a small pan containing finely crushed gunpowder. The sparks thus produced were directed into the flashpan.

The resulting flash passed through the flashhole and ignited the main charge behind the projectile. The development of the flintlock took several hundred years and gave rise to different variations. One variation was the snaphaunce lock. This system actually consisted of two hammers. The first had a kind of vice, in which a piece of flint was held. This hammer was cocked against the tension of a hammer spring.

A second hammer, consisting of a kind of anvil, was fitted immediately above the touchhole. When the trigger was pulled the hammer and flint struck this striking plate producing a spark that was directed into the flashhole. This ignited the fine powder in the flashpan and hence fired the main charge in the barrel. Another sensational

A weapon with the flint system

The percussion system with its funnel

development in this area was the true flintlock. Since the snaphaunce was rather weather-sensitive, a cover was devised to shield the flashpan. The vertical section of this cover also served as striking plate for the flint.

A real revolution was the invention of the percussion cap. In 1799, the English chemist Howard developed fulminate of mercury and in 1807 the Scottish minister Alexander Forsyth from Belhelvie in Aberdeenshire was granted a patent for the percussion cap. Fulminate could be detonated by a sharp blow and from here it was not such a big step to the development of the percussion cap, which is fulminate in a soft-metal container. The problem of naked flame for ignition therefore became a thing of the past.

Firearms at this time were still based on the old principles: an iron tube closed at one end. The barrel chamber, into which the powder was inserted, still had to be loaded with powder and ball via the muzzle, but the percussion cap was now placed on a hollow nipple connected to the chamber formed by the rear end of the barrel.

This nipple was called a funnel. To enable the percussion cap to be given a sharp blow, a striker mechanism was designed, based on the cock shape of the flintlock. This was fitted immediately behind or alongside the barrel chamber. This hammer, or cock, was rocked back against a spring's tension and locked. When the trigger was pulled, this lock was released. The cock then struck a percussion cap with force, detonating the explosive charge in the cap. This produced a flash through the flash channel in the funnel, igniting a powder charge in the chamber. This system was long used in rifles, pistols and later also in the more modern 5 or 6-round black-powder revolvers. In the late eighteenth and early nineteenth century, the bullet was developed.

At this time too, rifled barrels appeared with grooves and lands to impart a spin and thereby more stable trajectory on the bullet, creating greater accuracy and predicability.

The next important step was the development of a cartridge. Initially with a wrapping of paper or cardboard and later of brass, the components (projectile, gunpowder, percussion cap and case) were combined to form a single unit. These cartridges, however, were no longer loaded through the muzzle, but had to be inserted into the barrel chamber via the breech. This meant that the breech of the chamber had to be capable of being opened so that the weapon could be loaded. After the cartridge was placed in position, the barrel had to be capable of being tightly closed again. This system is nowadays called the breech lock.

Variations in ammunition development are the rimfire cartridge and the pinfire system. In the rimfire cartridge, the primer charge, the detonator powder, is not located in a brass cup, but is poured inside the rim of the cartridge case itself. This rimfire ammunition is still very popular for smallbore weapons.

The pinfire cartridge also has the primer charge inside the case and is detonated by the blow of the hammer on a protruding pin at the rear of the cartridge case. The popularity of this system soon declined.

Percussion military rifle (Hege)

Remington rimfire cartridge

The third important step in arms development was the invention of the chemical compound nitrocellulose. This enabled far higher development and pressure of gas. This enabled some of the gas pressure to be used to open the breech block automatically.

This gave rise to development of semi-automatic weapons such as pistols, sub-machine-guns, rifles and carbines. While the basic principle of chamber, gunpowder, bullet, gunpowder ignition and barrel remain unchanged, there have been major developments in terms of the weapons and the ammunition used and these developments are ongoing. Examples include electronic ignition and caseless cartridges. In the early years of firearms a great deal of time was needed to prepare a weapon for firing and conditions needed to be dry and preferably calm to permit the gunpowder to be ignited.

Accuracy was often more a question of luck than judgment. Nowadays firearms are made with rates of fire in excess of 600 rounds per minute that can be used in all weather with a high degree of accuracy and reliability. Cartridge magazines can be changed in fractions of a second. The modern combatant is issued with hands-free communications equipment consisting of a helmet microphone and ear-piece. The members of a platoon are thus constantly in contact with each other.

Developments

Austrian armaments maker Steyr heralded a new era with a modern weapon concept in 1975 when they introduced the Steyr Armee Universal Gewehr (AUG). In 1977, this weapon was introduced as the Austrian army's standard weapon. The futuristic AUG, in 5.56 x 45 mm NATO (.223 Rem.) caliber, is largely made of synthetic material. Besides the rifle version, this modular firearm can also be fitted out as a sub-machine-gun and light machine gun. In addition to the Austrian armed forces those of Australia, Ireland, Morocco, New Zealand and Saudi Arabia also use this weapon.

The FN machine gun/carbine with the Five-Seven pistol, both 5.7 x 28 mm caliber ammo

Another modern weapon system is the FN-P90. Belgium's FN-Herstal factory opted for a combination of sub-machine-gun and carbine in one, in the newly developed 5.7 x 28 mm caliber. An interesting fact is that this line of firearms is supplemented by the Five-Seven pistol in the same caliber. The market for military rifles has long been dominated by the Colt M16 and related models and licensed versions. In 1982, the US Army Material Command (AMCOM) began preparations for a new military rifle for the twenty-first century. This weapon was eventually meant to replace the current M16. This Advanced Combat Rifle (ACR) project is being supervised by the Joint Services Small Arms Program (JSSAP) department. The basic principle is to bring about a considerable improvement in the common soldier's effectiveness. A number of manufacturers have been invited to develop

The present American M16A2 military rifle (archive of R.H.G. Koster)

several weapons and matching ammunition and these are to be comprehensively tested and compared. These weapons are still largely prototypes.

AAI ACR

The ACR, made by the American AAI Corporation, bears the closest resemblance to the present M16 rifle. It is gas-operated and shoots a special steel arrow projectile in a .223 Remington caliber cartridge. The rifle is fitted with both the standard sighting devices and an optical 4:1 Arsmon scope.

The AAI ACR during field tests (archive of R.H.G. Koster)

The Advanced Combat Rifle (ACR) from AAI Corp. (archive of R.H.G. Koster)

The Colt ACR with Elcan scope (archive of R.H.G. Koster)

Colt ACR

The Colt ACR is derived from the Colt M16 models. It is gas-operated and also has a rotating bolt head. In spite of the modern trend towards 3-round bursts, the Colt shoots semi- and fully automatically, though this could change.

The Colt ACR (archive of R.H.G. Koster)

The ammunition selected by Colt is the .223 Remington standard caliber, but with a duplex bullet. This means that not one, but two bullets are located in the cartridge case. Every target struck thus takes two hits. The rifle is fitted as standard with the well-known Elcan 3.5:1 scope.

Heckler & Koch ACR

The ACR, made by Heckler & Koch, of Germany, is derived from an earlier design, the G11.

The Heckler & Koch ACR, based on the HK G11 (archive of R.H.G. Koster)

The Heckler & Koch ACR, based on the HK G11 (archive of R.H.G. Koster)

The ACR from the Austrian firm of Steyr (archive of R.H.G. Koster)

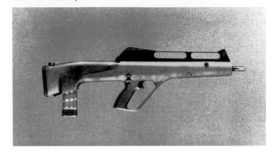

The Heckler & Koch ACR at the ready (archive of R.H.G. Koster)

The cartridge is caseless. This means that the bullet is packed in a solid compressed block of nitrocellulose. This cartridge is derived from the G11: 4.7 mm. The Americans use the caliber designation 4.92 mm, but this is purely a question of measurement: 4.7 mm is the outside diameter of the bullet and 4.92 mm is the diameter between the grooves in the bore. An interesting feature is that the scope has two different positions: 1:1 for close range and 3.5:1 for ranges of up to 300 meters (984 ft).

Steyr ACR

Although the Steyr AUG rifle already looks futuristic in comparison to other models, the company nevertheless wanted to develop a special weapon for the ACR program. On the Steyr ACR, a steel arrow cartridge was also opted for, but in a composite cartridge case. The rifle has a scope with two positions: 1.5:1 for close range and 3.5:1 for distance. The ACRs are still at the research stage and no decision

is expected before the year 2000. It is evident, however, that other NATO countries will not stay behind if the US armed forces decide to purchase the ACR.

Future developments

Another imminent development is the SDA program. The Soldier Digital Assistant (SDA) consists of a palmtop computer with a touch-operated screen. The software will include the Global Positioning System (GPS), which employs satellites to determine the user's own position very accurately on a digital map of the area in which he is operating. Many other positions, such as those of platoon members and vehicles, can also be shown on the screen.

In addition, the SDA can be used to request and direct aerial or artillery support. Digitalization is now also used in the field of sighting systems. Laser sighting devices are almost out-of-date nowadays. In the near future, the soldier will have a

The futuristic ACR Bullpup from Steyr (archive of R.H.G. Koster)

mini-screen in front of one eye, into which the gun sight is projected. The image will be automatically adapted to take account of poor visibility or darkness. The soldier of the future may no longer even have to aim his rifle. Once he has a target in his eye-screen, a sign for "friend or foe" will be generated automatically and then all he has to do is pull the trigger, press a button or simply think the word "fire" to give a mental command.

Arms technology

Before discussing the technical details of the firearms to be dealt with in this book, I will first give a general introduction to arms technology. This is useful for those readers who are not so familiar with this subject or who would like to refresh their knowledge.

It is also important for an understanding of the technical explanations accompanying the weapons. In order to appreciate a firearm as a piece of technology, you must first understand how it works. The various parts must also be called by their correct names, to avoid a Babel-like confusion.

For example, misunderstandings can arise when modern and obsolete terms are used. This is the case when the term magazine is used. A magazine is a removable holder into which cartridges are inserted. A blind magazine is a fixed internal storage space for cartridges. However, you needn't be afraid of being swamped beneath mounds of technical details about the workings of numerous catches, pins, springs and other bits and pieces. These fall outside the scope of this book and belong more in a manual for trained gunsmiths.

The names of the weapons discussed in this book are general terms. Presumably everyone knows roughly what a sub-machine-gun is. And yet it is difficult to give a concise definition of one. The same applies to the terms rifle and carbine. What exactly is the difference? In this section I have tried to give as clear a

Sig SG 551-1P military rifle

description as possible. These descriptions are not exhaustive, since modern firearms are sometimes a combination of two different types. The FN P90, for instance, is a sub-machine-gun, but can also be used as a carbine.

And the situation is even more complex as regards the weapons from ITM. How are you supposed to classify a firearm that looks like a sub-machine-gun, but has two barrels, one of which actually shoots rifle cartridges?

Rifle

A rifle is typically a shoulder-fired weapon. It has a rifled barrel, i.e. one with grooves and lands, so as to impart to the bullet rotation about its longitudinal axis and make for a stable trajectory. A rifle is normally more than 100 cm (39.4 ") long, though not always.

Rifles are often classified by locking system and/or repeating system. Thus, there are bolt-action rifles, hinged-barrel rifles, pump-action repeating rifles, semi-automatic and fully automatic rifles. Modern military rifles sometimes belong to a "weapon family". This means that one type of weapon is designed as a sub-machine-gun, carbine, rifle and light machine gun.

All versions shoot semi-automatically, often also with a three-shoot burst and automatically.

Ruger Mini-14/20 GB Government carbine

is often used in a carbine, but there are also carbines in pistol and revolver calibers. A carbine in a rifle caliber is usually a shortened version of a large rifle in the same caliber. This is often a very irritating gun to shoot, since the greater inertia (weight) of the big brother is lacking.

Anyone who has ever fired a "Juliana-Mauser", 8 x 57 mm caliber, or the Lee Enfield No. 5 "jungle carbine" in .303 British, will know exactly what I mean.

More modern carbines using .223 Remington caliber ammunition do not have this drawback.

Carbine

A carbine is actually a short, lightweight rifle with a barrel length of up to 56 cm (22"). The total length is less than 100 cm (39.4"). It is normally fired from the shoulder.

A carbine may have the following firing systems: bolt-action, semi-automatic and/or fully automatic. Rifle ammunition

Machine-gun

A machine-gun can best be described as an overgrown rifle. The weapon normally has a folding bipod. The majority of machine guns can be fitted with a magazine, a cartridge drum or a cartridge belt. Many machine guns shoot only automatically, but there are types which can also

FN Minimi (M249 SAW) machine-gun

fire a three-round burst and semi-auto-matically. Machine guns can be classified as heavy machine guns, such as those for use on a vehicle, ship or aircraft or in a fixed position on a tripod. A second type is the "light" machine gun, which is easier to handle.

Sub-machine-gun

This is a short firearm that can be fired semi-automatically or fully automatic from the hip or shoulder.
The weapon normally shoots pistol cartridges. When the weapon is being loaded and cocked, the bolt may remain in the rear position (open system) or be locked against the chamber of the barrel (closed system).
With the open system, when the trigger is pressed, the bolt lock is released and spring tension forces the bolt forward. This type often has a fixed firing pin. With the closed system, the trigger unlocks the hammer via a sear. The hammer strikes the rear of the firing pin, which in turn hits the primer in the bottom of the cartridge case.

Riot gun

A riot gun is a short shotgun, normally with a single barrel. Riot guns can be hinged-barrel, pump-action, semi-auto-matic or occasionally may even shoot automatically. Buckshot or a single lead slug is generally used as ammunition and

Uzi sub-machine-gun

Mossberg 500 USA Mil-Specs military riot gun

most riot guns have a smooth bore, although some rifled barrel riot guns also exist for firing single projectiles, called slugs.
They are used because of their tremendous hitting power and reasonable accuracy up to a range of about 100-150 meters (328–984 ft).

Sniper rifle

The name tells us at once what the purpose of this rifle is. It is for eliminating an enemy target at long range and with great preci-sion.
This objective places great demands on the technology. Such a weapon is thus usually fitted with a special barrel, a special receiver and bolt. Sniper rifles come in a variety of forms: as a bolt-action rifle, but also semi-automatic.
A sniper rifle is often designed for shooting rifle cartridges, but sometimes for .50 BMG caliber ammo, the cartridge used in the Browning machine-gun. These heavy sniper rifles have been specially developed for ranges of between 1000 and 2000 and they shoot with incredible accuracy. A sniper rifle is always fitted with a special military scope, often with a range finding system.

Mauser SR 97 sniper rifle

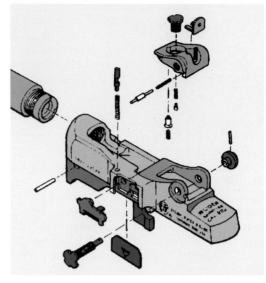

Component groups

A firearm consists of a number of component groups. The type and number of component groups depend to some extent on the type and system of the weapon. Examples of such component groups are:

a. receiver or the mechanism housing;
b. bolt or breechblock;
c. trigger system or firing system;
d. barrel and cartridge chamber;
e. sight or scope;
f. stock;
g. magazine.

THE RECEIVER

The receiver is the housing for the bolt of a rifle. The barrel is attached to this receiver.
The bolt can be moved backwards and forwards in the receiver to provide the rifle's repeating action. In the forward position, the bolt closes off the barrel chamber. Fixed to the underside of the receiver is the trigger group. In multi-

round weapons, space is left at the bottom of the receiver for the blind magazine or the removable magazine. The safety catch, the magazine catch and the bolt catch are also normally fitted in or on the receiver, but more about these later. The term receiver is often used with reference to bolt-action rifles, but there are also semi-automatic and fully automatic weapons that have a receiver, such as the Ruger Mini-14.
The difference between a receiver and a receiver housing can clearly be seen in the figures.

THE RECEIVER HOUSING

For many automatic and semi-automatic weapons, the term receiver housing is used instead of receiver. Housed in the closed section of the receiver housing is the repeating system, along with the trigger group and the magazine.

Manufacturing stages of a Zoli breech

Receiver housing of the Sig SG 551 rifle

A receiver housing is often made of stamped sheet-steel parts. The receiver housing accommodates all vital components of the repeating and firing mechanism, such as the trigger group, the bolt, the safety catch and the magazine catch. However, a receiver housing does not necessarily need to be made of steel parts. The following is an example of a synthetic housing for the entire weapon system: the Steyr AUG assault rifle.

Numerous control buttons or catches can be housed in the receiver housing, such as the bolt catch. This catch enables the bolt to be locked in its rearmost position. This can be useful, for instance, for inspecting the cartridge chamber.

In some cases this occurs automatically as soon as the last cartridge has been fired from the magazine. The bolt is then held in the rearmost position. When a full magazine is inserted into the weapon and the bolt catch is pressed, the bolt moves forward and at the same time pushes a fresh cartridge out of the magazine and into the barrel chamber.

A similar system is also found in riot guns. The purpose of this is often to lock the bolt so that an extra cartridge can be inserted by hand, for example of a different shot or slug type.

The receiver housing also accommodates a catch for removing the magazine. The magazine catch of the Colt AR-15 is shown on page 18. The serrated edge of the bolt rod for the "forward assist" is indicated by a red arrow.

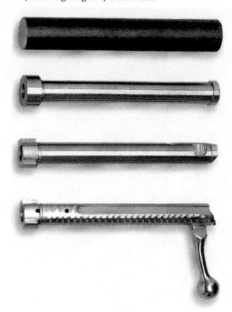

Magazine catch on the Colt AR-15 and M16 models

THE RECEIVER

A receiver or frame is the housing of a shotgun or hinged-barrel rifle. It contains not only the trigger group and sometimes the cartridge feeding system, but also the hinge that allows the barrel or barrels to be opened and closed.

THE BOLT OR BREECHBLOCK

On bolt-action rifles, we speak of a bolt.

This is a solid block of steel whose purpose is to close and lock the cartridge chamber in the barrel. To load the rifle, a cartridge is pushed into the barrel chamber by the bolt. The bolt is then rotated through a certain angle by a bolt lever attached to it.

To this end, a number of lugs on the bolt engage with corresponding recesses in the receiver. The figure shows the case extractor in red.

The spent-case ejector, here in the form of a spring-loaded catch in the bolt face, is shown in purple. The cartridge is now enclosed in the barrel chamber and the system is safely locked. The firing pin, which is cocked during the locking action, is also housed in the bolt. When the trig-

Bolt lever of the CZ 700 sniper rifle

Receiver of the H & R hinged-barrel survival rifle

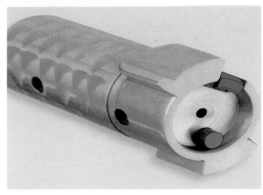

ger is pulled, the firing pin is released. The pressure exerted by the firing pin spring propels the firing pin forward against the primer in the bottom of the cartridge case. The cartridge is then fired.

The following illustration of a section of the Zoli AZ-1900 bolt-action rifle shows: 1. safety catch; 2. firing pin; 3. extractor; 4. barrel chamber; 5. bolt lugs; 6. magazine release catch; 7. firing mechanism. When the bullet has left the bore, the bolt with the bolt lever are rotated by one turn and can then be pulled back. Since the extrac-

tor is also located at the front of the bolt, the empty cartridge case is drawn out of the barrel chamber and ejected. In front of the bolt or breech block are the bolt lugs, the firing pin hole, the extractor and sometimes also the (spring-loaded) ejector, which ejects the spent case. The number of lugs on a bolt varies according to make and type.

The breech block, also a kind of bolt, may be operated by the recoil reaction of the shot or by gas pressure. After the cartridge in the barrel chamber has been fired, the bullet is driven by the gas pressure through the bore to the muzzle. Somewhere in the bore, often halfway along, there is a small gas vent.

As long as the bullet is moving along the bore, a small proportion of the gas pressure is drawn off. This gas pressure is directed into a small cylinder above or below the barrel. This cylinder contains a piston, which drives a piston rod, and this in turn is connected to the breech block or gives it a sharp blow.

This forces the breech block back and unlocks the system. The breech block thus has the same characteristics as the bolt,

Exploded model of a Zoli bolt-action rifle

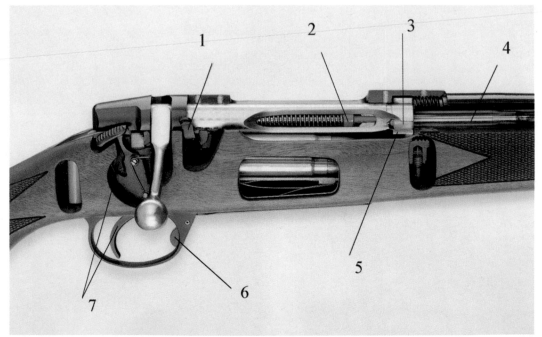

including bolt lugs, firing pin and extractor. The breech block on the Ruger Mini-14 is shown below. The bolt lugs are yellow. The spent case is removed from the chamber by the extractor and ejected from the weapon by a certain type of ejector; sometimes through the open top of the receiver, as on the Winchester .30-M1 carbine, for instance.

With a closed receiver housing, this ejection process is normally carried out via an ejection port cover, as in the AR-15/M16 system. An ejection port cover on the Bushmaster XM15-E2S is shown below.
The backwards motion of the bolt carrier compresses a bolt spring.
As soon as the bolt carrier is halted in the rearmost position, the pressure of the bolt spring forces it forward again. As it moves

forward, it strips a new cartridge from the magazine and pushes it into the barrel chamber. During the repeating action, the firing pin is again cocked. If the trigger is then pulled, the cartridge will be fired and the cycle is repeated.

A breech block is also provided with lugs. Semi-automatic and fully automatic weapons often have a rotating bolt locking system. This means that the bolt carrier runs backwards and forwards along a guide rail and that the attached bolt head is able to turn by a certain amount. As a result of this rotating motion, the bolt lugs

Ejection port cover on the Bushmaster XM15-E2S

Ruger Mini-14 breechblock: 1. ejector with spring; 2. extractor; 3. extractor pin with spring; 4. breechblock; 5. firing pin

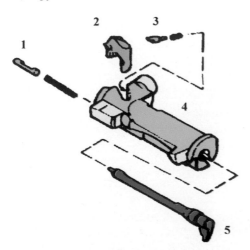

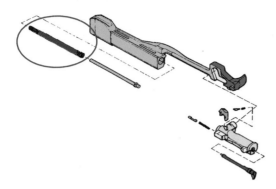

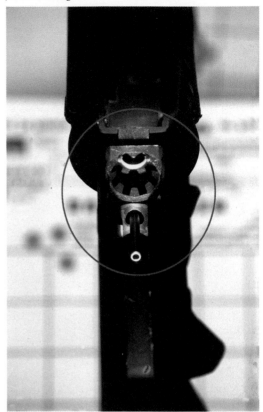

on the bolt head engage in corresponding recesses in the rear of the barrel chamber or in the receiver housing itself. The locking action is thus complete.

Some weapons make use of a different system, for example with a vertically sliding block. With this system, there is a locking block that runs along a guide rail above or below the receiver. When it is in the forward position, the locking block falls into a recess, thus locking the mechanism.

After the shot, an unlocking pin, connected in some way to the piston rod, depending on the system used, presses against the vertically sliding block and pushes it back into the breech block. The system is thus unlocked and the locking block is free to move back. On some military weapons, like the Colt M16 and types derived from it, the bolt carrier can be given additional forward assistance. The receiver housing is fitted with an "accelerator button".

Breechblock on the Benelli riot gun

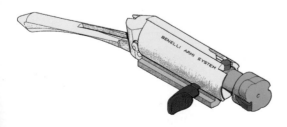

If the bolt carrier sticks in its forward position, this button can be used to give it an extra blow. The main reason for a rifle failing to lock is accumulation of dirt. The forward assist button arose out of experience of Vietnam where it proved to be a dire necessity. Unlike a bolt, the breech block is not operated by a bolt lever, but by a cocking lever for the initial loading of the weapon.

After that, the repeating cycle takes place automatically. Depending on the make and type of weapon, a cocking lever may come in various forms. A fine example is the cocking handle on the Steyr AUG rifle. Another example is the double-sided cocking lever on the CZ Skorpion sub-machine-gun.

On the Colt M16/AR-15 and related models, the cocking lever is on the rear of the receiver housing, below the carrying handle. In some cases an entire block is

Forward assist button on a Bushmaster rifle

Cocking lever on the CZ Skorpion sub-machine-gun

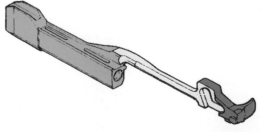

T-shaped cocking lever of a DPMS AR-15 rifle type

attached to the cocking lever; this block also serves as a kind of inertia mechanism of the locking system. Due to its weight, the block starts off relatively slowly, only after the bullet has left the bore. The short piston in the gas pressure cylinder strikes this block, thus propelling it backwards.

The drawing shows a cocking lever and block of this kind on the Ruger Mini-14. A similar system is found on the Winchester .30-M1 carbine, as well as on many other rifles and carbines.

Cocking lever on the Steyr AUG

Ruger Mini-14 cocking lever

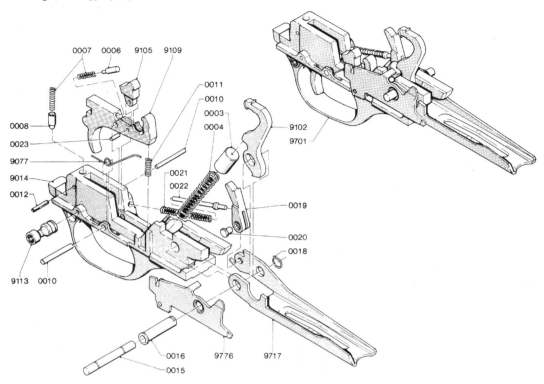

THE TRIGGER SYSTEM OR FIRING SYSTEM

The trigger group is attached to the receiver or fitted inside the receiver housing. It consists of the trigger itself, of course, but also of numerous catches, pins and springs.

I won't tire you with the names of all these parts. Broadly speaking, the firing process works as follows, starting with pulling the trigger on a cocked system. The trigger has a release lug, inside which there is a sear. The sear forms the connection between the trigger and the hammer, or cock. Such an intermediate connection would appear to be superfluous, but for example it reduces the pressure resistance of the trigger.

As soon as the trigger moves backwards, the sear is released by the trigger and disengages the lock of the cocked hammer. The hammer then moves forward and strikes the back of the firing pin. The firing pin passes through the firing pin channel in the breech block or bolt and hits the back of the primer in the bottom

Exploded view of the Ruger Mini-14 trigger group

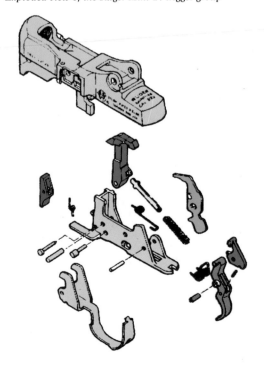

of the cartridge in the barrel chamber, which is then fired. The trigger group normally also houses the safety catch. Various locking systems, discussed below, are used to render a weapon safe.

THE BARREL AND THE CARTRIDGE CHAMBER

The barrel of a weapon normally consists of a round steel tube, but some older types of rifle may have an octagonal barrel. Modern rifle barrels, particularly those on sniper rifles, may have fluting. These flutes in the longitudinal direction of the barrel at least double the surface area of the bore and hence its cooling capacity. When the barrel heats up due to firing, air turbulence occurs above it.

Where a scope is used, this obscures the image. Besides the fluted barrel, a mirage band is sometimes used on sniper rifles to eliminate this effect.

This is a canvas band stretched between the gunsight and the muzzle which diverts the heat turbulence around the sight's field of vision. Another method of counteracting the heat haze above the barrel is the so-called bull barrel, an extra thick barrel. This barrel is also very rigid, which enhances accuracy. Competition rifles are often fitted with a thick barrel of this type. When a bullet is forced along the grooves

Barrel with fluting on the CZ 700 sniper rifle

Bushmaster: cross section of the barrel, with barrel chamber and bolt carrier

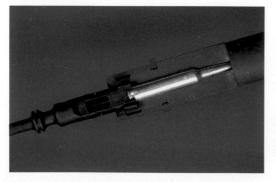

Sig SG 550 sniper with mirage band

and lands of the bore, the same phenomenon in fact occurs as when a hard blockage is pushed through a plastic garden hose: you can see the bump move through it.

In a rifle barrel, of course, this process goes somewhat faster, causing vibrations in the material. To combat this effect, competition barrels often have an extra thick construction. A disadvantage of this for military weapons is that the weapon is much heavier.

The inside of the barrel has spiral grooves, called grooves and lands. The purpose of these grooves and lands is to make the bullet spin about its longitudinal axis during the passage through the barrel. The bullet is forced along the grooves and lands by the gas pressure. The speed of this rotation is affected by the length and

Bull barrel of a DPMS rifle

sharpness of these spiral grooves. This rotation is known as "twist". A twist of 305 mm (12"), for example, means that the grooves and lands make an entire revolution of 360 degrees over a distance of 305 mm. To make the bullet spin properly, its outside diameter is slightly larger than the inside diameter between the lands.

The bullet is thus forced along the deeper grooves and the lands cut through the soft outer jacket of the bullet. This causes the spin. Anyone who has ever held a spent bullet in his hand will undoubtedly have noticed the oblique longitudinal scratches on it.

This spin is necessary to give the bullet greater stability in its trajectory. Otherwise, it might wobble and twirl due to the air resistance, causing a reduction in accuracy. The chamber is the first part of the barrel in which the cartridge to be fired is housed.

Its wall, called the chamber wall, is thicker than the eventual barrel wall. The reason for this is that when the cartridge is detonated a high gas pressure and high temperature are produced. This gas pressure may even reach very high levels, as much as 4000 bar. If the wall of the cartridge chamber were too thin, it could even burst or crack.

The internal shape of the barrel chamber also ensures that the cartridge is correctly positioned. It must be properly enclosed inside the chamber so that it cannot move too far along the bore. Otherwise the point of the firing pin would be unable to reach the primer.

The barrel is screwed into the receiver or receiver housing. This entire metal unit is enclosed in the stock. This fitting process is no simple matter. Many precision sniper rifles, and sometimes military rifles too, have a so-called free floating barrel. The receiver or receiver housing and the barrel chamber are connected rigidly to the stock, but the barrel itself is completely free.

When the shot is fired, i.e. while the bullet is moving through the bore, a high degree of vibration is produced. The barrel vibrates strongly because the bullet is being forced through the grooves and lands. It was found with competition rifles that the precision of the bullet was favorably affected if the barrel was not in contact with the stock. This is why the barrel, especially on sniper rifles, is often completely free. On most military rifles an attachment is mounted at the muzzle. This

Cross-section through barrel showing chamber of a Bushmaster rifle.

Free floating barrel on a Mauser sniper rifle

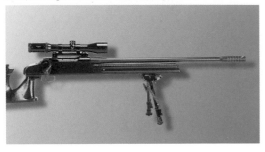

Another example of a muzzle damper on a Harris sniper rifle

attachment may have a variety of functions, but it is often a flash suppresser, by means of which the extent of the muzzle flash from the fired cartridge is reduced. This makes it harder for the shooter's position to be pinpointed and also improves his sight image, especially in the dark.

Flash suppresser on a DMPS rifle

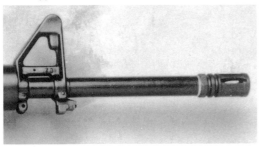

Another application is the muzzle damper. With heavier calibers in particular, the recoil force is sometimes so fierce that it can cause problems for the shooter. The muzzle damper utilizes some of the gas

Muzzle damper on a Harris .50 BMG sniper rifle

pressure to reduce the recoil action before the bullet flies out of the muzzle. An intermediate form of flash suppresser and muzzle damper is the compensator system.
In the final section of the barrel, just before the muzzle, a number of holes are

drilled. These holes are of a particular shape and bore direction. This is where the gas pressure escapes just before the bullet exits the barrel at a point where gas pressure is still high.
A fairly new system that is surprisingly little used on sniper rifles, is the Winchester Boss system. Its purpose is to increase accuracy and it works as follows. While

Muzzle with compensator holes on a Remington

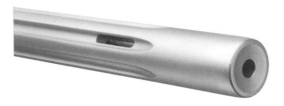

the bullet moves through the barrel it produces considerable vibration. This is inevitable because the bullet is forced trough grooves and lands at tremendous speed and force.
This vibration ceases only when the bullet leaves the muzzle. When the bullet reaches the muzzle, the vibration is at its greatest and a certain deviation is therefore imparted to the bullet, since vibration is not always exactly the same for every shot.
Long-range rifles therefore often have very thick, heavy barrels to reduce the effects of vibration. With the Winchester-Boss system the development of this vibration

Winchester Browning Boss compensation system

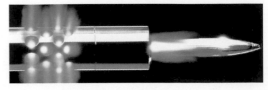

can be modified. It is not the amplitude of the vibration that is altered but its frequency. This Boss system also acts as a muzzle damper, reducing recoil force by about 30 to 50 percent. In 1996, Winchester brought out the new Boss-CR system which has a similar action to the standard Boss but without muzzle-dampening holes.

On many military rifles and carbines, the barrel is fitted with a bayonet stud. Modern weapons often have a bayonet with a barrel ring at the bayonet guard, which can be slid over the round barrel. The rear of the bayonet then fits into a locking lug on the barrel.

The repeating action of many fully and semi-automatic weapons operated by gas pressure. Some of the gas pressure is diverted through a small port in the barrel while the bullet is still being forced through the barrel. This pressure is directed via a gas vent to a small pressure cylinder with a piston.

This piston is forced out of the cylinder by pressure of gas, delivering a sharp blow to

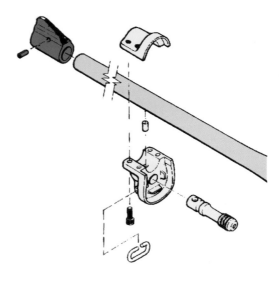

Drawing of the Ruger Mini-14 gas block

CZ 700 sniper with silenced barrel

Bayonet stud of the CZ 2000 military rifle

the piston rod. This blow is transmitted to the repeating system, setting the reloading cycle in motion. This system is dealt with in greater detail below.

Various accessories, such as the silencer, are available for specific applications of different military weapons. Situations are conceivable in which certain targets have to be eliminated.

Often, the surrounding area in which the operation takes place must not be alarmed. For this reason, some sniper rifles are fitted with a silencer. The same applies for sub-machine-guns. It goes without saying that for operations of this kind special ammunition must also be

used. The bullet used as standard ammunition travels at a velocity greater than the speed of sound (330 meters per second/1082 ft per second). The resulting sonic "boom" would negate the effect of the silencer. These special cartridges are normally termed subsonic ammunition.

HK MP5-SD sub-machine-gun with silencer

The gunsight and the scope

Sighting devices are fitted on the barrel and normally on the receiver or receiver housing. The rear gunsight on the receiver housing or receiver is often a device that is adjustable both for elevation and for windage. Military rifles normally have a sight that extends from 100 to 600 or more meters (328 ft to 656 yd or more) and can be adjusted in intervals of 50 or 100 meters (164 or 328 ft). There are various standard sights that are found on the majority of weapon models.

Tangent rear sight
The tangent rear sight is one of the most common types. The range of the sight shown here on the CZ 2000 military rifle is adjustable in intervals of 100 meters (328 ft).

Aperture sight
Aperture sights are also used a great deal. With this system, a rotatable ring is mounted on the receiver housing or receiver. In this ring there are a number of apertures at various heights. By rotating the ring, the range can be set to 100, 200 or more meters (328, 656 ft or more).

Carrying handle sight
Another type of aperture sight can be found on the Colt M16 type rifle. In this

Slide sight with protective hoods on the CZ 2000 rifle

Detail of the tangent rear sight

version, the sight is held in the carrying handle on top of the receiver housing. This type of sight is also adjustable both for elevation and for windage.

Ghostring
On riot guns, a different type of sight is often used, in combination with a special front sight on the barrel. A good example of this is the so-called ghost ring, which gives a good sight field of vision and yet at the same time a reasonable terrain overview. The figure shows the Benelli ghost ring sight.

Track-lock sight
Another example is the track-lock aperture sight with which Scatter-gun riot guns are fitted.
Two tritium points are attached on either side of the aperture as low-visibility markings. The same kind of point is located on the front sight and as long as these three points are in line in the sight field of vision during twilight or darkness, everything is fine. The bead is at the front of the barrel,

Heckler & Koch aperture sight

the ring bead. This type of model is used on most Heckler & Koch and SIG weapons. A steel ring is fitted around the actual front sight as protection. Such a ring also helps to improve the sight field of vision.

There's so much to say about the scope and the special mountings for it on the

Front sight of the Benelli M3 Super 90

usually close to the muzzle, though not necessarily so. You see as an example the front sight of the CZ 2000 military rifle. The actual bead is in fact barely visible, since it is protected on either side by two wings.

Another example is the front sight of the Benelli M3 Super 90 riot gun. In this case, the front sight is mounted on a low bead directly on the barrel. A typical front sight with a high bead mount is the Colt M16 type, shown here on an AR-15 rifle made by DPMS. A completely different type is

Benelli Ghostring sight for riot guns

Front sight of an AR-15 type rifle made by DPMS

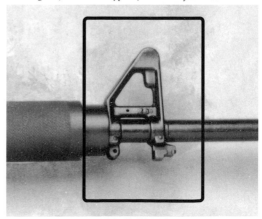

special sniper's scope, the Dakota Long-bow with a Leupold Mark 4 Ultra M-1 16 x 42 scope, is shown.

THE STOCK

Stocks come in many types, sizes and materials. The greatest variety of stocks is to be found in sporting guns, but there's plenty of choice in military weapons, too. There are a number of standard types that are used not only for rifles, but also for sub-machine-guns and riot guns. The caliber of the type of weapon thus makes little difference.

weapon that this subject will be dealt with separately. As an example of a scope with a special Picatinny mounting rail, a very

The most common type of stock is the fixed stock, with or without a separate pistol grip. On military weapons, the stock is often made of wood. This is a rigid and durable material which, when treated correctly, requires little maintenance.

Dakota Longbow sniper rifle with Picatinny mounting rail

Wooden stock of the Ruger Mini-14/20 GB Government carbine

Synthetic stock on the M24-A1 sniper rifle made by Arms Technology

In the past, wood was almost always used. The stocks on sniper rifles are usually made of synthetic material or wood. Shown below is a fine example of the CZ 700 sniper rifle.

The stock is made of laminated wood, a kind of multiply. The advantages of laminated wood are the material's relatively low weight and rigidity, and freedom from the "working" of natural timber. Many modern weapons have a synthetic stock. Synthetics are durable and have the added advantage of being maintenance-free. The stock shown at top right belongs to the Arms Technology M24 sniper rifle. It has an adjustable and extending butt plate. Most sniper rifles made by the American firm of Robar are fitted with a synthetic stock, available in a variety of camouflage colors.

In addition, a hollow synthetic stock can accommodate a variety of accessories. For example, Scatter-gun and Mossberg have even fitted some riot gun models with a so-called speed-lock stock containing an additional magazine for cartridges. The latest sniper rifle from Erma, the SR-100,

Synthetic camouflaged sniper stock made by Robar

has a fully adjustable stock with a special thumb hole in it. This strengthens the shooter's grip on the weapon. A number of sniper models from Mauser are fitted with a skeleton stock. In addition to wood and/or synthetic material, aluminum is used in this rifle.

In addition to wood, synthetic material is also often used for stocks on riot guns. Here you see a stock for the Benelli riot gun. It is made of synthetic material and has a separate pistol grip. A completely

CZ 700 sniper stock

Stock with Speed-lock system on a Mossberg riot gun

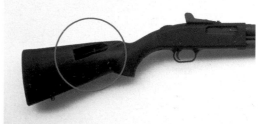

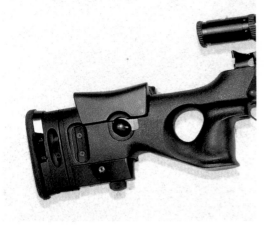

Mauser sniper stock

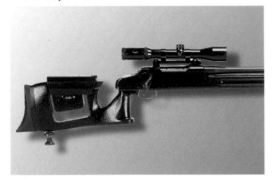

rifle. The modern tendency in military stocks is the folding stock. This makes the weapon considerably smaller, which is useful for paratroopers and vehicle crew. It is sometimes claimed that this type of stock is not so strong. Here you see an example of a synthetic folding stock for the Harris M93 sniper, using the super-heavy .50 BMG caliber ammo.

Besides synthetic material, steel or steel tubing is also frequently used for folding stocks. The Benelli M-3T Super 90 Combat riot gun has a tubular steel frame as the folding stock and a separate synthetic pistol grip. The CZ 2000 weapon family too is fitted with a folding stock consisting of a tubular steel frame. The same applies to the Ruger Mini-14 with a tubular steel folding frame.

The interesting thing about this weapon is that Ruger have made the stock from a single tube. The stock folds sideways. Moreover, the steel butt plate itself can

different concept is the "bullpup" rifle. The stock forms as it were a combination with the receiver housing. Various makes have a system of this kind, but one of the nicest examples is the stock of the Steyr AUG

Stock on a Benelli M-3T Super 90 Combat riot gun

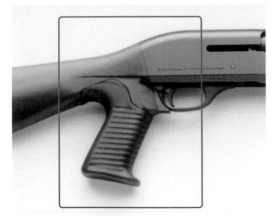

Folding stock on the Harris M93 .50 BMG sniper

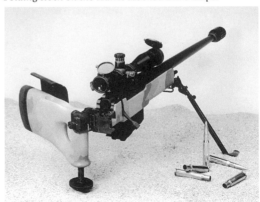

Forward hinged stock on the CZ Skorpion

Tubular frame on the Benelli M-3T Super 90 Combat

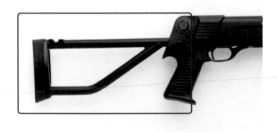

CZ 2000 folding stock

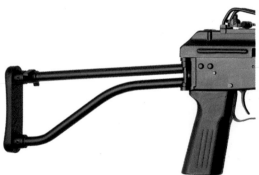

Steel folding stock on the Ruger Mini-14

also be folded. Apart from folding stocks that can hinge sideways, there are also models in which the stock folds away along the bottom or top. This is the "forward hinged stock", as found on the CZ Skorpion sub-machine-gun. Another example is the foldable stock on the Uzi sub-machine-gun.

This ingenious steel stock can be collapsed and folded away to such an extent that there's hardly anything left. The American firm of Stoner opted for a tubular tele-

scopic stock. With the stock shoved in, the weapon becomes extremely short and when pushed out it forms an exceedingly strong steel stock. On military weapons, the barrel in front of the chamber is often protected in addition to the stock – for the sake of the shooter's hands rather than the barrel.

During rapid fire barrels can get quite hot and it would not be wise, to say the least, to grasp the barrel with bare hands. To avoid this problem, these weapons are fitted with a hand grip, sometimes made of wood but more often of perforated sheet steel or synthetic material. Military weapons must be readily portable. Almost all military firearms are therefore fitted with carrying slings.

This is true not just of rifles, carbines and sub-machine-guns but also of tactical riot guns. A tried-and-tested method is the recess in the stock, as used on many military rifles since the Second World War. A more modern version is that of Benelli.

Hand grip on the CZ 2000

The other end of the sling is often attached to a swivel located to the tubular magazine of riot guns.

A different method can be seen clearly on the Steyr AUG rifle, with its rotating swivels. Precision military rifles, especially those used by snipers, are often fitted with a bipod. This can normally be folded to

Tubular stock on the Stoner SR-25K

Recess for a swivel on the Benelli riot gun

Swivel at the front of the tubular magazine of a Benelli riotgun

Swivel on the Steyr AUG

Harris extending bipod on a DPMS AR-15 rifle type

those that can be fitted to SIG rifles. A particularly robust model is the bipod developed by CZ for the CZ 2000 military rifle and light machine gun.

make the weapon easier to transport. Many sniper rifles have a bipod made by the firm of Harris. For special purposes Harris even make bipods with longer legs, as shown. Various manufacturers have also developed their own bipods such as

Harris bipod under the M24-A1 sniper from Arms Technology

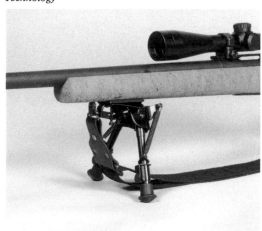

Special folding Sig bipod

Folding bipod for the CZ 2000

Magazine with integrated catch on the Remington Model 700 sniper

THE MAGAZINE AND THE BLIND MAGAZINE

The term magazine sometimes causes confusion. A repeating rifle, whether it be fully automatic, semi-automatic, or bolt-action, has a magazine well or magazine housing into which a detachable magazine can be inserted. Cartridges are held in the magazine.

Some rifles, whatever type of internal magazine they have, are closed underneath with a removable or hinged magazine base plate. In the case of an internal magazine, the cartridges are held in the bottom of the receiver, within the stock. A disadvantage of this system is the rather limited cartridge capacity.

Moreover, in most cases the internal magazine has to be loaded via the top, the bolt aperture. The advantage is that the rifle retains its slender shape and with no annoying protrusion in the form of a magazine. An intermediate solution is the

detachable magazine used for a sniper's rifle. While detachable it does fits inside the stock. However, it has the same disadvantage as the internal magazine of small cartridge capacity. The magazine catch attached to the magazine is indicated here by a red circle.

The advantage of a removable magazine is that it can be loaded outside the weapon. The magazine is then inserted into the magazine well and snapped closed with the magazine catch. This catch, for removing the magazine, is normally positioned close to the magazine well or the trigger group.

Another advantage is that the weapon can be reloaded very quickly with a fresh magazine when it has been emptied. Mili-

Synthetic cartridge holder for Sig military rifles; three clipped together

Synthetic magazine on the CZ 2000 military rifle

Drawing of the Ruger Mini-14 magazine. The numbers indicate: 1. Magazine housing; 2. follower; 3. magazine spring; 4. magazine locking plate; 5. Magazine base plate

Tubular magazine of the Benelli M3 Super 90

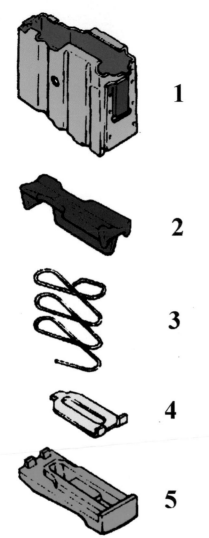

1

2

3

4

5

Tubular magazine extension from Scatter-gun Technologies

fitted, into which the cartridges are loaded one by one. With riot guns this is usually done through the rear, at the bottom of the receiver housing.

To give a riot gun a larger magazine capacity, the tubular magazine can often be extended by adding an attachment. Here you see a version that was designed by the firm of Scatter-gun.

Light machine-guns can generally operate well with a magazine. The problem, however, is that a magazine is quickly emptied. This type of weapon is therefore often fitted with a supply box with a larger cartridge capacity. Such a box may be made of synthetic material, which may rattle when moving.

For this reason, a drum magazine is also used, in which the cartridges are held by

Drum magazine on the CZ 200 light machine gun

tary rifles in particular are preferred with a detachable magazine. A disadvantage is that a detachable magazine, certainly one of the larger types, protrudes quite a way below the weapon. This can cause problems when firing from a prone position or with the weapon resting on an object; in addition, systems of this kind are prone to damage.

A different system is the tubular magazine. This is often used on riot guns. Underneath the barrel, a tubular magazine is

Canvas cartridge bag for the FN Minimi light machine-gun

Box magazine on the Calico sub-machine-gun

Magazine catch on the CZ 2000 military rifle

Magazine catch on the Steyr AUG

spring tension. Another solution is a canvas cartridge bag that can be snapped onto the weapon. On machine-guns that are mainly used in a fixed position, cartridges are fed by a cartridge belt. The cartridges are connected by links, forming a long chain.

Cartridge belts are normally kept in a steel box. If the gun is fired for a lengthy period, one cartridge belt is linked to the next one and so on. Another example of a box magazine is the magazine box used on Calico weapons.

Here, a filled synthetic box containing 50 or 100 cartridges is snapped on top of the weapon. The magazine must be easy to remove from the weapon. This is achieved by means of the magazine catch, which is located close to the magazine. The magazine normally has a recess somewhere in its housing and the catch in the mechanism casing then falls into this aperture. Sometimes this catch is in the form of a button. Here you see the magazine catch

Cartridge belt in the FN MAG machine-gun

of the CZ 700 sniper rifle, on which the button is built into the side of the stock. Yet another example is the large squeeze

Magazine button on the CZ 700 sniper rifle

catch on the Steyr AUG rifle. Here, the magazine catch is behind the magazine in the bullpup stock.

Safety systems

The purpose of a safety system on a weapon is to prevent a shot from being fired accidentally. The safety system is therefore always connected to a weapon's firing mechanism. With most systems, the trigger is locked when the safety system is selected. Alternatively, the external hammer or the internal striker can be locked.

With bolt-action rifles, the action of the bolt is sometimes blocked. As an extra safety measure, on some weapons the sear is disengaged from the trigger or the firing pin is secured. There are firing systems in which several safety features are combined. In addition to manual safety measures, there are also automatic safety systems, which are overridden, either mechanically or otherwise, when the trigger is pulled, for example an automatic firing pin security system. A number of safety systems are discussed below.

The safety catch on the Mauser SR 94 sniper rifle. The trigger system here is ready to fire (red dot)

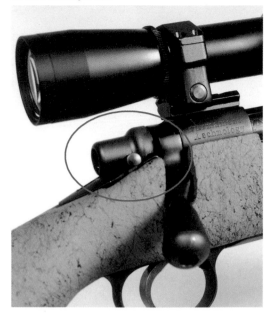

The safety catch behind the bolt lever of the American AT-M24-A1 sniper rifle

Safety systems

Safety systems that are often used on military and police weapons are:
- safety catch
- wing safety catch
- rotating safety catch
- rotating catch/firing selector
- safety slide
- pushbutton safety
- "loaded" indicator
- grip safety
- gas pressure valve
- lock safety.

THE SAFETY CATCH
A safety catch must be operated by hand. Depending on the weapon's make, type and model, it blocks the hammer or the internal striker and/or the sear and/or the trigger and sometimes the breech block or bolt as well. In addition, a combination of several methods may be used in one weapon.
On most bolt-action rifles, the safety catch is on the receiver, right next to the bolt lever. When the safety catch is in the firing position, a red dot is usually visible (see example). The safety catch on this Mauser

Safety catch in the front side of the trigger guard on the Ruger Mini-14

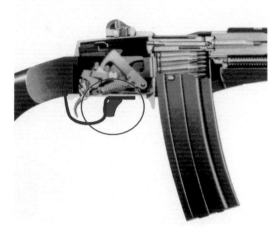

has been imitated by many manufacturers. A good example of this is the wing catch on Dakota's unusual sniper rifle, the Longbow.

THE ROTATING SAFETY CATCH

An example of the rotating catch used as a safety can be seen on the Winchester .30-M1 carbine. This catch is fitted in the front of the trigger guard and is operated using the index finger. The catch in front of it is the magazine catch.

THE ROTATING SAFETY CATCH/FIRING SELECTOR

On modern military rifles, carbines and sub-machine-guns, the safety catch is often combined with the firing selector. As the name indicates, the firing selector is

Rotating safety catch on the Winchester .30-M1 carbine

SR94 sniper rifle is in the firing position. A second example is the safety catch on the Armament Technology M24-A1 sniper rifle.

A similar catch, but in the form of a slide, is used on CZ's sniper rifle, the CZ 700. On the Ruger Mini-14 carbine, Ruger use another type of safety catch. It is housed in the front of the trigger guard and can thus be operated with the trigger finger. This system is derived from the Garand military rifle.

THE WING SAFETY CATCH

The wing safety is found primarily on bolt-action rifles. It is usually a rotating wing catch on the rear of the bolt. The system locks both the firing pin and the bolt, but not the trigger. One of the first manufacturers to use this system was Mauser, on their K98 military rifle. This type of safety

The combined rotating safety catch/firing selector on a Bushmaster XM15E25 rifle

In the safety position, the trigger is normally locked, but other parts of the firing system can also be blocked or disengaged.

THE SLIDING SAFETY CATCH

While this type of safety is most commonly found on hunting rifles, it also occurs on bolt-action, fully and semi-automatic weapons. The sliding catch is sometimes located in the top of the pistol grip of the stock, also called the neck, in the extension of the receiver. The safety slider usually locks the trigger and/or the sear. Below is an example of the sliding catch in the neck of the stock on the Mauser SR96

used for setting the firing mode. The rotating catch/firing selector depicted is used on the Bushmaster AR-15 rifle type. In many cases, the catch can be clicked to various positions: semi-automatic, 3-round burst, fully automatic or safe. A good example of this is the rotating safety catch/firing selector on the CZ 2000 military rifle.

Sliding safety on the Mauser SR96 rifle

Good example of the combined rotating safety catch/firing selector on the CZ 2000 military rifle

The sliding safety catch/firing selector on the Uzi

Browning's pushbutton safety. Note the red rim

and a red one in the firing position. Another example of a pushbutton safety can be seen on a Browning rifle. The red ring, the firing position, is clearly visible. Another type of pushbutton safety is used on the Steyr AUG. On this weapon, the pushbutton is not incorporated in the trigger guard, but is positioned in the receiver housing. Yet another example of

Pushbutton safety catch on the Steyr AUG

sniper rifle. The sliding safety catch may also be fitted on the side of the receiver housing. An example of this is the sliding safety catch/firing selector on the Uzi sub-machine-gun. It is shown above: the "S" stands for safe, the "R" for repeat or semi-automatic fire and the "A" means fully automatic fire.

THE PUSHBUTTON SAFETY

This type of safety is often housed in the trigger guard, as it usually locks only the trigger. This catch is a push-through button that can be pushed through from one side to the other side of the trigger guard. Often, a white ring around the pushbutton is visible in the safety position

Pushbutton safety and firing selector on the FN-P90

The Mossberg pushbutton safety

42

a pushbutton safety is the one on the FN-P90 submachine gun. On this weapon, the safety pushbutton is combined with the firing selector for semi- or full automatic fire.

THE "LOADED" INDICATOR

A "loaded" indicator shows whether the firing system is loaded and cocked. On Benelli shotguns and riot guns, a catch protrudes from the receiver housing as soon as the weapon is cocked by pump action or semi-automatically. This means that a full cartridge is in the chamber and that the firing system is ready to fire. A similar system is sometimes used on bolt-action rifles. In this case, a pin protruding from the rear of the bolt provides the "loaded" indicator.

THE GRIP SAFETY

The grip safety is an unusual system that is normally used only with pistols or sub-machine-guns. With this type of safety, the trigger, the cocking lever and/or the sear is locked if the grip safety is not pressed. This does not present any problems, however, as this safety is usually housed in the pistol grip. As soon as the weapon is firmly grasped, this catch is automatically pressed. This safety device is often combined with a separate safety catch or safety catch/firing selector, as on the Uzi sub-machine-gun (see example, Beretta sub-machine-gun).

THE GAS PRESSURE VALVE

Military weapons of course are designed for extreme conditions. This means not just very high or low temperatures but also high air humidity. In tropical jungles such

Grip safety on the Beretta sub-machine gun

Safety gas release valve in the barrel chamber of the Armament Technology M24-A1 sniper rifle

as those of South America or Asia, where humidity is some 95-99%, a military weapon must be able to function flawlessly. Despite the fact that modern ammunition is virtually waterproof and vapor-proof, misfires can happen. A misfire is when the shooter pulls the trigger and nothing happens.

The shot does not go off at once, but sometimes a little later. It may also happen that due to the extremely high temperature the gas pressure rises to such a level that a section of the case tears. To prevent this from presenting a hazard to the shooter, sniper rifles in particular are fitted with so-called gas valves. Apertures are made in the barrel chamber or in the bolt and/or in the bolt lever, through which extreme gas pressure can safely escape. The locking system can then "vent off" this excess gas pressure without the weapon

Benelli "loaded" indicator

43

Locking, repeating and firing systems

The following topics are discussed below:

Locking systems:
- recoil system
- locking lug system
- rotating lock system
- roller lock system

Repeating systems:
- gas pressure system
- pump-action system

Firing systems:
- the trigger group
- the firing selector

The terms "bolt" and "breechblock" will be dealt with first.

exploding. Here you see an example of a gas release aperture in the chamber of the AT-M24-A1 sniper rifle and an extra safety system on the CZ 700 sniper. In the latter case, not only is the barrel chamber provided with safety valves, but the bolt is too.

THE LOCK SAFETY

Almost all rifles and carbines have a lock safety that prevents a cartridge from being fired when the breech block or bolt is not fully closed. This may happen, for example, due to dirt or because a cartridge, for whatever reason, does not chamber properly. On most weapons, this safety system works as follows: a lug on the triggerbar should drop into a recess on the lower inside of the receiver or bolt. If this fails, i.e. if the breech block is not entirely in the foremost locked position, then the triggerbar is prevented from functioning properly and cannot reach the sear or hammer, so no shot can be fired. With manually operated systems, the internal or external hammer is blocked or cannot move forward to strike the firing pin. Other systems with no internal or external hammer work with a sear that makes direct contact with a firing lug on the firing pin. As long as the bolt is not fully closed, the connection between the sear and the firing pin is not made.

Bolt

A bolt is a solid steel block that is operated manually by means of a bolt lever. When closed, the bolt must be locked firmly to the receiver, so that the high gas pressure can be withstood. This locking action is normally effected by the so-called locking lugs on the bolt.

When locked, these lugs engage with corresponding recesses in the receiver or with an extension of the barrel. We speak of a receiver when the bolt or breech block is housed in a partially open "guide rail".

Breechblock

On a semi-automatic weapon it is usual to refer to a breech block. This too is a solid steel block that is driven by gas pressure or recoil action to effect the reloading cycle of the weapon.

The breech block is housed in a receiver housing. This is a largely sealed housing in which the breech block can move backwards and forwards. Usually, the trigger

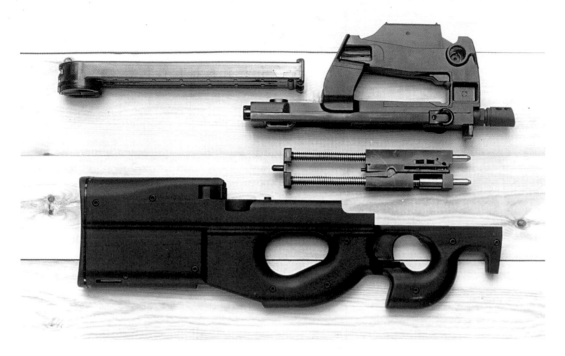

group and the magazine are also integrated in the receiver housing.

Locking systems

There are various kinds of locking systems.

BLOWBACK SYSTEM

On military weapons, recoil systems are normally found on sub-machine-guns and sometimes on carbines with a pistol caliber. The locking of this type of weapon is achieved by the weight or inertia of the breech block and by the action or main spring which ensures the breech block remains in the foremost, closed position. Due to the tension of the main spring, the breech block is pressed against the rear of the cartridge chamber in the barrel. The action of the weapon is as follows. When the shot is fired, gas pressure is produced. This forces the bullet out of the case and along the grooves and lands of the bore. The detonation and the gas pressure, the initial movement of the bullet and the forced passage through the bore produce

counter-pressure against the inner rear part of the case. Due to the pressure and temperature the case expands, sealing the chamber gas-tight.

This causes the case to try to fly backwards out of the chamber but this is prevented by the breech block. The tension of the main spring, combined with the weight (inertia) of the steel breech block, is so designed that this recoil reaction is delayed and commences only after the bullet has left the barrel. Only then can the mechanism be safely unlocked. As soon as the weight of the breech block has been set in motion it continues until this rearward recoil is halted. The action takes place in the following sequence:
- the shot is fired;
- the breech block moves backwards under pressure from the gas released;
- this more or less simultaneously cocks the firing pin and its spring and hammer plus spring, together with the main spring;
- when the breech block is propelled backwards, the spent case is removed from the chamber by the extractor and thrown clear by the ejector;

- since the bolt spring is fully depressed, it wants to release itself when the breech block reaches its rearmost position and is halted there;
- this in turn pushes the breech block forward again;
- as it moves forward, the breech block strips a new cartridge from the magazine and pushes it into the chamber in the barrel.

The main spring is usually located at the rear of the breech block. A FN P90 submachine-gun that has been disassembled into main groups is shown here. In the center is the solid breech block, which on the P90 has not one but two main springs.

LOCKING LUG SYSTEM

With a locking lug system, the bolt is provided with a number of locking lugs at the front and/or back of the bolt. During the closing or locking action, these lugs engage in recesses in the rifle receiver. As a result, the barrel chamber is sealed and the bolt and receiver are firmly locked together.

You see here an example of the CZ 700 sniper rifle, in which the locking lugs are located at the rear of the bolt. It is a robust and reliable locking system, which can withstand very high gas pressures and can thus shoot heavy ammunition. Depending on the make and system, one bolt may be provided with from one to as many as nine lugs.

On smallbore weapons, a single locking lug is often used. For the extra heavy Weatherby rifles, for instance, nine lugs

Detailed photo of the bolt of the CZ 700 sniper rifle

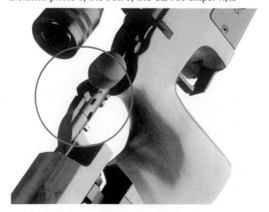

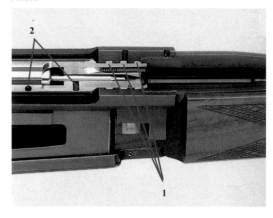

Bolt of a Weatherby rifle: 1. locking lugs; 2. gas valves

Krico receiver with bolt

are used on the bolt. On some makes, both the front and the rear of the bolt are provided with several locking lugs, so that the bolt can be locked tightly to the receiver, for example in a Krico receiver with bolt.

The locking lugs at the front of the bolt are clearly visible here. Yet another variation is the 360-degree spreading bolt, used on the Blaser R93 rifle. The locking lugs are arranged in a circle behind the bolt head. The locking lugs consist of eighteen narrow segments which, when the bolt is closed, are pressed outwards and engage in all directions in a collar around the barrel chamber.

ROTATING LOCK SYSTEM

The rotating lock system is often used on rifles and carbines and also on some semi-automatic shotguns and riot guns. The breech block in the receiver or receiver housing is provided at the front with a number of locking lugs. When the system is locked, these lugs rotate into corre-

Drawing of the Ruger Mini-14 breechblock: 1. extractor; 2. extractor pin; 2a. extractor pin spring; 3. bolt; 4. firing pin; 5. firing-pin guide lug; 6. ejector; 6a. ejector spring; A. locking lugs

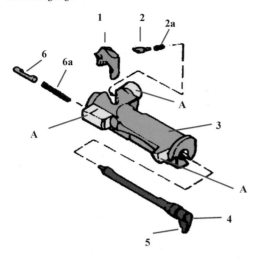

Detachable Benelli bolt. Note the purple lug in the top of the bolt. It is responsible for the rotation of the bolt head

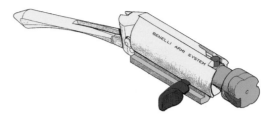

lugs and the cartridge in the barrel chamber can clearly be seen here. In the center of the breech block, a section of the firing pin is visible.

sponding recesses in the receiver or at the rear of the barrel. Through the recoil energy or the tapped gas pressure generated by the fired cartridge, the bolt head is rotated through a certain number of degrees following the shot. This releases the locking lugs from the recesses and the bolt is able to move back to unlock the system.

In the exploded view of a Benelli semi-automatic shotgun and the detachable bolt head, the purple lug in the top of the bolt is responsible for the rotation of the bolt head. Another example of a rotating lock system can be seen in a model of a Bushmaster bolt carrier. Both the locking

System drawing of the Benelli semi-automatic shotgun

ROLLER LOCK SYSTEM

Roller locking is associated with the German arms manufacturer Heckler & Koch. The action of the roller lock system is as follows. Lateral extensions of the barrel contain two semicircular recesses into which two steel rollers fall. These rollers are also attached to the bolt. When the rifle is locked two steel rollers drop into the recesses at the side of the barrel. After the shot is fired, the bolt is forced back by the recoil energy.

The two rollers swing inwards and when the disengagement is completed the bolt continues backwards on its own. The cycle of ejection and reloading then takes place. The advantage of this system is two-fold: firstly, when the cartridge is fired, the locking system is extremely stable; secondly, the recoil occurs with a delay, as the two rollers first have to swing inwards.

Bushmaster bolt carrier

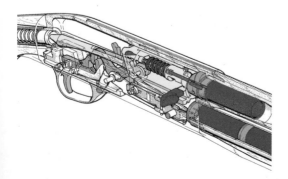

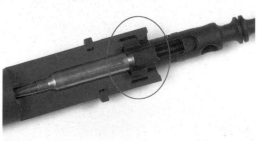

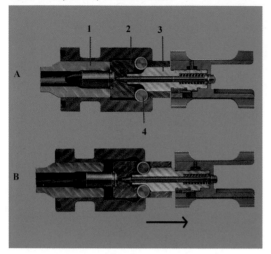

A disadvantage of this method is the high cost of production because of the fine tolerances demanded.

A further drawback is the sensitivity of this mechanism to variations in ammunition. Here you see a schematic representation of this locking system. In A, the locking system is closed; in B, the weapon is disengaged. The numbers refer to: 1. barrel and chamber; 2. bolt carrier; 3. bolt head; 4. locking rollers.

Repeating systems

GAS PRESSURE SYSTEM

Firearms with a repeating action operated by gas pressure are not a recent development. Experiments were conducted with this method as long ago as the nineteenth century.

An example is the Italian Cei-Rigotti rifle, which was demonstrated to the Italian army as early as 1895. In Germany various prototypes of this genre were made from 1901 onwards. In Britain the army command of the time rejected the Farquhar-Hill automatic rifle because it was too complex. The gas pressure principle really only became popular after the First World War. Broadly speaking, the action of the "gas-operated rifle" is as follows. When a cartridge is fired in the chamber, a high gas pressure is developed.

This pressure forces the bullet out of the cartridge case and through the barrel towards the muzzle. About halfway along the barrel there is a small port or gas vent. Since the bullet has not yet left the barrel, the gas pressure inside the barrel remains high. A small portion of this gas pressure escapes through this gas vent and is directed into a small cylinder containing a piston. Due to the sudden powerful gas pressure impact, the piston in the cylinder is thrust backwards.

A piston rod is normally connected to the piston and this piston rod is in turn connected to the breech block. Due to the thrust action of the piston, the breech block is propelled backwards. In the meantime, the bullet has left the barrel. The bore is therefore open at the muzzle and the gas pressure returns to the normal level. The motion of the breech block has by this time already been initiated and continues. In most cases, the breech block rotates by means of lugs and a lug guide or rail. This disengages the breech block from the barrel or receiver. At the same time, the case is extracted from the chamber and then ejected. The firing pin and/or the hammer (or the internal striker) is cocked, whereupon the breech block is held in the rearmost position. By now, the main spring has been tensioned by the backward motion of the breech block. The breech block now shoots forward again under the pressure of this main spring, strips a new cartridge from the magazine and pushes it into the barrel chamber. If the cartridge is then fired, the cycle will be repeated. Depending on the make and type, the gas vent and the cylinder area are fitted either below the barrel (30-M1 carbine) or above it (Kalashnikov AK-47).

Gas vent and gas tube on the CZ 2000 rifle

Strictly speaking, the gas pressure system is not a locking system, but a drive or repeating system. The true locking action takes place by means of locking lugs on the rotating breech block. This gas pressure system is used in several variations on rifles, carbines, machine guns, sub-machine-guns and shotguns. The numbers on the exploded view of the Ruger Mini-14 gas pressure system stand for: 1. the barrel; 2. gas block cover; 3. gas vent; 4. gas block; 5. piston.

PUMP-ACTION REPEATING SYSTEM

The action of the pump-action repeating system is by and large comparable to the gas pressure repeating system. The main difference is the drive. With the pump-action system, the repeating action is initi-

ated by pulling the forearm, underneath or around the barrel, backward by hand and then pushing it forward again. The breech block, with rotating locking lugs or with a vertically sliding block locking system, is then disengaged. The empty case is ejected and the firing pin or striker is cocked again. During the forward motion, a new cartridge is fed from the magazine and pushed into the barrel chamber.

The breech block is then rotated again and the locking lugs engage in the recesses in the receiver housing. This system is frequently used in shotguns. From an engineering point of view, the combination of semi-automatic and pump-action is interesting.

Benelli has used this combi system in its M3 Super 90 shotguns. At the front of the forearm there is a switch. In one position the weapon works semi-automatically on the basis of recoil energy and in the other position it is a pump-action system. Franchi used a similar concept for the SPAS-12 and SPAS-15 riot guns. With these weapons, the action can be switched from semi-automatic to pump-action by pressing a button in the forearm.

Detailed drawing of the Ruger gas pressure system

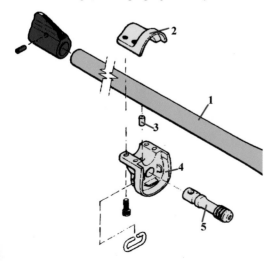

Switch on the Benelli M3 Super 90 riotgun for semi-automatic or pump-action

49

Firing systems

Military weapons are fitted with a variety of firing systems. Broadly speaking, a firing system consists of the trigger group and, if applicable, the firing selector.

THE TRIGGER GROUP

A trigger group on a semi-automatic weapon works as follows. The shooter inserts a magazine into the gun. He then cocks the weapon by pulling the charging handle backwards. The breech block, which is connected to this handle, moves back with it. As a result, the main spring is pressed back. The hammer or the internal striker is also tilted, so that the hammer spring is pressed back. The hammer is held in the tilted position by the sear, which in turn is connected to the trigger. As soon as the shooter releases the charging handle, it moves forward under the pressure of the main spring. In the process, the breech block strips a cartridge from the magazine and places it in the barrel chamber. The weapon is now ready to be fired by pulling the trigger.

When the trigger is pulled, it pivots around the trigger axis. The sear is located inside the trigger foot. When the trigger is tilted, the sear rises. The sear is in turn connected to the hammer or the internal striker. Since the sear is pushed upwards by the motion of the trigger, the hammer is released. Under the pressure of the hammer spring, the hammer moves forward to strike the firing pin, which hits the primer in the bottom of the cartridge in the barrel chamber. This causes the cartridge to be fired. The breech block is then unlocked by the recoil energy or the gas pressure. The breech block moves backwards and extracts the spent case

from the chamber. While the breech block is moving backwards, the main spring is also pressed back. When the shooter releases the trigger, it returns to its former position. The hammer or striker is tilted backwards by the breech block, so that the hammer spring or striker spring is also tensioned. The sear then falls back into its recess in the hammer. Sometimes this recess is located in the foot of the hammer, but it may also be on the hammerhead, as can be seen in the drawing below. Once the breech block has been halted in its backwards motion, the depressed main spring wants to release itself. The main spring presses the breech block forward again. In "passing", it strips a new cartridge from the magazine and pushes it in the chamber of the barrel. The weapon is now ready for the next shot. The following parts are shown on the drawing of the trigger group of a Ruger Mini-14 carbine: 1. hammer; 2. hammer spring guide rod; 3. hammer spring or plunger spring; 4. safety catch; 5. safety-catch spring; 6. sear; 7. hammer pin; 8. trigger; 9. trigger spring; 10. trigger pin bushing; 11. trigger pin; 12. trigger guard; 13. magazine catch; 14. Magazine catch spring; 15. Magazine catch pin; 16. safety-catch pin. The red dotted line indicates the connection

Drawing of a Ruger Mini-14 trigger group

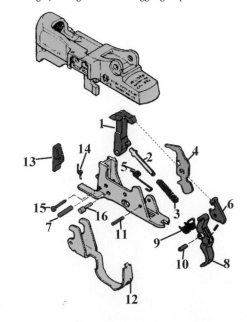

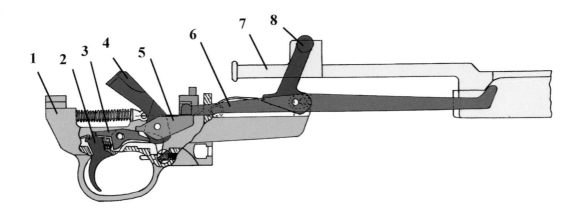

between the sear recess on the hammer and the sear.

THE FIRING SELECTOR

On an automatic weapon, the repeating action operates more or less as described above, except that in this case the sear is

Firing selector on the Ruger AC556K carbine

retained by the firing selector, so that it does not latch onto the hammer. The firing system thus simply continues to "rattle away" until the magazine is empty or the shooter releases the trigger. A simple but excellent system can be seen on the Winchester .30-M2 carbine. The large release lever (6) is clearly visible in the trigger group (1). It is connected to the selector button (8) and its end, via the release(5), presses the sear (3) out of operation. The sear recess of the sear thus no longer engages in the foot of the hammer (4). The numbered parts in the drawing above are: 1. trigger housing; 2. trigger; 3. sear; 4. hammer; 5. release; 6. release lever; 7. cocking lever; 8. firing selector. The catch for the firing selector on a weapon is

Firing selector on the automatic Ruger AC556 carbine

Sighting systems

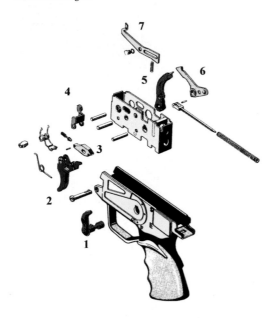

A sighting system incorporates a part or parts that enable the weapon to be aimed at a target so that the bullet hits its intended target. Sighting systems range from a simple steel sight to advanced laser sighting devices.

The sighting systems covered here are:
- steel sight;
- aperture sight;
- front sight;
- scope;
- light amplification sight;
- laser;
- mounting systems;
- aiming light.

Steel sight

often located close to the trigger group, since it has to be convenient to operate. Given below are two examples of the selector system employed by Ruger, starting with the firing selector on the Ruger AC556K carbine.

Using the selector catch, the firing system can be switched from semi-automatic to 3-round burst. Then comes the selector catch of the Ruger AC556, with three positions: semi-automatic, fully automatic and 3-round burst.

Just how the trigger system of an automatic weapon works can be seen clearly on the above drawing of the Heckler & Koch MP5 sub-machine-gun. The sear engages in the sear recess, which on this system is in the hammer foot. During automatic firing, the sear is switched off and is therefore unable to retain the hammer before each shot.

The bolt catch does do this, but on each shot it is pressed away again at lightning speed by the release lever. The bolt catch acts as a kind of retarder.

The names of the numbered parts are: 1. firing selector; 2. trigger; 3. sear; 4. bolt catch; 5. hammer; 6. release lever; 7. ejector.

Sights are fitted on the barrel and often on the receiver. With simple sights, the steel sight is usually positioned at the rear, close to the receiver.

The rear sight is a more or less vertical plate or sight plate with a rectangular notch in the center.Advanced steel sights can be adjusted for elevation and for windage, so that the point of impact can be set precisely.

This type of sight is known as a tangent rear sight. With this system, the sight can be set to fixed ranges.

Rear sight on the Ruger Police carbine

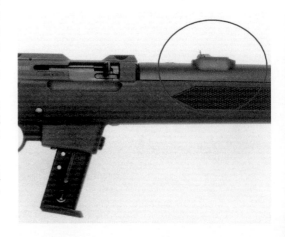

Tangent rear sight on the CZ 2000 military rifle

Aperture sight on the Ruger AC556 carbine

Detail of the CZ 2000 tangent rear sight

APERTURE SIGHT

An aperture sight normally consists of a foot supporting a round plate with a small hole in its center. With simple versions, such as those on military rifles, there are folding versions for the various distances or the plate can be shifted along an angled base plate for different ranges. A Scatter-gun trak-lock aperture sight with accompanying front sight for a riot gun is shown.

Trak-lock aperture sight and front sight on Scatter-gun

The aperture sight can be fitted on the receiver or the receiver housing, as can be clearly seen on the Ruger Mini-14 carbine types.

Sometimes an aperture sight of this type is incorporated in the rifle's carrying handle, as on the AR-15 and M16 rifle models.

Benelli uses ghost ring sights for its riot guns. This sight consists of a small ring protected on either side by wings, which

Aperture sight in the carrying handle of the DPMS A-15

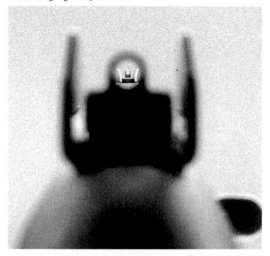

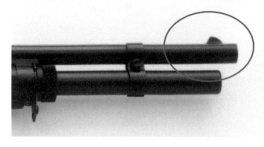

Front sight with base on the Benelli M3 Super 90

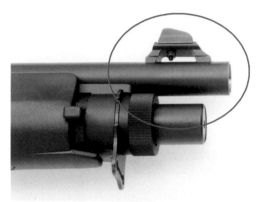

also function as a kind of sighting aid. Aiming is fast with this type of sight and at the same time the shooter gets a good overall view of the field of fire. Other systems consist of a rotating cylinder with several apertures at different heights for the various ranges.

Front sight

At the end of the barrel, near the muzzle, there is a vertical bead or pin. By positioning the top of the bead in the V or U-shaped notch of the rear sight, the weapon can be aimed at the target. Depending on the make and model of the weapon, the front sight may come in a variety of shapes.

Sometimes it is mounted flat on the barrel, but often it is on a raised base. On military weapons, the front sight is often protected against being knocked or dropped by a protective ring fitted around it. Some

Aperture drum sight from Heckler & Koch

weapons have a protective wing on either side of the front sight instead of this ring. On the AR-15/M16 rifle types, the front sight is housed in a high base. This is necessary as the aperture sight, which is also high on the weapon, is fitted in the carrying handle. Modern versions of the AR-15 rifle sometimes have a detachable carrying handle.

A mounting rail for a scope can be installed on the receiver housing instead. Since the front sight would then be in the

Ring bead on Sig military weapons

Front sight with wings on the CZ 2000 rifle

Optical sight on the FN P90 sub-machine-gun

DPMS front sight on the AR-15/M16 type

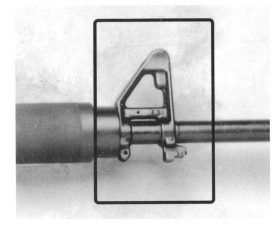

Optical sight on the HK G36E rifle

ArmaLite Picatinny rail for the detachable front sight base

Optical sight on the Steyr AUG family

way, the front sight with its base is also detachable.

Scope

Scopes, or telescopic sights, come in many types and sizes, depending on the purpose for which they are to be used. An assault rifle is sometimes fitted with a simple scope, often housed in the carrying handle. A large scope on this type of weapon would be too prone to damage in the field. An exception, or rather an inter-

Elcan scope on a DPMS A-15 rifle

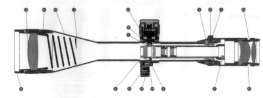
Cross-sectional drawing of the Springfield Government 3rd Generation scope

example. This type of scope is used for targets at between 300 meters (984 ft) up to as far as 2000 meters (2187 yd) away, depending on the caliber of the rifle. Tactical scopes, as sniper scopes are often called, normally have advanced setting features. This applies not only to setting the point of impact, but also to setting the

Sig SG 551 Swat with Trijicon ACOR scope

Harris M-86 sniper with Leupold Police scope

Nikkon Monarch scope

mediate form between the sniper sight and a combat sight, is the Elcan. On top of the scope there is also a simple auxiliary sight in the form of a fixed rear sight and front sight.

A similar combat scope is the Trijicon ACOR, used on SIG weapons, for example. This scope has as a sighting device a red dot, the intensity of which can be adjusted. Large scopes are usually found on sniper rifles. The magnification factor, which is often adjustable from four to fourteen times, is necessary for getting a target accurately in sight at long range. A scope is a complex optical instrument. The cross-sectional drawing of the Springfield Government 3rd Generation scope is an

Burris Black Diamond Tactical Mil-Dot scope

Adjusting ring for the magnification factor of a Leupold

Leupold Vari-X-III Long Range Tactical 4.5-14 X 50 scope

Springfield 4-14 X 56 3rd Generation Government Model 7.62 mm

range. Sometimes such a scope is also provided with a range finding system, which enables the scope to be set to a distant target with great accuracy. Large scopes can be fitted with all kinds of reticules.

These are sometimes simple cross wires, but more often a complex system with a range finding feature. For twilight, the cross wires can also be fitted with an adjustable LED dot. On a number of scope types, a red LED dot can be switched on in the middle of the reticule. This LED dot is intended as an aid when light conditions are poor. A long-distance scope is often unnecessary for sub-machine-guns, but what is required is an optical sight enabling rapid aiming. One of the sights used for this purpose is the special Aimpoint sight. These scopes have no reticule, only a red LED dot that has to be

Springfield 6-20 X 56 Mil-Dot Government Model Long Range

Springfield 5.56 Tactical reticle with range finding system

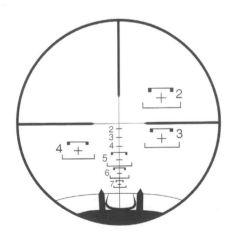

Springfield 4-14 X 56 Mil-Dot Government Model 7.62 mm

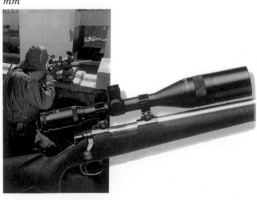

Night sights

pointed at the target. The intensity of this LED dot can usually be adjusted. Springfield 4-14 X 56 Mil-Dot Government Model 7.62 mm

A night sight is a scope that enables the light to be electronically intensified by thousands of times.

At twilight or at night, just moonlight or starlight may be sufficient for a good sight

Springfield 2nd Generation Tactical reticle with range finding system

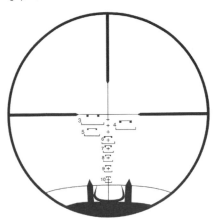

Burris scope with LED dot in reticle

Springfield 7.62 Mil-Dot with illuminated reticle and range finding system

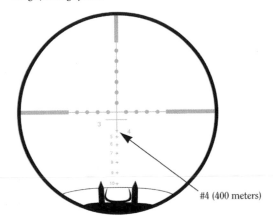

#4 (400 meters)

Aimpoint COMP scope on an HK MP5 sub-machine-gun

image. The well-known German firm of Zeiss, now a subsidiary of Hensoldt AG, makes the Orion 80II night sight.
At night, this 2nd-generation scope ampli-

Springfield 10 X 56 Mil-Dot with illuminated reticle and range finding system

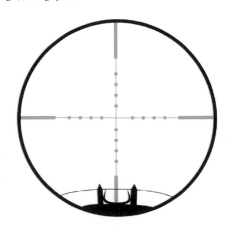

Scope systems for Sig military rifles

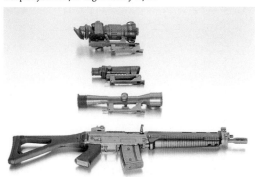

The Zeiss Orion 80II night sight on a Heckler & Koch PSG-1 sniper rifle

The HK PSG-1 with the Orion 80II at the ready

A port wharf at night

The same port wharf made visible with the Orion 80II

port wharf at night. Below is the same picture, but with the Orion 80II.

Laser

Laser sighting devices are used increasingly in combat situations at short range. The laser is not an optical scope, but more an aiming aid. The shooter does not have to look through anything, but simply aims the laser beam from his weapon at the target. As soon as a bright red light dot falls onto the target, the weapon is aimed. Sometimes a laser is also used in combination with a normal scope.

Mounting systems

Most military weapons are modified in some way for the use of optical sighting devices. For light calibers, it is sufficient to

Knight's RIS system with laser on the top rail

fies moonlight and starlight by 20,000 times. These night sights are often used by military and police units for sniper purposes.

The photos show the effect that these sights have. Little detail can be seen on a

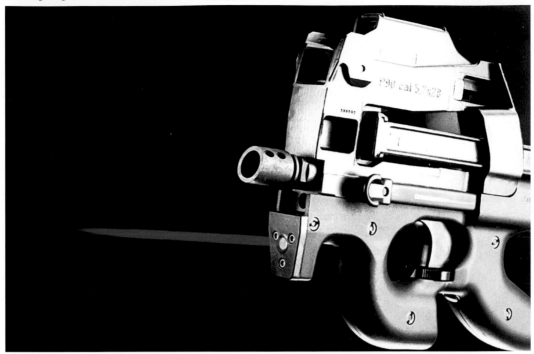

have a guide rail in the form of a dovetail to which the scope is attached with rings. The scope is fastened to the guide and mounting rail with scope rings. Two or more rings are fitted around the scope housing. Underneath, these rings have claws, which engage with the dovetail of the rail.

There are also scope rings that have threaded holes or a special lug that can be clicked into a recess in the mounting rail. A system such as this is not adequate for heavier calibers. Owing to the heavy recoil of the weapon, the scope could jump out of its rail. Rifles therefore either have special recesses or holes drilled and tapped in the top of the receiver. A scope mounting (a base) suitable for that particular rifle can then be attached to these holes. There are currently several types of mounting from which a scope can quickly be removed. This is useful for transport or movements in the field. An example is the Picatinny mounting rail. Provided a scope

Burris 30M Signature scope rings

Remington mounting rail

Mounting rail for the military Arms Technology M24 sniper

is always put back in the same position, the settings remain the same and the scope does not have to be recalibrated every time.

Another solution for this can be seen on the scope mounting for the CZ 700 sniper. This is a so-called tip-off attachment. First, the front ring is placed crosswise in the ring base and then rotated a quarter turn, so that the scope is straight. The rear base is then fastened. A system that somewhat resembles the Picatinny rail is the Rail

Picatinny rail

Interface System (RIS) made by Knight's Armament. This system consists of a horizontal top rail and one or more vertical side rails. Scopes can be attached in the top rail.

A laser or aiming light can be fitted on the side rail. The mounting slots on the RIS are numbered. This means, for example, that after being removed a scope can quickly be put back in precisely the same position. The scope does not then have to be newly adjusted every time.

Aiming light

An aiming light is particularly useful when searching buildings and is used mainly for short ranges.

When the aiming light is accurately set in respect of the weapon, it also functions as a sighting device. An aiming light of this kind, often a Mag-Lite torch, can sometimes be switched on and off separately by means of a switch on the forearm or on the pistol grip. It can easily be clicked onto

Knight's Rail Interface System (RIS)

the RIS. On other types of weapons like the Scatter-gun riot gun, such an aiming light is sometimes integrated in the fore-arm.

Ammunition for military weapons

Cartridges for rifles, carbines, sniper rifles, machine guns, sub-machine-guns and riot guns come in many types and sizes. A number of calibers can be used in several types of weapon. This is true, for example, of rifle ammunition, which can also be

Group of full-jacketed rifle cartridges from Remington

fired by machine guns. Cartridges for machine guns, however, often include special bullets (tracers) that enable the path of the bullets to be aimed at the target by producing a trail of light. Not all of the cartridges in a cartridge belt or box are tracer bullets: just one every "so many". Due to the high firing rate of 600 to 800 rounds a minute, one tracer bullet per 10 cartridges is easily enough to produce a clearly visible trail of light.

Only commonly used ammunition will be discussed here, plus some special kinds. The available number of calibers, sorts and types is so great that a separate book could be written on this topic.

How the cartridge works

Almost all cartridges are made up of four components:
- the case,
- the primer,
- the gunpowder,
- the bullet.

When a cartridge is fired, the following process takes place. The shooter has a loaded weapon, aims it at the target and pulls the trigger. The trigger is connected to a sear. This sear forms the connection between the trigger and the hammer. The sear is latched into the foot of the hammer. As the trigger moves backwards, the sear is lifted out of a notch in the hammer foot, thus releasing the hammer. The loading action had placed this hammer in the cocked position, thereby tensioning the trigger spring. When the hammer is released, it is thrust forward by the force of the hammer spring and strikes the end of the firing pin. The firing pin of the weapon strikes the primer, which is held in the bottom of the cartridge. The primer is

Cross section of primer (Remington)

filled with a small amount of detonator powder. This is a highly flammable mixture that can be ignited by a slight blow. In a few milliseconds, the small primer charge detonates, resulting in a short, fierce flash. Since the primer has either one hole (Boxer system) or several holes (Berdan system), the flash is directed through the flashholes into the gunpowder charge.

This gunpowder charge is now ignited and it burns out in a fraction of a second, thus generating a high gas pressure. This gas pressure is entirely enclosed, since the case is closed in on every side: at the back against the bolt or breech block, at the sides by the walls of the chamber and at the front by the bullet. The cartridge case is usually made of brass, a soft, elastic material. Since during the gunpowder ignition process the case expands and is pressed against the chamber wall, a tight gas seal is created.

This is necessary, since all the available gas pressure needs to be used to propel the bullet. The gas pressure can only escape at the front, but here the bullet is in the way. This high gas pressure forces the bullet out of its case. The force and the time required for this, which is very short, is called the bullet pull. In a short space of time, the bullet achieves tremendous acceleration, since the gas pressure expands as the bullet is forced further along the barrel. The gas pressure released during the combustion of the gunpowder may reach high levels, depending on the caliber and the gunpowder charge. An 8 x 57 mm Mauser cartridge has a moderate

gas pressure of 35,000 psi, or 2,465 kg/cm2, equivalent to 2.381 atmospheres. Just compare that with the pressure in your car tire. A more modern cartridge, such as the .223 Remington, develops a higher gas pressure, which may reach as much as 55,000 psi (equivalent to 3.742 atmospheres). A heavier caliber does not however necessarily mean that the gas pressure rises to "magnum proportions". A heavy magnum cartridge, such as the .458 Winchester Magnum, gets no higher than approximately 3.600 atmospheres. Depending on the caliber and type of weapon, the bullet will travel from several hundred meters up to as far as thousands of meters.

The acceleration due to the gas pressure ensures that the bullet travels towards the target at great velocity. A reasonable rule of thumb with rifle and carbine cartridges is that the lighter the bullet weight, the higher the bullet velocity, though this is not always the case. A lightweight .233-caliber Remington bullet attains a velocity of some 1000 meters (1093 ft) per second, measured at the muzzle. A .308 Winchester bullet also attains a velocity of around 1000 meters (1093 ft) per second. This bullet velocity is rather underestimated, certainly in popular television series, where the leading players easily manage to dodge a bullet as it zings towards them. When they hear the report, they pull their head back behind the wall just in time and the bullet shoots past them without causing any harm. In reality things are a little bit different.

Velocity of the bullet

From the moment the shooter decides to fire, it takes about 0.2 seconds for the trigger finger to obey the "order" from the brain. Some 0.0005 seconds later, the firing pin strikes the primer of the cartridge. The gunpowder in the cartridge case then ignites in 0.0004 seconds, making a total of 0.2054 seconds. The propellant charge is detonated by the flash from the primer and the gas pressure begins to develop. This chemical reaction continues, even after the bullet has left the barrel. After some 0.004 seconds, the bullet is pulled from the case and begins its passage through the bore. The bullet leaves the barrel at a velocity of some 1000 meters (1093 yd) per second, after being forced through the bore in a time of approximately 0.0012 seconds. Depending on the twist and a number of other factors, the bullet rotates at about 3000 revolutions per second after it leaves the barrel.

If the target is, say, 100 meters (328 ft) away, the bullet will reach it in 0.15 seconds. All told, the process from firing until the bullet hits the target takes just 0.3606 seconds. An interesting fact is that the shooter does not feel the recoil from the weapon until 0.2 seconds after the bullet has left the barrel.

Cross-sectional drawing of the 9 mm Para Gold Sabre Hollow-Point made by Remington

tics is the study of the behavior of the cartridge in the chamber and of the bullet in the barrel. External ballistics deals with the behavior of the bullet after it has left the barrel. There is also a third form of ballistics: terminal or wound ballistics, which is the study of the effect of the bullet on or in the target. Internal and external ballistics sometimes overlap. The speed at which a bullet leaves the barrel is called the muzzle velocity of the bullet. This depends on the cross section and, to a rather lesser extent, the shape of the bullet, as well as on the type of cartridge. A cartridge with a large propellant charge will generally reach a higher speed, since a high level of gas pressure is produced. This bullet velocity is often important, since it partly determines the kinetic energy of the bullet. For a handgun cartridge, this velocity is not normally of interest, since all that matters in this case is the precision up to 25 or 50 meters (49 or 164 ft). For long-range shooters, for example at 300 meters (984 ft), this velocity is important, since it also determines the range of the bullet. A high bullet velocity is also often responsible for a flat bullet trajectory. The kinetic bullet energy, expressed in joules, is calculated using a simple equation: bullet velocity2 x bullet weight (grams) / 2000 = number of joules.

Cross section of a bullet (Remington)

Ballistics

The science of the motion of ammunition is called ballistics. Broadly speaking, there are three types of ballistics. Internal ballis-

Broadly speaking, standard ammunition, when fired from standard rifles, is used up to ranges of 100 to 300 (328 to 984 ft). Special sniper rifles have an effective range that easily reaches up to 300 meters (984 ft) and even further. Modern large-bore snipers, such as the .50-caliber BMG (Browning machine-gun: derived from the machine gun cartridge), attain ranges of up to 2500 meters (2734 yd) with great accuracy. Marksmen with match rifles shoot groups of 3 to 5 cm in diameter at 300 meters (984 ft).

In addition to the shooter's know-how and experience, precision shooting also depends on the propellant charge, the type of bullet, the type of primer and the sort of weapon used.

The inside of the bore of a rifle or carbine has spiral grooves and lands. As a result, rotation is imparted to the bullet during its passage through the bore. This spinning motion gives the bullet the stability required to maintain its trajectory, as otherwise it would quickly begin to "yaw" after leaving the barrel.

Below, we give a general description of the most common calibers of rifles and carbines, with illustrations of the corresponding cartridges. The abbreviations used in the tables stand for:

VO: bullet velocity measured at the moment the bullet exits the muzzle (V = velocity at 0 metres);
fps: feet per second;
m/s: metres per second;
E0: bullet energy, calculated on the basis of bullet velocity at the muzzle (E = energy at 0 metres);
joules: joules: unit used to express the bullet energy. It is the work energy required to move an object weighing 1 kg by 1 metre. Work force is also expressed in Newtons. In this case this is straightforward, since 1 joule is 1 Newton;
ft./lb.: a unit of bullet energy. It is the work done when a force of 1 pound is applied over a distance of 1 foot.

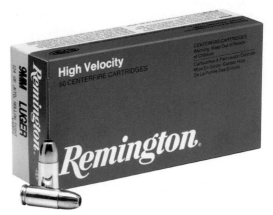

9 mm Para (Luger) caliber

The 9 mm Parabellum, 9 mm Luger, also called 9 x 19 mm cartridge came on the market in 1902 in combination with the Luger semi-automatic pistol. In 1904, the weapon and cartridge entered service with the German navy and in 1908 with the Germany army. For this reason the pistol is still designated the P08. Since then, many military pistols in this caliber have been introduced. In 1985, even the US Army switched from the tried-and-trusted .45 ACP cartridge for their Colt M1911-A1 pistol to the 9 mm Para (9 x 19 mm NATO) for the Beretta M92-F (M9). Government departments in other parts of the world also use this caliber. Only the bullet may vary from country to country. Many countries have introduced the ordinary full-jacketed cartridge, but there are also governments that have opted for a certain shape of a hollow-point bullet. Versions also exist for specialized usage. The 9 mm Para is now the NATO standard caliber for pistols and for the majority of sub-machine-guns.

Caliber	Bullet weight		VO		E0	
	Grains	grams	fps	m/s	joules	ft. lb.
9 mm Para FMJ	115	7.5	1,150	350	460	340
9 mm Para FMJ	124	8.0	1,120	340	462	341

Remington Disintegrator cartridge

In 1998, Remington developed a new police cartridge, the Disintegrator, used in 9 mm

Para, .40 S&W and .45 ACP caliber ammo. The bullet of this cartridge is made of a hard copper jacket filled with compressed metal particles. The bullet tip fragments completely when it strikes hard targets. A great advantage is the lack of the usual lead bullet core. A further advantage is that the bullet traps on the police shooting ranges do not suffer so much. The ballistics of this cartridge is the same as that of the normal full-jacketed cartridge.

Caliber	Bullet weight		V0		E0	
	Grains	grams	fps	m/s	joules	ft. lb.
9 mm Para	105	6.8	1,100	335	382	282
.40 S&W	145	9.4	1,085	331	515	379
.45 ACP	175	11.3	1,020	310	543	401

9 mm Para Action-3 police cartridge

For the past few years, the Dutch police have been using the special 9 mm Para Action-3 cartridge.

It has a bullet, made of solid brass, with a large cavity in the front. This hollow point is sealed with a green plastic cap, which is blown off several meters after the bullet is fired. The cartridge is used for several police weapons, such as the Walther P5 pistol and various Heckler & Koch carbines and sub-machine-guns.

.45 ACP cartridge from Winchester

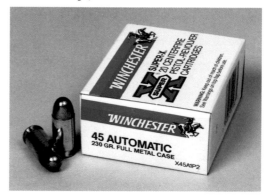

.45 ACP (Automatic Colt Pistol) caliber

This cartridge was developed in 1905 by John M. Browning for his Colt 1911 pistol. Until 1985, this cartridge was the official caliber for the US armed forces handgun. Later they switched to the 9 mm Para cartridge in combination with the Beretta 92F pistol.

Caliber	Bullet weight		V0		E0	
	Grains	grams	fps	m/s	joules	ft. lb.
.45 ACP-FMJ	230	14.9	850	260	504	372

5.45 x 39 (Russian) caliber

This Russian military cartridge was introduced in 1974 for the new AK-74 military rifle, the successor to the famous Kalashnikov AK-47. This cartridge was first written about in 1980 in the arms magazine Soldier of Fortune by author Galen Geer. He had seen the cartridge and the weapon in Afghanistan.

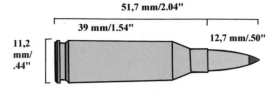

The first version of the cartridge had a steel case with a Berdan primer. In addition, the steel bullet was not entirely filled with a lead core, but had a small empty space in the tip. As a result, when the bullet hit the target it became so unstable that it started to tumble, causing serious injury.

Caliber	Bullet weight		VO		EO
	Grains-grams		fps	m/s	joules-ft. lb.
5.45 x 39	54	3.5	2,950	899	1,414 1,044

5.56 x 45 mm NATO / .223 Remington caliber

The development of the .223 Remington cartridge is related to that of the American military rifle in this caliber, the AR-15 or later the M-16. This Armalite rifle was designed by Eugene Stoner. The cartridge was developed by Robert Hutton, one of the authors of the American arms magazine Guns & Ammo.

On the basis of the existing .222 Remington cartridge, Hutton and Stoner developed a new cartridge. The requirement laid down by the US Army was that the bullet had to have a velocity of 330 meters

The 5.56 x 45 mm NATO or .223 Rem. from MagTech/CBC

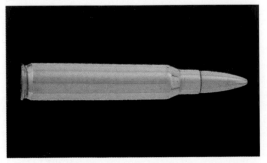

(1082 ft) per second at 500 meters (546 yd). In 1964, this caliber officially entered service with the US Army as the 5.56-mm Ball M193 cartridge. The 55 grain (3.56 gram) bullet attained a muzzle velocity of 3250 feet per second (990 meters per second).

The cartridge, in combination with the M16 military rifle, was tested extensively under war conditions in Vietnam. Various complaints eventually resulted in the cartridge being modified in 1980. Initially, the barrel of the M16 had a twist of 1:12", i.e. one complete circle over a distance of 12" (30.5 cm).

In 1980, Belgium's FN factory came up with a striking improvement to the weapon's accuracy. This involved making the twist of the bore faster: 1:7" (17.8 cm). The new cartridge for this was called the M855. It has a 62 grain (4.0 gram) bullet, designated the SS109, with a muzzle velocity of 3100 fps (945 m/s). This cartridge is currently NATO's official standard rifle caliber. The modern tendency is also to introduce light machine guns in this caliber into the armed forces.

In the past there have been many strange tales about this caliber. One of them is that a hit in, say, a leg or arm would be enough to eliminate a person for good. This was supposed to be the consequence of the enormous shock wave or hitting power. However, when you consider that for example a .308 Win. cartridge develops twice the bullet energy, you will realize that this is a fairy-tale.

Caliber	Bullet weight		VO		EO
	Grains-grams		fps	m/s	joules-ft. lb.
5.56 mm M193	55	3,6	3,250	990	1.764 1.302
5.56 mm M855	62	4,0	3,100	945	1.786 1.318

Note: as early as 1979, SAAMI (the Sporting Arms and Ammunition Manufacturers Institute) issued a warning regarding the use of military ammunition in commercial semi-automatic rifles in this caliber.

Because of the slightly different dimensions of the barrel chamber and the barrel throat (space between the start of the bore and the rifling), too high a pressure can develop in the chamber on a sports rifle.

5.7 x 28 mm FN-P90 (SS190)

This caliber was developed around 1985 by the Belgian arms group FN for their new sub-machine-gun, the P90, and the accompanying military pistol, the Five Seven. The idea, at least Fn.'s idea, is that this cartridge will replace the 9 mm Para as NATO ammunition. This caliber has an effective range of 200 meters (656 ft) and is capable of piercing a 48-layer Culver bullet-proof vest.

Caliber	Bullet weight Grains-grams		VO fps	m/s	EO joules-ft. lb.	
5.7 x 28 mm	93	6	2,346	715	1,533	1,131

7.5 x 55 mm (Swiss) caliber

This caliber was developed in 1885 for the Swiss Schmidt-Rubin military rifle. The weapon and cartridge entered service with the Swiss army in 1889.
Initially, the cartridge was provided with a 213 grain (13.8 gram) bullet and had a muzzle velocity of 1970 fps (600 m/s). In 1903, the cartridge was modified and

The new 5.7 x 28 mm cartridge from FN for the FN-P90

The Swiss 7.5 x 55 mm cartridge

given a 190 grain (12.3 gram) bullet. In 1911, a new bullet was introduced, weighing 174 grains (11.3 grams).

Caliber	Bullet weight Grains-grams		VO fps	m/s	EO joules-ft. lb.	
7.5 x 55 mm	174	11.3	2,560	780	3,437	2,537

.30-M1 Carbine caliber

The carbine was meant to replace the Colt 1911-A1 .45 ACP military pistol and was therefore actually intended to be a compromise between a handgun and a normal-sized military rifle.

Following the Second World War, many carbines were disposed of by the army and

The popular .30-M1 carbine cartridge (Winchester)

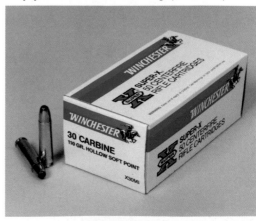

became available for sport shooting. The .30-M1 carbine was largely developed by David Marshall "Carbine" Williams of the Winchester Repeating Arms Company.

During the Second World War, .30-M1 carbines were made by several manufacturers, such as Inland, Underwood, Quality Hardware and Machine Corporation (HMC), Rock-Ola, Irwin-Pedersen, Saginaw, National Postal Meter, Standard Products and IBM.
The cartridge is usually designated the .30 US Carbine.

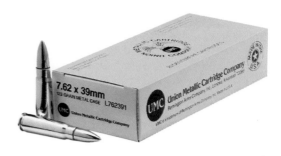

The 7.62 x 39 mm cartridge (MagTech/CBC)

Caliber	Bullet weight		V0		E0	
	Grains	grams	fps	m/s	joules	ft. lb.
.30-M1 Carbine	110	7.1	1,975	602	1,287	950

7.62 x 39 mm M43 (Russian) caliber

This cartridge is the Russian equivalent of the .308 Winchester caliber, also called 7.62 x 51 NATO. This caliber was developed as early as 1943, during the Second World War. Initially, the cartridge was intended for the Russian SKS carbine, but later it was also used for the Kalashnikov AK-47. Most old military ammunition is still provided with a lacquered steel case. Since the Cold War and the fall of the "Iron Curtain", this caliber has been permitted in all Western countries. The prime example of reconciliation is that Colt markets its civilian version of the M16 military rifle in this caliber as well. The same also applies, incidentally, to Ruger with its Mini-Thirty carbine.

Caliber	Bullet weight		V0		E0	
	Grains	grams	fps	m/s	joules	ft. lb.
7.62 x 39 M43	122	7.9	2,330	710	1,991	1,469

.303 British caliber

This cartridge was used in the nineteenth century in the far-flung British Empire. It was developed in 1887 and entered service with the British army in 1888. The ammunition has seen service in all the former British colonies, for example in Africa and India. Originally, the 215 grain (13.9 gram) round-nosed bullet was propelled by black powder. The myth of the "dum-dum bullet" is related to this cartridge. The official version is as follows. Complaints were received from various fronts about the low effectiveness of the round-nosed bullet against insurgents. Army Captain B. Clay, who worked as an arms engineer at the State Arsenal in the town of Dum Dum in India, developed an expanding bullet, in which the bullet jacket did not continue to the tip, but to the point where the lead core remained free. The unofficial version of the story is that British soldiers were exasperated with the cartridge and filed off the full-jacketed point for reasons of self-preservation. This produced the same expanding result. When this operation was discovered, it was a simple matter to modify the bullet in the factory. In 1892, the cartridge was modified for smokeless powder. The round-nosed bullet was

The .303 British rifle cartridge (Winchester)

replaced in 1910 by a pointed-nose bullet, called the Mk VII. This bullet, with a lead core, had a point filled with aluminum or synthetic fiber. The .303 British caliber was initially designed for the Lee-Metford Mk I military rifle. In 1895, this rifle was succeeded by the Lee-Enfield, whose bore had deeper grooves and lands. Some time after World War II this caliber became obsolete as a military cartridge and was superseded by the 7.62 x 51 mm (NATO) or .308 Winchester caliber.

Caliber	Bullet weight		VO		EO	
	Grains-grams		fps	m/s	joules-ft. lb.	
.303 Br.Mk VII	174	11.3	2,440	744	3,127	2,308

.30-06 Springfield (US) caliber

This cartridge entered service in 1906 with the US armed forces for the Springfield Model 1903 bolt-action rifle. The name comes from a cartridge with a .30 caliber (.308 in to be precise) dating from 1906, hence .30-06. The additional name "Springfield" comes from the US Springfield Arsenal, which was a state institution until the 1950s. Initially the "1903 cartridge" had a round-nosed bullet weighing 220 grains (14.3 grams), with a muzzle velocity of some 2300 fps (700 m/s). This was later changed to a 150 grain (9.7 gram) pointed bullet. Officially it was designated Ball Cartridge, caliber 30, Model of 1906, abbreviated to .30-06. In 1926, the caliber was again modified and a 172 grain (11.1 gram) bullet was used. This new cartridge was designated the Ball, caliber 30, M1. In 1940, the older 150 grain bullet returned as the Cartridge, Ball, caliber 30, M2. This cartridge was used during the Second World War for the semi-automatic Garand military rifle, because the Garand was unable to take the heavier 172 grain bullet. Eventually, this caliber was succeeded by the 7.62 x 51 NATO caliber.

Caliber	Bullet weight		VO		EO	
	Grains-grams		fps	m/s	joules-ft. lb.	
.30-06 M1903	220	14.3	2,300	700	3,504	2,586
.30-06 M1	172	11.1	2,640	805	3,597	2,655
.30-06 M2	150	9.7	2,730	832	3,357	2,477

.308 Winchester caliber

This cartridge was developed after the Second World War by the US Army's Ordnance Department. The military name for this caliber is 7.62 x 51 mm NATO, since in 1953 it was officially introduced as a NATO caliber.
In 1952, Winchester was given permission to market this cartridge in a civilian version under the name .308 Winchester. The US Army used this cartridge for its M1A rifle or the Springfield M14 and for the M60 machine gun.
In Europe, this cartridge was used in the FN-FAL military rifle and the FN-MAG machine gun. This caliber remained in use by the NATO armed forces until 1980. After this date, the 5.56 x 45 mm cartridge was introduced as the NATO standard. The .308 Win. was retained for various machine guns as well as for snipers.

Caliber	Bullet weight		VO		EO	
	Grains-grams		fps	m/s	joules-ft. lb.	
Ball M80	150	9.7	2,750	838	3,405	2,513
Ball M852	168	10.9	2,660	811	3,585	2,646

The .30-06 Springfield cartridge (MagTech/CBC)

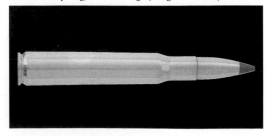

The .308 Win. or 7.62 x 51 mm Nato (MagTech/CBC)

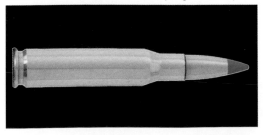

.300 Winchester Magnum caliber

The .300 Winchester Magnum was originally developed as a hunting cartridge. In 1963, it was brought onto the market by Winchester in combination with the Winchester Model 70 bolt-action rifle. The cartridge is derived from the heavy .338 Winchester Magnum. In military circles, this caliber has actually never been particularly popular, but nowadays this cartridge is used for police sniper rifles.

Caliber	Bullet weight		V0		E0	
	Grains-grams		fps	m/s	joules-ft. lb.	
.300 WM	150	9.72	3,290	1,003	4,889	3,605
.300 WM	180	11.66	2,960	902	4,743	3,500

7.62 x 54R caliber

The Russian 7.62 x 54R is also designated the 7.62 x 53R. The cartridge dates from 1891 and was designed for the Mosin-Nagant Model 1891 bolt-action rifle. Initially, it had a round bullet, but in 1909 a 150 grain pointed bullet was introduced.

This cartridge was the Russian standard caliber during the Second World War. Nowadays it is used for machine guns and the SVO Dragunov sniper rifle.

Caliber	Bullet weight		V0		E0	
	Grains-grams		fps	m/s	joules-ft. lb.	
Ball 150	150	9.72	2,800	853	3,536	2,620

8 x 57 mm Mauser caliber

The 7.9 x 57 mm Mauser cartridge is almost always designated the 8 x 57 mm Mauser or 8 mm Mauser. This military cartridge was developed in 1888. Originally, the caliber was derived from the Austrian Mannlicher cartridge. Another designation for this caliber was 8 x 57 mm-J or I for infantry. The original diameter of the bullet was 8.08 mm (.318").

The Mauser 8 x 57 mm cartridge (Winchester)

This round-nosed bullet weighed 226 grains (14.6 grams) and had a muzzle velocity of some 2,090 fps (637 m/s). In 1905, the cartridge was modified, with the caliber designation being retained, but with the suffix "S", i.e. the 8 x 57 mm-S or JS.

This cartridge has a bullet diameter of 8.20 mm (.323 in). A confusing business, then, because firing an "S" cartridge in a "J" rifle has particularly nasty consequences.The S or JS cartridge has a sharp tip, weighs 154 grains (9.97 grams) and has a muzzle velocity of 2,880 fps (878 m/s). Most Mauser rifles of the 98 type have been built for this new caliber. The Mauser 1888 Commission rifle always fires the old "J" caliber.

Caliber	Bullet weight		VO		EO
	Grains-grams		fps	m/s	joules-ft. lb.
8 x 57 mm J	226	14.6	2,090	637	2,962 2,186
8 x 57 mm JS	154	9.97	2,880	878	3,843 2,836

.338 Winchester Magnum

Winchester introduced the .338 Winchester Magnum cartridge in 1958, in combination with the Winchester Model 70 Alaskan bolt-action rifle. This weapon was primarily intended as a long-range "polar bear rifle".

Some years later, Remington also used this cartridge for its Model 700 rifles. On the basis of this, various sniper models have been introduced by Remington on several occasions, especially for police applica-

The .338 Winchester Magnum sniper cartridge

tions. The cartridge is less powerful than the .338 Lapua Magnum, but is used for police snipers in the USA and South America in particular.

Caliber	Bullet weight		VO		EO
	Grains-grams		fps	m/s	joules-ft. lb.
.338 Win.Mag.	200	12.96	2,960	902	5,272 3,890
.338 Win.Mag.	250	16.2	2,660	811	5,328 3,920

.338 Lapua Magnum caliber

Commissioned by the US Navy, the research institute of Research Armament Co. began development of a new, powerful sniper cartridge in 1983. Eventually, the neck of a .416 Rigby big-game cartridge was adapted to a .338 in bullet. The idea was to give a 250 grain (16.2 gram) bullet a muzzle velocity of around 3,000 fps (approx. 915 m/s).

The hitting power of this cartridge was enormous, certainly for those days. In 1985, the cartridge was ready. The bullet was manufactured by Hornady, the cartridge case by Brass Extrusions Labs Ltd., with the bolt-action rifle being built by Research Armament. Eventually, Lapua took on the commercial production of this cartridge and lent its name to it.

Caliber	Bullet weight		VO		EO
	Grains-grams		fps	m/s	joules-ft. lb.
.338 Lap.Mag.	250	16.2	3,000	915	6,782 5,005

.50 BMG (Browning Machine Gun) caliber

This cartridge was developed as early as 1921 by the well-known American arms

The .338 Lapua Magnum sniper cartridge

The large .50 BMG (Browning Machine Gun) from MagTech/CBC)

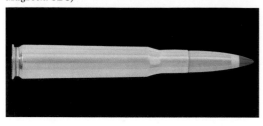

The large .50 BMG (Browning Machine Gun) from MagTech/CBC)

designer John Moses Browning. The caliber was intended for his .50 machine gun. In 1923, this weapon was introduced into the US Army.

It is striking that after more than 75 years of service this weapon is still used by NATO for arming armored vehicles, tanks and as an aircraft machine gun. This caliber is nowadays also used for heavy sniper rifles for ranges over 1500 meters (1640 yd). The bullet energy is tremendously high. Only heavily armored vehi-

cles, such as modern tanks, are capable of withstanding such force. The first manufacturers that built such rifles in this caliber were the American firms of Barrett, McMillan and Harris.

Caliber	Bullet weight Grains-grams		VO fps	m/s	EO joules-ft. lb.	
.50 BMG-M33	668	43.2	2,900	884	16,880	12,398
.50 BMG-M2	720	46.7	2,800	853	16,990	12,539

Riotgun ammunition

A large number of cartridge types exist for the short riot- gun. The best-known is the slug. In Europe, the brand name Brenneke has actually become more of a generic name. In the USA, various ammunition manufacturers also make similar slug cartridges, such as Remington and Federal. Government departments also

Buckshot cartridge from Remington

Collection of target discs from Remington

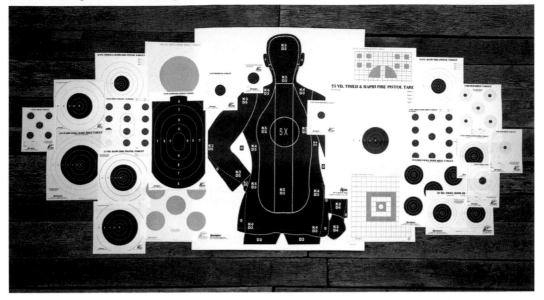

Brenneke slug cartridge from Rottweil

Flechettes are a kind of arrow-shaped projectiles. Sabots consist of a wedge-shaped or conical lead projectile. The slug is usually shot using cylindrical smooth-bore guns. There are however also gun types in caliber 12 with rifled bores for this type of ammunition. It is used for shooting at ranges of 100 (328 ft) up to as far as 300 meters (984 ft) for special purposes.

sometimes use the so-called Buckshot. This "shotgun cartridge" usually has 7 to 9 lead balls. In addition, several ammunition factories have developed various kinds of prototypes, such as flechettes and sabots.

Caliber	Bullet weight		VO		EO
	Grains-grams		fps	m/s	joules-ft. lb.
12/76 Brenneke	39	460	4,126	3,045	
12/76 Remingt.	1 oz.	28.35	1,600	488	3,375 2,491

The Remington slug cartridge

Cross section of the Brenneke slug cartridge and the Express buckshot cartridge from Rottweil

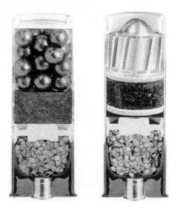

Exploded views

Expressions are used in this encyclopedia that may be confusing to the reader. Certain parts can quickly be found in the technical drawings. Most firearms function using roughly the same system, making it easier to understand the operation of the weapon.

Semi-automatic shotgun (riotgun)

See exploded view of a Benelli semi-automatic shotgun. The numbers in the drawing indicate the following parts:

1. tubular magazine
2. barrel chamber
3. cocking handle
4. breechblock
5. 5. safety pushbutton

Cross-sectional drawing of a Benelli riotgun

6. main spring guide rod
7. main spring
8. hammer
9. firing pin
10. bolt head

Semi-automatic rifle

The following exploded view shows the FN FAL rifle.
The most important parts are indicated by numbers. They are:

1. stock
2. pistol grip
3. magazine floor plate
4. magazine spring
5. follower
6. magazine housing
7. safety catch/firing selector
8. trigger
8a. trigger guard
9. sear

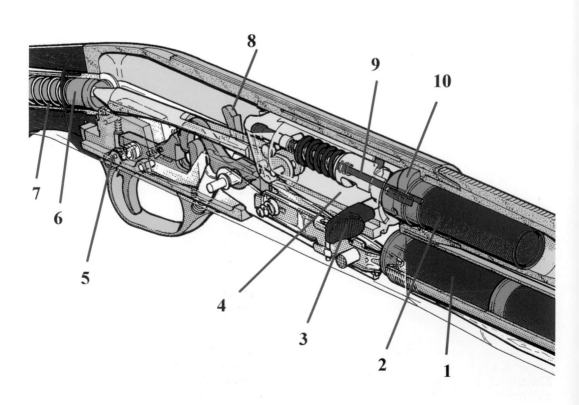

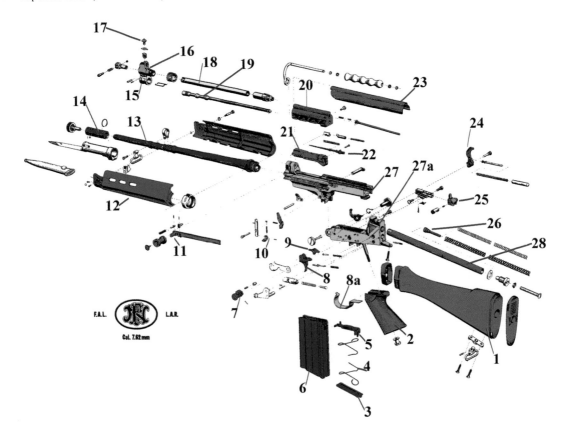

10. magazine catch
11. cocking handle
12. hand guard
13. barrel
14. flash suppresser
15. gas block
16. bead mounting
17. front sight
18. gas tube
19. piston rod
20. breechblock
21. vertical locking block
22. firing pin
23. receiver cover
24. hammer
25. aperture sight
26. main spring guide rod
27. receiver
27a. trigger housing
28. main spring tube

Carbine

An exploded view of the Ruger Mini-14 is shown as a comparison between a rifle and a carbine.
The numbers indicate the following parts:

1. trigger
2. sear
3. safety catch
4. hamer
5. trigger housing
6. trigger guard
7. magazine catch
8. magazine housing
9. follower
10. magazine spring
11. magazine base plate lock
12. magazine base plate
13. bolt catch

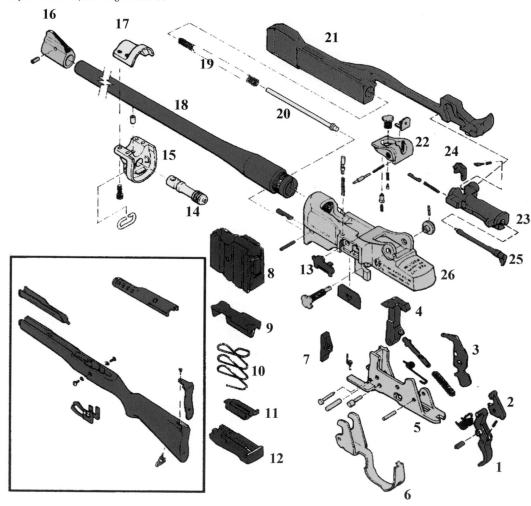

14. piston
15. gas block
16. front sight
17. gas block cover
18. barrel
19. main spring
20. main spring guide rod
21. cocking lever with inertia block
22. aperture sight
23. bolt
24. extractor
25. firing pin
26. receiver

Automatic rifle

An exploded view of the Beretta AR 70 is shown as an example of an automatic rifle. Part no. 43 is the release lever, which presses the sear (no. 56) outside the reach of the hammer (no 45), so that the weapon can fire automatically as long as the trigger remains pressed. Another interesting feature is that the main spring (no. 3) is fitted around the piston rod (no. 2), which provides the repeating action.
The illustrated parts of the Beretta AR 70 are:

1. barrel
2. piston rod

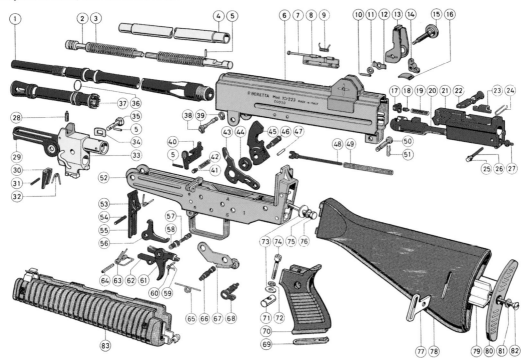

Exploded view of the Beretta AR 70 rifle

3. main spring	30. grenade launcher catch
4. piston rod tube	31. grenade launcher catch pin
5. cotter pin	32. grenade launcher catch spring
6. receiver housing	33. gas block
7. ejector port hinge pin	34. gas regulator spring
8. ejector port cover	35. gas regulator
9. ejector port cover spring	36. locking ring for rifle grenade
10. aparture sight pin	37. attachment for rifle grenade
11. ring for aperture sight	38. pivoting pin
12. spring for adjusting knob for aperture sight	39. pivoting pin rings (two)
13. aperture sight housing	40. bolt catch
14. aperture sight	41. bolt catch lock pin
15. adjusting knob for aperture sight	42. bolt catch spring
16. aperture sight spring	43. release lever (automatic firing)
17. extractor	44. hammer pin bushing
18. extractor pin	45. hammer
19. extractor spring	46. hammer pin
20. breechblock	47. hammer spring lock pin
21. receiver housing	48. hammer spring guide rod
22. cocking lever	49. hammer spring
23. cocking lever catch	50. receiver housing lock pin
24. cocking handle catch spring	51. receiver housing lock pin spring
25. firing pin lock shaft ring	52. trigger housing
26. firing pin lock shaft	53. magazine catch spring
27. firing pin	54. magazine catch shaft
28. front sight	55. magazine catch
29. lever for grenade device	56. sear
	57. trigger pin

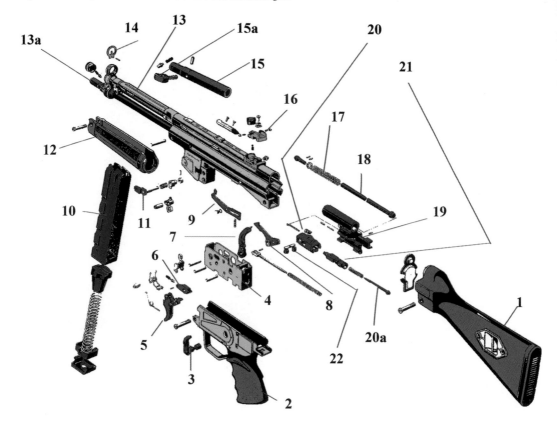

58. trigger pin bush
59. sear spring pin
60. sear spring
61. trigger
62. release lever catch
63. trigger spring
64. trigger spring pin
65. release lever spring
66. release lever pin
67. locking plate for release lever pin
68. combined rotating firing selector/
    safety catch
69. pistol grip buttplate
70. pistol grip
71. pistol grip locking nut
72. locking ring
73. washers (two)
74. pistol grip bolt
75. locking ring
76. stock bolt
77. sling swivel
78. stock

79. butt plate nut guide bushing
80. butt plate
81. locking nut
82. butt plate screw
83. hand grip

Sub-machine-gun

The next exploded view is of the Heckler
& Koch MP5 sub-machine-gun. Note in
particular part no. 8: the release lever,
which ensures that the weapon can fire
automatically by disabling the sear.

1. stock
2. pistol grip with receiver housing
3. safety catch/firing selector
4. trigger housing
5. trigger
6. sear
7. hammer

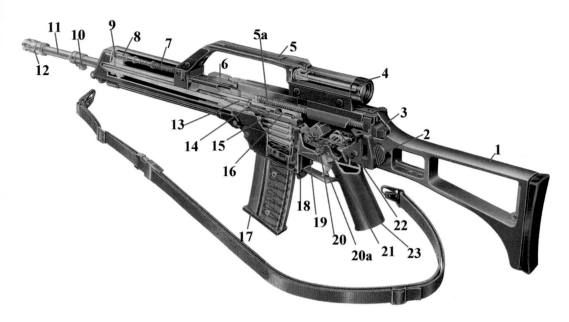

8.	release lever	1.	folding stock
9.	ejector	2.	locking button for folding stock
10.	magazine	3.	locking button for receiver housing
11.	magazine catch		(opening rifle)
12.	hand guard	4.	scope
13.	receiver housing	5.	carrying handle
13a.	barrel	5a.	main spring with main spring guide
14.	front sight		rod
15.	cocking rod	6.	cocking handle
15a.	cocking lever	7.	piston rod
16.	drum sight	8.	piston
17.	main spring	9.	gas vent
18.	main spring guide rod	10.	bayonet lug
19.	bolt carrier	11.	barrel
20.	bolt head	12.	flash suppresser
20a.	firing pin	13.	barrel chamber
21.	guide block for locking rollers	14.	bolt lugs
22.	locking rollers	15.	breechblock
		16.	firing pin
		17.	magazine
		18.	magazine catch
		19.	bolt catch
		20.	hammer
		20a.	trigger
		21.	safety catch/firing selector
		22.	release lever
		23.	pistol grip

Automatic rifle

Finally, an exploded view of the new Heckler & Koch G36E military rifle. In this drawing, the interrelationship between all parts can clearly be seen. The most important parts are indicated by numbers.

Military rifles and sub-machine-guns from A-Z

A a

Accuracy International

The English firm of Accuracy International, of Portsmouth in Hampshire, produces mainly sniper rifles for government departments. In 1982, owner and director Malcolm Cooper developed the PM (Precision Magazine) sniper rifle. This rifle was introduced into the British army in 1986 as the L96A1. A few years later, a modified version followed, which entered service as the L97A1. This rifle was fitted with the Schmidt & Bender 6 x 42 scope. The PM sniper came in several versions: the PM Counter-Terrorist, with a Schmidt & Bender 6 x 42 or 2.5-10 x 56 scope; the PM Covert, with a folding stock; and the PM Infantry Rifle. Later versions also consisted of the PM Long Range Sniper rifle, in 7 mm Remington Magnum or .300 Winchester Magnum caliber, with an S&B 12 x 42 scope, the PM Moderate Rifle with silencer for subsonic ammunition, and the PM Super Magnum, in .338 Lapua Magnum caliber. In 1992, the AW (Arctic Warfare) sniper rifle was developed, based

Accuracy International, logo

on the PM. In the late 1980s, the Swedish army was the first to receive this rifle, designated the PSG-90. As well as the military AW version, the AW series also consists of the AWP-Police, in .308 Winchester or .243 Winchester caliber. AI introduced the weapon in 1997. The rifle, which has a stainless-steel barrel, has an S&B 3-12 x 50 scope. The AWS, in which the S stands for Silenced, and the AWM, the Super Magnum that uses .338 Lapua Magnum or .300 Winchester Magnum caliber ammo, are for quieter work. The stock of the rifle consists of two synthetic dish sections fixed together by Allen screws around the receiver. In 1997, the company opened a new factory in Oak Ridge, Tennessee: Accuracy International North America Inc.

Accuracy International AW (Arctic Warfare)

SPECIFICATIONS

Caliber	: .223 Rem. (5.56 NATO) or .308 Win. (7.62 NATO)
Magazine	: detachable magazine
Cartridge capacity	:.308: 10 cartridges; .223: 8 cartridges
Magazine catchl	: in front of trigger guard
Action	: bolt-action
Cocking system	: bolt lever
Firing system	: single round
Locking system	: 3-lug locking

AI AW (Arctic Warfare)

AI AW in box

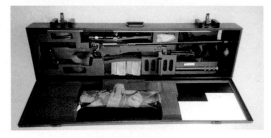

AI AWM in .338

Length	: 118 cm (46.5")
Barrel length	: 66 cm (26")
Weight	: .223: 6.2 kg (13.5 lb); .308: 5.9 kg (13 lb.)
Sight	: Schmidt & Bender 6 x 42 or 10 x 42 MKII scope
Safety	: wing catch behind and to the right of bolt lever; firing pin safety
Stock	: green synthetic stock with thumb hole

PARTICULARS

Green coating; folding bipod; special flash suppresser /recoil compensator; special construction against ice formation to -40 °C. It comes in a metal box. The stock can be lengthened as required by means of spacers.

This sniper rifle has been introduced into many army units associated with NATO. The weapon is also used by police units in many countries.

Accuracy International AWM (Arctic Warfare Super Magnum)

SPECIFICATIONS

Caliber	: .300 Win. Mag. or .338 Lapua Mag.
Magazine	: detachable magazine
Cartridge capacity	: 5 cartridges
Magazine catch	: in front of trigger guard
Action	: bolt-action
Cocking system	: bolt lever
Firing system	: single round
Locking system	: 6-lug locking

AI AWM

Length	: .300: 120 cm (47"); .338: 123 cm (48.4")
Barrel length	: .300: 66 cm (26") or .338: 68.6 cm d(27")
Weight	: .300: 7.1 kg (15.6 lb.); .338: 6.8 kg (15.1 lb.)
Sight	: Schmidt & Bender 10 x 42, 3-12 x 50 or 4-16 x 50 MKII scope
Safety	: wing catch behind and to the right of bolt lever; firing pin safety
Stock	: green or dark-grey synthetic stock with thumb hole

PARTICULARS

Green or dark-gray coating; folding bipod; special flash suppresser/recoil compensator; special construction against ice formation to -40 °C. It comes in a metal box. The stock can be lengthened as required by means of spacers. The AWM, in .300 Win. Mag. caliber ammo, has a fluted barrel. It is intended for ranges of approx. 1000 meters (1093 yd).

Accuracy International AWP (Arctic Warfare Police)

SPECIFICATIONS

Caliber	: .243 Win. or .308 Win. (7.62 NATO)
Magazine	: detachable magazine
Cartridge capacity	: 10 cartridges
Magazine catch	: in front of trigger guard
Action	: bolt-action
Cocking system	: bolt lever
Firing system	: single round

AI AWP

AI AWP police sniper

Locking system	: 3-lug locking
Length	: 112 cm (44")
Barrel length	: 61 cm (24")
Weight	: 6.5 kg (14.3 lb.)
Sight	: Schmidt & Bender 3-12 x 50 MKII scope
Safety	: wing catch behind and to the right of bolt lever; firing pin safety
Stock	: black synthetic stock with thumb hole

PARTICULARS

Black coating; folding bipod; special construction against ice formation to -40 °C. It comes in a metal box. The stock can be lengthened as required by means of spacers. The rifle is made particularly for police and special units.

Accuracy International AWS (Arctic Warfare Silencer)

SPECIFICATIONS

Caliber	: .308 Win. (subsonic)
Magazine	: detachable magazine
Cartridge capacity	: 10 cartridges
Magazine catch	: in front of trigger guard
Action	: bolt-actione

AI AWS

Cocking system	: bolt lever
Firing system	: single round
Locking system	: 3-lug locking
Length	: 120 cm (47")
Barrel length	: 66 cm (26")
Weight	: 6 kg (13.2 lb.)
Sight	: Schmidt & Bender 6 x 42 or 3-12 x 50 MKII scope
Safety	: wing catch behind and to the right of bolt lever; firing pin safety
Stock	: :green synthetic stock with thumb hole

PARTICULARS

Green coating; folding bipod; special silenced barrel; special construction against ice formation to -40 °C. It comes in a synthetic box.
The stock can be lengthened as required by means of spacers. This sniper rifle is made particularly for special operations.

Accuracy International AW50 (Arctic Warfare)

SPECIFICATIONS

Caliber	: .50 BMG
Magazine	: detachable magazine
Cartridge capacity	: 5 cartridges
Magazine catchl	: in front of trigger guard
Action	: bolt-action
Cocking system	: bolt lever
Firing system	: single round
Locking system	: heavy 6-lug lock
Length	: 142 cm (56"); with collapsed stock: 117 cm (46")
Barrel length	: 68.6 cm (27")
Weight	: 15 kg (33 lb.)
Sight	: Schmidt & Bender 10 x 42, 3-12 x 50 or 4-16 x 50 MKII scope
Safety	: wing catch behind and to the right of bolt lever; firing pin safety
Stock	: green synthetic folding stock with thumb hole

AI AW50

AI AW50

PARTICULARS
Green coating; folding bipod with extra leg under stock; special flash suppresser and built-in recoil damper; special construction against ice formation to -40 °C. It comes in a metal box. This sniper rifle is designed particularly for very long ranges.

ArmaLite

The ArmaLite Division was set up in 1954 as a subsidiary of the Fairchild Engine & Airplane Corporation. The group's plan was for ArmaLite to develop a line of weapons using aluminum alloys and synthetics, which were already used in the aircraft industry. The first concept was the AR-3, developed by chief designer Eugene Stoner. This design eventually resulted in the AR-10 and later the AR-15 rifles. The AR-10, designed by Stoner, was made by the Nederlandse Artillerie-Inrichtingen (Dutch artillery organization) in Zaandam under license from ArmaLite. Following a series of tests and modifications in 1955, 1956 and 1957, the line of weapons was extended in 1958 to include a version of a carbine/sub-machine-gun, a sniper rifle and a light machine gun. In 1959, a worldwide representation was even set up. Artillerie-Inrichtingen/Eurometaal Zaandam was to make the rifle under license

and ArmaLite was hopeful of large army orders. During the final test by the Dutch army, the test weapon developed a fatal jam after several hundred shots. As a result, the proposed purchase of the AR-10 was dropped. The story goes that a top army officer purposely disrupted the test because the top brass and politicians had other plans. In the end, the Dutch army opted for the Belgian FN-FAL. The stock of AR-10s was sold to Sudan, Portugal and Guatemala. In 1957, the Department of Defense stipulated a number of requirements that a new military rifle had to meet. It had to be a smallbore rifle weighing not more than 2.7 kg (6 lb.), with ballistic characteristics that were equal to the .30 cartridge up to 300 yards. The AR-10 rifle was modified by ArmaLite for the .222 Remington cartridge.

There was one problem, however: the US Army made the requirements more stringent. The ballistic requirement was increased from 300 to 500 yards. This was solved by developing a new cartridge, the .222 Rem. Special, later the .223 Remington. The rifle was designated the AR-15. Tests conducted in March 1958 showed that this rifle met the requirements with flying colors, though a few modifications were regarded as necessary. For instance, the carrying handle had to be fitted at the back of the receiver housing and a flash suppresser was attached to the barrel. Originally, the rifle had a 30-round magazine. To reduce the weight to within the stipulated requirements, a 20-round magazine was designed. Nevertheless, in 1958 the army selected the M14 in .308 Win. caliber. As a result, ArmaLite lost all interest in the AR-15 and sold the license to

ArmaLite, logo

Colt. The Colt factory continued development of the AR-15 and came on the market in 1959 with the AR-15-01. This rifle was first sold to India and Malaysia. The U.S. Air Force, however, saw potential in this weapon and, despite opposition in Congress, the rifle became the official standard weapon in 1962 for the air force, the Navy Seals and special military advisors in Vietnam. The US Army also revived its interested. In the autumn of 1962, the rifle was again tested under the name XM-16.

This resulted in the purchase of 100,000 AR-15 rifles for airborne landing troops and special units. In 1963, the twist of the rifling was modified from 1:14 in to 1:12 in for improved bullet ballistics. In the same year, at the request of the army, the rifle was provided with a "forward assist plunger". This button was attached to the right-hand side of the receiver housing, under the cocking lever. The purpose of this is to give the breech block a thump if it fails to close completely. This type was given the military designation XM16E1. At the end of 1963, Colt received the first official government order for 85,000 XM16E1 rifles for the army and 19,000 M16 rifles for the air force. The first complaints from the troops in Vietnam started to come in 1965. Many of them could be explained by a lack of maintenance, but there were also problems with the extractor and the breech block recoil after locking.

These problems were corrected in 1966 by a modified main spring and buffer spring and the use of a different type of propellant for the ammunition. In June 1966, Colt received a second order for over 835,000 rifles. The XM16E1 rifle was renamed the M16A1 in 1967. Because the extraction problems were still occurring, from May 1967 the barrel chamber was chrome-plated. However, the Department of Defense was not happy about having just one manufacturer and so in June 1967 it bought Colt's entire production rights for US$4,500,000 and an extra payment for every rifle made under government license. The rifles were then also made by Hydra-Matic Division, a subsidiary of General Motors, and by Harrington &

Richardson. In 1982, a new version of the rifle was introduced, the M16A1E1, later called the M16A2. This weapon had a modified aperture sight and a heavy barrel with a 1:7 twist.

The pistol grip, the stock and the flash suppresser were also altered. In addition, the trigger mechanism was changed from fully automatic to 3-round burst. One of the last versions was the M16A3, with a flat-top receiver and fully automatic firing mechanism (Model 901), and the same weapon with a 3-round-burst system (Model 905).

Altogether, the AR-15 or M16 has had many variations, more than twenty of the standard model and over ten of the Heavy Barrel model. There are more than ten variations of the carbine version. The M16 in the form of a sub-machine-gun has fifteen versions, including several Commando models, such as the XM177, XM177E1 and XM177E2 for special army units. The AR-15/M16 has been exported to many countries, from Australia to Zaire. In 1996, ArmaLite was taken over by Eagle Arms. Both firms continued under the ArmaLite name.

ArmaLite AR-10A2

SPECIFICATIONS

Caliber	: .308 Win.
Magazine	: detachable magazine
Cartridge capacity:	10 or 20 cartridges
Magazine catch	: in left-hand side of magazine housing
Action	: gas pressure
Cocking system	: cocking lever
Firing system	: semi-automatic
Locking system	: rotating bolt head with 6 locking lugs and 1 safety lug

ArmaLite AR-10A2

Length	: 104 cm (41")
Barrel length	: 50.8 cm (20")
Weight	: 4.5 kg (9.8 lb.)
Sight	: carrying handle with adjustable rear and front sights of M16 type
Safety	: rotating catch on left-hand side of receiver housing
Stock	: synthetic stock and pistol grip

PARTICULARS
Synthetic hand grip; matt black coating.
Stainless-steel barrel.

ArmaLite AR-10A4 Special Purpose Rifle

SPECIFICATIONS

Caliber	: .308 Win.
Magazine	: detachable magazine
Cartridge capacity	: 10 or 20 cartridges
Magazine catch	: in left-hand side of magazine housing
Action	: gas pressure
Cocking system	: cocking lever
Firing system	: semi-automatic
Locking system	: rotating bolt head with 6 locking lugs and 1 safety lug
Length	: 104 cm (41")
Barrel length	: 50.8 cm (20"); HBAR match barrel
Weight	: 4.35 kg (9.8 lb.)
Sight	: Picatinny mounting rail
Safety	: rotating catch on left-hand side of receiver housing
Stock	: synthetic stock and pistol grip

PARTICULARS
Synthetic hand grip; matt black coating.
Chrome-steel barrel.

ArmaLite AR-10A4 Carbine Stainless

SPECIFICATIONS

Caliber	: .308 Win.
Magazine	: detachable magazine
Cartridge capacity	: 10 or 20 cartridges
Magazine catch	: in left-hand side of magazine housing

ArmaLite AR-10A4 Special Purpose Rifle

ArmaLite AR-10A4 Carbine Stainless

Action	: gas pressure
Cocking system	: cocking lever
Firing system	: semi-automatic
Locking system	: rotating bolt head with 6 locking lugs and 1 safety lug
Length	: 94.2 cm (37.1")
Barrel length	: 40.6 cm (16")
Weight	: 4.1 kg (9 lb.)
Sight	: Picatinny mounting rail
Safety	: rotating catch on left-hand side of receiver housing
Stock	: synthetic stock and pistol grip

PARTICULARS
Synthetic hand grip; matt black coating.
Stainless-steel barrel.

ArmaLite AR-10(T)

SPECIFICATIONS

Caliber	: .308 Win.
Magazine	: detachable magazine
Cartridge capacity	: 10 or 20 cartridges
Magazine catch	: in left-hand side of magazine housing
Action	: gas pressure
Cocking system	: cocking lever
Firing system	: semi-automatic
Locking system	: rotating bolt head with 6 locking lugs and 1 safety lug
Length	: 110.5 cm (43.5")

ArmaLite AR-10(T)

Barrel length	: 61 cm (24")
Weight	: 4.7 kg (10.4 lb.)
Sight	: base for front sight; Picatinny
Safety	: rotating catch on left-hand side of receiver housing
Stock	: synthetic stock and pistol grip

PARTICULARS

Free floating hand guard; matt black coating. Thick, stainless-steel barrel.

ArmaLite AR-10(T) Carbine

SPECIFICATIONS

Caliber	: .308 Win.
Magazine	: detachable magazine
Cartridge capacity	: 10 or 20 cartridges
Magazine catch	: in left-hand side of magazine housing
Action	: gas pressure
Cocking system	: cocking lever
Firing system	: semi-automatic
Locking system	: rotating bolt head with 6 locking lugs and 1 safety lug
Length	: 94.2 cm (37.1")
Barrel length	: 40.6 cm (16")
Weight	: 3.9 kg (8.5 lb.)
Sight	: base for front sight; Picatinny mounting rail
Safety	: rotating catch on left-hand side of receiver housing
Stock	: synthetic stock and pistol grip

PARTICULARS

Free floating hand grip; matt black coating. Thick, stainless-steel barrel.

ArmaLite M15A2 Carbine

SPECIFICATIONS

Caliber	: .223 Rem.
Magazine	: detachable magazine
Cartridge capacity	: 7 cartridges

ArmaLite AR-10(T) Carbine

ArmaLite M15A2 Carbine

Magazine catch	: in left-hand side of magazine housing
Action	: gas pressure
Cocking system	: cocking lever
Firing system	: semi-automatic
Locking system	: 7-lug rotating bolt head
Length	: 90.4 cm (35.6")
Barrel length	: 40.6 cm (16")
Weight	: 3.2 kg (7 lb.)
Sight	: carrying handle with adjustable rear and front sights of M16 type
Safety	: rotating catch on left-hand side of receiver housing
Stock	: synthetic stock and pistol grip

PARTICULARS

Synthetic hand guard; matt black coating.

ArmaLite M15A2 HBAR

SPECIFICATIONS

Caliber	: .223 Rem.
Magazine	: detachable magazine
Cartridge capacity	: 7 cartridges
Magazine catch	: in left-hand side of magazine housing
Action	: gas pressure
Cocking system	: cocking lever
Firing system	: semi-automatic
Locking system	: 7-lug rotating bolt head
Length	: 97.5 cm (38.4")
Barrel length	: 50.8 cm (20")
Weight	: 4.1 kg (9 lb.)

ArmaLite M15A2 HBAR

Auto-Ordnance Thompson Model 1927A-1C Lightweight

Auto-Ordnance Thompson Model 1927A-5

Auto-Ordnance Thompson Model 1927A-1C Lightweight

SPECIFICATIONS

Caliber	: .45 ACP
Magazine	: detachable magazine or drum
Cartridge capacity	: 30-round detachable magazine, 50 or 100-round cartridge drum
Magazine catch	: lever on left of receiver housing above trigger
Action	: recoil energy
Cocking system	: cocking lever
Firing system	: semi-automatic
Locking system	: inertia locking system
Length	: 104 cm (41")
Barrel length	: 45.7 cm (18")
Weight	: 4.3 kg (9.5 lb.)
Sight	: adjustable rear sight
Safety	: safety rotating catch on left of receiver housing above pistol grip
Stock	: detachable walnut stock with pistol grip and separate forearm

PARTICULARS

One of the famous Tommy Gun sub-machine-gun models. Light-metal receiver housing and receiver housing. Cocking handle with centerslot (for sight line) on top of receiver housing. Fluted barrel with compensator.

Auto-Ordnance Thompson Model 1927A-5

SPECIFICATIONS

Caliber	: .45 ACP
Magazine	: detachable magazine or drum
Cartridge capacity	: 30-round detachable magazine, 50 or 100-round cartridge druml
Magazine catch	: lever on left of receiver housing above trigger
Action	: recoil energy
Cocking system	: cocking lever
Firing system	: semi-automatic
Locking system	: inertia locking system
Length	: 66 cm (26")
Barrel length	: 34.3 cm (13.5")
Weight	: 3.2 kg (7 lb.)
Sight	: adjustable rear sight
Safety	: safety rotating catch on left of receiver housing above pistol grip
Stock	: walnut pistol grip and separate forearm

PARTICULARS

Pistol version of the famous Tommy Gun sub-machine-gun. Cocking handle with center slot (for sight line) on top of receiver housing. Fluted barrel with compensator.

Auto-Ordnance Thompson Model 1928

SPECIFICATIONS

Caliber	: .45 ACP
Magazine	: detachable magazine or drum
Cartridge capacity	: 30-round detachable magazine, 50 or 100-round cartridge drum
Magazine catch	: lever on left of receiver housing above trigger
Action	: trecoil energy
Cocking system	: cocking lever
Firing system	: semi-automatic and automatic
Locking system	: inertia locking system
Length	: 87.6 cm (34.5")
Barrel length	: 26.7 cm (10.5")
Weight	: 5.2 kg (11.5 lb.)
Sight	: adjustable rear sight
Safety	: safety rotating catch on left of receiver housing above pistol grip

Auto-Ordnance Thompson Model 1928

Barrel length	: 61 cm (24")
Weight	: 4.7 kg (10.4 lb.)
Sight	: base for front sight; Picatinny
Safety	: rotating catch on left-hand side of receiver housing
Stock	: synthetic stock and pistol grip

PARTICULARS
Free floating hand guard; matt black coating. Thick, stainless-steel barrel.

ArmaLite AR-10(T) Carbine

SPECIFICATIONS

Caliber	: .308 Win.
Magazine	: detachable magazine
Cartridge capacity	: 10 or 20 cartridges
Magazine catch	: in left-hand side of magazine housing
Action	: gas pressure
Cocking system	: cocking lever
Firing system	: semi-automatic
Locking system	: rotating bolt head with 6 locking lugs and 1 safety lug
Length	: 94.2 cm (37.1")
Barrel length	: 40.6 cm (16")
Weight	: 3.9 kg (8.5 lb.)
Sight	: base for front sight; Picatinny mounting rail
Safety	: rotating catch on left-hand side of receiver housing
Stock	: synthetic stock and pistol grip

PARTICULARS
Free floating hand grip; matt black coating. Thick, stainless-steel barrel.

ArmaLite M15A2 Carbine

SPECIFICATIONS

Caliber	: .223 Rem.
Magazine	: detachable magazine
Cartridge capacity	: 7 cartridges

ArmaLite M15A2 Carbine

Magazine catch	: in left-hand side of magazine housing
Action	: gas pressure
Cocking system	: cocking lever
Firing system	: semi-automatic
Locking system	: 7-lug rotating bolt head
Length	: 90.4 cm (35.6")
Barrel length	: 40.6 cm (16")
Weight	: 3.2 kg (7 lb.)
Sight	: carrying handle with adjustable rear and front sights of M16 type
Safety	: rotating catch on left-hand side of receiver housing
Stock	: synthetic stock and pistol grip

PARTICULARS
Synthetic hand guard; matt black coating.

ArmaLite M15A2 HBAR

SPECIFICATIONS

Caliber	: .223 Rem.
Magazine	: detachable magazine
Cartridge capacity	: 7 cartridges
Magazine catch	: in left-hand side of magazine housing
Action	: gas pressure
Cocking system	: cocking lever
Firing system	: semi-automatic
Locking system	: 7-lug rotating bolt head
Length	: 97.5 cm (38.4")
Barrel length	: 50.8 cm (20")
Weight	: 4.1 kg (9 lb.)

ArmaLite AR-10(T) Carbine

ArmaLite M15A2 HBAR

Sight	: carrying handle with adjustable rear and front sights of M16 type
Safety	: rotating catch on left-hand side of receiver housing
Stock	: synthetic stock and pistol grip

PARTICULARS

Synthetic hand grip; matt black coating. Heavy stainless-steel match barrel with flash suppresser.

ArmaLite M15A2 National Match

SPECIFICATIONS

Caliber	: .223 Rem.
Magazine	: detachable magazine
Cartridge capacity	: 7 cartridges
Magazine catch	: in left-hand side of magazine housing
Action	: gas pressure
Cocking system	: cocking lever
Firing system	: semi-automatic
Locking system	: 7-lug rotating bolt head
Length	: 97.5 cm (38.4")
Barrel length	: 50.8 cm (20")
Weight	: 4.1 kg (9 lb.)
Sight	: carrying handle with adjustable rear and front sights of M16 type
Safety	: rotating catch on left-hand side of receiver housing
Stock	: synthetic stock and pistol grip

PARTICULARS

Free floating synthetic hand grip; matt black coating. Heavy stainless-steel National Match barrel; special NM trigger group.

ArmaLite M15A4 Carbine

SPECIFICATIONS

Caliber	: .223 Rem.
Magazine	: detachable magazine

ArmaLite M15A2 National Match

ArmaLite M15A4 Carbine

Cartridge capacity	: 7 cartridges
Magazine catch	: :in left-hand side of magazine housing
Action	: gas pressure
Cocking system	: cocking lever
Firing system	: semi-automatic
Locking system	: 7-lug rotating bolt head
Length	: 90.4 cm (35.6")
Barrel length	: 40.6 cm (16")
Weight	: 3.2 kg (7 lb.)
Sight	: base for front sight; Picatinny mounting rail
Safety	: rotating catch on left-hand side of receiver housing
Stock	: synthetic stock and pistol grip

PARTICULARS

Synthetic hand grip; matt black coating.

ArmaLite M15A4 Special Purpose Rifle

SPECIFICATIONS

Caliber	: .223 Rem.
Magazine	: detachable magazine
Cartridge capacity	: 7 cartridges
Magazine catch	: in left-hand side of magazine housing
Action	: gas pressure
Cocking system	: cocking lever
Firing system	: semi-automatic
Locking system	: 7-lug rotating bolt head
Length	: 100.3 cm (39.5")
Barrel length	: 50.8 cm (20")

ArmaLite M15A4 Special Purpose Rifle

ArmaLite M15A4(T)

Weight	: 3.5 kg (7.8 lb.)
Sight	: base for front sight; Picatinny mounting rail
Safety	: rotating catch on left-hand side of receiver housing
Stock	: synthetic stock and pistol grip

PARTICULARS

Free floating hand grip; matt black coating. Heavy chrome-steel match barrel.

ArmaLite M15A4(T)

SPECIFICATIONS

Caliber	: .223 Rem.
Magazine	: detachable magazine
Cartridge capacity	: 7 cartridges
Magazine catch	: in left-hand side of magazine housing
Action	: gas pressure
Cocking system	: cocking lever
Firing system	: semi-automatic
Locking system	: 7-lug rotating bolt head
Length	: 107.7 cm (42.4")
Barrel length	: 61 cm (24")
Weight	: 4.2 kg (9.2 lb.)
Sight	: base for front sight; Picatinny mounting rail
Safety	: rotating catch on left-hand side of receiver housing
Stock	: synthetic stock and pistol grip

PARTICULARS

Free floating hand grip; matt black coating. Heavy stainless-steel barrel.

ArmaLite M15A4(T) Carbine

SPECIFICATIONS

Caliber	: .223 Rem.
Magazine	: detachable magazine
Cartridge capacity	: 7 cartridges
Magazine catch	: in left-hand side of magazine housing
Action	: gas pressure
Cocking system	: cocking lever
Firing system	: semi-automatic

ArmaLite M15A4(T) Carbine

Locking system	: 7-lug rotating bolt head
Length	: 90.2 cm (35.5")
Barrel length	: 40.6 cm (16")
Weight	: 3.4 kg (7.6 lb.)
Sight	: base for front sight; Picatinny mounting rail
Safety	: rotating catch on left-hand side of receiver housing
Stock	: synthetic stock and pistol grip

PARTICULARS

Free floating hand grip; matt black coating. Stainless-steel barrel.

Armament Technology

Armament Technology is a small company specializing in long-range sniper rifles. The firm was started in 1988 by a number of match shooters and sharpshooters and is based in Halifax, Canada. The founders had the nerve to try to improve the US Army's famous sniper rifle, the M24, and they were extraordinarily successful in their attempt. Five-shot groups at 100 meters (328 ft) with a diameter of between 7.4 mm (0.292 in) and 9.3 mm (0.366 in) with Norma Match 168 grain HPBT

Armament Technology, logo

cartridges are standard! The rifle is based on the Remington 700 Model. The barrel has been specially made with clockwise 5-groove rifling, with a twist of the firm's own design. The mounting rail for the scope is made to NATO specifications. The synthetic stock is Kevlar-reinforced, with the receiver embedded in a block of aircraft aluminum. Arms Technology supplies its snipers not only to sports shooters, but also to special government departments throughout the world.

Arms Technology AT1-M24 Tactical Sniper Type 1

SPECIFICATIONS

Caliber	: 7.62 x 51 mm NATO or .300 Win. Mag.
Magazine	: blind magazine or detachable magazine
Cartridge capacity	: 5 cartridges (magazine); 5 or 10 cartridges
Magazine catch	: N/A. or on left under magazine opening
Action	: bolt lever
Cocking system	: bolt lever
Firing system	: single round
Locking system	: 2-lug Remington M700
Length	: 115 cm (45.3")
Barrel length	: 66 cm (26")
Weight	: 6 kg (13.2 lb.)
Sight	: Bausch & Lomb 10x scope or as preferred
Safety	: safety catch on right behind bolt lever
Stock	: Kevlar-reinforced synthetic stock

PARTICULARS

Matt black barrel and receiver; Harris bipod.

Arms Technology AT1-M24 Sniper Type 2

SPECIFICATIONS

Caliber	: 7.62 x 51 mm NATO or .300 Win. Mag.
Magazine	: blind magazine or detachable magazine
Cartridge capacity	: 5 cartridges (magazine); 5 or 10 cartridges
Magazine catch	: N/A. or on left under magazine opening
Action	: bolt lever
Cocking system	: bolt lever
Firing system	: single round
Locking system	: 2-lug Remington M700
Length	: 115 cm (45.3") or as preferred
Barrel length	: 66 cm (26") or as preferred
Weight	: 6 kg (13.2 lb.)
Sight	: Bausch & Lomb 10x scope or as preferred
Safety	: safety catch on right behind bolt lever
Stock	: Kevlar-reinforced synthetic stock with extending and adjustable butt plate

PARTICULARS

Matt black barrel and receiver; Harris bipod.

Arms Technology AT1-M24 Sniper Type 2

Auto-Ordnance Corporation

The name Auto-Ordnance is always associated first and foremost with the "Tommy Gun". This sub-machine-gun was designed at the end of the First World War by Brigadier General John T. Thompson. The firm of Auto-Ordnance introduced the weapon in 1919 as the Model 1921. Initially, the sub-machine-gun was known as a gangster weapon. In 1928, the US government bought a series of a later model for the Marines and the Coast Guard.

After the Second World War broke out, this weapon was in such great demand that Auto-Ordnance was unable to manufacture it in sufficient numbers, so the Colt company took over most of the production. During this period, Colt made some 15,000 Thompson sub-machine-guns for the US Army. In 1940, Britain also placed a major order for the Model M1928-1. Auto-Ordnance contracted Savage Arms for the production of this order. The later models, such as the M1 and the M1A1, were also part of this British contract. Altogether, Savage made more than 1.5 million of these weapons.

The first models of the Tommy Gun were fitted with the Blish locking system. This system consists of two steel bolt blocks that slide past one another, thereby retarding the return of the breech block. This system was rejected by the US government, whereupon the inertia locking system was used. The Tommy Gun was succeeded at the end of 1942 by the US-M3 sub-machine-gun, nicknamed "Grease Gun". The M3 could be mass-produced at considerably lower cost than could the Tommy Gun. This weapon was designed by George Hyde and Frederick Sampson of the Inland Manufacturing Division, a unit of General Motors. Auto-Ordnance continued to exist as a company. Since the Second World War, Thompson sub-machine-guns in various versions have continued to be made for army and police units. Several models of the M1911-A1 pistol are also produced.

Auto-Ordnance Thompson Model 1927A-1

SPECIFICATIONS

Caliber	: .45 ACP
Magazine	: detachable magazine or drum
Cartridge capacity	: 30-round detachable magazine, 50 or 100-round cartridge drum
Magazine catch	: lever on left of receiver housing above trigger
Action	: recoil energy
Cocking system	: cocking lever
Firing system	: semi-automatic
Locking system	: inertia locking system
Length	: 104 cm (41")
Barrel length	: 45.7 cm (18")
Weight	: 5.9 kg (13 lb.)
Sight	: adjustable rear sight
Safety	: safety rotating catch on left of receiver housing above pistol grip
Stock	: detachable walnut stock with pistol grip and separate forearm

PARTICULARS

One of the famous Tommy Gun sub-machine-gun models. Cocking handle with center slot (for sight line) on top of receiver housing. Fluted barrel with compensator.

Auto-Ordnance Corporation, logo

Auto-Ordnance Thompson Model 1927A-1

Auto-Ordnance Thompson Model 1927A-1C Lightweight

Auto-Ordnance Thompson Model 1927A-5

Auto-Ordnance Thompson Model 1927A-1C Lightweight

SPECIFICATIONS

Caliber	: .45 ACP
Magazine	: detachable magazine or drum
Cartridge capacity	: 30-round detachable magazine, 50 or 100-round cartridge drum
Magazine catch	: lever on left of receiver housing above trigger
Action	: recoil energy
Cocking system	: cocking lever
Firing system	: semi-automatic
Locking system	: inertia locking system
Length	: 104 cm (41")
Barrel length	: 45.7 cm (18")
Weight	: 4.3 kg (9.5 lb.)
Sight	: adjustable rear sight
Safety	: safety rotating catch on left of receiver housing above pistol grip
Stock	: detachable walnut stock with pistol grip and separate forearm

PARTICULARS

One of the famous Tommy Gun sub-machine-gun models. Light-metal receiver housing and receiver housing.Cocking handle with centerslot (for sight line) on top of receiver housing. Fluted barrel with compensator.

Auto-Ordnance Thompson Model 1927A-5

SPECIFICATIONS

Caliber	: .45 ACP
Magazine	: detachable magazine or drum
Cartridge capacity	: 30-round detachable magazine, 50 or 100-round cartridge druml
Magazine catch	: lever on left of receiver housing above trigger
Action	: recoil energy
Cocking system	: cocking lever
Firing system	: semi-automatic
Locking system	: inertia locking system
Length	: 66 cm (26")
Barrel length	: 34.3 cm (13.5")
Weight	: 3.2 kg (7 lb.)
Sight	: adjustable rear sight
Safety	: safety rotating catch on left of receiver housing above pistol grip
Stock	: walnut pistol grip and separate forearm

PARTICULARS

Pistol version of the famous Tommy Gun sub-machine-gun. Cocking handle with center slot (for sight line) on top of receiver housing. Fluted barrel with compensator.

Auto-Ordnance Thompson Model 1928

SPECIFICATIONS

Caliber	: .45 ACP
Magazine	: detachable magazine or drum
Cartridge capacity	: 30-round detachable magazine, 50 or 100-round cartridge drum
Magazine catch	: lever on left of receiver housing above trigger
Action	: trecoil energy
Cocking system	: cocking lever
Firing system	: semi-automatic and automatic
Locking system	: inertia locking system
Length	: 87.6 cm (34.5")
Barrel length	: 26.7 cm (10.5")
Weight	: 5.2 kg (11.5 lb.)
Sight	: adjustable rear sight
Safety	: safety rotating catch on left of receiver housing above pistol grip

Auto-Ordnance Thompson Model 1928

Auto-Ordnance Thompson Model 1928

Stock : detachable walnut stock with pistol grip and separate forearm

PARTICULARS

One of the famous Tommy Gun sub-machine-gun models. Separate firing selector catch next to safety catch. Cocking handle with center slot (for sight line) on top of receiver housing. Fluted barrel with compensator. Rate of fire approximately 700 rounds a minute (fully automatic).

Auto-Ordnance Thompson Model M1

SPECIFICATIONS

Caliber : .45 ACP
Magazine : detachable magazine
Cartridge capacity: 30 cartridges
Magazine catch : lever on left of receiver housing above trigger
Action : recoil energy
Cocking system : cocking lever
Firing system : semi-automatic and automatic
Locking system : inertia locking system
Length : 81.3 cm (32")
Barrel length : 26.7 cm (10.5")
Weight : 5 kg (11 lb.)
Sight : fixed rear sight
Safety : safety rotating catch on left of receiver housing above pistol grip
Stock : detachable walnut stock with pistol grip and forearm

Auto-Ordnance Thompson Model M1

Auto-Ordnance Thompson Model M1A1

PARTICULARS

One of the famous Tommy Gun sub-machine-gun models. Separate firing selector catch next to safety catch. Round barrel, without fluting or compensator. Shown here is the Thompson M1A1 model.

Auto-Ordnance Thompson Model M1 Carbine

SPECIFICATIONS

Caliber : .45 ACP
Magazine : detachable magazine
Cartridge capacity: 30 cartridges
Magazine catch : lever on left of receiver housing above trigger
Action : recoil energy
Cocking system : cocking lever
Firing system : semi-automatic
Locking system : inertia locking system
Length : 96.5 cm (38")
Barrel length : 42 cm (16.5")
Weight : 5.2 kg (11.5 lb.)
Sight : fixed rear sight
Safety : safety rotating catch on left of receiver housing above pistol grip
Stock : detachable walnut stock with pistol grip and forearm

PARTICULARS

Carbine model of the famous Tommy Gun sub-machine-gun. Round barrel, without fluting or compensator.

Auto-Ordnance Thompson Model M1 Carbine

Benelli M3 Super 90 Kromo

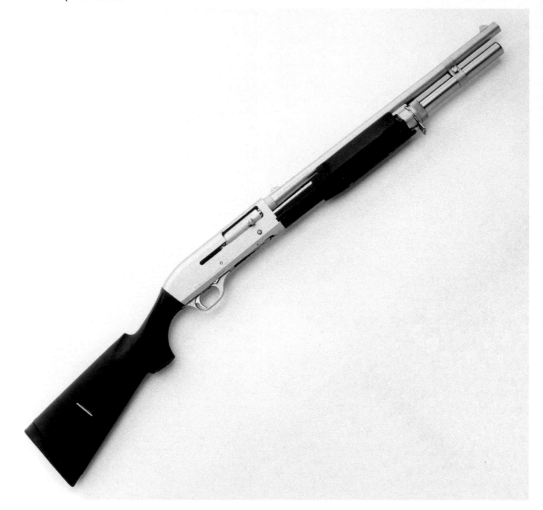

Benelli M1 Super 90 riot gun

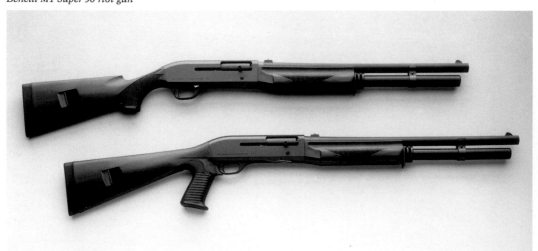

B b

Baikal/Izhevsky Mekhanichesky Zavod

The Russian arms factory Izhevsky Mekhanichesky Zavod dates from 1885. The government of the day commissioned the arms factories in Tula, Izhevsk and Sestroretsk to manufacture civilian weapons as well as military firearms. The revolution in 1917 was a turbulent time for arms factories. The Red Army commandeered the arms stocks of the Russian Tsarist army, but there were still great shortages of arms and ammunition. During the period from 1918 to 1920, the arms factories in Izhevsky produced a total of almost 1,300,000 rifles, 15,000 machine guns and 175,000 Nagant revolvers. They also made some 840,000,000 cartridges of various calibers for these weapons. In the Second World War, the production capacity was utilized for military equipment. In 1949, the Izhevsky Mekhanichesky Zavod

Baikal/Izhevsky Mekhanichesky Zavod, logo

factory again began to produce sport rifles and shotguns. The Izh-49 double-barreled shotgun was based on the Sauer Model 9. In 1954, Baikal introduced the Izh-54 double-barreled shotgun, which had been designed by the engineers Leonid Pugachyev and Anatoly Klimov. The most popular "Baikal" shotgun, the Izh-27, based on a design by Sergei Khuzyakhmetov, came onto the market in 1973. The Baikal rifles are also designated with the letters "IJ", e.g. the "IJ-27".

The company currently makes a range of shotguns and rifle/shotgun combinations under the name of "Izh", which is better known in the West by the brand name Baikal. Izhevsky also produces airguns, including the futuristic Izh-62, with a skeleton stock and Red-Point scope. Baikal weapons are very inexpensive, very robust and reliable.

Baikal Degtyarev DP

SPECIFICATIONS

Caliber	: 7.62 x 54R
Magazine	: drum magazine
Cartridge capacity	: 47 cartridges
Magazine catch	: N/A.
Action	: gas pressure
Cocking system	: cocking lever
Firing system	: automatic
Locking system	: spring-loaded locking lugs on both sides of the breechblock engage in recesses in the receiver housing (Kjellman Frijberg system)
Length	: 127 cm (50")
Barrel length	: 60.5 cm (23.8")
Weight	: 11.9 kg (26.2 lb.)
Sight	: tangent rear sight
Safety	: on the right behind receiver housing
Stock	: wooden stock

Baikal Degtyarev DP

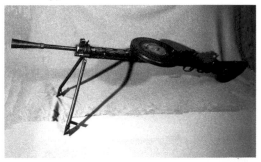

PARTICULARS

Entered service with the Russian troops in 1926.

Its successor was the DPM, in which the main spring protruded at the back of the receiver housing. The DT model, when used as a machine gun on vehicles, has a 60-round drum magazine and a steel stock.

Baikal IZH-81KM Pump-action rifle

SPECIFICATIONS

Caliber	: 12/76 (3")
Magazine	: detachable magazine
Cartridge capacity	: 5 cartridges
Magazine catch	: in front of trigger guard
Action	: pump-action
Cocking system	: forearm
Firing system	: single round
Locking system	: vertically sliding block locking system
Length	: 109 to 123 cm (42.9 to 48.4")
Barrel length	: 56 to 70 cm (22 to 27.6")
Weight	: 3.4 kg (7.5 lb.)
Sight	: front sight
Safety	: pushbutton in rear of trigger guard
Stock	: birch, beech or walnut, with or without separate pistol grip

PARTICULARS

Light-metal receiver housing.

Baikal IZH-81M Pump-action rifle

SPECIFICATIONS

Caliber	: 12/76 (3")
Magazine	: tubular magazine
Cartridge capacity	: 4 or 6 cartridges
Magazine catch	: N/A.
Action	: pump-action
Cocking system	: forearm

Baikal IZH-81KM Pump-action rifle

Baikal IZH-81M Pump-action rifle

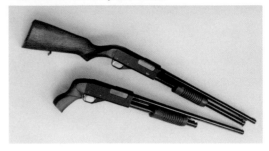

Firing system	: single round
Locking system	: vertically locking block
Length	: 109 to 123 cm (42.9 to 48.4")
Barrel length	: 56 to 70 cm (22 to 27.6")
Weight	: 3.4 kg (7.5 lb.)
Sight	: front sight
Safety	: pushbutton in rear of trigger guard
Stock	: birch, beech or walnut, with or without separate pistol grip

PARTICULARS

Light-metal receiver housing.

Baikal Model K-50M

SPECIFICATIONS

Caliber	: 7.62 x 25 mm (Russian)
Magazine	: detachable magazine
Cartridge capacity	: 35 cartridges
Magazine catch	: folding catch behind magazine well
Action	: recoil action
Cocking system	: cocking lever
Firing system	: semi- and fully-automatic
Locking system	: inertia locking system
Length	: with unfolded stock: 75 cm (29.5") when folded: 57.2 cm (22.5")
Barrel length	: 26.9 cm (10.6")
Weight	: 3.4 kg (7.5 lb.)
Sight	: fixed rear and front sights

Baikal Model K-50M

Safety : combined safety catch and firing selector in
trigger guard
Stock : steel wire stock

PARTICULARS
System derived from the Russian PPSh-41 sub-machine-gun, combined with the metal wire stock of the French MAT-38.

Developed and produced by China and North Vietnam.

Baikal Model PPSh-41

SPECIFICATIONS
Caliber : 7.62 x 25 mm (Russian)
Magazine : detachable magazine or drum
Cartridge capacity: 35 or 71 cartridges
Magazine catch : folding catch behind magazine well
Action : recoil action
Cocking system : cocking lever
Firing system : semi- and fully-automatic
Locking system : inertia locking system
Length : 84.2 cm (33.15")
Barrel length : 26.9 cm (10.6")
Weight : 4.2 kg (9.2 lb.)
Sight : fixed rear and front sights
Safety : combined safety catch and firing selector in
trigger guard
Stock : wooden stock

PARTICULARS
Developed by the Russian arms engineer Georgi Shpagin. Steel hand grip with cooling perforations around the barrel. Made in large quantities after the German invasion in 1941.

Baikal Simonov SKS carbine

SPECIFICATIONS
Caliber : 7.62 x 39 mm
Magazine : detachable magazine
Cartridge capacity: 10 cartridges

Baikal PPSh-41

Baikal Simonov SKS

Magazine catch : in front of magazine well
Action : gas pressure
Cocking system : cocking lever
Firing system : semi-automatic
Locking system : vertically locking block
Length : 102 cm (40.2")
Barrel length : 52 cm (20.5")
Weight : 3.9 kg (8.5 lb.)
Sight : tangent rear sight
Safety : on right-hand side of receiver
Stock : wooden stock

PARTICULARS
Precursor of the AK-47 rifle system; usually fitted with a folding bayonet. The SKS was the first Russian weapon to use 7.62 x 39 mm caliber ammo.
Known in China as the Type 56 and in former Yugoslavia as the M59. The weapon depicted is a modern version made by Norinco.

Baikal Tokarev Model 1940 (SVT40)

SPECIFICATIONS
Caliber : 7.62 x 54R
Magazine : detachable magazine
Cartridge capacity: 10 cartridges
Magazine catch : behind magazine
Action : gas pressure
Cocking system : cocking lever
Firing system : semi-automatic
Locking system : vertically locking block
Length : 122.6 cm (48.3")
Barrel length : 61 cm (25")
Weight : 3.9 kg (8.6 lb.)
Sight : tangent rear sight
Safety : in rear of trigger guard

for hunting and sport shooting, Benelli also carries a small range of compact riot guns for the army and other government departments.

Stock	: wooden stock and forearm, metal hand grip with cooling perforations

PARTICULARS
Barrel with large flash suppresser. The SVT40 has a single barrel band between the hand grip and the forearm. Its predecessor, the SVT38, has two barrel bands. Like the SVT38, the Tokarev SVT40 depicted also has a cleaning rod underneath the barrel. This was discontinued on later models of the SVT40.

Benelli

Benelli, logo

The firm of Benelli is based in the Italian town of Urbino. Filippo and Giovanni Benelli founded the company at the start of the twentieth century. The factory used to be known mainly for its mopeds, but machinery, tools and, since 1967, firearms are also made here. In addition to pistols, Benelli has an extensive range of semi-automatic shotguns.

From an engineering point of view, the M-3 Super 90 type is the most interesting. This shotgun can easily be switched from semi-automatic to pump-action and, of course, vice versa. To do this, a knob at the front of the forearm simply has to be rotated a quarter turn. Besides shotguns

Benelli M-3 Super 90 Combat

SPECIFICATIONS

Caliber	: 12/76 (3")
Magazine	: tubular magazine
Cartridge capacity	: 6 cartridges
Magazine catch	: N/A.
Action	: pump-action/recoil energy
Cocking system	: forearm/cocking lever
Firing system	: single round or semi-automatic
Locking system	: rotating bolt head
Length	: 104.5 cm (41.1")
Barrel length	: 50 cm (19.7"); cylindrical choke
Weight	: 3.5 kg (7.7 lb.)
Sight	: rear and front sights
Safety	: pushbutton in rear of trigger guard; cocking indicator on the right above trigger guard
Stock	: glass-fibre-reinforced synthetic stock and forearm

PARTICULARS
Matt black coating; barrel also suitable for slugs. The action on this unusual rifle can be switched from semi-automatic to pump-action by rotating the ring at the front of the forearm (near the swivel).

Benelli M-3 Super 90 Kromo

SPECIFICATIONS

Caliber	: 12/76 (3")
Magazine	: tubular magazine
Cartridge capacity	: 6 cartridges
Magazine catch	: N/A.
Action	: pump-action/recoil energy
Cocking system	: forearm/cocking lever
Firing system	: single round or semi-automatic
Locking system	: rotating bolt head

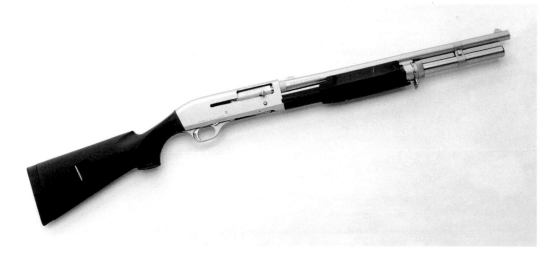

Length	: 104.5 cm (41.1")
Barrel length	: 50 cm (19.7"); cylindrical choke
Weight	: 3.5 kg (7.7 lb.)
Sight	: rear and front sights
Safety	: pushbutton in rear of trigger guard; cocking indicator on the right above trigger guard
Stock	: glass-fibre-reinforced synthetic stock and forearm

PARTICULARS

Matt chrome-plated; barrel also suitable for slugs.
The action on this unusual rifle can be switched from semi-automatic to pump-action by rotating the ring at the front of the forearm (near the swivel).

Benelli M-1 Super 90 Tactical

SPECIFICATIONS

Caliber	: 12/76 (3")
Magazine	: tubular magazine
Cartridge capacity:	7 cartridges
Magazine catch	: N/A.
Action	: recoil energy
Cocking system	: cocking lever
Firing system	: semi-automatic
Locking system	: rotating bolt head
Length	: 101.5 cm (40")
Barrel length	: 47 cm (18.5"); cylindrical choke
Weight	: 3.1 kg (6.8 lb.)
Sight	: rear and front sights
Safety	: pushbutton in rear of trigger guard; cocking indicator on the right above trigger guard

Benelli M-1 Super 90 Tactical

Stock	: glass-fibre-reinforced synthetic stock and forearm

PARTICULARS

Matt black coating; barrel also suitable for slugs.
Depicted are the Benelli M-1 Super 90 Tactical with a normal stock and the version with a special pistol grip.

Benelli M-3T Super 90 Combat Folding Stock

SPECIFICATIONS

Caliber	: 12/76 (3")
Magazine	: tubular magazine
Cartridge capacity:	6 cartridges
Magazine catch	: N/A.
Action	: pump-action/recoil energy
Cocking system	: forearm/cocking lever
Firing system	: single round or semi-automatic
Locking system	: rotating bolt head

Benelli M-3T Super 90 Combat Folding Stock

Length	: 78 cm (folded stock) and 104.5 cm (30.7" and 41.1")
Barrel length	: 50 cm (19.7"); cylindrical choke
Weight	: 3.5 kg (7.7 lb.)
Sight	: adjustable combat sight
Safety	: pushbutton in rear of trigger guard; cocking indicator on the right above trigger guard
Stock	: metal tubular stock, glass-fibre-reinforced synthetic pistol grip and forearm

PARTICULARS
Matt black coating; barrel also suitable for slugs. The stock is folded upwards over the receiver housing. The action on this unusual rifle can be switched from semi-automatic to pump-action by rotating the ring at the front of the forearm (near the swivel).

Benelli M-3T Super 90 Short Combat Folding Stock

SPECIFICATIONS

Caliber	: 12/76 (3")
Magazine	: tubular magazine
Cartridge capacity	: 6 cartridges
Magazine catch	: N/A.
Action	: pump-action/recoil energy
Cocking system	: forearm/cocking lever
Firing system	: single round or semi-automatic
Locking system	: rotating bolt head
Length	: 63.5 cm (folded stock) and 90 cm (25" and 35.4")
Barrel length	: 35.5 cm (14"); cylindrical choke
Weight	: 3.4 kg (7.5 lb.)

Benelli M-3T Super 90 Short Combat Folding Stock

Sight	: adjustable combat sight
Safety	: pushbutton in rear of trigger guard; cocking indicator on the right above trigger guard
Stock	: metal tubular stock, glass-fibre-reinforced synthetic pistol grip and forearm

PARTICULARS
Matt black coating; barrel also suitable for slugs. The stock is folded upwards over the receiver housing. The action on this unusual rifle can be switched from semi-automatic to pump-action by rotating the ring at the front of the forearm (near the swivel).

Beretta

As early as the fifteenth century, Bartolomeo Beretta had a small arms workshop in Gardone, in the Val Trompia region. He made mainly gun barrels for other gunsmiths. His son, Giovannino, succeeded his father and became a renowned master gunsmith. At that time, the company made primarily rifles and shotguns. At the end of the eighteenth century, Pietro Beretta was in charge of the firm.

He received large orders for supplying rifles to Napoleon's army. After the Battle of Waterloo, the arms market rapidly declined. Beretta switched to the production of sport and hunting weapons. Pietro's son, Giuseppe, was blessed with great business acumen and in the period from 1840 to 1865 developed the company into a large concern. At the start of the twentieth century, his son, also called Pietro, introduced modern production techniques. A later generation, Giuseppe and Carlo Beretta, transformed Beretta

Beretta, logo

into a true multinational, with subsidiaries in the United States, France, Brazil and Greece. The company is currently run by Ugo Gussalli Beretta. The firm enjoys a great reputation in the field of military weapons, shotguns and sport rifles and pistols.

In the early 1960s, Beretta developed the BM 59 rifle. This was a modified version of the Garand M1. The changes comprised a different barrel, using .308 Winchester caliber ammo, a modified receiver for the detachable magazine, a stainless-steel gas block and a modified trigger system for semi-automatic and fully automatic firing with a firing selector on the left-hand side of the receiver housing. In 1984, Beretta introduced a new rifle family, the model 70/90, which entered service with the Italian army in July 1990. A major breakthrough in 1986 was the US Army's selection of the Beretta M92-F pistol, using 9 mm Para caliber ammo. To meet American objections that the government had chosen a foreign military pistol, a separate firm, Beretta USA Corporation, was set up, with its head office in Accokeek, Maryland.

Beretta BM 59 Ital

SPECIFICATIONS

Caliber	: .308 Win.
Magazine	: detachable magazine
Cartridge capacity	: 15, 20 or 25 cartridges
Magazine catch	: in front of the trigger guard
Action	: gas pressure
Cocking system	: cocking lever
Firing system	: semi-automatic and fully automatic
Locking system	: rotating bolt head
Length	: 109.5 cm (43.1")
Barrel length	: 49 cm (19.3")

Weight	: 4.4 kg (9.7 lb.)
Sight	: aperture sight, adjustable for elevation and for windage
Safety	: safety catch in front side of trigger guard
Stock	: wooden stock, forearm and hand grip

PARTICULARS

This rifle is an improved version of the Garand rifle. The barrel has a flash suppresser and compensator apertures; folding bipod; firing selector on the left-hand side of the receiver behind the hand grip; folding winter trigger guard; grenade sight that folds over the front sight. The detachable magazine can also be loaded with cartridge clips via the top of the receiver.

There is room in the butt plate for a maintenance kit. There is a bayonet lug on the barrel, in front of the gas block.

Beretta BM 59 Ital-A

SPECIFICATIONS

Caliber	: .308 Win.
Magazine	: detachable magazine
Cartridge capacity	: 15, 20 or 25 cartridges
Magazine catch	: in front of the trigger guard
Action	: gas pressure
Cocking system	: cocking lever
Firing system	: semi-automatic and fully automatic
Locking system	: rotating bolt head
Length	: with unfolded stock: 112 cm (43.7") collapsed: 72.5 cm (28.5")
Barrel length	: 47 cm (18.3")
Weight	: 4.5 kg (9.9 lb.)
Sight	: aperture sight, adjustable for elevation and for windage
Safety	: safety catch in front side of trigger guard
Stock	: steel tubular stock, wooden forearm and hand grip, synthetic pistol grip

Beretta BM 59 Ital-A

Beretta BM 59 Ital

PARTICULARS

This rifle is an improved version of the Garand rifle. It has a detachable barrel section for grenades with a flash suppresser, compensator apertures and bayonet lug; folding bipod; firing selector on the left-hand side of the receiver behind the hand grip; folding winter trigger guard; grenade sight that folds over the front sight. The detachable magazine can also be loaded with cartridge clips via the top of the receiver.

Beretta BM 59 Ital Mark I

Beretta BM 59 Ital-Alpini

SPECIFICATIONS

Caliber	: .308 Win.
Magazine	: detachable magazine
Cartridge capacity	: 15, 20 or 25 cartridges
Magazine catch	: in front of the trigger guard
Action	: gas pressure
Cocking system	: cocking lever
Firing system	: semi-automatic and fully automatic
Locking system	: rotating bolt head
Length	: with unfolded stock: 111 cm (43.7") folded: 85.5 cm (33.7")
Barrel length	: 49 cm (19.3")
Weight	: 4.5 kg (9.8 lb.)
Sight	: aperture sight, adjustable for elevation and for windage
Safety	: safety catch in front side of trigger guard
Stock	: steel tubular stock, wooden forearm and hand grip, synthetic pistol grip

PARTICULARS

This rifle is an improved version of the Garand rifle. The barrel has a flash suppresser and compensator apertures; folding bipod; firing selector on the left-hand side of the receiver behind the hand grip; folding winter trigger guard; grenade sight that folds over the front sight. The

Beretta BM 59 Ital-Alpini

detachable magazine can also be loaded with cartridge clips via the top of the receiver. There is a bayonet lug on the barrel, in front of the gas block.

Beretta BM 59 Ital Mark I

SPECIFICATIONS

Caliber	: .308 Win.
Magazine	: detachable magazine
Cartridge capacity	: 15, 20 or 25 cartridges
Magazine catch	: in front of the trigger guard
Action	: gas pressure
Cocking system	: cocking lever
Firing system	: semi-automatic and fully automatic
Locking system	: rotating bolt head
Length	: 104 cm (40.5")
Barrel length	: 44.5 cm (17.4")
Weight	: 4.1 kg (9.1 lb.)
Sight	: aperture sight, adjustable for elevation and for windage
Safety	: safety catch in front side of trigger guard
Stock	: wooden stock, forearm and hand grip

PARTICULARS

This rifle is an improved version of the Garand rifle. The barrel has a flash suppresser and compensator apertures; firing selector on the left-hand side of the receiver behind the hand grip; folding winter trigger guard. The detachable magazine can also be loaded with cartridge clips via the top of the receiver. There is room in the butt plate for a maintenance kit. There is a bayonet lug on the front of the gas block.

Beretta BM 59 Ital Mark II

SPECIFICATIONS

Caliber	: .308 Win.

Magazine	: detachable magazine
Cartridge capacity	: 15, 20 or 25 cartridges
Magazine catch	: in front of the trigger guard
Action	: gas pressure
Cocking system	: cocking lever
Firing system	: semi-automatic and fully automatic
Locking system	: rotating bolt head
Length	: 104 cm (40.5")
Barrel length	: 44.5 cm (17.4")
Weight	: 4.3 kg (9.4 lb.)
Sight	: aperture sight, adjustable for elevation and for windage
Safety	: :safety catch in front side of trigger guard
Stock	: wooden stock, forearm, hand and pistol grip

PARTICULARS

This rifle is an improved version of the Garand rifle. The barrel has a flash suppresser and compensator apertures; firing selector on the left-hand side of the receiver behind the hand grip; folding winter trigger guard. It has a folding bipod. The bayonet lug is on the front of the gas block. The detachable magazine can also be loaded with cartridge clips via the top of the receiver. There is room in the butt plate for a maintenance kit.

Beretta BM 59 Ital Mark III

SPECIFICATIONS

Caliber	: .308 Win.
Magazine	: detachable magazine
Cartridge capacity	: 15, 20 or 25 cartridges
Magazine catch	: in front of the trigger guard
Action	: gas pressure
Cocking system	: cocking lever
Firing system	: semi-automatic and fully automatic
Locking system	: rotating bolt head
Length	: with unfolded stock: 105.5 cm (41") folded: 80.5 cm (31.7")
Barrel length	: 44.5 cm (17.4")

Weight	: 4.3 kg (9.4 lb.)
Sight	: aperture sight, adjustable for elevation and for windage
Safety	: safety catch in front side of trigger guard
Stock	: steel tubular stock, wooden forearm and hand grip, synthetic pistol grip

PARTICULARS

This rifle is an improved version of the Garand rifle. The barrel has a flash suppresser and compensator apertures; folding bipod; firing selector on the left-hand side of the receiver behind the hand grip; folding winter trigger guard. The detachable magazine can also be loaded with cartridge clips via the top of the receiver. There is a bayonet lug on the front of the gas block.

Beretta BM 59 Ital Mark IV

SPECIFICATIONS

Caliber	: .308 Win.
Magazine	: detachable magazine
Cartridge capacity	: 15, 20 or 25 cartridges
Magazine catch	: in front of the trigger guard
Action	: gas pressure
Cocking system	: cocking lever
Firing system	: semi-automatic and automatic
Locking system	: rotating bolt head
Length	: 113 cm (44.5")

Beretta BM 59 Ital Mark IV

Barrel length	: 49 cm (19.3")
Weight	: 5.5 kg (12.1 lb.)
Sight	: aperture sight, adjustable for elevation and for windage
Safety	: safety catch in front side of trigger guard
Stock	: wooden stock, forearm and hand grip; synthetic pistol grip

Beretta BM 59 Ital SL

PARTICULARS

This rifle is an improved version of the Garand rifle. The barrel has a flash suppresser and compensator apertures; ·heavy folding bipod; firing selector on the left-hand side of the receiver behind the hand grip; folding winter trigger guard; grenade sight that folds over the front sight. The detachable magazine can also be loaded with cartridge clips via the top of the receiver. There is room in the butt plate for a maintenance kit.

PARTICULARS

This rifle is an improved version of the Garand rifle. The barrel has a flash suppresser and compensator apertures; folding bipod; firing selector on the left-hand side of the receiver behind the hand grip; folding winter trigger guard; grenade sight that folds over the front sight. The detachable magazine can also be loaded with cartridge clips via the top of the receiver. There is a bayonet lug on the barrel, in front of the gas block.

Beretta BM 59 Ital-Paratrooper

SPECIFICATIONS

Caliber	: .308 Win.
Magazine	: detachable magazine
Cartridge capacity	: 15, 20 or 25 cartridges
Magazine catch	: in front of the trigger guard
Action	: gas pressure
Cocking system	: cocking lever
Firing system	: semi-automatic and fully automatic
Locking system	: rotating bolt head
Length	: with unfolded stock: 122.5 cm (48.2") folded: 72.5 cm (28.5")
Barrel length	: 46.8 cm (18.4")
Weight	: 4.6 kg (10 lb.)
Sight	: aperture sight, adjustable for elevation and for windage
Safety	: safety catch in front side of trigger guard
Stock	: steel tubular stock, wooden forearm and hand grip, synthetic pistol grip

Beretta BM 59 Ital SL

SPECIFICATIONS

Caliber	: .308 Win.
Magazine	: detachable magazine
Cartridge capacity	: 15, 20 or 25 cartridges
Magazine catch	: in front of the trigger guard
Action	: gas pressure
Cocking system	: cocking lever
Firing system	: semi-automatic
Locking system	: rotating bolt head
Length	: 109 cm (43")
Barrel length	: 44.5 cm (17.4")
Weight	: 4.6 kg (10.1 lb.)
Sight	: aperture sight, adjustable for elevation and for windage
Safety	: safety catch in front side of trigger guard
Stock	: wooden stock, forearm, continuous hand grip

Beretta BM 59 Ital-Paratrooper

PARTICULARS

This rifle is an improved version of the Garand rifle. It has a folding winter trigger guard. There is room in the butt plate for a maintenance kit. There is a bayonet lug on the barrel, in front of the gas block.

Beretta M 12

SPECIFICATIONS

| Caliber | : 9 mm Para |

Beretta M 12

Magazine : detachable magazine
Cartridge capacity: 32 cartridges
Magazine catch : under front of trigger guard
Action : recoil action
Cocking system : cocking lever
Firing system : semi-automatic and fully automatic
Locking system : inertia locking system with telescopic breechblock
Length : with unfolded stock: 64.5 cm (25.4");
folded: 41.8 cm (16.5")
Barrel length : 20 cm (7.9")
Weight : 3.0 kg (6.6 lb.)
Sight : laterally adjustable folding aperture for 150 and 250 metres(492 and 820 yd); front sight adjustable for elevation
Safety : separate pushbutton for firing selector and push-

button safety catch above pistol grip; grip safety
Stock : folding steel tubular stock with butt plate, synthetic pistol grip and forearm. Also available with fixed wooden stock

PARTICULARS
Matt black; special mounting for scope, night sights or laser; special forearm with built-in torch available and spare barrel with silencer.

Beretta PM 12S

SPECIFICATIONS
Caliber : 9 mm Para
Magazine : detachable magazine
Cartridge capacity: 32 cartridges
Magazine catch : under front of trigger guard
Action : recoil action
Cocking system : cocking lever
Firing system : semi-automatic and fully automatic
Locking system : inertia locking system with telescopic breechblock
Length : with unfolded stock: 66 cm (26");
folded: 41.8 cm (16.5")
Barrel length : 20 cm (7.9")
Weight : 3.4 kg (7.5 lb.)
Sight : folding aperture for 100 and 200 metres (328 and 656 ft); fully adjustable front sight

Beretta PM 12S

Safety	: combined firing selector and safety rotating catch on left-hand side of receiver housing; grip safety
Stock	: folding steel tubular stock with butt plate, synthetic pistol grip and forearm

Beretta 70/90 AS LMG (Light Machine Gun)

PARTICULARS

Matt black; special mounting for scope, night sights or laser; special forearm with built-in torch available and spare barrel with silencer.

Beretta 70/90 AR Assault Rifle Standard

SPECIFICATIONS

Caliber	: .223 Rem.
Magazine	: detachable magazine
Cartridge capacity	: 30-rounds
Magazine catch	: at front of trigger guard
Action	: gas pressure
Cocking system	: cocking lever
Firing system	: semi-automatic, 3-round burst and fully automatic
Locking system	: rotating bolt head
Length	: 99.8 cm (39.3")
Barrel length	: 45 cm (17.7")
Weight	: 4 kg (8.8 lb.)
Sight	: folding aperture 250/400 metres (830/1312 ft); laterally adjustable; front sight adjustable for elevation
Safety	: ambidextrous combined firing selector/safety rotating catch
Stock	: synthetic stock, hand grip and pistol grip

PARTICULARS

Matt black coating; adjustable gas regulator for normal and heavy-duty conditions; bayonet lug under gas block; can be fitted with folding bipod. Folding trigger guard (winter trigger). Carrying handle with mounting for scope, night sights or laser.

Beretta 70/90 AS LMG (Light Machine Gun)

Beretta 70/90 AR Assault Rifle Standard

SPECIFICATIONS

Caliber	: .223 Rem.
Magazine	: detachable magazine
Cartridge capacity	: 30-rounds
Magazine catch	: at front of trigger guard
Action	: gas pressure
Cocking system	: cocking lever
Firing system	: semi-automatic and fully automatic
Locking system	: rotating bolt head
Length	: 100 cm (39.4")
Barrel length	: 46.5 cm (18.3")
Weight	: 5.4 kg (11.9 lb.)
Sight	: micrometer sight 300-800 metres (984 ft–874 yd)
Safety	: tambidextrous combined firing selector/safety rotating catch
Stock	: synthetic stock and pistol grip, steel hand grip

PARTICULARS

Matt black coating; adjustable gas regulator for normal and heavy-duty conditions; folding bipod. Folding trigger guard (winter trigger). Bayonet lug under gas block. Carrying handle with mounting for scope, night sights or laser.

Beretta 70/90 SC Carbine

SPECIFICATIONS

Caliber	: .223 Rem.
Magazine	: detachable magazine
Cartridge capacity	: 30-rounds
Magazine catch	: at front of trigger guard
Action	: gas pressure
Cocking system	: cocking lever
Firing system	: semi-automatic, 3-round burst and fully automatic
Locking system	: rotating bolt head
Length	: with unfolded stock: 98.6 cm (38.8"); with folded stock: 75.1 cm (29.6")
Barrel length	: 45 cm (17.7")
Weight	: 4.0 kg (8.8 lb.)

Beretta 70/90 SC Carbine

Sight	: folding aperture 250/400 metres (820/1312 ft); laterally adjustable; front sight adjustable for elevation
Safety	: ambidextrous combined firing selector/safety rotating catch
Stock	: steel folding stock, synthetic hand grip and pistol grip

PARTICULARS
Matt black coating; adjustable gas regulator for normal and heavy-duty conditions; bayonet lug under gas block; can be fitted with folding bipod.
Folding trigger guard (winter trigger). Carrying handle with mounting for scope, night sights or laser.

Beretta 70/90 SCS Carbine

SPECIFICATIONS

Caliber	: .223 Rem.
Magazine	: detachable magazine
Cartridge capacity	: 30-rounds
Magazine catch	: at front of trigger guard
Action	: gas pressure
Cocking system	: cocking lever

Beretta 70/90 SCS Carbine

Firing system	: semi-automatic, 3-round burst and fully automatic
Locking system	: rotating bolt head
Length	: with unfolded stock: 87.6 cm (34.5"); with folded stock: 64.7 cm (25.5")
Barrel length	: 35.2 cm (13.9")
Weight	: 3.8 kg (8.4 lb.)
Sight	: folding aperture 250/400 metres (820/1312 ft); laterally adjustable; front sight adjustable for elevation
Safety	: ambidextrous combined firing selector/safety rotating catch
Stock	: steel folding stock, synthetic hand grip and pistol grip

PARTICULARS
Matt black coating; adjustable gas regulator for normal and heavy-duty conditions. Folding trigger guard (winter trigger). Carrying handle with mounting for scope, night sights or laser.

Blaser

Blaser, logo

Blaser

The German firm of Blaser Jagdwaffen GmbH is based in Isny in the Allgäu region of the state of Baden Württemberg, on the border of southern Bavaria and Austria, near the Allgäuer Alps. This company was founded in 1977 by Horst Blaser and was taken over in 1986 by Blaser's master gunsmith Gerhard Blenk. Blaser specializes in quality hunting rifles, often with very unusual engravings. Most models have a self-cocking hinged system, as used on shotguns.
These rifles are often fitted with a scope. Blaser uses only high-quality scopes from famous makes, such as Zeiss, Swarovski, Schmidt & Bender and Leupold. Blaser rifles can be fitted with the Mag-Na-Port recoil damper system or a Kickstop recoil damper in the stock, as preferred. In 1993, at IWA, the international arms fair in

Nuremberg, Germany, a new type of rifle was introduced: the single-round R-93 UIT Standard and the 10-round R-93 CISM bolt-action rifle, both match rifles for 300 meters (984 ft). In 1997, a special sniper version of this rifle was introduced. This bolt-action rifle has an unusual locking system.

The bolt lever can be pulled straight back to disengage and so does not have to be rotated by a certain amount first. Further, the bolt head is provided with a 360-degree ring with twelve lug segments that when the weapon is closed or locked are pushed outwards into a circular ridge round the barrel chamber.

By means of a spare barrel system, the R-93 rifle can quickly be fitted with a different caliber. Blaser has also developed a special technique for countering the rusting process in weapons. During the production process, the steel components are treated with the so-called Blaser-Q technique, whereby nitrogen gas is applied to the components and penetrates deep into the surface of the steel(approx. 0.2 mm).

Blaser R 93 Tactical

SPECIFICATIONS

Caliber	: .308 Win.
Magazine	: detachable magazine
Cartridge capacity	: 10 cartridges
Magazine catch	: on the right, below magazine
Action	: bolt-action
Cocking system	: bolt lever
Firing system	: single round
Locking system	: special 360-degree locking system
Length	: 112 cm (44.1")
Barrel length	: 60 cm (23.6"), including muzzle brake
Weight	: 7.3 kg (16.1 lb.), including scope and bipod

Blaser R 93 Tactical

Sight	: none; special sight mounting
Safety	: sliding catch on rear of bolt
Stock	: aluminium with synthetic; adjustable cheek piece and butt plate

PARTICULARS

Matt black finish; free floating Lothar Walther fluted barrel; special detachable bipod with hand-grip. It is shown with a Leupold Mark 4 16 x scope.

Brown

Brown, logo

Chet Brown is the founder of the American firm of Brown Precision Inc. The company is based in Los Molinos in California. Chet Brown was originally a custom gunsmith, who made special rifles to order. In 1970, he was one of the first gunsmiths to experiment with synthetic rifle stocks. These stocks soon became popular with bench-rest shooters, for whom it was important to have a stock that is insensitive to all weather conditions. In addition, a synthetic stock is considerably lighter than a wooden one. Otherwise, Brown uses mainly stainless steel.

Steel components are chemically nickel-plated or Teflon-coated. Brown rifles are built on the basis of a Remington 700 or 40X or Winchester M70 receiver with bolt. These receivers are provided by Brown with a stainless-steel Shilen match barrel and, if required, various types of muzzle flash suppresser. The customer determines the caliber, the barrel length, the type of stock and the finish. All mechanical parts are carefully hand-tuned. The above-mentioned synthetic stocks are made of Kevlar or fiber glass. Brown also makes a special sniper rifle.

Brown Tactical Elite

SPECIFICATIONS

Caliber	: .223 Rem. .308 Win. .300 Win. Mag. or as preferred
Magazine	: blind magazine or detachable magazine
Cartridge capacity	: 3 to 5 cartridges
Magazine catch	: in front side of trigger guard
Action	: bolt-action
Cocking system	: bolt lever
Firing system	: single round
Locking system	: 2-lug bolt (Remington 700 system)
Length	: 103 cm (40.6")
Barrel length	: 61 cm (24")
Weight	: 4.5 kg (9.9 lb.), excluding scope
Sight	: none
Safety	: safety catch at rear of receiver on the right, behind bolt lever
Stock	: black Kevlar synthetic stock with pistol grip and adjustable butt plate

PARTICULARS

Special folding bipod; matt black protective coating.

Brown Tactical Elite

Bushmaster

The Quality Parts Company is based in Windham, in the state of Maine. Since 1979 they have made arms components

Bushmaster, logo

for the US Army and the police. They also manufacture numerous products for the civilian arms market, especially components for the AR-15/M16 rifle. In addition, they make accessories for FAL, Heckler & Koch, Ruger and AK-47 rifles and special components for the Colt .45 ACP pistol and for Uzi pistols and carbines. Bushmaster Firearms Inc., a subsidiary, makes special versions of the AR-15 rifle under the name XM15.

During the Gulf War, operation Desert Storm, the company received a large contract to produce the M16-A2-M4 carbine for the US Army. For the civilian market, Bushmaster makes XM15-E2S rifles and carbines. The suffix "S" stands for semi-automatic. Bushmaster even makes special match versions of this type for ranges up to 800 meters (874 yd). As on the Colt M16, on the right of the receiver housing there is an auxiliary button with which extra pressure can be exerted on the bolt to force it forward. This is because the repeating action may be retarded by dirt or heat from the barrel chamber.

The suffix "S" for Bushmaster rifles XM15-E2S indicates that these weapons fire only semi-automatically. Fully automatic rifles are sold only to government bodies or to private individuals with a special license.

Bushmaster XM 15 E2S "Dissipator" carbine

Bushmaster XM 15 E2S "Dissipator" V-Match carbine

Bushmaster XM 15 E2S "Dissipator" carbine

SPECIFICATIONS

Caliber	: .223 Rem.
Magazine	: detachable magazine
Cartridge capacity: 30 cartridges	
Magazine catch	: magazine catch on right-hand side of magazine housing
Action	: gas pressure
Cocking system	: cocking lever
Firing system	: XM-15 E2 version: semi-automatic and fully automatic; XM-15E2S version: semi-automatic only
Locking system	: 7-lug rotating bolt head
Length	: 87.6 cm (34.5")
Barrel length	: 40.6 cm (16")
Weight	: 3.4 kg (7.4 lb.)
Sight	: adjustable aperture sight in carrying handle
Safety	: safety catch on left-hand side of receiver housing, also firing position indicator on right-hand side
Stock	: synthetic stock and forearm

PARTICULARS
Black phosphate finish. This rifle has a hand grip ("forearm") provided with a special heat dissipater.

Bushmaster XM 15 E2 "Dissipator" V-Match carbine

SPECIFICATIONS

Caliber	: .223 Rem.
Magazine	: detachable magazine
Cartridge capacity: 30 rounds	
Magazine catch	: magazine catch on right-hand side of magazine housing
Action	: gas pressure
Cocking system	: cocking lever
Firing system	: XM-15 E2 version: semi-automatic and fully automatic; XM-15E2S version: semi-automatic only
Locking system	: 7-lug rotating bolt head

Length	: 87.6 cm (34.5")
Barrel length	: 40.6 cm (16")
Weight	: 3.4 kg (7.4 lb.)
Sight	: none; guide rail for sight mounting
Safety	: safety catch on left-hand side of receiver housing, also firing position indicator on right-hand side
Stock	: synthetic stock and forearm

PARTICULARS
Black phosphate finish. Forearm hand grip is designed to dissipate heat.

Bushmaster XM-15 E2 HBAR Law Enforcement

SPECIFICATIONS

Caliber	: .223 Rem.
Magazine	: detachable magazine
Cartridge capacity: 30 rounds	
Magazine catch	: magazine catch on right-hand side of magazine housing
Action	: gas pressure
Cocking system	: cocking lever
Firing system	: XM-15 E2 version: semi-automatic and fully automatic; XM-15E2S version: semi-automatic only
Locking system	: 7-lug rotating bolt head
Length	: 100 cm (39.5")

Bushmaster XM 15 E2S HBAR Law Enforcement

Barrel length	: 51 cm (20")
Weight	: 3.9 kg (8.6 lb.)
Sight	: adjustable aperture sight in carrying handle
Safety	: safety catch on left-hand side of receiver housing, also firing position indicator on right-hand side
Stock	: synthetic stock and forearm

PARTICULARS

Black phosphate finish. Barrel with flash suppresser and bayonet lug. Rifle is also available as a carbine with telescopic tubular stock, a total length of 86.4 cm (34") and a barrel length of 40.6 cm (16").

Bushmaster XM 15 E2 "Shorty" carbine

SPECIFICATIONS

Caliber	: .223 Rem.
Magazine	: detachable magazine
Cartridge capacity:	30 rounds
Magazine catch	: magazine catch on right-hand side of magazine housing
Action	: gas pressure
Cocking system	: cocking lever
Firing system	: XM-15 E2 version: semi-automatic and fully automatic; XM-15E2S version: semi-automatic only
Locking system	: 7-lug rotating bolt head
Length	: 88.3 cm (34.75")
Barrel length	: 40.6 cm (16")
Weight	: 3.2 kg (6.97 lb.)
Sight	: adjustable aperture sight in carrying handle

Bushmaster XM 15 E2S Target Rifle

Bushmaster XM 15 E2S "Shorty" carbine

Safety	: safety catch on left-hand side of receiver housing, also firing position indicator on right-hand side
Stock	: synthetic stock and forearm

PARTICULARS

Black phosphate finish.

Bushmaster XM-15 E2 Target Rifle

SPECIFICATIONS

Caliber	: .223 Rem.
Magazine	: detachable magazine
Cartridge capacity:	30 rounds
Magazine catch	: magazine catch on right-hand side of magazine housing
Action	: gas pressure
Cocking system	: cocking lever
Firing system	: XM-15 E2 version: semi-automatic and fully automatic; XM-15E2S version: semi-automatic only
Locking system	: 7-lug rotating bolt head
Length	: 97 cm (38.25")

113

Barrel length : 51 cm (20")
Weight : 3.9 kg (8.6 lb.)
Sight : adjustable aperture sight in carrying handle
Safety : safety catch on left of receiver housing and firing indicator on right
Stock : synthetic stock and forearm

PARTICULARS

Black phosphatised finish. Rifle is also available with barrel lengths of 61 cm (24") or 66 cm (26").

Bushmaster XM 15 E2 V-Match Competition rifle

SPECIFICATIONS

Caliber : .223 Rem.
Magazine : detachable magazine
Cartridge capacity: 30 rounds
Magazine catch : on right of magazine housing
Action : gas pressure
Cocking system : cocking lever
Firing system : XM-15 E2 version: semi-automatic and fully automatic; XM-15E2S version: semi-automatic only
Locking system : 7-lug rotating bolt head
Length : 97 cm (38.25")
Barrel length : 51 cm (20")
Weight : 3.8 kg (8.3 lb.))
Sight : none; guide rail for scope mounting
Safety : safety catch on left-hand side of receiver housing, also firing position indicator on right-hand side
Stock : synthetic stock

PARTICULARS

Black phosphatised finish; receiver housing has no carrying handle. Rifle is also available with a 61-cm (24") or 66-cm (26") barrel.

Bushmaster X17 Bullpup rifle

SPECIFICATIONS

Caliber : .223 Rem.
Magazine : detachable magazine
Cartridge capacity: 30 rounds
Magazine catch : on left-hand side of magazine housing
Action : gas pressure
Cocking system : cocking lever
Firing system : X17 version: semi-automatic and fully automatic; X17S version: semi-automatic only
Locking system : 7-lug rotating bolt head
Length : 76 cm (30")
Barrel length : 54.6 cm (21.5")
Weight : 3.8 kg (8.4 lb.)
Sight : fixed iron sight in carrying handle; guide rail for scope mounting
Safety : safety catch on right-hand side of receiver housing, also firing position indicator on left-hand side
Stock : synthetic bullpup stock

PARTICULARS

Black phosphate finish. Detachable magazine located in the rear of the stock.

Bushmaster X17S Bullpup rifle

CZ 700 Subsonic sniper rifle

CZ Skorpion sub-machine-gun

C c

Calico

The California Instrument Company is based in Bakersfield, in the state of California. The company was set up in 1982. Initially, it designed and produced specialist tools for the oil industry. From this background, the firm decided in May 1985 to start developing a line of weapons. The company developed light automatic and semi-automatic weapons with a very unusual detachable magazine. This is a box magazine positioned on top of the weapon. Spiral rows of cartridges are forced forward by a spring as a result of the rotating motion of a magazine follower. At the front, the cartridges are pressed one by one out of the magazine and into the barrel chamber. When the rifle is fired, the rotating rows of cartridges are forced forward, since a space is created here after every round.

The first weapon made by Calico was a 100-round smallbore pistol in .22 LR. In June 1989, a 50 and 100-round 9 mm Para carbine was introduced, with a detachable magazine based on the same spiral principle. Then came the two sub-machine-guns, fitted with an extending stock and two synthetic pistol grips. Housed at the front of the trigger guard are both a separate firing selector and the safety catch. Calico relies primarily on sales to government departments and exports. In its own country, the company's weapons may not be sold on the civilian market because of the large magazine capacity.

Calico Liberty 50 carbine

SPECIFICATIONS

Caliber	: 9 mm Para
Magazine	: box magazine
Cartridge capacity	: 50 cartridges
Magazine catch	: pushbutton at rear of box magazine
Action	: recoil energy
Cocking system	: cocking lever
Firing system	: semi-automatic
Locking system	: inertia locking system
Length	: 87.6 cm (34.5")
Barrel length	: 40.9 cm (16.1")
Weight	: 3.2 kg (7 lb.)
Sight	: rear sight and adjustable front sight on bracket above box magazine
Safety	: ambidextrous safety pushbutton
Stock	: stock, grip and box magazine made of impact-resistant synthetic

PARTICULARS

Matt black protective coating; special position for inspecting the barrel chamber without having to cock the weapon or feed the cartridge into the chamber.

Calico Liberty 100 carbine

SPECIFICATIONS

Caliber	: 9 mm Para
Magazine	: box magazine
Cartridge capacity	: 100 cartridges
Magazine catch	: pushbutton at rear of box magazine
Action	: recoil energy
Cocking system	: cocking lever
Firing system	: semi-automatic
Locking system	: inertia locking system
Length	: 87.6 cm (34.5")
Barrel length	: 40.9 cm (16.1")
Weight	: 3.2 kg (7 lb.)

Calico Liberty 50 carbine

Calico, logo

Calico Liberty 100 carbine

Sight	: fixed rear sight, adjustable front sight
Safety	: ambidextrous safety pushbutton
Stock	: stock, grip and box magazine made of impact-resistant synthetic

PARTICULARS

Matt black protective coating; special position for inspecting the barrel chamber without having to cock the weapon or feed the cartridge into the chamber.

Calico M-955A sub-machine-gun

SPECIFICATIONS

Caliber	: 9 mm Para
Magazine	: box magazine
Cartridge capacity	: 50 or 100 cartridges
Magazine catch	: pushbutton at rear of box magazine
Action	: recoil energy
Cocking system	: cocking lever
Firing system	: semi-automatic and automatic
Locking system	: inertia locking system
Length	: 63.5 cm (25") (folded stock)
Barrel length	: 27.9 cm (11")
Weight	: 2.4 kg (5.3 lb.)
Sight	: fixed rear sight, adjustable front sight
Safety	: ambidextrous safety pushbutton; firing selector in front side of trigger guard
Stock	: extending stock, two synthetic pistol grips; light-metal receiver housing

PARTICULARS

Matt black; adjustable combined muzzle flash suppresser and recoil damper. Stan-

Calico M-955A sub-machine-gun

dard firing rate 600-700 rounds a minute, but can be set to a different rate.

Calico M-960A sub-machine-gun

SPECIFICATIONS

Caliber	: 9 mm Para
Magazine	: box magazine
Cartridge capacity	: 50 or 100 cartridges
Magazine catch	: pushbutton at rear of box magazine
Action	: recoil energy
Cocking system	: cocking lever
Firing system	: semi- and fully automatic
Locking system	: inertia locking system
Length	: 53.3 cm (21") (folded stock)
Barrel length	: 17.8 cm (7")
Weight	: 2.1 kg (4.6 lb.)
Sight	: fixed rear sight, adjustable front sight
Safety	: ambidextrous safety pushbutton; firing selector in front side of trigger guard
Stock	: extending stock, two synthetic pistol grips; light-metal receiver housing

PARTICULARS

Matt black; adjustable combined muzzle flash suppresser and recoil damper. Standard firing rate 600-700 rounds a minute, but can be set to a different rate.

Carcano/Mannlicher Carcano

The Mannlicher Carcano arms family covers a period of almost fifty years. The Model 1891 bolt-action rifle was developed by Salvatore Carcano, who was an artillery lieutenant-colonel and arms engineer at the Italian state arsenal in Turin. For this rifle, he used a modified form of

Calico M-960A sub-machine-gun

the Mauser 1888 locking system, combined with the Mannlicher magazine that could be loaded with a 6-round cartridge clip. The logo is the official hallmark of the Turin arsenal. In 1892, the weapon entered service with the Italian army. A shorter carbine, the Model 91 Carbine, was also derived from this rifle. This carbine has an interesting folding bayonet.

The models dating from 1891 were made for 6.5 x 52 mm Mannlicher-Carcano caliber. The Mannlicher Carcano design had many weaknesses. One of them was the cartridge clip, which allowed the magazine to get dirty quickly. Several submodels of this rifle are known, because the weapon concept was modified on a number of occasions, namely in 1895, 1897, 1907 and 1912.

In 1938, a new series of rifles and carbines was introduced. In various battles, such as in Ethiopia, the 6.5 mm cartridge proved to have too little power. The caliber was therefore increased to 7.35 x 51 mm Carcano. Strangely enough, at the start of the Second World War the 6.5 x 52 mm caliber was re-introduced by the Italian army and a large number of rifles that used 7.35 caliber ammo were converted to 6.5 mm.

The Mannlicher Carcano rifle achieved worldwide fame with the assassination of President John F. Kennedy. He was shot by Lee Harvey Oswald on 22 November 1963 with a 6.5 mm Model 91/38 rifle. It

was a bolt-action rifle converted from 7.35 mm caliber to 6.5 mm. At the end of the Second World War, a small number of Carcanos using 8 x 57 mm Mauser caliber were made for various German army units. The Mannlicher Carcano continued to be used for a long time by the Italian armed forces.

The weapon was succeeded by the Beretta BM59, a modified Garand with a detachable magazine using 7.62 x 51 NATO caliber ammo.

Carcano M1891

SPECIFICATIONS

Caliber	: 6.5 x 52 mm Mannlicher-Carcano
Magazine	: blind magazine
Cartridge capacity	: 6 cartridges in a clip
Magazine catch	: N/A.
Action	: bolt-action
Cocking system	: bolt lever
Firing system	: single round
Locking system	: 2-lug locking system (Mauser type)
Length	: carbine: 92 cm (36.2"); rifle: 129 cm (50.8")
Barrel length	: carbine: 45 cm (17.7"); rifle: 78 cm (30.7")
Weight	: carbine: 3.0 kg (6.6 lb.); rifle: 3.9 kg (8.6 lb.)
Sight	: tangent rear sight 500 to 1500 metres/546 to 1640 yd (rifle: 500 to 2000 metres/546 to 2187 yd)
Safety	: wing catch on rear of bolt
Stock	: wooden stock

PARTICULARS

The bolt lever is located in front of the split rear receiver bridge. The carbine has a long folding spike bayonet. The twist of the rifling becomes shorter towards the muzzle.

Carcano M1891

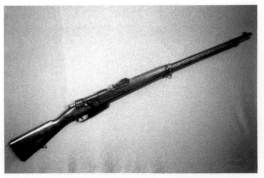

Carcano M1891 carbine

Carcano M1938

SPECIFICATIONS

Caliber	: 6.5 x 52 mm Mannlicher-Carcano or 7.35 x 51 mm Carcano
Magazine	: blind magazine
Cartridge capacity	: 6 cartridges in a clip
Magazine catch	: N/A.
Action	: bolt-action
Cocking system	: bolt lever
Firing system	: single round
Locking system	: 2-lug locking system (Mauser type)
Length	: carbine: 92 cm (36.2"); rifle: 102 cm (40.2")
Barrel length	: carbine: 45 cm (17.7"); rifle: 53 cm (20.9")
Weight	: 6.5 mm carbine: 3.0 kg (6.6 lb.); 7.35 mm: 2.95 kg (6.5 lb.); 6.5 mm rifle: 3.5 kg (7.6 lb.); 7.35 mm: 3.4 kg (7.5 lb.)
Sight	: fixed sight
Safety	: wing catch on rear of bolt
Stock	: wooden stock

PARTICULARS

The bolt lever is located in front of the split rear receiver bridge. Folding bayonet.

Carcano M1938

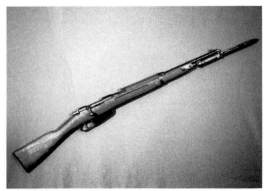

CETME

CETME stands for Centro de Estudios de Materiales Especiales. This Spanish state-owned company developed a new assault rifle for the Spanish armed forces after the Second World War. The former Mauser employee and arms engineer Vorgrimmler designed this weapon on the basis of the Mauser Sturmgewehr 45M prototype dating from early 1945. There is an interesting tale associated with this development.

This rifle already had a roller locking system, as was later to be used on Heckler & Koch weapons. Originally, the Spanish weapon used 7.62 x 51 CETME caliber ammo, a lighter version of the 7.62 x 51 NATO cartridge. In the early 1950s, the Dutch firm of NWM, an arms factory in Den Bosch, acquired the production license for the CETME rifle. At that time, NWM was part of an international partnership in the area of defense. The license was valid worldwide, except in Germany, which at the time did not yet have its own army.

In 1956, Germany was given permission by the Allies to set up its own armed forces. A selection procedure was set in motion for choosing a new military rifle. Four rifles were candidates: the Belgian FAL, as R1, the SIG rifle, as R2, the CETME rifle, as R3, and the American/Dutch AR10, as R4. Owing to the close ties between Spain and Germany and the fact that after the war many Germany arms engineers had found work in Spain, it was clear from the very start that the CETME rifle would be the Germans' preferred choice.

With the help of Rheinmetall's development department, the CETME concept was modified to meet the German requirements and converted to the eventual R3 rifle. Production of this new military rifle was contracted out to the German firm of Heckler & Koch. Interest developed abroad in the R3 and Heckler & Koch had to keep turning down these customers and referring them to the Dutch

NWM factory. The German government felt that this situation was not ideal and took steps to (in their view) rectify matters. Following intense negotiations, NWM was forced to cede the license rights to Heckler & Koch. Due to the enormous success of this type of roller locking system, it is fair to say that, from the Dutch point of view, this was a historic blunder. The Spanish CETME had in the meantime also switched to the standard NATO Caliber and in 1958 entered service with the Spanish troops as the Model 58. Even more interesting from an arms engineering point of view is the fact that the barrel chamber has horizontal grooves. This prevents the case from "sticking" in the chamber.

This problem apparently occurred at the time, though in other weapon designs, such as the FN-FAL, this measure was not necessary. The derived CETME M58 rifle has no wooden or synthetic hand grip and has a tangent rear sight. Later types do have such a hand grip made of wood, synthetic material or stamped sheet steel and a rotating aperture sight drum, as used for the Heckler & Koch weapons.

CETME Model 58

SPECIFICATIONS

Caliber	: 7.62 x 51 mm NATO
Magazine	: detachable magazine
Cartridge capacity	: 20 cartridges
Magazine catch	: magazine housing at rear, in front of trigger guard
Action	: gas pressure

Cocking system	: cocking lever
Firing system	: semi-automatic and fully automatic
Locking system	: roller locking system
Length	: 101.5 cm (39.9")
Barrel length	: 45 cm (17.7")
Weight	: 4.5 kg (9.9 lb.)
Sight	: early models: tangent rear sight; later models: rotatable aperture drum (Heckler & Koch type)
Safety	: combined rotating safety catch and firing selector on left-hand side of receiver housing
Stock	: wooden stock and hand grip or with sheet-steel hand grip and synthetic pistol grip

PARTICULARS

Folding bipod; carrying handle and bead ring. The cocking lever is connected to the piston rod and is located in the (gas) tube above the barrel.

CETME Model FR-8 Cetmeton

SPECIFICATIONS

Caliber	: .308 Win.
Magazine	: blind magazine
Cartridge capacity	: 5 cartridges
Magazine catch	: N/A.
Action	: bolt-action
Cocking system	: bolt lever
Firing system	: single round
Locking system	: Mauser lug locking system
Length	: 98.1 cm (38-5/8")
Barrel length	: 45 cm (17.75")
Weight	: 3.6 kg (7.9 lb.)
Sight	: notched and aperture sight
Safety	: Mauser wing catch on rear of bolt
Stock	: wooden stock and hand grip

PARTICULARS

The weapon resembles a gas-operated rifle due to the tube below the barrel. However,

CETME Model 58

CETME Model FR-8 Cetmeton

this tube is a storage compartment for the cleaning rod and the oil tube.

CETME Model L

SPECIFICATIONS

Caliber	: 5.56 x 45 mm NATO (.223 Rem.)
Magazine	: detachable magazine
Cartridge capacity	: 30 cartridges
Magazine catch	: on right-hand side of magazine housing
Action	: gas pressure
Cocking system	: cocking lever
Firing system	: semi-automatic and fully automatic
Locking system	: roller locking system
Length	: rifle (Model L): 101.5 cm (39.9"); carbine (Model LC): 86 cm (33.9")
Barrel length	: rifle (Model L) 45 cm (17.7"); carbine (Model LC): 32 cm (12.6")
Weight	: rifle (Model L): 4.5 kg (9.9 lb.); carbine (Model LC): 3.2 kg (7.1 lb.)
Sight	: early models: tangent rear sight; later models: rotatable aperture drum (Heckler & Koch type)
Safety	: combined rotating safety catch and firing selector on left-hand side of receiver housing
Stock	: synthetic stock and hand grip or with sheet-steel hand grip and pistol grip

PARTICULARS

Folding bipod; carrying handle and bead ring. The carbine version, Model LC, has a steel extending stock. The total length with folded stock is 66.5 cm (26.2 in).

Colt

Colt, logo

Colt's Manufacturing Company Inc. is situated in Hartford, in the state of Connecticut, on the east coast of the United States. The company has been making firearms for over 160 years: at first only revolvers, but at the start of the twentieth century the range was extended to include, among other weapons, semi-automatic pistols.

The renowned Colt Model 1911 .45 ACP pistol, designed by the famous John Moses Browning, was introduced by Colt in 1911. In the military area, Colt is best known for its M16/AR-15. Tens of thousands of pages in hundreds of books have been written about the history of the AR-15 and its military counterpart, the M16. Some books are full of praise for it, while others express sharp criticism, stemming from the war experiences in Vietnam. In spite of everything, the M16, together with the AK-47, has been produced and copied more than any other rifle. Many variations of the M16 are known.

ne of the standard works about this rifle is The Black Rifle by R.B. Stevens and E.C. Ezell. In 416 pages, the history of the M16 is covered. Over the years, Colt has made a number of civilian versions of the famed Colt M16 automatic military rifle under the brand name of Colt AR-15. The M16 was designed for the ArmaLite company by the American arms designer Eugene Stoner in 1956.

At that time, ArmaLite was part of the Fairchild Engine and Airplane group and Stoner worked there as chief engineer. In 1959, Colt took over the production activities. During the Vietnam War, the M16 was also produced for the US Army by Harrington & Richardson and General Motors.

Altogether, some 3,440,000 Colt M16s were made in several models. The present Colt rifle line consists of the Colt Match Target rifle in seven different versions. This weapon is a modified civilian version of the Colt M16 military rifle. The Colt Match Target rifle is available in calibers .223 Rem., 9 mm Para and the Russian caliber 7.62 x 39 mm.

Colt M4 carbine

SPECIFICATIONS

Caliber	: .223 Rem.
Magazine	: detachable magazine
Cartridge capacity	: 20 or 30 rounds
Magazine catch	: on right-hand side of magazine housing
Action	: gas pressure
Cocking system	: cocking lever
Firing system	: semi-automatic, 3-shot burst or fully automatic
Locking system	: 7-lug rotating bolt head
Length	: with telescoped stock: 81.3 cm (32") or 88.9 cm (35") with unfolded stock
Barrel length	: 38.8 or 40.6 cm (14.5 or 16")
Weight	: 2.6 kg (5.7 lb.) (with 38.8 cm/14.5" barrel)

Colt M4 with RIS and Remington Model 870 Police

Sight	: adjustable A2 aperture sight in detachable carrying handle with MilSpec Picatinny or Knight RIS mounting rail
Safety	: combined firing selector/safety catch on left-hand side of receiver housing
Stock	: telescopic steel tubular stock, can be set in four positions

PARTICULARS

Modular rifle: various configuration options. The photo shows the Colt M4 with RIS mounting rail, Elcan scope, laser and MagLite torch. Below, the Colt M4 with RIS and Remington Model 870 Police riot gun below the barrel.

Colt M16A2

SPECIFICATIONS

Caliber	: .223 Rem.
Magazine	: detachable magazine
Cartridge capacity	: 20 or 30 rounds
Magazine catch	: on right-hand side of magazine housing
Action	: gas pressure
Cocking system	: cocking lever
Firing system	: semi-automatic and 3-shot burst

M4 with Elcan scope and M203 40-mm grenade launcher

Colt M16A2

Locking system	: 7-lug rotating bolt head
Length	: 100.6 cm (39.6")
Barrel length	: 50.8 cm (20")
Weight	: 3.6 kg (7.9 lb.)
Sight	: adjustable aperture sight in carrying handle
Safety	: combined firing selector/safety catch on left-hand side of breechblock housing
Stock	: synthetic stock, pistol grip and hand grip

PARTICULARS
Differences between the M16A2 and the M16A1: adjustable aperture sight, improved pistol grip and hand grip, new combined flash suppresser and compensator, a case buffer behind the ejection port (for left-handed shooters). The A2 also does not have a fully automatic firing system, as the M16A1 does.

Colt Match Target Competition HBAR Flattop (R6700)

SPECIFICATIONS

Caliber	: .223 Rem.
Magazine	: detachable magazine
Cartridge capacity	: 5, 20 or 30 rounds
Magazine catch	: on right-hand side of magazine housing
Action	: gas pressure
Cocking system	: cocking lever
Firing system	: semi-automatic
Locking system	: 7-lug rotating bolt head

Colt Match Target Competition HBAR Flattop (R6700)

Length	: 99.1 cm (39")
Barrel length	: 51 cm (20")
Weight	: 3.9 kg (8.5 lb.)
Sight	: flattop receiver housing with adjustable aperture sight in carrying handle
Safety	: safety catch on left-hand side of breechblock housing
Stock	: synthetic stock and forearm

PARTICULARS
Matt black phosphate finish. Twist of the barrel is 1:9.

Colt Match Target HBAR (Heavy Barrel)

Colt Match Target HBAR (Heavy Barrel)

SPECIFICATIONS

Caliber	: .223 Rem.
Magazine	: detachable magazine
Cartridge capacity	: 5, 20 or 30 rounds
Magazine catch	: on right-hand side of magazine housing
Action	: gas pressure
Cocking system	: cocking lever
Firing system	: semi-automatic
Locking system	: 7-lug rotating bolt head
Length	: 99.1 cm (39")
Barrel length	: 51 cm (20")
Weight	: 3.9 kg (8.5 lb.)
Sight	: adjustable aperture sight in carrying handle
Safety	: safety catch on left-hand side of receiver housing
Stock	: synthetic stock and forearm

PARTICULARS
Matt black phosphate finish. This rifle is also available in calibers 9 mm Para and 7.62 x 39 mm and in the 3.0-kg (6.7-lb) lightweight version. The twist of the barrel is 1:9 (Model MT6700) or 1:7 (Model MT6601).

Colt Match Target HBAR II (Heavy Barrel)

Colt Sporter Competition HBAR Flattop (R6700CH)

Colt Match Target HBAR II (Heavy Barrel)

SPECIFICATIONS

Caliber	: .223 Rem.
Magazine	: detachable magazine
Cartridge capacity	: 5, 20 or 30 rounds
Magazine catch	: on right-hand side of magazine housing
Action	: gas pressure
Cocking system	: cocking lever
Firing system	: semi-automatic
Locking system	: 7-lug rotating bolt head
Length	: 87.6 cm (34.5")
Barrel length	: 40.9 cm (16.1")
Weight	: 3.2 kg (7.1 lb.)
Sight	: adjustable aperture sight in carrying handle
Safety	: safety catch on left-hand side of receiver housing
Stock	: synthetic stock and forearm

PARTICULARS

Matt black phosphatised. Twist of the barrel is 1:9.

Colt Sporter Competition HBAR Flattop (R6700CH)

SPECIFICATIONS

Caliber	: .223 Rem.
Magazine	: detachable magazine
Cartridge capacity	: 5, 20 or 30 rounds
Magazine catch	: on right-hand side of magazine housing
Action	: gas pressure
Cocking system	: cocking lever
Firing system	: semi-automatic
Locking system	: 7-lug rotating bolt head
Length	: 99.1 cm (39")
Barrel length	: 51 cm (20")

Weight	: 4.8 kg (10.5 lb.), including scope
Sight	: flattop receiver housing with 3-9X scope with rubber protective sleeve
Safety	: safety catch on left-hand side of receiver housing
Stock	: synthetic stock and forearm

PARTICULARS

Matt black phosphate finish. Twist of the barrel is 1:9.

Colt Sporter HBAR (Heavy Barrel)

SPECIFICATIONS

Caliber	: .223 Rem.
Magazine	: detachable magazine
Cartridge capacity	: 5, 20 or 30 rounds
Magazine catch	: on right-hand side of magazine housing
Action	: gas pressure
Cocking system	: cocking lever
Firing system	: semi-automatic
Locking system	: 7-lug rotating bolt head
Length	: 99.1 cm (39")
Barrel length	: 51 cm (20")
Weight	: 3.4 kg (7.5 lb.)
Sight	: adjustable aperture sight in carrying handle
Safety	: safety catch on left-hand side of receiver housing
Stock	: synthetic stock and forearm

PARTICULARS

Matt black phosphate finish.

Colt Sporter HBAR (Heavy Barrel)

Colt Sporter Lightweight 9 mm (MT6430)

SPECIFICATIONS

Caliber	: 9 mm Para
Magazine	: detachable magazine
Cartridge capacity: 5 or 20 rounds	
Magazine catch	: on right-hand side of magazine housing
Action	: recoil energy
Cocking system	: cocking lever
Firing system	: semi-automatic
Locking system	: inertia locking system
Length	: 87.6 cm (34.5")
Barrel length	: 40.6 cm (16")
Weight	: 3.2 kg (7.1 lb.)
Sight	: adjustable aperture sight in carrying handle
Safety	: safety catch on left-hand side of receiver housing
Stock	: synthetic stock and forearm

Colt Sporter Lightweight 9 mm (MT6430)

PARTICULARS

Matt black phosphate finish. Twist of the barrel is 1:10.
The weapon is used in many countries, including the United States, as a police carbine.

Colt Sporter Match Target Lightweight (MT6530)

SPECIFICATIONS

Caliber	: .223 Rem.
Magazine	: detachable magazine
Cartridge capacity: 5, 20 or 30 rounds	
Magazine catch	: on right-hand side of magazine housing
Action	: gas pressure
Cocking system	: cocking lever
Firing system	: semi-automatic
Locking system	: 7-lug rotating bolt head
Length	: 87.6 cm (34.5")
Barrel length	: 40.6 cm (16")
Weight	: 3.0 kg (6.7 lb.)
Sight	: adjustable aperture sight in carrying handle
Safety	: safety catch on left-hand side of receiver housing
Stock	: synthetic stock and forearm

PARTICULARS

Matt black phosphate finish. Twist of the barrel is 1:7.

CZ

CZ stands for Ceska Zbrojovka. The company is based in Uhersky Brod, a small town in the foothills of the Carpathians in the south of Moravia, in the Czech Republic. After the First World War, Czechoslovakia had an extensive arms industry, since the national army had to be re-equipped on a large scale. Factories such as Zbrojovka Brno, Ceska Zbrojovka Strakonice and Zavody Skoda are the best known of these. The company from Brno (or Brunn) was responsible for developing the Brno ZB-26 light machine gun. In 1937, a production license was sold to the British state-owned company of Enfield Lock. A modified version, the Bren Gun, using .303 British caliber ammo, was supplied to many countries by Britain. The present company of Ceska Zbrojovka, or CZ, was founded in July 1936 as a result of the threat of war from Nazi Germany. Eventually, Czechoslovakia was annexed to Germany anyway, and in the period from 1939 to 1945 the arms factories were forced to make machine guns for the German army. After the Second World War, when the country had fallen within the Russian sphere of influence, Kalashnikov rifle models were produced on a large scale. In the sixty years that the company has existed in its present form, production has been extended to include a series of pistols and rifles. CZ's current range consists of a comprehensive series of bolt-action rifles, semi-automatic pistols, shotguns, air-guns and military weapons.

CZ, logo

In the world of sport shooting, CZ as a brand name is famed for its excellent CZ-75 and CZ-85 pistol series. The company is now one of the largest manufacturers of lightweight weapons and it exports to over 70 countries throughout the world.

CZ/AK-47

CZ/AK-47

SPECIFICATIONS

Caliber	: 7.62 x 39 mm
Magazine	: detachable magazine
Cartridge capacity	: 30 cartridges
Magazine catch	: in front of trigger guard
Action	: gas pressure
Cocking system	: cocking lever
Firing system	: fully automatic or semi-automatic
Locking system	: rotating bolt head
Length	: 88.1 cm (34.7")
Barrel length	: 41.4 cm (16.3")
Weight	: 3.45 kg (7.6 lb.)
Sight	: adjustable tangent rear sight and front sight
Safety	: safety catch on right-hand side of receiver housing
Stock	: hardwood stock in various models

PARTICULARS

Matt black coating on receiver housing and barrel. The weapon is a specific Czech version of the Russian Kalashnikov AK-47.

CZ 537 Sniper

SPECIFICATIONS

Caliber	: .308 Win.
Magazine	: blind magazine
Cartridge capacity	: 4 cartridges
Magazine catch	: N/A.
Action	: bolt-action
Cocking system	: bolt lever
Firing system	: single round

CZ 537 Sniper

CZ 700 Sniper

Locking system	: 2-lug bolt (Mauser type)
Length	: 115 cm (45.3")
Barrel length	: 65 cm (25.6")
Weight	: 5.25 kg (11.6 lb.)
Sight	: none; special sight mounting
Safety	: safety catch on right, behind bolt lever
Stock	: stock with pistol grip and adjustable cheek and butt plate

PARTICULARS

Adjustable, folding bipod; 5-round group of up to 120 mm (4.72") at 300 meters (984 ft).

CZ 700 Sniper

SPECIFICATIONS

Caliber	: .308 Win.
Magazine	: detachable magazine
Cartridge capacity	: 10 cartridges
Magazine catch	: in right-hand side of stock
Action	: bolt-action
Cocking system	: bolt lever
Firing system	: single round
Locking system	: 3-lug bolt

CZ 700 Sniper Subsonic

Length	: 121.5 cm (47.8")
Barrel length	: 65 cm (25.6")
Weight	: 6.2 kg (13.7 lb.), including scope and bipod
Sight	: none; special sight mounting; scope as preferred
Safety	: safety catch on right, behind bolt lever
Stock	: stock of laminated wood with pistol grip and adjustable cheek and butt plat

PARTICULARS

Adjustable, folding bipod as preferred; special fluted barrel; receiver and bolt provided with gas vents. Stock color or coating as preferred

CZ 700 Sniper Subsonic

SPECIFICATIONS

Caliber	: .308 Win.
Magazine	: detachable magazine
Cartridge capacity	: 10 cartridges
Magazine catch	: in right-hand side of stock
Action	: bolt-action
Cocking system	: bolt lever

CZ 2000 Assault Rifle

Firing system	: single round
Locking system	: 3-lug bolt
Length	: 123 cm (48.4")
Barrel length	: 45 cm (17.7")
Weight	: 6.7 kg (14.8 lb.), including scope and bipod
Sight	: none; special sight mounting; scope as preferred
Safety	: safety catch on right, behind bolt lever
Stock	: stock of laminated wood with pistol grip and adjustable cheek and butt plate

PARTICULARS

Adjustable, folding bipod as preferred; special fluted barrel; receiver and bolt provided with gas vents. Stock color or coating as preferred. The barrel is fully integral with a silencer.

CZ 2000 Assault Rifle

SPECIFICATIONS

Caliber	: .223 Rem.
Magazine	: detachable magazine
Cartridge capacity	: 30 cartridges
Magazine catch	: in front of trigger guard
Action	: gas pressure (Kalashnikov system)
Cocking system	: cocking lever
Firing system	: fully automatic, 3-shot burst and semi-automatic
Locking system	: rotating bolt head
Length	: with unfolded stock: 85 cm (33.5"); folded: 61.5 cm (24.2")
Barrel length	: 38.2 (15")
Weight	: 3.1 kg (6.8 lb.)
Sight	: fully adjustable and protected tangent rear sight (100 to 800 metres/328 ft to 874 yd) and front sight; special scope mounting
Safety	: combined safety catch/firing selector on left-hand side of receiver housing
Stock	: folding steel skeleton stock, synthetic pistol grip and hand grip

PARTICULARS

Matt black coating; synthetic detachable magazine; barrel fitted with a lugged attachment for bipod, bayonet lug; both can also be used for attaching the rifle grenade launcher. Sight with 3-dot low-visibility markings.

CZ 2000 Assault Rifle Short

SPECIFICATIONS

Caliber	: .223 Rem.
Magazine	: detachable magazine
Cartridge capacity	: 30 cartridges
Magazine catch	: in front of trigger guard
Action	: gas pressure (Kalashnikov system)
Cocking system	: cocking lever
Firing system	: fully automatic, 3-shot burst and semi-automatic
Locking system	: rotating bolt head
Length	: with unfolded stock: 67.5 cm (26.6"); folded: 43.5 cm (17.1")
Barrel length	: 18.5 (7.3")
Weight	: 2.7 kg (6 lb.)
Sight	: fully adjustable and protected tangent rear sight (100 to 800 metres) and front sight; special scope mounting
Safety	: combined safety catch/firing selector on left-hand side of receiver housing
Stock	: folding steel skeleton stock, synthetic pistol grip and hand grip

PARTICULARS

Matt black coating; synthetic detachable magazine. Sight with 3-dot low-visibility markings.

CZ 2000 LMG Light Machine Gun

SPECIFICATIONS

Caliber	: .223 Rem.
Magazine	: detachable magazine
Cartridge capacity	: 30 cartridges or synthetic 200-cartridge drum
Magazine catch	: in front of trigger guard
Action	: gas pressure (Kalashnikov system)
Cocking system	: cocking lever
Firing system	: fully automatic, 3-shot burst and semi-automatic
Locking system	: rotating bolt head
Length	: with unfolded stock: 105 cm (41.3"); folded: 81 cm (31.9")
Barrel length	: 57.7 (22.7")
Weight	: 4.2 kg (9.3 lb.)

CZ 2000 LMG Light Machine Gun

Sight	: fully adjustable and protected tangent rear sight (100 to 1,000 metres/328ft to 1093 yd) and front sight; special scope mounting
Safety	: combined safety catch/firing selector on left-hand side of receiver housing
Stock	: folding steel skeleton stock, synthetic pistol grip and hand grip

PARTICULARS

Matt black coating; synthetic detachable magazine; barrel fitted with lugged attachment for bipod. Sight with 3-dot low-visibility markings.

CZ/Lada Assault Rifle

SPECIFICATIONS

Caliber	: 5.45 x 39, 5.56 x 45 NATO
Magazine	: detachable magazine
Cartridge capacity	: 30 cartridges
Magazine catch	: in front side of trigger guard
Action	: gas pressure
Cocking system	: cocking lever
Firing system	: fully automatic, semi-automatic and 3-shot burst
Locking system	: rotating bolt head
Length	: 85 cm (33.5")
Barrel length	: 38.2 (15")
Weight	: 3.0 kg (6.6 lb.)

CZ/Lada Assault Rifle

Sight   : adjustable tangent rear sight and front sight; mounting rails for scope
Safety   : combined firing selector and safety catch on left-hand side of receiver housing
Stock   : folding steel tubular stock

PARTICULARS
Matt black coating, synthetic hand grip, folding bipod optional.

CZ/Lada Carbine

SPECIFICATIONS
Caliber   : 5.45 x 39, 5.56 x 45 NATO
Magazine   : detachable magazine
Cartridge capacity : 30 cartridges
Magazine catch   : in front side of trigger guard
Action   : gas pressure
Cocking system   : cocking lever
Firing system   : fully automatic, semi-automatic and 3-shot burst
Locking system   : rotating bolt head
Length   : 67.5 cm (26.6")
Barrel length   : 118.5 cm (7.3")
Weight   : 2.6 kg (5.7 lb.)
Sight   : adjustable tangent rear sight and front sight
Safety   : combined firing selector and safety catch on left-hand side of receiver housing
Stock   : folding steel tubular stock

PARTICULARS
Matt black, synthetic hand grip.

CZ/Lada Light Machinegun

SPECIFICATIONS
Caliber   : 5.45 x 39, 5.56 x 45 NATO
Magazine   : detachable magazine
Cartridge capacity : 30 cartridges
Magazine catch   : in front side of trigger guard
Action   : gas pressure
Cocking system   : cocking lever
Firing system   : fully automatic, semi-automatic and 3-shot burst
Locking system   : rotating bolt head
Length   : 105 cm (41.3")
Barrel length   : 57.7 (22.7")
Weight   : 4.1 kg (9.04 lb.)
Sight   : adjustable tangent rear sight up to 1000 metres (1093 yd) and front sight; mounting rails for scope or night sight

CZ/Lada Light Machinegun

Safety	: combined firing selector and safety catch on left-hand side of receiver housing
Stock	: folding steel tubular stock

PARTICULARS

Matt black, synthetic hand grip, folding bipod.

CZ Scorpion Model 82/Model 83/ Model 61E

SPECIFICATIONS

Caliber	: 9 mm Makarov (Model 82), 9 mm Short/.380 ACP (Model 83) or 7.65 mm Browning/.32 ACP (Model 61E)
Magazine	: detachable magazine
Cartridge capacity	: 12, 24 or 30 cartridges
Magazine catch	: in left-hand side of receiver housing
Action	: recoil energy
Cocking system	: ambidextrous cocking lever
Firing system	: fully automatic and semi-automatic
Locking system	: inertia locking system
Length	: with unfolded stock: 51.7 cm (20.4"); folded: 27 cm (10.6")
Barrel length	: 11.3 (4.4") (82/83) or 11.5 cm (4.5") (61E)
Weight	: 1.44 kg (3.2 lb.) (82/83) or 1.28 kg (2.8 lb.) (61E)

CZ Scorpion Model 82/Model 83/Model 61E

Sight	: folding aperture sight 75 and 150 metres
Safety	: combined firing selector and safety catch on left-hand side of receiver housing
Stock	: folding metal wire stock and synthetic or hardwood pistol grip

PARTICULARS

Matt black. Theoretical rate of fire: 750 cartridges/min.

DPMS Bull Twenty-Four Special Sniper

Soldier behind machine gun

D d

D&L MR30 PG (Professional Grade) Tactical Rifle

D&L Sports Inc.

D&L Inc. is based in Gillette, in the state of Wyoming, and was founded by Dave Lauck. The company has specialized in adapting and converting existing weapons. In addition, very special and accurate sniper rifles are made here.

The weapons are modified or built entirely to the specifications of the individual customer or government body. The firm also has training facilities for long-range weapons.

Previously, when he worked as a policeman, Dave Lauck trained sniper teams and SWAT units. As a shooter, he won numerous competitions in Sniper and Counter-Sniper matches. His main customers are competition shooters and special police teams.

D&L MR30 PG (Professional Grade) Tactical Rifle

SPECIFICATIONS

Caliber	: .308 Win.
Magazine	: blind magazine
Cartridge capacity	: 5 cartridges
Magazine catch	: front of trigger guard
Action	: bolt-action
Cocking system	: bolt lever

D&L Sports Inc., logo

Firing system	: single round
Locking system	: lug locking system
Length	: 112 cm (44")
Barrel length	: 61 cm (24")
Weight	: 6.8 kg (15 lb.)
Sight	: none; scope mounting with double rings
Safety	: safety catch on right-hand side of receiver, behind bolt lever
Stock	: specially constructed Kevlar synthetic stock with adjustable cheek and butt plate

PARTICULARS

Sniper rifle made on the basis of a Remington model 700 breech; special stainless-steel Hart barrel with fluting; special flash suppresser and recoil damper; Harris bipod. This rifle has a special trigger system.

D&L MR30 Tactical Rifle

SPECIFICATIONS

Caliber	: .308 Win.
Magazine	: blind magazine
Cartridge capacity	: 5 cartridges
Magazine catch	: front of trigger guard

D&L MR30 Tactical Rifle

Action   : bolt-action
Cocking system   : bolt lever
Firing system   : single round
Locking system   : lug locking system
Length   : 112 cm (44")
Barrel length   : 61 cm (24")
Weight   : 7.0 kg (15.4 lb.)
Sight   : none; scope mounting with double rings
Safety   : safety catch on right-hand side of receiver, behind bolt lever
Stock   : specially constructed skeleton stock with pistol grip and adjustable cheek and butt plate

PARTICULARS
Sniper rifle made on the basis of a Remington model 700 breech; special stainless-steel thick barrel, special flash suppresser and recoil damper; Harris bipod. This rifle has a special trigger system.

D&L Professional Perimeter Carbine

SPECIFICATIONS
Caliber   : .223 Rem.
Magazine   : detachable magazine
Cartridge capacity : 20 or 30 rounds

D&L Professional Perimeter Carbine

Magazine catch   : on left-hand side of receiver housing
Action   : gas pressure
Cocking system   : cocking lever
Firing system   : semi-automatic
Locking system   : rotating locking system
Length   : 87 cm (34.25")
Barrel length   : 42 cm (16.5")
Weight   : 4.1 kg (9 lb.)
Sight   : none; special scope mounting
Safety   : on left-hand side of receiver housing
Stock   : synthetic stock, pistol grip and free floating hand grip

PARTICULARS
Color finish as preferred; one or more torch mountings on front of hand grip; Harris bipod; special stainless-steel bull barrel; modified trigger system. The rifle can be fitted with a flash suppresser or silencer.

Daewoo

Daewoo, logo

◍ DAEWOO

The South Korean arms factory Daewoo Precision Industries Ltd. is located in Seoul and is part of the large Daewoo group. The parent company has many production subsidiaries in machine building, shipbuilding and aircraft building, as well large car plants. Daewoo makes a number of rifles, as well as pistols. The DR200 rifle in .223 Rem. caliber ammo, introduced in 1985, is a striking combination of techniques featured on the Colt M16 and the AK-47 rifles. This rifle is exported mainly to North America. In 1997, a special version of this weapon was introduced, the DR 300, using the Russian Caliber 7.62 x 39 mm. Daewoo is not an unknown player in the field of arms and has been producing light weapons for more than fifteen years. The first models were the Max-1 and Max-2 in .223 Rem caliber. The Max-1 has a telescopic stock,

while the Max-2 is fitted with a folding stock. All Daewoo weapons use AR-15/Colt M-16 detachable magazines. The Daewoo AR-100 rifle in .223 Rem. caliber was introduced in 1985.

Daewoo DR 200 Rifle

SPECIFICATIONS
Caliber	: .223 Rem.
Magazine	: detachable magazine
Cartridge capacity	: 5, 10 or 20-round AR-15 detachable magazines
Magazine catch	: right-hand side of receiver housing
Action	: gas pressure (Coltsystem)
Cocking system	: cocking lever
Firing system	: fully automatic or semi-automatic
Locking system	: rotatielocking system
Length	: 99.6 cm (39.2")
Barrel length	: 46.5 cm (18.3")
Weight	: 4.1 kg (9 lb.), excluding scope
Sight	: military aperture sight and front-sight tunnel; special scope mounting available
Safety	: ambidextrous safety catch on receiver housing above pistol grip
Stock	: synthetic stock with pistol grip and thumb hole

PARTICULARS
Matt black phosphate finish. The rifle is supplied without magazines, but is suitable for all Colt and ArmaLite .223 Rem. detachable magazines.

Dakota

The Dakota Arms Company Inc. is a small-scale and relatively young American arms factory. Until 1984, Don Allen, the company's founder, worked as a commercial pilot on a Northwest Airlines Boeing 727. Since 1962 his hobby had been building special rifles based on the Winchester Model 70. When he retired in 1984, he and his wife set up the present firm of Dakota Arms Inc., based in Sturgis in the state of South Dakota. The first rifle type that Allen put into production was the Dakota Model 76 bolt-action rifle, which he introduced in 1987. Allen also developed six different rifle calibers with special characteristics for hunting medium to big game, the 7 mm Dakota, .300 Dakota, .330 Dakota, .375 Dakota, .416 Dakota and .450 Dakota. In the autumn of 1995, Don Allen brought a traditional side-by-side shotgun onto the market, the American Legend. On the basis of the Model 76, Dakota built a special long-range sniper rifle, the Dakota Longbow, which has an effective range of up to 1500 meters (1640 yd). This rifle has a Lothar Walther barrel and shoots with great accuracy, with a guaranteed 3-round group of 13 mm (0.51") at 100 meters (328 ft).

Dakota Longbow

SPECIFICATIONS
Caliber	: .338 Lapua Magnum, .300 Dakota Magnum or .330 Dakota Magnum
Magazine	: blind magazine
Cartridge capacity	: 5 cartridges
Magazine catch	: N/A.
Action	: bolt-action
Cocking system	: bolt lever
Firing system	: single round
Locking system	: heavy 2-lug bolt
Length	: 127 cm (50")
Barrel length	: 71 cm (28")
Weight	: 6.2 kg (13.7 lb.), excluding scope
Sight	: none; Picatinny mounting rail for scope
Safety	: wing catch on rear of bolt
Stock	: McMillan A2 synthetic stock with adjustable cheek and butt plate

PARTICULARS

Lothar Walther barrel; attachment for bipod on front end of forearm.

S.W. Daniel Inc.

The American firm of S.W. Daniel Inc., of Atlanta, began producing the Cobray M11 sub-machine-gun in 1990. This weapon was derived directly from the famous Ingram M10 sub-machine-gun. As early as 1946, arms designer Gordon B. Ingram had developed a sub-machine-gun for the US Army. Since then, this type of weapon has entered service with several army units under the names US-M1, US-M2, US-M3 and US-M4.

When Ingram attempted to conquer the civilian market, he named this model the Ingram M5. Several models then followed, designated 6 to 9. In 1969, Ingram designed the entirely new model MAC-10, using 9 mm Para and .45 ACP caliber ammo, and the MAC-11 model, using 9 mm Short (.380 ACP) caliber ammo. The weapons were produced for Ingram by the Military Armament Corp., of Marietta, Georgia.

Because no major orders were forthcoming, partly due to the stiff competition from the Heckler & Koch MP5, the firm went bankrupt in 1975. A new attempt was made by the firm of RPB Industries, of Atlanta, but when the American BATF (Bureau for Alcohol, Tobacco and Firearms) banned production, in 1983, this spelled the end of the company. One of the shareholders of RPB Industries, however, thought this weapon concept had commercial potential and set up S.W. Daniel Inc.

The new model was called the Cobray M-11/Nine. The model has several variants, such as a semi-automatic and fully automatic version, and several calibers, such as 9 mm Para and 9 mm Short (.380 ACP). Apparently the firm supplies to a number of governments, judging from a newspaper report dated 17 September 1998. Remarkably, the same article claimed that the Dutch government had bought a series of Cobray sub-machine-guns for subsequent delivery to the Palestinian Authority.

The Israeli Prime Minister Netanyahu did not approve, and confiscated these weapons.

SWD Cobray M-11/Nine

SPECIFICATIONS

Caliber	: 9 mm Para (M-11) or 9 mm Short (.380 ACP) (M-12)
Magazine	: detachable magazine
Cartridge capacity	: 13 or 32 cartridges
Magazine catch	: in rear of grip
Action	: recoil energy
Cocking system	: cocking lever
Firing system	: full and/or semi-automatic
Locking system	: inertia locking system
Length	: 28.7 cm (11.3")
Barrel length	: 13.6 cm (5.4")
Weight	: 1.6 kg (3.5 lb.)
Sight	: fixed aperture sight
Safety	: combined safety catch and firing selector on right-hand side of receiver housing
Stock	: none, or with forward hinged stock

PARTICULARS

Matt black coating, front end of barrel threaded for compensator or silencer.

SWD Cobray M-11/Nine

Diemaco

Diemaco, logo

A DEVTEK AEROSPACE CO.

Diemaco Inc., based in the Canadian town of Kitchener in the province of Ontario, is a subsidiary of the Devertek Aerospace Co. This company produces several variants of the AR-15/M16 military rifle under license and enjoys considerable success with them. One of their customers is the Dutch army, which ordered various versions of the Diemaco to replace the FN-FAL rifle. The fact that Diemaco, rather than license-holder Colt, makes these weapons is due to the various problems Colt has had in recent years. Like most modern military weapons, the Diemaco is actually an entire family of weapons.

The product range consists of a standard assault rifle, a sniper version, a carbine and a light machine gun. All models are made for 5.56 x 45 mm NATO caliber, i.e. the military variant of the .223 Remington cartridge. The C7 Combat rifle is intended for regular troops, while the C7A1 is meant for special units, such as the Marine Corps. A decision is due soon in several NATO countries regarding which light machine gun is to be selected. This will then replace the well-known FN-MAG machine gun. The Diemaco LSW may stand a good chance. Due to its extremely simple construction, which also requires little maintenance, the Stoner LMG is also one of the favorites.

Diemaco C7 Combat Rifle

SPECIFICATIONS

Caliber	: .223 Rem.
Magazine	: detachable magazine
Cartridge capacity	: 30 cartridges
Magazine catch	: on right-hand side of receiver housing
Action	: gas pressure
Cocking system	: cocking lever
Firing system	: semi-automatic and fully automatic
Locking system	: rotating bolt head

Diemaco C7 Combat Rifle

Length	: 100 cm (39.3")
Barrel length	: 50 cm (19.7")
Weight	: 3.4 kg (7.5 lb.)
Sight	: adjustable rear and front sights (M16 type)
Safety	: combined firing selector/safety catch on left-hand side of receiver housing with indicator on right-hand side
Stock	: synthetic stock, pistol grip and hand grip

PARTICULARS
Matt black; it may be fitted with an M203 grenade launcher below the rifle barrel.

Diemaco C7A1 Combat Rifle/Semi-Sniper

SPECIFICATIONS

Caliber	: .223 Rem.
Magazine	: detachable magazine
Cartridge capacity	: 30 cartridges
Magazine catch	: on right-hand side of receiver housing
Action	: gas pressure
Cocking system	: cocking lever
Firing system	: semi-automatic and fully automatic
Locking system	: rotating bolt head
Length	: 100 cm (39.3")
Barrel length	: 50 cm (19.7")
Weight	: 3.4 kg (7.5 lb.)
Sight	: optical sight; can be fitted with Elcan scope with various mounting rails (Weaver-Rarde-Picatinny-RIS)

Diemaco C7A1 Combat Rifle/Semi-Sniper

Safety	: combined firing selector/safety catch on left-hand side of receiver housing with indicator on right-hand side
Stock	: synthetic stock, pistol grip and hand grip

PARTICULARS
Matt black; intended for special units as a semi-sniper rifle.

Diemaco C8 Carbine

SPECIFICATIONS

Caliber	: .223 Rem.
Magazine	: detachable magazine
Cartridge capacity	: 30 cartridges
Magazine catch	: on right-hand side of receiver housing
Action	: gas pressure
Cocking system	: cocking lever
Firing system	: semi-automatic and fully automatic
Locking system	: rotating bolt head
Length	: 76 cm (29.9") with extended stock
Barrel length	: 37 cm (14.6")
Weight	: 2.7 kg (6 lb.)
Sight	: adjustable rear and front sights (M16 type)
Safety	: combined firing selector/safety catch on left-hand side of receiver housing with indicator on right-hand side
Stock	: steel extending stock, synthetic pistol grip and hand grip

PARTICULARS
Matt black.

Diemaco C8 Carbine

Diemaco LSW

Diemaco LSW

SPECIFICATIONS

Caliber	: .223 Rem.
Magazine	: detachable magazine
Cartridge capacity	: 30 cartridges
Magazine catch	: on right-hand side of receiver housing
Action	: gas pressure
Cocking system	: cocking lever
Firing system	: semi-automatic and fully automatic
Locking system	: rotating bolt head
Length	: 100 cm (39.3")
Barrel length	: 50 cm (19.7")
Weight	: 5.8 kg (12.8 lb.)
Sight	: adjustable rear and front sights (M16 type)
Safety	: combined firing selector/safety catch on left-hand side of receiver housing with indicator on right-hand side
Stock	: synthetic stock, pistol grip, extra forearm and hand grip

PARTICULARS

Matt black, folding bipod.

DPMS

DPMS, logo

Defense Procurement Manufacturing Services Inc.

DPMS A-15 Panther Pump Rifle

DPMS (Defense Procurement Manufacturing Services Inc.), established in 1986 by Randy Luth, operates as an intermediary for defense contracts with the arms industry. DPMS produce a range of different types of rifle based on the AR-15. The receivers are made for DPMS from 7075-T6 aircraft aluminum by the Sturm & Ruger Company. In addition, DPMS sell a wide range of accessories, including their own brand of optical sights, Leatherwood, as well as sights by other manufacturers, such as the famous Elcan military sights. DPMS also supply various types of flash suppressers and recoil dampers, bipods, synthetic stocks, optical sight mounting rails, and numerous small parts for rifles of the AR-15 type.

DPMS furthermore offer an optional special barrel hardening process which substantially increases the weapon's accuracy. The process involves cooling the barrel for 20 to 30 hours to a temperature of -184 °C.

The barrel is then heated to 148 °C after which it is slowly cooled to room temperature. This results in a highly increased density of the metal structure and a reduction of stresses in the metal. The DMPS AR-15 pump gun is a special weapon. It is similar to the AR-15, but features a pump repeater action. The weapon was designed for DPMS by the well-known gun designer, Les Branson.

DPMS A-15 Panther Pump Rifle

SPECIFICATIONS

Caliber	: .223 Rem.
Magazine	: detachable magazine
Cartridge capacity	: 10, 20, or 30 rounds
Magazine catch	: magazine catch on left-hand side of housing
Action	: pump-action

Cocking system   : forearm
Firing system   : single round
Locking system   : rotating bolt head
Length   : 100.3 cm (39.5")
Barrel length   : 50.8 cm (20")
Weight   : 3.9 kg (8.5 lb.)
Sight   : A-2 Sight/carrying handle and bead
Safety   : safety catch on left-hand side of housing
Stock   : Zytel synthetic stock

PARTICULARS
Matt black stock and aluminium forearm
for pump-action.

DPMS Arctic Panther Black

SPECIFICATIONS
Caliber   : .223 Rem.
Magazine   : detachable magazine
Cartridge capacity: 10, 20 or 30 rounds
Magazine catch   : magazine catch on left-hand side of
                     housing
Action   : gas pressure
Cocking system   : cocking lever
Firing system   : semi-automatic
Locking system   : rotating bolt head
Length   : 97 cm (38.25")
Barrel length   : 50.8 cm (20")
Weight   : 4.5 kg (10 lb.)
Sight   : none; special sight mounting
Safety   : safety catch on left-hand side of housing
Stock   : Zytel synthetic stock; pistol grip with palm
                       rest

PARTICULARS
Matt black stock and free floating
aluminum hand grip; adjustable Harris
bipod; stainless steel fluted barrel

DPMS Arctic Panther Black

DPMS Arctic White Panther

SPECIFICATIONS
Caliber   : .223 Rem.
Magazine   : detachable magazine
Cartridge capacity: 10, 20 or 30 rounds
Magazine catch   : magazine catch on left-hand side of
                     housing
Action   : gas pressure
Cocking system   : cocking lever
Firing system   : ssemi-automatic
Locking system   : rotating bolt head
Length   : 97 cm (38.25")
Barrel length   : 50.8 cm (20")
Weight   : 4.5 kg (10 lb.)
Sight   : none; special sight mounting
Safety   : safety catch on left-hand side of housing
Stock   : Zytel synthetic stock

PARTICULARS
Matt black stock; white powder coating
on receiver housing and aluminum hand
grip; barrel with matt black Teflon coating;
adjustable Harris bipod; stainless steel
fluted barrel

DPMS Bulldog

SPECIFICATIONS
Caliber   : .223 Rem.
Magazine   : detachable magazine
Cartridge capacity: 10, 20 or 30 rounds
Magazine catch   : magazine catch on left-hand side of housing
Action   : gas pressure
Cocking system   : cocking lever
Firing system   : semi-automatic
Locking system   : rotating bolt head
Length   : 100.3 to 110.5 cm (39.5 to 43.5")
Barrel length   : 50.8 cm (20")
Weight   : 5 kg (11 lb.)

DPMS Bulldog

Sight   : none; special sight mounting
Safety   : safety catch on left-hand side of
               housing
Stock   : Zytel synthetic stock with adjustable and
               extendable butt

PARTICULARS
Matt black stock and free floating
aluminum hand grip; stainless steel fluted
barrel

DPMS Panther Bull A-15

SPECIFICATIONS
Caliber   : .223 Rem.
Magazine   : detachable magazine
Cartridge capacity: 10, 20 or 30 rounds
Magazine catch   : magazine catch on left-hand side of
                   housing
Action   : gas pressure
Cocking system   : cocking lever
Firing system   : semi-automatic
Locking system   : rotating bolt head
Length   : 97 cm (38.25")
Barrel length   : 50.8 cm (20")
Weight   : 4.5 kg (10 lb.)
Sight   : none; special sight mounting

DPMS Panther Bull A-15

DPMS Panther Bull Gold

Safety   : safety catch on left-hand side of housing
Stock   : Zytel synthetic stock

PARTICULARS
Matt black stock and free floating
aluminum hand grip; adjustable Harris
bipod; stainless steel barrel

DPMS Panther Bull Gold

SPECIFICATIONS
Caliber   : .223 Rem.
Magazine   : detachable magazine
Cartridge capacity: 10, 20 or 30 rounds
Magazine catch   : magazine catch on left-hand side of
                   housing
Action   : gas pressure
Cocking system   : cocking lever
Firing system   : semi-automatic
Locking system   : rotating bolt head
Length   : 97 cm (38.25")
Barrel length   : 50.8 cm (20")
Weight   : 4.5 kg (10 lb.)
Sight   : none; special sight mounting
Safety   : safety catch on left-hand side of housing
Stock   : Zytel synthetic stock; with Pachmayr
                   Vindicator pistol grip

PARTICULARS
Stock, housing, mounting rail and hand
grip feature gold-colored coating;
adjustable Harris bipod; matt black stainless steel fluted barrel

DPMS Panther Bull SST Sixteen

SPECIFICATIONS
Caliber   : .223 Rem.
Magazine   : detachable magazine
Cartridge capacity: 10, 20 or 30 rounds
Magazine catch   : magazine catch on left-hand side of housing

DPMS Panther Bull SST Sixteen

Action	: gas pressure
Cocking system	: cocking lever
Firing system	: semi-automatic
Locking system	: rotating bolt head
Length	: 87 cm (34.25")
Barrel length	: 40.6 cm (16")
Weight	: 4.1 kg (9 lb.)
Sight	: none; special sight mounting
Safety	: safety catch on left-hand side of housing
Stock	: Zytel synthetic stockf

PARTICULARS

Matt black stock and free floating aluminum hand grip; adjustable Harris bipod; heavy stainless steel bull barrel. The rifle shown here features the Elcan EL-01 3.4 x 55 optical sight.

DPMS Panther Bull Twenty-Four Special

SPECIFICATIONS

Caliber	: .223 Rem.
Magazine	: detachable magazine
Cartridge capacity	: 10, 20 or 30 rounds
Magazine catch	: magazine catch on left-hand side of housing
Action	: gas pressure
Cocking system	: cocking lever
Firing system	: semi-automatic
Locking system	: rotating bolt headr
Length	: 107 cm (42.25")
Barrel length	: 61 cm (24")
Weight	: 5 kg (11 lb.)
Sight	: none; special sight mounting
Safety	: safety catch on left-hand side of housing
Stock	: Zytel synthetic stock; pistol grip with palm rest

DPMS Panther Bull Twenty-Four Special

PARTICULARS

Matt black stock and free floating aluminum hand grip; adjustable Harris bipod; heavy stainless steel barrel with fluting.

DPMS Panther Super Bull Twenty-Four

SPECIFICATIONS

Caliber	: .223 Rem.
Magazine	: detachable magazine
Cartridge capacity	: 10, 20 or 30 rounds
Magazine catch	: magazine catch on left-hand side of housing
Action	: gas pressure
Cocking system	: cocking lever
Firing system	: semi-automatic
Locking system	: rotating bolt head
Length	: 107 cm (42.25")
Barrel length	: 61 cm (24")
Weight	: 5 kg (11 lb.)
Sight	: none; special sight mounting
Safety	: safety catch on left-hand side of housing
Stock	: Zytel synthetic skeleton

PARTICULARS

Matt black stock and free floating aluminium hand grip; adjustable Harris bipod; extra heavy stainless steel bull barrel.

DPMS Panther Super Bull Twenty-Four

Ee

Erma-Suhl

Erma-Suhl, logo

The Erma company has its offices at Dachau, near Munich in the federal state of Bavaria, Germany. The name Erma is short for Erfurter Maschinenfabrik. The company was founded in 1922 and at the time had its offices at Erfurt. The original name of the company was Erma-Werke B. Geipel GmbH, named after its founder. A well-known product from that era is the Erma Schmeisser MP40 sub-machine-gun. Another weapon produced by Erma during the Second World War, in cooperation with Mauser and Haenel, was the MP44 assault rifle, for 7.92 Short (7.92 x 33 mm).

In 1945, right after the Second World War, the allied forces ordered the shutdown of the factory. The present company reopened its doors in 1949 and in 1952 moved to Dachau. During the first years of its existence, Erma manufactured arms components for the Allied Occupation Forces in Germany. When the German Bundeswehr was founded, the company received a number of orders for the construction of armored housings for fire control systems. Erma also became active in the field of competitive shooting.

At first the company produced small caliber versions of famous pistols like the Luger P08, and various small caliber models of the Walther PP and PPK. Great commercial success was achieved with a .22 LR version of the famous Winchester .30-M1 carbine. The company has since marketed a range of pistols with a style of their own, such as the Erma ESP-85. In addition to the small caliber M1 carbine, Erma manufacture various types of lever-action repeating carbines. One of the latest products is the Erma SR-100 sniper rifle.

The weapon features a modular construction, facilitating the exchange of various components. These include the barrel, caliber changes, silenced barrels, the stock, and a number of sighting systems. In 1998 the Erma company was taken over by Suhler Jagd- und Sportwaffen GmbH from Suhl, the makers of the famous Merkel sports guns.

Erma MP28/II

SPECIFICATIONS

Caliber	: 9 mm Para
Magazine	: detachable magazine
Cartridge capacity	: 20, 32 or 50 rounds (in drum magazine)
Magazine catch	: on magazine housing
Action	: recoil
Cocking system	: cocking lever
Firing system	: semi- and fully automatic
Locking system	: inertia lock
Length	: 81.2 cm (32")
Barrel length	: 19.6 cm (7.75")
Weight	: 3.9 kg (8.75 lb.)
Sight	: tangent rear sight
Safety	: push button above trigger guard
Stock	: wooden stock

PARTICULARS

Short sub-machine-gun with perforated steel hand grip around the barrel. It was produced by Haenel Waffen- und Fahrradfabrik, and by Pieper in Belgium for the Belgian army as Mitraillette Model 34. It

Erma MP28/II

has also been produced under license in Spain. In 1929 it was produced for Portugal chambered for 7.65 Para.

Erma Schmeisser MP40

SPECIFICATIONS

Caliber	: 9 mm Para
Magazine	: detachable magazine
Cartridge capacity	: 32 rounds
Magazine catch	: in right-hand side of magazine housing
Action	: recoil
Cocking system	: cocking lever
Firing system	: fully automatic
Locking system	: inertia lock
Length	: with unfolded stock: 83.2 cm 32.75"); folded: 62.9 cm (24.75")
Barrel length	: 24.8 cm (9.75")
Weight	: 3.9 kg (8.75 lb.)
Sight	: fixed notch sight, 50 meters (164 ft) with hinged notch sight blade for 100 meters (328 ft)
Safety	: recess for cocking lever notch at rear of receiver housing
Stock	: folding steel stock

PARTICULARS

Simplified form of the MP38 sub-machine-gun. It features a distinguishable folding support below the front end of the barrel. In spite of its name, the Schmeisser was designed by the German arms designer, Vollmer. It was produced by Erma, Haenel and the Austrian Steyr works.

Erma MP44

SPECIFICATIONS

Caliber	: 7.92 x 33 mm Short
Magazine	: detachable magazine
Cartridge capacity	: 30 rounds
Magazine catch	: on right-hand side of magazine housing
Action	: gas pressure

Erma MP44

7.92 x 33 mm Short cartridge

Barrel length : 41.8 cm (16.5")
Weight : 5.1 kg (11.24 lb.)
Sight : tangent rear sight
Safety : rotating catch on left-hand side above pistol
grip
Stock : wooden stock, pressed steel hand grip

PARTICULARS
Initially introduced as the MP43. Separate push button firing mode selector above pistol grip for semi- and fully automatic operation.
Related models are the MP43/1 with screw-on grenade launcher, MP44(P) with a 30 degrees curved barrel for use from trenches and foxholes, MP44(V) with a 40 degrees curved barrel and the MP44(K) featuring a barrel curved no less than 90 degrees. A round of the special 7.92 x 33 mm ammunition is shown.

Erma-Suhl SR 100 sniper rifle

SPECIFICATIONS
Caliber : .308 Win., .300 Win. Mag., .338 Lapua Mag.
or .50 BMG
Magazine : detachable magazine
Cartridge capacity: 10, 8, or 5 rounds resp.
Magazine catch : in right-hand side of stock
Action : bolt-action

Cocking system : cocking lever
Firing system : semi- and fully automatic
Locking system : sliding breech block
Length : 94 cm (37")

Erma-Suhl SR 100 sniper rifle

Cocking system	: bolt lever	
Firing system	: single round	
Locking system	: 3-lug bolt	
Length	: 124.5 to 134.5 cm (49 to 53")	
Barrel length	: 65 to 75 cm (25.6 to 29.5")	
Weight	: 6.9 to 7.5 kg (15.2 to 16.5 lb.)	
Sight	: none; special sight mounting; aperture emergency sight optional	
Safety	: wing-type safety catch at rear of bolt, drop safety	
Stock	: skeletonized synthetic stock	

PARTICULARS

Modular construction; matt blued finish. Receiver made of a special aircraft aluminum alloy. The caliber of the rifle can be changed by exchanging barrel, detachable magazine, and bolt. The trigger pull can be adjusted from 500 to 3000 g. Bipod. Special mounting rail for night sight with extendible mirage band. The Erma-Suhl SR100 with optical sight and aperture emergency sight is shown.

Erma-Suhl SR 100 sniper rifle

Ff

Feg

The predecessor of the Hungarian gun manufacturers Feg of Budapest dates back to 1891, with the name Fegyver & Gepayar Reszvenytarsasag. Besides arms, they manufactured machinery and tools. Feg was renowned for Frommer pistols. Until 1918 Hungary was part of the Austro-Hungarian empire. During the Second World War the production was used to re-arm the Hungarian army and for export. After the war, Feg focused on the manu-facture of Kalashnikov rifles and sports weapons. For decades, the company has produced a range of pistols based on the FN Browning High Power. Feg engineers added a number of improvements to the original design, which can be credited to the American gun designer John Moses Browning. These improvements include the double-action trigger system. Feg are less well known for the manufacture of rifles. In most cases, at the insistence of a number of importers, the arms manufac-tured by Feg were marketed under a variety of names. These days, the weapons manu-factured by Feg are marketed under the name Fegarmy. In addition to arms, the company now specialized in cast steel production of machinery components in accordance with the ISO-9002 standard.

Feg, logo

Feg SA-85

Feg SA-85

SPECIFICATIONS

Caliber	: 7.62 x 39 mm
Magazine	: detachable magazine
Cartridge capacity	: 30 rounds
Magazine catch	: in front of trigger guard
Action	: gas pressure
Cocking system	: cocking lever
Firing system	: fully or semi-automatic
Locking system	: lugged bolt
Length	: 89.5 or 93 cm (35.2 or 36.6")
Barrel length	: 41.5 cm (16.3")
Weight	: 3.4 or 3.8 kg (7.5 of 8.4 lb.)
Sight	: tangent rear sight
Safety	: large slider on right of reveiver housing
Stock	: hardwood stock and pistol grip, or closed stock with thumb hole

PARTICULARS

The SA-85 is based on the Kalashnikov AK-47 rifle. The bottom weapon shows the typical angled muzzle of the AK-47

Feg SA-85 Sniper

SPECIFICATIONS

Caliber	: 7.62 x 39 mm
Magazine	: detachable magazine
Cartridge capacity	: 30 rounds
Magazine catch	: in front of trigger guard
Action	: gas pressure
Cocking system	: cocking lever
Firing system	: fullyor semi-automatic
Locking system	: lugged bolt
Length	: 87 cm (34.25")
Barrel length	: 41.5 cm (16.3") +I

Feg SA-85 Sniper

Weight	: 3.95 kg (8.7 lb.)
Sight	: tangent rear sight and optical sight, similar to the Russian PSO-1
Safety	: large sliding catch on right-hand side of reveiver housing
Stock	: hardwood stock and pistol grip

PARTICULARS
Sniper rifle, based on the Kalashnikov AK-47. The optical sight is of Hungarian manufacture, similar to the PSO-1 sight of the Dragunov sniper rifle.

Feg SG KGP-9

SPECIFICATIONS

Caliber	: 9 mm Para
Magazine	: detachable magazine
Cartridge capacity	: 25 rounds
Magazine catch	: in front of trigger guard
Action	: recoil
Cocking system	: cocking lever
Firing system	: full and semi-automatic
Locking system	: inertia lock

Feg SG KGP-9

Length	: with unfolded stock: 64.5 cm (25.4"); folded: 38.5 cm (15.2")
Barrel length	: 19 cm (7.5")
Weight	: 2.7 kg (6 lb.)
Sight	: folding aperture sight for 100 and 200 metres (656 ft)
Safety	: in top of trigger guard, doubles as firing mode selector
Stock	: folding steel tube stock, synthetic pistol grip and forearm

PARTICULARS
Small sub-machine-gun with pressed steel receiver housing. An optional 25 cm (9.8 in) replacement barrel is available.

FN-Herstal

FN-Herstal, logo

The Belgian arms manufacturing company, Fabrique Nationale at Herstal near Liege, was founded in 1889. The first weapon produced by the company was the Model 1889 infantry rifle, chambered for 7.65 x 53 mm. This rifle had been developed by Mauser and was manufactured by FN under license. The next army weapon was the Model 1930, a version of the Browning Automatic Rifle (BAR) M1918, also chambered for 7.65 x 53 mm. An improved version was the Model FN-Browning Type D, chambered for 7.92 x 57 mm and .30-06. Even before the Second World War, FN designed the SAFN-Model 49, but war meant production had to wait until after 1945. This rifle was produced in various calibers, in semi-automatic, fully automatic,

FN-Herstal FAL

51 mm, and the large .50 M2HB-QCB machine-gun in .50 BMG (Browning machine-gun) caliber for mounting on vehicles and vessels. The present-day modern FN-Browning company, part of the French Giat Defense industry, has branches in the United States and Canada, and in addition is linked with ammunition giant Winchester. FN-Browning also leads the market in the field of rifles and shotguns for hunting and competitive shooting.

FN-Herstal FAL

SPECIFICATIONS

Caliber	: 7.62 x 51 mm
Magazine	: detachable magazine
Cartridge capacity	: 20 rounds
Magazine catch	: behind magazine well
Action	: gas pressure
Cocking system	: cocking lever
Firing system	: semi- and fully automatic
Locking system	: vertically sliding block
Length	: Standard-fixed stock: 109 cm (42.9")
	Standard-unfolded stock: 109.5 cm (43.1")
	Standard-folded stock: 84.5 cm (33.3")
Barrel length	: 55.3 cm (21.8")
Weight	: 3.9 or 4.3 kg (8.6 or 9.5 lb.)
Sight	: adjustable tangent rear sight for up to 600 meters (656 yd), or flip-up sight for 150 and 250 meters (492 and 820 ft), or fixed sight for 300 meters (984 ft) (Para)
Safety	: safety catch integrated with firing mode selector
Stock	: fixed synthetic stock or folding stock

and sniper models. The company gained fame with the High Power HP-35 pistol. This was developed by John Moses Browning in 1926, and FN acquired the production rights. The best-known army rifle must be the FN-FAL, short for Fusil Automatique Légère (light automatic rifle) chambered for the erstwhile NATO 7.62 x 51 mm (.308 Winchester) caliber. This rifle, introduced in 1950, came in three basic models, the Standard, the HB (Heavy Barrel) with bipod, and the Para with folding stock. Three models are still in production, the Standard with fixed stock, the Standard with folding stock, and the short Para with folding stock. In Brazil the FAL was produced under license by IMBEL until 1988. The successor was the FN-CAL, chambered for 5.56 x 45 mm, but this was only produced for a short period, until 1975. In 1980 FN introduced the improved , the FNC, for the new 5.56 x 45 mm NATO caliber. The FNC is also produced under license in Indonesia. The latest FN is the P90, a cross between a carbine and a submachine-gun, with newly developed 5.7 x 28 mm caliber. This futuristic weapon is extremely short with a large magazine, holding 50 rounds. Inside the detachable magazine, cartridges are arranged transversely in a double row. During loading, an ingenious system rotates the cartridge through 45 degrees to align with the barrel. Using the same caliber, FN have developed a new army pistol: the 20-shot Five-seven pistol. Heavier weapons produced by FN are the Minimi machine-gun, also designated M249 SAW, chambered for 5.56 x 45 mm, the older MAG (M240), chambered for 7.62 x

PARTICULARS

Folding carrying handle; folding bipod; muzzle flash suppresser doubles as bayonet socket; gas control selector for firing rifle grenades. The Belgian army model FN-FAL is shown.

FN-Herstal FAL

FN-Herstal FAL-HB

SPECIFICATIONS

Caliber	: 7.62 x 51 mm
Magazine	: detachable magazine
Cartridge capacity	: 20 rounds
Magazine catch	: behind magazine slot
Action	: gas pressure
Cocking system	: cocking lever
Firing system	: semi- and fully automatic
Locking system	: vertically sliding block
Length	: 115 cm (45.3")
Barrel length	: 55.3 cm (21.8")
Weight	: 6 kg (13.2 lb.)
Sight	: adjustable sight from 260 to 600 meters (853 ft to 656 yd
Safety	: safety catch integrated with firing mode selector
Stock	: fixed synthetic stock

PARTICULARS

Folding carrying handle; folding bipod; muzzle flash suppresser doubles as bayonet socket; gas control selector for firing rifle grenades.
The firing mode selector switches from semi- to fully automatic. The weapon's principal use was as an assault rifle and light machine-gun. This model is also designated as the FN-FALO.

FN-Herstal FAL-Para

SPECIFICATIONS

Caliber	: 7.62 x 51 mm
Magazine	: detachable magazine
Cartridge capacity	: 20 rounds
Magazine catch	: behind magazine slot
Action	: gas pressure
Cocking system	: cocking lever
Firing system	: semi- and fully automatic
Locking system	: vertically sliding block
Length	: Para-unfolded stock: 102 cm (40.2"); Para-folded stock: 77 cm (30.3")
Barrel length	: 45.8 or 55.3 cm (18 or 21.8")
Weight	: 3.75 or 3.9 kg (8.3 or 8.6 lb.)
Sight	: flip-up sight for 150 and 250 meters (492 and 820 ft), or fixed, 300 meters (984 ft) (Para)
Safety	: safety catch integrated with firing mode selector
Stock	: steel folding stock

PARTICULARS

Folding carrying handle; the muzzle flash suppresser doubles as bayonet socket; the gas control is selector for firing rifle grenades.

FN-Herstal FNC

SPECIFICATIONS

Caliber	: 5.56 x 45 mm
Magazine	: detachable magazine
Cartridge capacity	: 30 rounds
Magazine catch	: above trigger guard
Action	: gas pressure
Cocking system	: cocking lever
Firing system	: semi-, fully automatic, and 3-shot burst
Locking system	: rotating bolt head
Length	: Standard-fixed stock: 101 cm (39.8"); Standard-unfolded stock: 99.7 cm (39.3"); Standard-folded stock: 76.6 cm (30.2"); Para-unfolded stock: 91.1 cm (35.9"); Para-folded stock: 68 cm (26.8")
Barrel length	: 44.9 cm (17.7")

FN-Herstal FNC

Weight	: 4 to 4.1 kg (8.8 to 9 lb.)
Sight	: adjustable flip-up sight
Safety	: safety catch on left-hand side of receiver housing, integrated with firing mode selector
Stock	: fixed synthetic stock or folding stock

PARTICULARS

Flash suppresser with separate bayonet socket around barrel for standard M7 bayonet. Various optical sights and night sight.

FN-Herstal MAG (M240)

SPECIFICATIONS

Caliber	: 7.62 x 51 mm
Magazine	: cartridge belt
Cartridge capacity	: N/A
Magazine catch	: N/A
Action	: gas pressure
Cocking system	: cocking lever
Firing system	: fully automatic
Locking system	: vertically sliding block
Length	: 126 cm (49.6")
Barrel length	: 63 cm (24.8")
Weight	: 11 kg (24.3 lb.)
Sight	: 300 to 1,800 meters (84 ft to 1,968 yd)
Safety	: push-button in pistol grip
Stock	: fixed hardwood stock or no stock

PARTICULARS

Special vehicle-mounted models with electric firing system; adjustable gas control for rate of fire; barrel system with carrying handle.

FN-Herstal Minimi (M249SAW)

SPECIFICATIONS

Caliber	: 5.56 x 45 mm
Magazine	: detachable magazine, box or cartridge belt
Cartridge capacity	: 30 (detachable magazine) or 200 (box)
Magazine catch	: behind magazine well
Action	: gas pressure
Cocking system	: cocking lever

FN-Herstal Minimi (M249SAW)

FN-Herstal Minimi (M249SAW)

FN-Herstal Mauser M1924 carbine

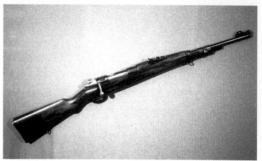

FN-Herstal Wilhelmina

Firing system	: fully automatic
Locking system	: rotating bolt head
Length	: Standard-fixed stock: 104 cm (40.9"); Para-unfolded stock: 91.4 cm (36"); Para-folded stock: 76.6 cm (30.2")
Barrel length	: Standard: 46.5 cm (18.3"); Para: 34.9 cm (13.7")
Weight	: 7.1 kg (15.6 lb.)
Sight	: adjustable 300-1000 meters (984 ft-1,093 yd)
Safety	: push-button above pistol grip; in older model also loading indicator
Stock	: telescopic, folding or fixed stock (MK2)

PARTICULARS
Barrel assembly with carrying handle, folding bipod; detachable magazines of FNC or M16 rifles can be used without modification; removable trigger guard.

FN-Herstal Mauser M1924 carbine

SPECIFICATIONS

Caliber	: 8 x 57 mm Mauser, 7 x 57 mm Mauser or 7.65 Mauser
Magazine	: blind magazine
Cartridge capacity	: 5 rounds
Magazine catch	: N/A
Action	: bolt-action
Cocking system	: bolt lever
Firing system	: single round
Locking system	: Mauser 2-lug bolt
Length	: 95 cm (37.4")
Barrel length	: 44 cm (17.3")
Weight	: 3.3 kg (7.3 lb.)
Sight	: tangent rear sight 200 to 1400 meters (656 to 1,531 yd)
Safety	: wing-type catch on rear of bolt
Stock	: wooden stock with straight butt plate and hand wouden guard

PARTICULARS
This Mauser system was manufactured by FN of Belgium after the Second World War as a carbine (M1924) and a rifle (M1924/30) with an overall length of 110 cm/43.3 in. Both models have been exported to many countries, including Argentina, Bolivia, Brazil, Chili, China, Columbia, Costa Rica, Ecuador, Iran, Yemen, Yugoslavia, Liberia, Lithuania, Luxembourg, Mexico, the Netherlands, Paraguay, Peru, Turkey, Uruguay, and Venezuela. The carbines shown were in use with the Dutch Police force. The top carbine features a large stamped 'J' and crown on the receiver bridge, dating from the reign of the Dutch queen Juliana. Below it is a similar weapon with a stamped 'W' and crown from the reign of the Dutch queen Wilhelmina.

FN-Herstal M1949 SAFN

SPECIFICATIONS

Caliber	: .30-06, 7 x 57 mm Mauser, 8 x 57 mm Mauser, or 7.65 mm Mauser
Magazine	: detachable magazine
Cartridge capacity	: 10 rounds

FN-Herstal M1949 SAFN

Magazine catch : on front of trigger guard
Action : gas pressure
Cocking system : cocking lever
Firing system : semi-automatic
Locking system : vertically sliding block
Length : 111 cm (43.7")
Barrel length : 59 cm (23.2")
Weight : 4.3 kg (9.5 lb.)
Sight : tangent rear sight
Safety : slide catch in rear of trigger guard
Stock : wooden stock and hand grip, or pressed steel hand grip

PARTICULARS

Although this weapon was designed in the late thirties of the twentieth century by Belgian gun designer Dieudonné, Saive, the Second World War caused production to be delayed until 1948.

The rifle has seen service with the armed forces of Argentina, Belgium, the Belgian Congo, Brazil, Columbia, Egypt, Luxembourg, Indonesia, the former Dutch Indies, and Venezuela. The weapon features the same gas pressure system as the later FN-FAL.

FN-Herstal P90

SPECIFICATIONS

Caliber : 5.7 x 28 mm (SS190)
Magazine : detachable magazine
Cartridge capacity : 50 rounds
Magazine catch : ambidextrous behind magazine
Action : recoil-action
Cocking system : cocking lever
Firing system : semi- and fully automatic
Locking system : inertia lock
Length : 50 cm (19.7")
Barrel length : 31 cm (12.2")

FN-Herstal P90

Weight : 3 kg (6.6 lb.)
Sight : tritium optical sight (non-enlarging)
Safety : ambidextrous under trigger
Stock : impact-resistant synthetic bullpup stock

PARTICULARS

Extremely compact weapon system. Can be fitted with optional enlarging optical sight, laser, or IR sighting system. Mounting rail on left-hand side for flashlight, night sight, etc. A silencer can be attached to the barrel.

Franchi

Franchi, logo

The Italian arms factory of Luigi Franchi is located at Fornaci, in the North Italian Brescia region, famous for its gunsmiths since the Middle Ages. Franchi manufacture a number of excellent over-and-under shotguns, and a few semi-automatic models. The company gained fame with its range of riot guns, such as the SPAS-12 (introduced in 1983) and the SPAS-15 for military and other government purposes.

Franchi Model Pump PA-8E

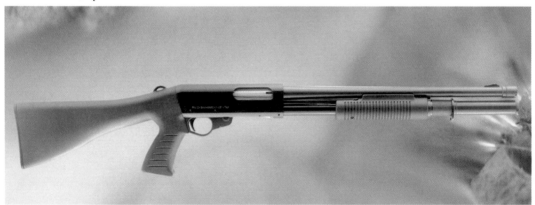

Both models operate either semi-automatically or in pump-action mode chosen by a push-button selector.

Franchi Model Pump PA-7

SPECIFICATIONS

Caliber	: 12/76 (3")
Magazine	: tubular magazine
Cartridge capacity	: 5 rounds; 7 with magazine extender
Magazine catch	: N/A
Action	: pump-action
Cocking system	: forearm
Firing system	: single round
Locking system	: vertically sliding block
Length	: 108 cm (42.5")
Barrel length	: 47.5 cm or 61 cm (18.7 of 24")
Weight	: 3.2 kg (7.1 lb.)
Sight	: bead
Safety	: push-button on front of trigger

Stock	: matt black finished hardwood stock and forearm

PARTICULARS
Matt black coating. Shown here with magazine extender.

Franchi Model Pump PA-8E

SPECIFICATIONS

Caliber	: 12/76 (3")
Magazine	: tubular magazine
Cartridge capacity	: 5 rounds; 7 with magazine extender
Magazine catch	: N/A
Action	: pump-action
Cocking system	: forearm
Firing system	: single round
Locking system	: vertically sliding block
Length	: 108 cm (42.5")
Barrel length	: 47.5 cm or 61 cm (18.7 of 24")

Weight	: 3.1 kg (6.8 lb.)
Sight	: bead
Safety	: push-button on front of trigger guard
Stock	: synthetic stock, forearm and pistol grip

PARTICULARS

Matt black coating. Shown here with a magazine extender.

Franchi Model Pump PA-8L

SPECIFICATIONS

Caliber	: 12/76 (3")
Magazine	: tubular magazine
Cartridge capacity:	5 rounds; 7 with magazine extender
Magazine catch	: N/A
Action	: pump-action
Cocking system	: forearm
Firing system	: single round
Locking system	: vertically sliding block
Length	: 107 cm (42.1")
Barrel length	: 47.5 cm or 61 cm (18.7 of 24")
Weight	: 3.0 kg (6.6 lb.)
Sight	: bead
Safety	: push-button on front of trigger guard
Stock	: metal folding stock with synthetic pistol grip

PARTICULARS

Matt black coating.

Franchi Model SPAS-12

Franchi Model SPAS-12

SPECIFICATIONS

Caliber	: 12/76 (3")
Magazine	: tubular magazine
Cartridge capacity:	7 rounds
Magazine catch	: N/A
Action	: semi-automatic using gas pressure and selector to pump-action
Cocking system	: cocking lever
Firing system	: semi-automatic or single round (pump-action)
Locking system	: vertically sliding block
Length	: 107 cm (42.1")
Barrel length	: 55 cm (21.7")
Weight	: 4.0 kg (8.8 lb.)
Sight	: rear sight and bead
Safety	: push-button on front of trigger guard
Stock	: metal folding stock or synthetic stock, with pistol grip

PARTICULARS

Matt black coating; in the center of the underside of the forearm a push-button has been incorporated which switches from pump-action to semi-automatic operation.

Shown are the Franchi SPAS-12 (top) and the SPAS-15 (bottom), both with fixed synthetic stock.

Franchi Model SPAS-15

Franchi Model SPAS-15

SPECIFICATIONS

Caliber	: 12/76 (3")
Magazine	: detachable magazine
Cartridge capacity	: 6 rounds
Magazine catch	: in front of trigger guard
Action	: semi-automatic using gas pressure and switchable to pump-action
Cocking system	: cocking lever
Firing system	: semi-automatic or single round (pump-action)
Locking system	: vertically sliding block
Length	: 98 or 100 cm (38.6 or 39.4")
Barrel length	: 45 cm (17.7")
Weight	: 3.9 or 4.1 kg (8.6 or 9.0 lb.)
Sight	: notch rear sight and bead
Safety	: safety catch in left front of the trigger guard and grip safety in the front of the pistol grip
Stock	: metal folding stock or matt black finished hardwood stock, with pistol grip

PARTICULARS

Matt black; carrying handle on receiver housing; in the center of the top of the forearm a push-button has been incorporated which switches from pump-action to semi-automatic operation.

Gibbs

The Gibbs Rifle Company was established in 1991 by Val Forgett Jr. and operates from Martinsburg in West Virginia. In less than a year a tract of wasteland grew into a factory of more than 3700 square meters (4425 sq. yd).
The company acquired the rights of the famous Parker-Hale factory in Birmingham, England and of the Midland Gun Company. Gibbs is continuing the production of both gun makes. The Parker-Hale rifles are based on the Mauser 98 system, while the Midland rifles were derived from the Springfield 1903 rifle design. In addition, the company manu-

Gibbs, logo

Gibbs Parker-Hale M-85 Sniper

factures the M-85 sniper rifle, which was first used by the British elite forces, the S.A.S. Since then the rifle has been purchased for a large number of government services all over the world. The company thanks a major part of its commercial success to the trade in old army rifles, which are bought from surplus stores, restored at the company works, and sold to the civilian arms trade for competitive shooting and collectors.

Gibbs Parker-Hale M-85 Sniper

SPECIFICATIONS

Caliber	: .308 Win.
Magazine	: detachable magazine
Cartridge capacity	: 10 rounds
Magazine catch	: on front of magazine slot
Action	: bolt-action
Cocking system	: bolt lever
Firing system	: single round
Locking system	: 3-lug bolt
Length	: 114.3 cm (45")
Barrel length	: 61 cm (24")
Weight	: 5.7 kg (12.6 lb.), incl. optical sight
Sight	: flip-up sight; suitable for sight mounting
Safety	: safety catch on right, behind bolt lever, loading indicator by means of protruding pin at rear of bolt
Stock	: special fibreglass McMillan stock

PARTICULARS
Matt blued finish, bipod. The stock is available in six different camouflage colors: NATO green, desert, urban, black, jungle, and arctic.

GOL

The abbreviation GOL stands for Gottfrieds Originelle Lösung (Gottfried's original solution). Gottfried is the first name of the German master gunsmith Gottfried Prechtl from the town of Wein-

Gol, logo

heim, to the northeast of Mannheim. Using the Mauser 98 system as a basis, Prechtl manufactures a range of precision and sniper rifles of high quality. The best-known rifle is the GOL Sniper, which is available with a variety of stock types. This .308 Winchester rifle is capable of shooting 10-shot patterns with a diameter of only 12 to 14 mm (0.47 to 0.55") at a range of 100 meters (328 ft). Another famous product by GOL is the so-called StoCon skeleton stock, made of laminated wood. A second GOL rifle, model 'S', is based on the new Sako M591/L691 receiver system. The Lithuanian army was the first to introduce this sniper rifle.

GOL-Sniper Rifle Model Standard-Synthetic

SPECIFICATIONS

Caliber	: .308 Win.
Magazine	: blind magazine
Cartridge capacity	: 5 rounds
Magazine catch	: N/A
Action	: bolt-action
Cocking system	: bolt lever
Firing system	: single round
Locking system	: 2-lug Mauser bolt
Length	: approx. 118.4 cm (46.6")
Barrel length	: 65 cm (25.6 in), exc. muzzle damper or flash suppresser
Weight	: approx. 5.5 kg (12.1 lb.), incl. optical sight
Sight	: none; suitable for sight mounting
Safety	: safety catch on the right, behind bolt lever
Stock	: matt black synthetic stock with pistol grip

PARTICULARS

Matt black barrel and receiver; forearm with Harris bipod. Timney trigger system. The receiver is based on the Mauser 98 system.

GOL-Sniper Rifle Model Standard-Synthetic

GOL-Sniper Rifle Model S

GOL-Sniper Rifle Model S

SPECIFICATIONS

Caliber	: .308 Win., .300 Win. Mag.
Magazine	: none
Cartridge capacity	: single shot
Magazine catch	: N/A
Action	: bolt-action
Cocking system	: bolt lever
Firing system	: single round
Locking system	: 2-lug Sako bolt
Length	: 123 cm (48.4")
Barrel length	: 65 cm (25.6")
Weight	: approx. 6.6 kg (14.6 lb.)
Sight	: none; suitable for sight mounting
Safety	: safety catch on the right, behind bolt lever
Stock	: special laminated open StoCon stock, laminated solid standard stock, or matt black synthetic stock with pistol grip

PARTICULARS

Sako receiver system; stainless, nickel-plated, or matt black barrel. Tests have shown this rifle capable of firing 5-shot groups at 100 meters (328 ft) with a diameter of 11 to 14 mm (0.43 to 0.55").

Sniper in wetlands

Soldier behind machine-gun

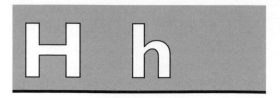

Harrington & Richardson (H&R)/New England Firearms (NEF)

The American arms manufacturing company of Harrington & Richardson was founded in 1871 by Gilbert Henderson Harrington and Franklin Wesson. Previously, Harrington worked for a small revolver factory, the Ballard & Fairbanks Company at Worcester, Massachusetts. Franklin Wesson started with a small gun workshop where he manufactured rifles. In view of the great demand for double-barreled shotguns, the company decided to manufacture these. Both partners obtained a license from the English company of Anson & Deely. Since the demand for H&R-revolvers increased greatly, and the company did not have the necessary production capacity, production of shotguns ceased in 1886. In 1888 the company was drastically reorganized, and the name changed to Harrington & Richardson Arms Company. Both directors died shortly after one another in 1897. A triumvirate consisting of Mr. Brooks, the former accountant of the company, the 20-year old son of the founder, Edwin C. Harrington, and daugh-

ter Mary A. Richardson, continued the company. After its long association with Worcester, the factory moved to Gardner, Massachusetts. The current H&R range comprises single-barreled shotguns and rifles as well as revolvers. In addition, the company produces arms under the name of its subsidiary, New England Firearms. The company has designed a simplified carbine version to be included in survival sets for various US Army units. This weapon is sold in a various rifle and shotgun calibers/gauges in the civilian market.

H&R/NEF Survivor 357 MAG

SPECIFICATIONS

Caliber	: .357 Magnum/.38 Special
Magazine	: none
Cartridge capacity	: N/A
Magazine catch	: N/A
Action	: hinged
Cocking system	: hinge
Firing system	: single round
Locking system	: lug bolt behind hammer
Length	: 91.4 cm (36")
Barrel length	: 55.9 cm (22")
Weight	: 2.7 kg (6 lb.)
Sight	: adjustable notch rear sight
Safety	: none; transfer bar between hammer and firing pin
Stock	: synthetic stock with pistol grip and thumb hole

PARTICULARS

Stock contains compartment for survival kit; ammunition storage space in the forearm.

H&R/NEF Survivor 223

SPECIFICATIONS

Caliber	: .223 Rem.

Harrington & Richardson (H&R)/(NEF), logo

H&R/NEF Survivor 357 MAG

Magazine	: none
Cartridge capacity	: N/A
Magazine catch	: N/A
Action	: hinged
Cocking system	: hinge
Firing system	: single round
Locking system	: lug bolt behind hammer
Length	: 91.4 cm (36")
Barrel length	: 55.9 cm (22")
Weight	: 2.7 kg (6 lb.)
Sight	: mounting rail for optical sight
Safety	: none; transfer bar between hammer and firing pin
Stock	: synthetic stock with pistol grip and thumb hole

PARTICULARS
Stock contains compartment for survival kit; ammunition storage space in the forearm.

Harris Gunworks

The American company of Harris Gunworks Inc. has its offices in Phoenix, Arizona. The company's main products consist of sniper rifles in various calibers for government use. Precision rifles for competition shooting are also produced. The Harris sniper rifles are intended for 'surgical operations' at ranges of 800 meters (874 yd) and over. Harris also produce several sniper models in the .50 BMG (Browning machine-gun) caliber for ranges over 1500 meters (1640 yd). Another well-known Harris product is the multi-barreled Combo sniper rifle. This system enables the user to change the weapon's caliber simply by selecting another barrel. This set comprises three barrels, chambered for .308 Win., .30-06 Spr., and .300 Win. Mag. The rifle can be fitted with a silencer. A folding stock .50 BMG caliber model is also offered, the sole purpose of the folding stock being to facilitate transport. A special sniper rifle is the Long Range Phoenix in the specially developed .30 Phoenix caliber, capable of shooting extremely tight patterns.

Harris Long Range Phoenix Sniper Rifle

SPECIFICATIONS

Caliber	: ..300 Phoenix and other .30 Magnum calibers
Magazine	: blind magazine
Cartridge capacity	: 5 rounds
Magazine catch	: N/A
Action	: bolt-action
Cocking system	: bolt lever
Firing system	: single round
Locking system	: 2-lug bolt
Length	: 127 cm (50")
Barrel length	: 73.7 cm (29")
Weight	: 5.7 kg (12.6 lb.)
Sight	: none; suitable for sight mounting
Safety	: safety catch, on right-hand side behind bolt
Stock	: fibreglass stock with adjustable butt

PARTICULARS
Matt black coating; special free floating barrel; Harris bipod.

Harris Long Range Phoenix Sniper Rifle

Harris Gunworks, logo

Harris M-86 Sniper Rifle

SPECIFICATIONS

Caliber	: .308 Win., .300 Win. Mag.
Magazine	: detachable magazine
Cartridge capacity	: 5 or 10 rounds
Magazine catch	: on front of trigger guard
Action	: bolt-action
Cocking system	: bolt lever
Firing system	: single round
Locking system	: 2-lug bolt
Length	: 105 cm (41.3")
Barrel length	: 61 cm (24")
Weight	: 6.1 kg (13.4 lb.)
Sight	: optical sight to order
Safety	: safety catch on right-hand side along rear of bolt
Stock	: fibreglass stock with pistol grip

PARTICULARS
Matt black phosphate finish; shown with the Leupold Police 3.5-10 X optical sight; Harris bipod optional.

Harris M-87 Sniper Rifle

SPECIFICATIONS

Caliber	: .50 BMG
Magazine	: detachable magazine
Cartridge capacity	: 5 rounds
Magazine catch	: in front of trigger guard
Action	: bolt-action
Cocking system	: bolt lever
Firing system	: single round
Locking system	: heavy 2-lug bolt
Length	: 135 cm (53.2")
Barrel length	: 74 cm (29.1"), incl. muzzle brake
Weight	: 9.5 kg (21 lb.)
Sight	: optical sight to order
Safety	: safety catch on right-hand side along rear of bolt
Stock	: fibreglass stock with pistol grip and thumb hole

PARTICULARS
Matt black; designed as a sniper rifle for use against light vehicles and helicopters at ranges over 1500 meters (1640 yd).

Harris M-89 Sniper Rifle

SPECIFICATIONS

Caliber	: .308 Win.
Magazine	: detachable magazine
Cartridge capacity	: 5, 10 or 20 rounds
Magazine catch	: at rear of magazine slot
Action	: bolt-action
Cocking system	: bolt lever
Firing system	: single round
Locking system	: 2-lug bolt
Length	: 83.5 cm (32.9")
Barrel length	: 45.7 cm (18")
Weight	: 7.0 kg (15.4 lb.)
Sight	: optical sight to order
Safety	: safety catch on right-hand side along rear of bolt
Stock	: fibreglass stock with pistol grip

PARTICULARS
Matt black.

Harris M-89 Sniper Rifle

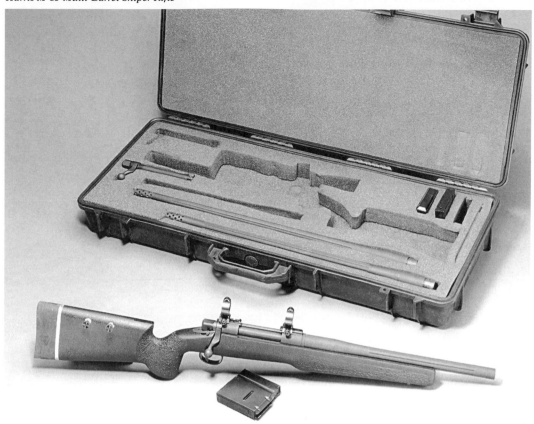

Harris M-89 Multi-Barrel Sniper Rifle

SPECIFICATIONS

Caliber	: .308 Win. and exchangeable barrels for .300 Win. Mag. and .30-06 Spr.
Magazine	: detachable magazine
Cartridge capacity	: 5, 10 or 20 rounds to order
Magazine catch	: on front of trigger guard
Action	: bolt-action
Cocking system	: bolt lever
Firing system	: single round
Locking system	: 2-lug bolt
Length	: 97.4 cm (38.4")
Barrel length	: 45.7 cm (71 cm with recoil damper) (18"/ 28")
Weight	: 5.2 kg (11.5 lb.)
Sight	: none; suitable for sight mounting
Safety	: safety catch, on right-hand side along rear of bolt
Stock	: fibreglass stock

PARTICULARS

Matt black; supplied in case with two exchangeable barrels in .300 Win. Mag. and .30-06 Spr. calibers.

Harris M-89 Multi-Barrel Stainless Sniper Rifle

SPECIFICATIONS

Caliber	: .308 Win. and exchangeable barrels for .300 Win. Mag. and .30-06 Spr.
Magazine	: detachable magazine
Cartridge capacity	: 5, 10 or 20 rounds to order
Magazine catch	: on front of trigger guard
Action	: bolt-action
Cocking system	: bolt lever
Firing system	: single round
Locking system	: 2-lug bolt
Length	: 97.4 cm (38.4")
Barrel length	: 45.7 cm (18")
Weight	: 5.2 kg (11.5 lb.)
Sight	: none; suitable for sight mounting
Safety	: safety catch on right-hand side, along rear of bolt
Stock	: fiberglas stock

Harris M-89 Multi-Barrel Stainless Sniper Rifle

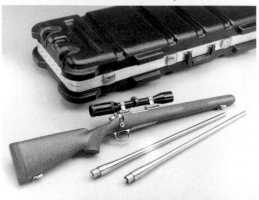

PARTICULARS

Matt finish stainless steel barrel and receiver.

Harris M-92 BMG Bullpup Long Range Sniper

SPECIFICATIONS

Caliber	: .50 BMG
Magazine	: N/A
Cartridge capacity	: single round
Magazine catch	: N/A
Action	: bolt-action
Cocking system	: bolt lever
Firing system	: single round
Locking system	: heavy 2-lug bolt
Length	: 105 cm (41.3")
Barrel length	: 64 cm (25.2"), incl. muzzle brake
Weight	: 10.9 kg (24 lb.)
Sight	: optical sight to order
Safety	: safety catch on right-hand side along rear of bolt
Stock	: short fibreglass stock with pistol grip and thumb hole

PARTICULARS

Matt black; designed as a sniper rifle

Harris M-92 BMG Bullpup Long Range Sniper

for use against light vehicles and helicopters at ranges over 1500 meters (1640 yd).

Purpose-designed long-range sniper rifle (1500 meters/1640 yd plus) for special units like the US Navy Seals.

Harris M-93 Sniper

Harris M-93 Sniper

SPECIFICATIONS

Caliber	: .50 BMG
Magazine	: detachable magazine
Cartridge capacity	: 10 or 20 rounds
Magazine catch	: on front of trigger guard
Action	: bolt-action
Cocking system	: bolt lever
Firing system	: single round
Locking system	: heavy 2-lug bolt
Length	: 135 cm (53")
Barrel length	: 73.7 cm (29")
Weight	: 9.5 kg (21 lb.)
Sight	: none; suitable for sight mounting
Stock	: fibreglass stock with pistol grip. The stock can be folded for easier transport

Harris M-93 Sniper folding stock

PARTICULARS

Matt black; special folding bipod; designed as a sniper rifle for range over 1500 meters (1640 yd).

Harris M-95 Ultra Light

SPECIFICATIONS

Caliber	: .50 BMG
Magazine	: detachable magazine
Cartridge capacity:	10 or 20 rounds
Magazine catch	: on front of trigger guard
Action	: bolt-action
Cocking system	: bolt lever
Firing system	: single round
Locking system	: heavy 2-lug bolt
Length	: 135 cm (53")
Barrel length	: 73.7 cm (29"), incl. muzzle brake
Weight	: 8.2 kg (18 lb.)
Sight	: none; suitable for sight mounting
Safety	: safety catch on right along rear of bolt
Stock	: fibreglass stock with pistol grip and thumbhole

Length	: 142.2 cm (56")
Barrel length	: 73.6 cm (29"), incl. muzzle brake
Weight	: 11.3 kg (25 lb.)
Sight	: sight mounting
Safety	: safety catch on left-hand side of receiver housing
Stock	: aluminium and synthetic

PARTICULARS

Matt black finish; titanium receiver, carbon steel barrel; purpose-designed sniper rifle for range up to 2000 meters (2187).

Harris M-96 Long Range Sniper

PARTICULARS

Cocking handle can be transferred to other side; special bipod; adjustable gas pressure; designed as a sniper rifle for ranges up to 2000 meters (2187 yd).

Harris RBLP

SPECIFICATIONS

Caliber	: .50 BMG
Magazine	: detachable magazine
Cartridge capacity:	5 rounds
Magazine catch	: on front of trigger guard
Action	: gas pressure
Cocking system	: cocking lever
Firing system	: semi-automatic
Locking system	: vertically sliding block

SPECIFICATIONS

Caliber	: .308 Win.
Magazine	: geen
Cartridge capacity:	N/A
Magazine catch	: N/A
Action	: bolt-action
Cocking system	: bolt lever

Harris RBLP

Harris M-95 Ultra Light

Firing system	: single round
Locking system	: 2-lug bolt
Length	: 113 cm (44.5")
Barrel length	: 66 cm (26")
Weight	: 5.3 kg (11.7 lb.)
Sight	: optical sight to order
Safety	: safety catch on right-hand side along rear of bolt
Stock	: fibreglass stock with pistol grip

Heckler & Koch HK 11E Machine Gun

PARTICULARS
Matt black; the RBLP designation stands for Right-hand Bolt, Left-side Port.

Heckler & Koch

Heckler & Koch, logo

The German company of Heckler & Koch was founded in 1949. After the formation of the German Bundeswehr in the early fifties of the twentieth century, the company received a commission to develop an automatic army rifle using the .308 Winchester caliber. The Heckler & Koch rifle was derived from the Spanish CETME rifle. In cooperation with the Rheinmetall development department the CETME concept was adapted to the German requirements and reshaped into the G3 army rifle.

This rifle uses the famous roller lock. Heckler & Koch was one of the first companies to use the polygon barrel profile. Instead of rifling, this type of barrel has a polygon profile with a certain twist which gives the bullet its rotation. The Dutch arms factory, NWM, initially held the Spanish license rights, but was forced under political pressure to cede these to Heckler & Koch. Many of the technical innovations incorporated in the army weapons can also be found in the Heckler & Koch competition and hunting rifles, including the roller lock mentioned above, the military aperture sight with preset rotary range adjustment, and the polygon barrel. In addition to the famous HK MP5 sub-machine-gun, in its many guises, H&K produce a small range of sniper rifles. In the mid eighties of the twentieth century, H&K developed a special army rifle, the G-11, which used caseless ammunition. In late 1990 the company came under financial pressure when certain government orders did not materialize.

The decision of the US armed forces to adopt the Beretta M-92 pistol instead of the Heckler & Koch P7-M13 pistol was a serious setback. Furthermore, the G-11 rifle project did not raise sufficient interest. In March 1991 the company was taken over by the British company, Royal Ordnance, a subsidiary of British Aerospace. In 1995 the company was taken over, by the German Wischo concern. HK scored a big hit with the USP pistol, which was selected by the US Navy Seals and other special units of the US armed services.

Heckler & Koch offer a wide range of options. Rifles, carbines and sub-machine-guns can easily be adapted using optional trigger assemblies, stocks, grenade launchers, flash suppressers, and sight mountings. In 1997 Heckler & Koch developed a totally new rifle concept, the HK G36E. This new rifle family comprises an assault rifle, a light machine-gun, and a carbine model. Surprisingly, Heckler & Koch have dropped the roller locking system for this new rifle model. The HK 36E is fitted with a rotating bolt head lock.

Heckler & Koch HK 11E Machine Gun

SPECIFICATIONS

Caliber	: 7.62 x 51 mm NATO
Magazine	: detachable magazine
Cartridge capacity	: 20 rounds
Magazine catch	: in front of trigger guard
Action	: retarded recoil
Cocking system	: cocking lever
Firing system	: semi-automatic, 3-shot burst and fully automatic
Locking system	: roller lock
Length	: 103 cm (40.6")
Barrel length	: 45 cm (17.7"), without flash suppresser
Weight	: 8.15 kg (18 lb.)
Sight	: adjustable aperture drum 100 to 1000 metres; Stanag sight mounting; optical sight 4 x 24
Safety	: ambidextrous safety catch/firing mode selector above trigger guard
Stock	: synthetic stock with pistol grip and pressed steel hand grip

PARTICULARS

Matt black; vertically adjustable and folding bipod. Folding carrying handle; detachable magazines can be linked together with lugs. The weapon features a lock assist lever for low-noise cocking. An easy to fit spare barrel is included.

Heckler & Koch HK 21E Machine Gun

SPECIFICATIONS

Caliber	: 7.62 x 51 mm NATO
Magazine	: cartridge belt or cartridge box
Cartridge capacity	: 100 round box
Magazine catch	: in front of trigger guard
Action	: retarded recoil
Cocking system	: cocking lever

Heckler & Koch HK 21E Machine Gun

Firing system	: semi-automatic, 3-shot burst, and fully automatic
Locking system	: roller lock
Length	: 114 cm (44.9")
Barrel length	: 56 cm (22")
Weight	: 9.3 kg (20.5 lb.)
Sight	: adjustable aperture drum 100 to 1200 metres; Stanag sight mounting; optical sight 4 x 24
Safety	: ambidextrous safety catch/firing mode selector above trigger guard
Stock	: synthetic stock with pistol grip and pressed steel hand grip

PARTICULARS

Matt black; vertically adjustable and folding bipod; folding carrying handle. Optional extra pistol grip under forearm. The weapon features a lock assist lever for low-noise cocking. An easy to fit spare barrel is included.

Heckler & Koch HK 23E Machine Gun

SPECIFICATIONS

Caliber	: 5.56 x 45 mm
Magazine	: box magazine or cartridge belt
Cartridge capacity	: 200 rounds box magazine
Magazine catch	: on right-hand side, in front of magazine slot
Action	: retarded recoil
Cocking system	: cocking lever
Firing system	: semi-automatic, 3-shot burst and fully automatic
Locking system	: roller lock
Length	: 103 cm (40.6")
Barrel length	: 45 cm (17.7"), without flash suppresser
Weight	: 8.8 kg (19.4 lb.)
Sight	: adjustable aperture sight; Stanag sight mounting

Heckler & Koch HK 23E Machine Gun

Safety	: ambidextrous safety catch/firing mode selector above trigger guard
Stock	: synthetic stock with pistol grip

PARTICULARS

Matt black; vertically adjustable and folding bipod.

Heckler & Koch HK 33E

SPECIFICATIONS

Caliber	: 5.56 x 45 mm
Magazine	: detachable magazine
Cartridge capacity	: 25 or 30 rounds
Magazine catch	: on front of trigger guard
Action	: retarded recoil
Cocking system	: cocking lever
Firing system	: semi-automatic, 3-shot burst, and fully automatic
Locking system	: roller lock
Length	: 92 cm (36.2") with fixed stock; 92 cm (36.2") with extended stock; 74 cm (29.1") with retracted stock
Barrel length	: 41 cm (16.1"), without muzzle flash suppressor
Weight	: 3.9 kg (8.6 lb.)
Sight	: adjustable aperture sight; special sight mounting
Safety	: ambidextrous safety catch/firing mode selector above trigger guard
Stock	: fixed synthetic stock or telescopic steel stock with synthetic butt, available in a number of colours, like green camouflage for bush combat, yellow camouflage for desert duties and white camouflage for arctic conditions.

Heckler & Koch HK 33E

Heckler & Koch HK 33E in camouflage colours and a telescopic stock

Heckler & Koch HK 33E with the HK 79-A1 40 mm grenade launcher

PARTICULARS

Matt black or in various camouflage colors. Other firing systems available: semi- plus fully automatic; semi-automatic plus 3-shot burst. The rifle can be fitted with the HK 79-A1 40 mm grenade launcher under the barrel.

Heckler & Koch HK 33EK

SPECIFICATIONS

Caliber	: 5.56 x 45 mm
Magazine	: detachable magazine
Cartridge capacity	: 25 or 30 rounds

Heckler & Koch HK 33EK

Magazine catch	: on front of trigger guard
Action	: retarded recoil
Cocking system	: cocking lever
Firing system	: semi-automatic, 3-shot burst and fully automatic
Locking system	: roller lock
Length	: 86.5 cm (34.1 in) with extended stock; 67 cm (26.4 in) with retracted stock
Barrel length	: 34 cm (13.4"), without muzzle flash suppresser
Weight	: 3.9 kg (8.6 lb.)
Sight	: adjustable aperture sight
Safety	: ambidextrous safety catch/firing mode selector above trigger guard
Stock	: telescopic steel stock with synthetic butt, available in a number of colours

PARTICULARS

Matt black or in various camouflage colors. Other firing systems available: semi- plus fully automatic; semi-automatic plus 3-shot burst.

Heckler & Koch HK 33E-GR3

SPECIFICATIONS

Caliber	: 5.56 x 45 mm
Magazine	: detachable magazine
Cartridge capacity	: 25 or 30 rounds
Magazine catch	: on front of trigger guard
Action	: retarded recoil
Cocking system	: cocking lever
Firing system	: semi-automatic, 3-shot burst and fully automatic

Locking system	: roller lock
Length	: 92.5 cm (36.4")
Barrel length	: 39 cm (15.4"), without muzzle flash suppressor
Weight	: 3.9 kg (8.6 lb.)
Sight	: adjustable aperture sight; special sight mounting
Safety	: tambidextrous safety catch/firing mode selector above trigger guard
Stock	: synthetic stock available in a number of colours

PARTICULARS

Matt black or in various camouflage colors. Other firing systems available: semi- plus fully automatic; semi-automatic plus 3-shot burst.

Heckler & Koch HK 33E Sniper

SPECIFICATIONS

Caliber	: 5.56 x 45 mm
Magazine	: detachable magazine
Cartridge capacity	: 25 or 30 rounds
Magazine catch	: on front of trigger guard
Action	: retarded recoil
Cocking system	: cocking lever
Firing system	: semi-automatic, 3-shot burst and fully automatic
Locking system	: roller lock
Length	: 92 cm (36.2")
Barrel length	: 41 cm (16.1"), without muzzle flash suppressor
Weight	: 4.6 kg (10.1 lb.)

Heckler & Koch HK 33E Sniper

Sight	: adjustable aperture sight and 4 x 24 optical sight; special sight mounting, suitable for aperture sight
Safety	: ambidextrous safety catch/firing mode selector above trigger guard
Stock	: synthetic stock available in a number of colours

PARTICULARS
Matt black or in various camouflage colors. The weapon has a vertically adjustable and folding bipod.

Heckler & Koch HK 53A3

SPECIFICATIONS

Caliber	: 5.56 x 45 mm
Magazine	: detachable magazine
Cartridge capacity:	25 or 30 rounds
Magazine catch	: on front of trigger guard
Action	: retarded recoil
Cocking system	: cocking lever

Heckler & Koch HK 53A3

Firing system	: semi-automatic, 3-shot burst and fully automatic
Locking system	: roller lock
Length	: 76 cm (30") with extended stock; 56.4 cm (22.2") with retracted stock
Barrel length	: 21 cm (8.3")
Weight	: 3.7 kg (8.1 lb.)
Sight	: adjustable aperture sight; special sight mounting
Safety	: ambidextrous safety catch/firing mode selector above trigger guard
Stock	: telescopic steel stock with synthetic butt

PARTICULARS
Matt black. Special muzzle flash suppresser. Hybrid carbine/sub-machine-gun. The weapon is available with a fixed synthetic stock as the HK53A2.

Heckler & Koch HK G3A3

SPECIFICATIONS

Caliber	: .308 Win.
Magazine	: detachable magazine
Cartridge capacity:	5 of 20 rounds
Magazine catch	: on front of trigger guard
Action	: retarded recoil
Cocking system	: cocking lever
Firing system	: semi-automatic and fully automatic
Locking system	: roller lock
Length	: 102.6 cm (40.4")
Barrel length	: 45 cm (17.7")
Weight	: 4.4 kg (9.7 lb.)
Sight	: adjustable aperture sight; special sight mounting
Safety	: safety catch/firing mode selector on left-hand side of housing with indicator on right-hand side
Stock	: green fixed synthetic stock and forearm

PARTICULARS
Matt black. Special muzzle flash suppresser with rifle grenade attachment.

Heckler & Koch HK G3A3

German Bundeswehr model. The G3 rifle was the first HK weapon with the roller lock. The semi-automatic version of the G3, chambered for .308 Win., is designated HK91. The same model chambered for .223 Rem. is designated HK93.

Heckler & Koch HK G3KA4 Carbine

SPECIFICATIONS

Caliber	: .308 Win.
Magazine	: detachable magazine
Cartridge capacity	: 5 or 20 rounds
Magazine catch	: on front of trigger guard
Action	: retarded recoil
Cocking system	: cocking lever
Firing system	: semi-automatic and fully automatic
Locking system	: roller lock
Length	: 89.5 cm (35.25") with extended stock; 71.1 cm (28") with retracted stock
Barrel length	: 31.5 cm (12.4")
Weight	: 4.4 kg (9.7 lb.)
Sight	: adjustable aperture sight; special sight mounting
Safety	: ambidextrous safety catch/firing mode selector above trigger guard
Stock	: telescopic steel stock with synthetic butt

PARTICULARS

Matt black. Compact carbine model using .308 Win. Special muzzle flash suppresser. The weapon is available with a fixed synthetic stock as HK G3KA3.

Heckler & Koch HK G11

SPECIFICATIONS

Caliber	: 4.7 mm caseless
Magazine	: box magazine
Cartridge capacity	: 50 rounds

Heckler & Koch HK G3KA4 carbine

Heckler & Koch HK G11

Magazine catch	: push-button
Action	: gas pressure
Cocking system	: rotating knob
Firing system	: semi-automatic, 3-shot burst and fully automatic
Locking system	: 90 degrees cylinder bolt lock
Length	: 75 cm (29.5")
Barrel length	: 54 cm (21.3")
Weight	: 3.6 kg (7.9 lb.)
Sight	: optical 1:1 sight
Safety	: ambidextrous safety catch/firing mode selector above trigger guard
Stock	: synthetic stock, housing and pistol grip

PARTICULARS

Matt black; optional folding bipod. Further development of the G11 has been suspended. Production may well be taken up again in the twenty-first century. One of the last development models is shown.

Heckler & Koch HK G36E Assault Rifle

SPECIFICATIONS

Caliber	: 5.56 x 45 mm
Magazine	: detachable magazine
Cartridge capacity	: 30 rounds
Magazine catch	: on front of trigger guard
Action	: gas pressure
Cocking system	: cocking lever
Firing system	: semi- and fully automatic

Heckler & Koch HK G11-2

Heckler & Koch HK G36E Assault Rifle

Heckler & Koch HK G36E Carbine

Locking system : rotation bolt head
Length : 99 cm (39") with unfolded stock; 76 cm (29.9") with folded stock
Barrel length : 48 cm (18.9")
Weight : 3.3 kg (7.3 lb.)
Sight : 1.5 x optical sight in carrying handle; fixed auxiliary sight on carrying handle
Safety : ambidextrous safety catch/firing mode selector above trigger guard
Stock : folding light metal stock with rubber butt

PARTICULARS

Matt black. Free floating barrel with special muzzle flash suppresser. Synthetic housing, pistol grip, hand grip. Synthetic detachable magazines with linking lugs. The carrying handle is used for mounting special sights (night sight, infra-red, or laser). The rifle has a lever-type cocking lever for left-handed or right-handed use.

Heckler & Koch HK G36E Carbine

SPECIFICATIONS

Caliber : 5.56 x 45 mm
Magazine : detachable magazine
Cartridge capacity: 30 rounds
Magazine catch : on front of trigger guard
Action : gas pressure
Cocking system : cocking lever
Firing system : semi-automatic and fully automatic
Locking system : rotation bolt head
Length : 86 cm (33.9") with unfolded stock; 61.5 cm (24.2") with folded stock
Barrel length : 32 cm (12.6")
Weight : 3 kg (6.6 lb.)
Sight : 1.5 x optical sight in carrying handle; fixed auxiliary sight on carrying handle

Safety : ambidextrous safety catch/firing mode selector above trigger guard
Stock : folding light metal stock with rubber butt

PARTICULARS

Matt black. Free floating barrel with special muzzle flash suppresser. Synthetic housing, pistol grip, hand grip. Synthetic detachable magazines with linking lugs.
The carrying handle is used for mounting special sights (night sight, infra-red, or laser). The rifle has a lever-type cocking lever for left-handed or right-handed use.

Heckler & Koch HK G36E LSW (Light Support Weapon)

SPECIFICATIONS

Caliber : 5.56 x 45 mm
Magazine : detachable magazine of double drum
Cartridge capacity: 30 or 100 rounds
Magazine catch : on front of trigger guard
Action : gas pressure
Cocking system : cocking lever

Heckler & Koch HK G36E LSW (Light Support Weapon)

Firing system	: semi-automatic and fully automatic
Locking system	: rotating bolt head
Length	: 99 cm (39") with unfolded stock; 76 cm (29.9") with folded stock
Barrel length	: 48 cm (18.9")
Weight	: 3.5 kg (7.7 lb.)
Sight	: 1.5 x optical sight in carrying handle; fixed auxiliary sight on carrying handle
Safety	: ambidextrous safety catch/firing mode selector above trigger guard
Stock	: folding light metal stock with rubber butt

PARTICULARS

Matt black. Folding bipod. Free floating barrel with special muzzle flash suppresser. Synthetic housing, pistol grip, hand grip. Synthetic detachable magazines with linking lugs.

The carrying handle is used for mounting special sights (night sight, infra-red, or laser). The rifle has a lever-type cocking lever for left-handed or right-handed use.

Heckler & Koch HK MP5-A2/A4

SPECIFICATIONS

Caliber	: MP5-A2/A4: 9 mm Para; MP5-40A2: .40 S&W
Magazine	: detachable magazine
Cartridge capacity	: 15 or 30 rounds
Magazine catch	: on front of trigger guard
Action	: retarded recoil
Cocking system	: cocking lever
Firing system	: MP5-A2: semi- plus fully automatic; MP5-A4: semi-automatic, 3-shot burst and fully automatic
Locking system	: roller lock
Length	: 68 cm (26.8")
Barrel length	: 22.5 cm (8.9")
Weight	: 2.7 kg (6 lb.)
Sight	: adjustable aperture sight

Heckler & Koch HK MP5-A2/A4

Heckler & Koch HK MP5-A3/A5

Safety	: MP5-A2: safety catch/firing mode selector on left-hand side above trigger guard; MP5-A4: ambidextrous safety catch/firing mode selector above trigger guard
Stock	: fixed synthetic stock

PARTICULARS

Matt black; special police version as semi-automatic. The MP5-A4 is shown.

Heckler & Koch HK MP5-A3/A5

SPECIFICATIONS

Caliber	: MP5-A3/A5: 9 mm Para; MP5-10A3: 10 mm Auto
Magazine	: detachable magazine
Cartridge capacity	: 15 or 30 rounds
Magazine catch	: on front of trigger guard
Action	: retarded recoil
Cocking system	: cocking lever
Firing system	: MP5-A3: semi- plus fully automatic; MP5-A5: semi-automatic, 3-shot burst and fully automatic
Locking system	: roller lock
Length	: 68 cm (26.8") with extended stock; 49 cm (19.3") with retracted stock
Barrel length	: 22.5 (8.9")
Weight	: 2.7 kg (6 lb.)
Sight	: adjustable aperture sight
Safety	: MP5-A3: safety catch/firing mode selector on left-hand side above trigger guard; MP5-A5: ambidextrous safety catch/firing mode selector above trigger guard
Stock	: telescopic steel stock with synthetic butt

PARTICULARS

Matt black finish. The MP5-A5 is shown.

Heckler & Koch HK MP5-K/KA4 in suitcase

Cocking system	: cocking lever
Firing system	: MP5-K: semi- plus fully automatic; MP5-KA4: semi-automatic, 3-shot burst and fully automatic
Locking system	: roller lock
Length	: 32.5 cm (12.8")
Barrel length	: 11.5 cm (4.5")
Weight	: 2 kg (4.4 lb.)
Sight	: adjustable aperture sight
Safety	: MP5-K: safety catch/firing mode selector on left-hand side above trigger guard; MP5-KA4: ambidextrous safety catch/firing mode selector above trigger guard
Stock	: none; synthetic pistol and fore grips

PARTICULARS

Matt black. The MP5-KA4 is shown. The second illustration shows a special suitcase version for special services.

Heckler & Koch HK MP5-K/KA4

SPECIFICATIONS

Caliber	: 9 mm Para
Magazine	: detachable magazine
Cartridge capacity	: 15 or 30 rounds
Magazine catch	: on front of trigger guard
Action	: retarded recoil

Heckler & Koch HK MP5-KA1/KA5

SPECIFICATIONS

Caliber	: 9 mm Para
Magazine	: detachable magazine
Cartridge capacity	: 15 or 30 rounds
Magazine catch	: on front of trigger guard
Action	: retarded recoil

Heckler & Koch HK MP5-KA1/KA5

Cocking system	: cocking lever
Firing system	: MP5-KA1: semi- plus fully automatic; MP5-KA5: semi-automatic, 3-shot burst and fully automatic
Locking system	: roller lock
Length	: 32.5 cm (12.8")
Barrel length	: 11.5 cm (4.5")
Weight	: 2 kg (4.4 lb.)
Sight	: fixed notch sight
Safety	: MP5-KA1: safety catch/firing mode selector on left-hand side above trigger guard; MP5-KA5: ambidextrous safety catch/firing mode selector above trigger guard
Stock	: none; synthetic pistol and foregrip

PARTICULARS
Matt black. The MP5-KA5 is shown.

Heckler & Koch HK MP5K-PDW Navy

SPECIFICATIONS

Caliber	: 9 mm Para
Magazine	: detachable magazine
Cartridge capacity:	15 or 30 rounds
Magazine catch	: on front of trigger guard
Action	: retarded recoil

Heckler & Koch HK MP5K-PDW Navy

Cocking system	: cocking lever
Firing system	: semi- plus fully automatic
Locking system	: roller lock
Length	: 60.5 cm (23.8") with unfolded stock; 36.8 cm (14.5") with folded stock
Weight	: 2.8 kg (6.1 lb.)
Sight	: adjustable aperture sight
Safety	: ambidextrous safety catch/firing mode selector above trigger guard
Stock	: folding steel stock with synthetic butt, pistol grip and foregrip

PARTICULARS
Matt black; barrel with silencer thread. Special version for vehicle crews and security personnel.

Heckler & Koch HK MP5N Navy

Heckler & Koch HK MP5N Navy

SPECIFICATIONS

Caliber	: 9 mm Para
Magazine	: detachable magazine
Cartridge capacity:	15 or 30 rounds
Magazine catch	: on front of trigger guard
Action	: retarded recoil
Cocking system	: cocking lever
Firing system	: semi- plus fully automatic
Locking system	: roller lock
Length	: 69.2 cm (27.25") with extended stock; 53.3 cm (21") with retracted stock
Weight	: 2.9 kg (6.5 lb.)
Sight	: adjustable aperture sight; special sight mounting
Safety	: ambidextrous safety catch/firing mode selector above trigger guard
Stock	: telescopic steel stock with synthetic butt, pistol grip

PARTICULARS
Matt black; barrel with silencer thread. Special version for U.S. Navy Seals.

Heckler & Koch HK MP5-SD1/SD4

Heckler & Koch HK MP5-SD1/SD4

SPECIFICATIONS

Caliber	: 9 mm Para
Magazine	: detachable magazine
Cartridge capacity	: 15 or 30 rounds
Magazine catch	: on front of trigger guard
Action	: retarded recoil
Cocking system	: cocking lever
Firing system	: MP5-SD1: semi- plus fully automatic; MP5-SD4: semi-automatic, 3-shot burst and fully automatic
Locking system	: roller lock
Length	: 55 cm (21.7")
Barrel length	: 14.6 cm (5.7"), including silencer
Weight	: 2.9 kg (6.4 lb.)
Sight	: adjustable aperture sight; special sight mounting
Safety	: MP5-SD1: safety catch/firing mode selector on left-hand side above trigger guard; MP5-SD4: ambidextrous safety catch/firing mode selector above trigger guard
Stock	: none

PARTICULARS
Matt black. The MP5-SD4 is shown.

Heckler & Koch HK MP5-SD2/SD5

SPECIFICATIONS

Caliber	: 9 mm Para

Heckler & Koch HK MP5-SD2/SD5

Magazine	: detachable magazine
Cartridge capacity	: 15 or 30 rounds
Magazine catch	: on front of trigger guard
Action	: retarded recoil
Cocking system	: cocking lever
Firing system	: MP5-SD2: semi- plus fully automatic; MP5-SD5: semi-automatic, 3-shot burst and fully automatic
Locking system	: roller lock
Length	: 78 cm (30.7")
Barrel length	: 14.6 cm (5.7"), including silencer
Weight	: 3.1 kg (6.8 lb.)
Sight	: adjustable aperture sight; special sight mounting
Safety	: MP5-SD2: safety catch/firing mode selector on left-hand side above trigger guard; MP5-SD5: ambidextrous safety catch/firing mode selector above trigger guard
Stock	: fixed synthetic stock

PARTICULARS
Matt black. The MP5-SD5 is shown.

Heckler & Koch HK MP5-SD3/SD6

SPECIFICATIONS

Caliber	: 9 mm Para
Magazine	: detachable magazine
Cartridge capacity	: 15 or 30 rounds
Magazine catch	: on front of trigger guard
Action	: retarded recoil
Cocking system	: cocking lever
Firing system	: MP5-SD3: semi- plus fully automatic; MP5-SD6: semi-automatic, 3-shot burst and fully automatic
Locking system	: roller lock
Length	: 78 cm (30.7") with extended stock; 61 cm (24") with retracted stock
Barrel length	: 14.6 cm (5.7"), including silencer
Weight	: 3.4 kg (7.5 lb.)
Sight	: adjustable aperture sight; special sight mounting
Safety	: MP5-SD3: safety catch/firing mode selector on left-hand side above trigger guard; MP5-SD6: ambidextrous safety catch/firing mode selector above trigger guard

Heckler & Koch HK MP5-SD3/SD6

Heckler & Koch MSG90 Sniper Rifle

Stock   : telescopic steel stock with synthetic butt

PARTICULARS
Matt black. The MP5-SD6 is shown.

Heckler & Koch MSG90 Sniper Rifle

SPECIFICATIONS

Caliber	: .308 Win.
Magazine	: detachable magazine
Cartridge capacity	: 5 or 20 rounds
Magazine catch	: behind magazine housing
Action	: retarded recoil
Cocking system	: cocking lever
Firing system	: semi-automatic
Locking system	: roller lock
Length	: 116.1 cm (45.9")
Barrel length	: 60 cm (23.6")
Weight	: 6.4 kg (14.1 lb.)
Sight	: none; special PSG1 Hensoldt 10 x optical sight
Safety	: ambidextrous safety catch above trigger guard
Stock	: synthetic forearm and stock with adjustable cheek and butt plates; wooden pistol grip with adjustable palm rest

Heckler & Koch MSG90 Sniper Rifle

PARTICULARS
Matt black; special PSG1 match trigger and Anschütz mounting rail in forearm for hand-grip and adjustable bipod; Special battlefield version of the costly HK PSG1.

Heckler & Koch PSG1

SPECIFICATIONS

Caliber	: .308 Win.
Magazine	: detachable magazine
Cartridge capacity	: 5 or 20 rounds
Magazine catch	: behind magazine housing
Action	: retarded recoil
Cocking system	: cocking lever
Firing system	: semi-automatic
Locking system	: roller lock
Length	: 120.7 cm (47.5")
Barrel length	: 65 cm (25.6")
Weight	: 8.1 kg (17.8 lb.)
Sight	: none; special PSG1 Hensoldt 6 x 42 optical sight with rangefinder and illuminated cross-hairs
Safety	: safety catch on left-hand side above trigger guard with indicator on right-hand side of receiver housing
Stock	: synthetic forearm and stock with adjustable cheek and shoulder; wooden pistol grip with adjustable palm rest

PARTICULARS
Matt black; special match trigger and Anschütz mounting rail in forearm for hand stop and adjustable bipod; 3-shot test groups at 100 yards: 6.35 mm (.25"); at 200 yards: 28 mm (1.1"), and at 300 yards: 50.2 mm (1.975").

Heckler & Koch HK SL6

SPECIFICATIONS

Caliber	: .223 Rem.
Magazine	: detachable magazine

Heckler & Koch PSG1

Heckler & Koch PSG1

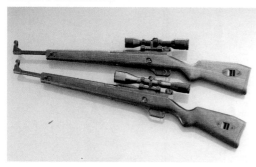

Heckler & Koch HK SL6

Cartridge capacity: 10 rounds
Magazine catch : on front of trigger guard
Action   : retarded recoil
Cocking system : cocking lever
Firing system   : semi-automatic
Locking system : roller lock
Length   : 101.5 cm (40")
Barrel length   : 45 cm (17.7")
Weight   : 3.9 kg (8.6 lb.)
Sight   : adjustable aperture sight; special sight
                  mounting
Safety   : safety catch on left-hand side with indicator in
                  right-hand side of stock
Stock   : wooden stock

PARTICULARS
Matt blued. The HK SL6 (top) and the HK
SL7 (bottom) are shown.

Heckler & Koch HK SL7

SPECIFICATIONS
Caliber   : .308 Win.
Magazine   : detachable magazine
Cartridge capacity: 10 rounds
Magazine catch : on front of trigger guard
Action   : retarded recoil
Cocking system : cocking lever
Firing system   : semi-automatic
Locking system : roller lock

Heckler & Koch HK SL7

Length   : 101 cm (39.8")
Barrel length   : 43 cm (16.9")
Weight   : 3.9 kg (8.6 lb.)
Sight   : adjustable aperture sight; special sight
                  mounting
Safety   : safety catch on left-hand side with indicator in
                  right-hand side of the stock
Stock   : wooden stock

PARTICULARS
Matt blued. The HK SL6 (top) and the HK
SL7 (bottom) are shown.

Hellenic Arms

Hellenic Arms, logo

Hellenic Arms Industry SA is a Greek
state arsenal established in 1977. Among
other locations, the company has offices
in Athens. It produces large numbers of
weapons, ammunition, and other military
supplies. These include the radar-guided
Artemis 30 mm anti-aircraft gun, 81 mm

mortars, fuel tanks and rocket launchers for jet fighters, as well as shells for the 8 inch Howitzer, 155 and 105 mm cannon, 81 mm and 4.2 inch mortars, and ammunition for the 105 mm, 90 mm, and 30 mm cannon. In addition, the company produces rounds for the 106 mm recoilless anti-tank gun, and various types of gunpowder for cannon ammunition. A subsidiary of the concern manufactures combat clothing, bullet-proof vests, and helmets. Hellenic also manufacture a series of light military weapons under license to Heckler & Koch, carrying the Hellenic-EBO trade name. The company has also developed a sniper rifle of its own, the Kefefs.

Hellenic G3A3 Assault Rifle

SPECIFICATIONS

Caliber	: 7.62 x 51 mm NATO (.308 Win.)
Magazine	: detachable magazine
Cartridge capacity	: 20 rounds
Magazine catch	: built into front of trigger guard
Action	: retarded recoil
Cocking system	: cocking lever
Firing system	: automatic and semi-automatic
Locking system	: roller lock
Length	: G3A3/G3A4: 102.5 cm (40.4"); G3A4 with retracted stock: 84 cm (33")
Barrel length	: 45 cm (17.7")
Weight	: 4.4 kg (9.7 lb.)
Sight	: aperture drum sight, 100, 200, 300 and 400 meters (328, 656, 984 and 1312 ft)
Safety	: combined rotary safety switch and firing mode selector
Stock	: synthetic stock, pistol grip and hand grip

PARTICULARS

This rifle is also available as the model G3A4 with telescopic stock. Optional 4 x optical sight with 6 fixed settings, or 100 to 600 meters (328 ft and 656 yd).

Hellenic HK11A1 LMG

SPECIFICATIONS

Caliber	: 7.62 x 51 mm NATO (.308 Win.)
Magazine	: detachable magazine
Cartridge capacity	: 20 rounds
Magazine catch	: built into front of trigger guard
Action	: retarded recoil
Cocking system	: cocking lever
Firing system	: full- and semi-automatic
Locking system	: roller lock

179

Hellenic HK11A1 LMG

Length	: 103 cm (40.6")
Barrel length	: 45 cm (17.7")
Weight	: 7.7 kg (17 lb.)
Sight	: aperture drum sight 200-1200 meters (656 ft–1312 yd)
Safety	: combined rotary safety catch and firing mode selector
Stock	: synthetic stock and pistol grip, pressed steel hand grip

PARTICULARS
Folding bipod, folding carrying handle , and extra barrel. Optional 4 x optical sight with 6 fixed settings, or 100 to 600 meters (328 ft to 656 yd).

Hellenic KEFEFS-M (Military) Sniper

SPECIFICATIONS

Caliber	: .308 Win.
Magazine	: blind magazine
Cartridge capacity:	5 rounds
Magazine catch	: N/A
Action	: bolt-action

Hellenic KEFEFS-M (Military) Sniper

Cocking system	: bolt lever
Firing system	: single round
Locking system	: 3-lug bolt
Length	: 120 cm (47.2")
Barrel length	: 65 cm (25.6")
Weight	: 4.75 kg (10.5 lb.)
Sight	: none; special sight mounting; optical sight to order
Safety	: safety catch on right-hand side behind bolt lever
Stock	: walnut Monte Carlo stock with camouflage coating

PARTICULARS
Adjustable and folding bipod; heavy match barrel; receiver features gas vent. Adjustable trigger pull.

Hellenic KEFEFS-P (Police) Sniper

SPECIFICATIONS

Caliber	: .308 Win.
Magazine	: blind magazine
Cartridge capacity:	5 rounds
Magazine catch	: N/A
Action	: bolt-action
Cocking system	: bolt lever
Firing system	: single round
Locking system	: 3-lug bolt
Length	: 120 cm (47.2")
Barrel length	: 65 cm (25.6")
Weight	: 5.45 kg (12 lb.)
Sight	: none; special sight mounting; optical sight to order
Safety	: safety catch on right-hand side behind bolt lever
Stock	: walnut Monte Carlo stock

PARTICULARS
Adjustable and folding bipod; special fluted barrel; receiver features gas vent. Adjustable trigger pull.

Hellenic KEFEFS-P (Police) Sniper

Hellenic MG3

SPECIFICATIONS

Caliber	: 7.62 x 51 mm NATO (.308 Win.)
Magazine	: none
Cartridge capacity	: cartridge belt feed
Magazine catch	: N/A
Action	: retarded recoil
Cocking system	: cocking lever
Firing system	: fully automatic
Locking system	: roller lock
Length	: 122.5 cm (48.2")
Barrel length	: 56.5 cm (22.2")
Weight	: 11.5 kg (25.4 lb.)
Sight	: tangent rear sight 200-1200 meters (656 ft–1312 yd)
Safety	: push-button in pistol grip
Stock	: synthetic stock and pistol grip, pressed steel hand grip

PARTICULARS

Heavy folding bipod, folding carrying handle and extra barrel. The weapon has an optional 4 x optical sight with 16 fixed settings for 100 to 1600 meters 328 ft to 1749 yd).

Hellenic MP5 sub-machine-gun

SPECIFICATIONS

Caliber	: 9 mm Para
Magazine	: detachable magazine
Cartridge capacity	: 30 rounds
Magazine catch	: built into front of trigger guard
Action	: retarded recoil
Cocking system	: cocking lever
Firing system	: full- and semi-automatic
Locking system	: roller lock
Length	: MP5 with fixed stock: 68 cm (26.8"); MP5 with extended stock: 66 cm (26"); MP5 with retracted stock: 49 cm (19.3")
Barrel length	: 22.5 cm (8.9")
Weight	: 2.5 to 2.9 kg (5.5 to 6.4 lb.)
Sight	: aperture drum sight
Safety	: combined rotary safety catch/firing mode selector
Stock	: synthetic stock, pistol grip and hand grip, or steel telescopic stock

PARTICULARS

Optional 4 x optical sight with 5 settings of 15, 25, 50, 75, and 100 meters (49, 82, 164, 246 and 328 ft).

Hembrug

In 1895, the Dutch army introduced the M95 rifle, caliber 6.5 x 53R mm. The weapon, produced by the Dutch Hembrug factory, was based on the Mannlicher bolt-action rifle. The rifle featured a 5-round blind magazine, loaded with a clip. Seven different carbine models derived from the M95 rifle were manufactured. The model 1917 is in fact the M95 adapted to accept the 7.92 Mauser caliber.

At that time, the Dutch army had a large ammunition stock of this caliber from its Schwarzlose machine-gun. In order to use this stock, a limited number of rifles were adapted to this caliber. A number of rifle

Locking system : bolt lugs
Length   : 129.5 cm (51")
Barrel length   : 79 cm (31.1")
Weight   : 4.4 kg (9.7 lb.)
Sight   : tangent rear sight
Safety   : wing-type catch on rear of bolt
Stock   : wooden stock

PARTICULARS
Based on the Steyr-Mannlicher rifle.

Hembrug Model M1914 Police Carbine

SPECIFICATIONS
Caliber   : 6.5 x 53R
Magazine   : blind magazine
Cartridge capacity : clips with 5 rounds
Magazine catch   : N/A
Action   : bolt-action
Cocking system   : bolt lever
Firing system   : single round
Locking system   : bolt lugs
Length   : 95 cm (37.4")
Barrel length   : 44.5 cm (17.5")
Weight   : 3,4 kg (7.5 lb.)
Sight   : tangent rear sight
Safety   : wing-type catch on rear of bolt
Stock   : wooden stock

PARTICULARS
Carbine for Dutch police units. The ramp of the tangent rear sight has been partly cut down.

and carbine models are shown, including a KNIL model (KNIL = Koninklijk Nederlands-Indisch Leger, the Royal Dutch Indies Army, which was stationed in the former Dutch Indies, now the Indonesian Republic) This type of carbine features a gas vent on the right-hand side of the barrel chamber. Following its independence, Indonesia converted a large number of KNIL carbines to the British .303 caliber.

Hembrug Model M1895 Rifle

SPECIFICATIONS
Caliber   : 6,5 x 53R
Magazine   : blind magazine
Cartridge capacity : clips with 5 rounds
Magazine catch   : N/A
Action   : bolt-action
Cocking system   : bolt lever
Firing system   : single round

Hembrug Model M1914 Police Carbine

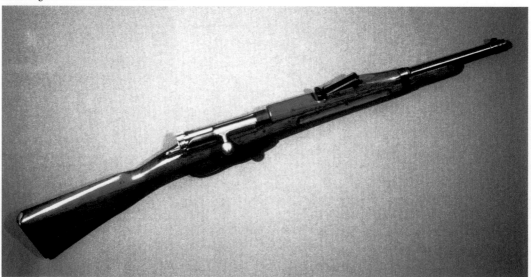

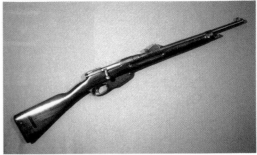

Hembrug Model M1917 Rifle

SPECIFICATIONS

Caliber	: 7.92 Mauser (8 x 57 mm Mauser)
Magazine	: blind magazine
Cartridge capacity	: 5 rounds
Magazine catch	: N/A
Action	: bolt-action
Cocking system	: bolt lever
Firing system	: single round
Locking system	: bolt lugs
Length	: 129.5 cm (51")
Barrel length	: 79 cm (31.1")
Weight	: 4.4 kg (9.7 lb.)
Sight	: tangent rear sight
Safety	: wing-type catch on rear of bolt
Stock	: wooden stock

PARTICULARS

Based on the Steyr-Mannlicher rifle, converted to accept the German 7.92 mm Mauser cartridge.

Hembrug Model M1919 KNIL Carbine

SPECIFICATIONS

Caliber	: 6.5 x 53R
Magazine	: blind magazine
Cartridge capacity	: clips with 5 rounds
Magazine catch	: N/A
Action	: bolt-action
Cocking system	: bolt lever
Firing system	: single round
Locking system	: bolt lugs
Length	: 95 cm (37.4")
Barrel length	: 44.5 cm (17.5")
Weight	: 3.4 kg (7.5 lb.)
Sight	: tangent rear sight
Safety	: wing-type catch on rear of bolt
Stock	: wooden stock

PARTICULARS

Carbine for Dutch Indies army. The bolt lever is curved, and a gas vent has been drilled on the right-hand side of the barrel chamber.

The weapon has a large sling swivel on the left-hand side of the forearm.

Hembrug Model M1939 Carbine

SPECIFICATIONS

Caliber	: 6.5 x 53R
Magazine	: blind magazine
Cartridge capacity	: clips with 5 rounds
Magazine catch	: N/A
Action	: bolt-action
Cocking system	: bolt lever
Firing system	: single round
Locking system	: bolt lugs
Length	: 95 cm (37.4")
Barrel length	: 44.5 cm (17.5")
Weight	: 3.4 kg (7.5 lb.)
Sight	: tangent rear sight
Safety	: wing-type catch on rear of bolt
Stock	: wooden stock

PARTICULARS

Carbine dating from the Dutch WWII mobilization. Due to the threat of war with Germany, a large number of weapons were assembled from parts in order to supply the Dutch troops.

Hesse Arms

Hesse Arms, logo

Hesse Arms from Inver Grove Heights in Maine started out as a manufacturer of components for military arms. The relatively young company produces a large number of rifles for the civilian market based on the FN-FAL and the M16/AR-15. Hesse Arms conduct a great deal of their marketing through the Internet: www.HesseArms.com. The different versions of the FN-FAL are especially noteworthy and include the Tactical Sniper, the FALO with a heavy bull barrel, the FAL Congo rifle, and the short Congo carbine with a 41 cm (16") heavy barrel. For police and army use, these variants can also be supplied as automatics and with a folding stock. Hesse Arms also supply separate components for the FAL and FALO, including the well-known bipod, various models of flash suppressers, the 20-round detachable magazine, and the original FAL optical sight mount. These are of special interest to collectors. Another successful model is the Omega Match Sniper, based on the flat top AR-15 with optical sight and Harris bipod. Hesse Arms do not supply military surplus goods, but components based on the originals, manufactured in their own works using CNC equipment. All weapons are manufactured to military specifications.

Hesse FAL-H Congo Rifle

SPECIFICATIONS

Caliber	: .308 Win. (1:12" RH)
Magazine	: detachable magazine
Cartridge capacity	: 20 rounds
Magazine catch	: behind magazine slot
Action	: adjustable gas pressure
Cocking system	: cocking lever
Firing system	: semi-automatic
Locking system	: vertically sliding block
Length	: 105 cm (41.3")
Barrel length	: 40.6 cm (16")
Weight	: 4.0 kg (8.8 lb.
Sight	: folding aperture sight 150 and 250 meters (492 and 820 ft)
Safety	: safety catch integrated with firing mode selector
Stock	: fixed synthetic stock; metal hand grip

PARTICULARS

With or without folding carrying handle, folding bipod optional.

Hesse FAL-H Standard Rifle

SPECIFICATIONS

Caliber	: .308 Win. (1:12" RH)
Magazine	: detachable magazine
Cartridge capacity	: 20 rounds
Magazine catch	: behind magazine slot
Action	: adjustable gas pressure
Cocking system	: cocking lever
Firing system	: semi-automatic
Locking system	: vertically sliding block
Length	: 115 cm (45.3")
Barrel length	: 53.3 cm (21")
Weight	: 4.3 kg (9.5 lb.)

Sight	: folding aperture sight 150 and 250 meters (492 and 820 ft)
Safety	: safety catch integrated with firing mode selector
Stock	: fixed synthetic stock with metal hand grip

PARTICULARS

With or without folding carrying handle, folding bipod optional.

Hesse FALO-H Congo Carbine

SPECIFICATIONS

Caliber	: .308 Win. (1:12" RH)
Magazine	: detachable magazine
Cartridge capacity	: 20 rounds
Magazine catch	: behind magazine slot
Action	: adjustable gas pressure

Hesse FALO-H Congo Carbine

Cocking system	: cocking lever
Firing system	: semi-automatic
Locking system	: vertically sliding block
Length	: 105 cm (41.3")
Barrel length	: 40.6 cm (16")
Weight	: 4.2 kg (9.3 lb.)
Sight	: folding aperture sight 150 and 250 meters (492 and 820 ft)
Safety	: safety catch integrated with firing mode selector
Stock	: fixed synthetic stock with special hand grip

PARTICULARS

Heavy barrel; with or without folding carrying handle. Shortened version, based on the Israeli FALO model.

Hesse FALO-H Heavy Barrel Rifle

SPECIFICATIONS

Caliber	: .308 Win. (1:12" RH)
Magazine	: detachable magazine
Cartridge capacity	: 20 rounds
Magazine catch	: behind magazine slot
Action	: adjustable gas pressure
Cocking system	: cocking lever
Firing system	: semi-automatic
Locking system	: vertically sliding block

Length	: 115 cm (45.3")
Barrel length	: 53.3 cm (21")
Weight	: 6.3 kg (13.9 lb.)
Sight	: folding aperture sight 150 and 250 meters (492 and 820 ft)
Safety	: safety catch integrated with firing mode selector
Stock	: fixed synthetic stock with special hand grip

PARTICULARS
Heavy barrel; with or without folding carrying handle, folding bipod optional. Based on the Israeli FALO model, in use as a light machine-gun.

Hesse FALO-H Tactical Sniper Rifle

SPECIFICATIONS

Caliber	: .308 Win. (1:12" RH)
Magazine	: detachable magazine
Cartridge capacity	: 20 rounds

Hesse FALO-H Tactical Sniper Rifle

Magazine catch	: behind magazine slot
Action	: adjustable gas pressure
Cocking system	: cocking lever
Firing system	: semi-automatic
Locking system	: vertically sliding block
Length	: 115 cm (45.3")
Barrel length	: 53.3 cm (21")
Weight	: 6.3 kg (13.9 lb.)
Sight	: folding aperture sight 150 and 250 meters (492 and 820 ft); special mounting rail for optical sight
Safety	: ssafety catch integrated with firing mode selector
Stock	: fixed synthetic stock with free floating light metal hand grip

PARTICULARS
Heavy barrel with special flash suppresser; with or without folding carrying handle, folding bipod.

Hesse HAR-15A2 Bull Gun

SPECIFICATIONS

Caliber	: .223 Rem., 7.62 x 39, 6 mm x .223, 6 mm PPC, .300 Fireball, or .50 AE (Action Express)
Magazine	: detachable magazine
Cartridge capacity	: 5, 10, 20, 30, or 40 rounds
Magazine catch	: in left-hand side of magazine housing
Action	: gas pressure
Cocking system	: cocking lever
Firing system	: semi-automatic
Locking system	: 7-lug rotating bolt head

Hesse HAR-15A2 Bull Gun

Length	: 101.6 cm (40")
Barrel length	: 50.8 cm (20")
Weight	: 3.6 kg (8 lb.)
Sight	: carrying handle with M16 type adjustable rear- and front sight
Safety	: rotating catch on left-hand side of housing
Stock	: synthetic stock and pistol grip

PARTICULARS

Synthetic hand grip; matt black coating.
Heavy stainless steel match barrel.

Hesse HAR-15A2 Carbine

SPECIFICATIONS

Caliber	: .223 Rem., 7.62 x 39, 6 mm x .223, 6 mm PPC, .300 Fireball or .50 AE (Action Express)

Magazine	: detachable magazine
Cartridge capacity	: 5, 10, 20, 30, of 40 rounds
Magazine catch	: in left-hand side of magazine housing
Action	: gas pressure
Cocking system	: cocking lever
Firing system	: semi-automatic
Locking system	: 7-lug rotating bolt head
Length	: 88.9 cm (35")
Barrel length	: 40.6 cm (16")
Weight	: 3.0 kg (6.7 lb.)
Sight	: carrying handle with M16 type adjustable rear- and front sight
Safety	: rotating catch on left-hand side of receiver housing
Stock	: light metal fixed stock derived from extending model, or original extending stock

PARTICULARS

Synthetic hand guard; matt black coating.

Hesse HAR-15A2 Dispatcher

SPECIFICATIONS

Caliber	: .223 Rem., 7.62 x 39, 6 mm x .223, 6 mm PPC, .300 Fireball, or .50 AE (Action Express)
Magazine	: detachable magazine
Cartridge capacity	: 5, 10, 20, 30, or 40 rounds
Magazine catch	: in left-hand side of magazine housing
Action	: gas pressure

Hesse HAR-15A2 Dispatcher

Cocking system	: cocking lever
Firing system	: semi-automatic
Locking system	: 7-lug rotating bolt head
Length	: 88.9 cm (35")
Barrel length	: 40.6 cm (16")
Weight	: 3.0 kg (6.7 lb.)
Sight	: carrying handle with M16 type adjustable sight and bead
Safety	: rotating catch on left-hand side of receiver housing
Stock	: synthetic stock and pistol grip

PARTICULARS
Long synthetic hand grip; matt black coating.

Hesse HAR-15A2 Omega Match Sniper Rifle

Hesse HAR-15A2 Omega Match Sniper Rifle

SPECIFICATIONS

Caliber	: .223 Rem., 7.62 x 39, 6 mm x .223, 6 mm PPC, .300 Fireball, or .50 AE (Action Express)
Magazine	: detachable magazine
Cartridge capacity	: 5, 10, 20, 30, or 40 rounds
Magazine catch	: in left-hand side of magazine housing
Action	: gas pressure
Cocking system	: cocking lever
Firing system	: semi-automatic
Locking system	: 7-lug rotating bolt head
Length	: 101.6 cm (40")
Barrel length	: 50.8 cm (20")
Weight	: 3.6 kg (8 lb.)
Sight	: none; flat top mounting rail for optical sight
Safety	: rotating catch on left-hand side of receiver housing
Stock	: kunststof stock en pistoolgreep

Hesse HAR-15A2 National Match Rifle

188

PARTICULARS
Free floating light metal hand grip; matt black coating. Heavy stainless steel match barrel. Adjustable trigger.

Hesse HAR-15A2 National Match Rifle

SPECIFICATIONS

Caliber	: .223 Rem., 7.62 x 39, 6 mm x .223, 6 mm PPC, .300 Fireball, or .50 AE (Action Express)
Magazine	: detachable magazine
Cartridge capacity	: 5, 10, 20, 30, or 40 rounds
Magazine catch	: iin left-hand side of magazine housing
Action	: gas pressure
Cocking system	: cocking lever
Firing system	: semi-automatic
Locking system	: 7-lug rotating bolt head
Length	: 101.6 cm (40")
Barrel length	: 50.8 cm (20")
Weight	: 3.6 kg (8 lb.)
Sight	: carrying handle with adjustable M16 type match sight
Safety	: rotary catch on left-hand side of receiver housing
Stock	: synthetic stock and pistol grip

PARTICULARS
Free floating synthetic hand grip; matt black coating. Heavy stainless steel match barrel with flash suppresser. Specially assembled match version with minimal tolerances.

Hesse HAR-15A2 Standard Rifle

SPECIFICATIONS

Caliber	: .223 Rem., 7.62 x 39, 6 mm x .223, 6 mm PPC, .300 Fireball, or .50 AE (Action Express)
Magazine	: detachable magazine
Cartridge capacity	: 5, 10, 20, 30 or 40 rounds
Magazine catch	: in left-hand side of magazine housing
Action	: gas pressure
Cocking system	: cocking lever
Firing system	: semi-automatic
Locking system	: 7-lug rotating bolt head
Length	: 101.6 cm (40")
Barrel length	: 50.8 cm (20")
Weight	: 3.6 kg (8 lb.)
Sight	: carrying handle with M16 type adjustable sight
Safety	: rotating catch on left-hand side of receiver housing
Stock	: synthetic stock and pistol grip

PARTICULARS
This rifle has a synthetic hand grip and a matt black coating; heavy match barrel with flash suppresser.

Machine-gun

Sub-machine-gun

I.M.I. (Israel Military Industries)

Following its formation, the young state of Israel immediately became involved in a number of armed conflicts. Upon the declaration of independence on 14 May 1948, war broke out with the adjoining Arab countries. Since this drove the country into political isolation at a time when it was hampered by a shortage of foreign currency, the new nation had to primarily rely on its own resources. It had the British Sten sub-machine-gun at its disposal, but additional armament was urgently required. In 1949, Israeli colonel Uziel Gal designed the famous Uzi sub-machine-gun, which in 1951 was introduced into the Israeli army on a massive scale. The design was of such a high quality that the Uzi was later adopted by the armies of many other countries. Several countries built the Uzi under license, e.g. the FN works at near Liege in Belgium. The Uzi was even adopted as official NATO armament. Following the Israel-Arab war of 1967, the Israeli army decided to develop a light rifle as a counterpart to the Russian AK-47 used by the Arab

forces. The Israelis opted for the AK-47 type gas pressure repeating system in combination with the NATO .223 Remington caliber. The designer of the weapon was the Sabra Israeli Galili, 44 years old at the time.

In view of the urgency of the requirement, a large consignment of arms components intended for the Valmet Model 62 army rifle was purchased in Finland. These were rebuilt in Israel into the Galil rifle. Current demand for Galil rifles is high, resulting in a large flow of foreign currency. The result is that the Israeli army has to be content with Colt M16 rifles. The company also produce ammunition under the brand names Uzi and Samson.

I.M.I. (Israel Military Industries), logo

ISRAEL MILITARY INDUSTRIES LTD (I.M.I)

FORMERLY TAAS

W e a p o n s   G r o u p

I.M.I. Galil AR

SPECIFICATIONS

Caliber	: .223 Rem. of .308 Win.
Magazine	: detachable magazine
Cartridge capacity	: .223: 35 or 50 rounds; .308: 25 rounds
Magazine catch	: rear of magazine housing
Action	: gas pressure
Cocking system	: folding cocking lever
Firing system	: full- and semi-automatic

I.M.I. Galil AR

Locking system	: rotating bolt head
Length	: unfolded stock: .223: 98 cm (38.6"); .308: 105 cm (41.3"); folded stock: .223: 74 cm (29.1"); .308: 81 cm (31.9")
Barrel length	: .223: 46 cm (18.1"); .308: 50.8 cm (20")
Weight	: 4.0 kg (8.8 lb.)
Sight	: folding aperture sight 300/500 meters (984 ft/546 yd)
Safety	: integrated with firing mode selector on right-hand side of receiver housing
Stock	: folding steel skeleton stock with black synthetic pistol grip and hand grip

PARTICULARS

Matt black model; caliber .308 with straight detachable magazine, and .223 with curved detachable magazine. Page 191 shows a photograph of a reconnaissance vehicle with the Negev LMG (top) and the Galil AR (bottom).

I.M.I. Galil ARM

SPECIFICATIONS

Caliber	: .223 Rem. of .308 Win.
Magazine	: detachable magazine
Cartridge capacity	: .223: 35 or 50 rounds; .308: 25 rounds
Magazine catch	: on rear of magazine housing
Action	: gas pressure
Cocking system	: folding cocking lever

I.M.I. Galil ARM

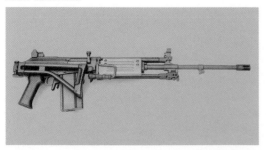

Firing system	: full- and semi-automatic
Locking system	: rotating bolt head
Length	: unfolded stock: .223: 98 cm (38.6"); .308: 105 cm (41.3"); folded stock: .223: 74 cm (29.1"); .308: 81 cm (31.9")
Barrel length	: .223: 46 cm (18.1"); .308: 50.8 cm (20")
Weight	: .223: 4.4 kg (9.7 lb.); .308: 4.5 kg (9.9 lb.)
Sight	: folding aperture sight 300/500 meters (984 ft/546 yd)
Safety	: integrated with firing mode selector on right-hand side of receiver housing
Stock	: folding steel skeleton stock with synthetic pistol grip and wooden hand grip

PARTICULARS

Matt black model; FN-FAL-like carrying handle; folding bipod; caliber .308 with straight detachable magazine, and .223 with curved detachable magazine.

I.M.I. Galil SAR

SPECIFICATIONS

Caliber	: .223 Rem. of .308 Win.
Magazine	: detachable magazine
Cartridge capacity	: .223: 35 or 50 rounds; .308: 25 rounds
Magazine catch	: rear of magazine housing
Action	: gas pressure
Cocking system	: folding cocking lever
Firing system	: automatic and semi-automatic
Locking system	: rotating bolt head
Length	: unfolded stock: .223: 84 cm (33.1"); .308: 91.5 cm (36"); folded stock: .223: 61 cm (24"); .308: 67.5 cm (26.6")
Barrel length	: .223: 33.2 cm (13"); .308: 40 cm (15.7")
Weight	: .223: 3.75 kg (8.3 lb.); .308: 3.85 kg (8.5 lb.)
Sight	: folding aperture sight 300/500 meters (984 ft/546 yd)
Safety	: integrated with firing mode selector on right-hand side of receiver housing
Stock	: folding steel skeleton stock with black synthetic pistol grip and hand grip

I.M.I. Galil SAR

I.M.I. Galil SASR: semi-automatic Sniper Rifle

PARTICULARS

Matt black model; caliber .308 with straight detachable magazine and in .223 with curved detachable magazine.

I.M.I. Galil SASR: semi-automatic Sniper Rifle

SPECIFICATIONS

Caliber	: .308 Win.
Magazine	: detachable magazine
Cartridge capacity:	25 rounds
Magazine catch	: on front of trigger guard
Action	: gas pressure
Cocking system	: folding cocking lever
Firing system	: semi-automatic
Locking system	: rotating bolt head
Length	: unfolded stock: 111.2 cm (43.8"); folded stock: 84.5 cm (33.3")
Barrel length	: 50.8 cm (20")
Weight	: 6.4 kg (14.1 lb.)
Sight	: aperture sight and Nimrod optical sight and sight mounting
Safety	: ambidextrous safety catch on receiver housing
Stock	: folding wooden stock with adjustable cheek and butt; synthetic pistol grip

I.M.I. Galil SASR: semi-automatic Sniper Rifle

PARTICULARS

Wooden forearm, folding bipod, extended flash suppresser/recoil damper

I.M.I. Negev LMG

SPECIFICATIONS

Caliber	: .223 Rem.
Magazine	: drum or belt feed
Cartridge capacity:	drum: 200 rounds
Magazine catch	: rear of magazine housing
Action	: gas pressure
Cocking system	: folding cocking lever
Firing system	: semi- and fully automatic
Locking system	: rotating bolt head
Length	: unfolded stock: 102 cm (40"); folded stock: 78 cm (30.7")
Barrel length	: 46 cm (18.1")
Weight	: 7.3 kg (16.1 lb.)
Sight	: adjustable aperture sight up to 1000 meters (1093 yd)
Safety	: integrated with firing mode selector on right-hand side of receiver housing
Stock	: folding steel skeleton stock with black synthetic pistol grip and hand grip

PARTICULARS

Matt black; folding bipod; synthetic carrying handle; special attachment points for mounting on vehicles or gun tripod.

I.M.I. Negev LMG Short

SPECIFICATIONS

Caliber	: .223 Rem.
Magazine	: Galil detachable magazine or drum
Cartridge capacity:	35 or 50 rounds; drum: 200 rounds
Magazine catch	: rear of magazine housing

I.M.I. Negev LMG

I.M.I. Negev LMG Short

Action	: gas pressure
Cocking system	: folding cocking lever
Firing system	: semi- and fully automatic
Locking system	: rotating bolt head
Length	: unfolded stock: 89 cm (35"); folded stock: 65 cm (25.6")
Barrel length	: 33 cm (13")
Weight	: 7.0 kg (15.4 lb.)
Sight	: adjustable aperture sight up to 1000 meters (1093 yd)
Safety	: integrated with firing mode selector on right-hand side of receiver housing
Stock	: folding steel skeleton stock with black synthetic pistol grip and hand grip

PARTICULARS
Matt black; folding bipod; synthetic carrying handle; shortened paratrooper model.

I.M.I. Uzi

SPECIFICATIONS

Caliber	: 9 mm Para with exchange sets for .45 ACP and .41 AE
Magazine	: detachable magazine
Cartridge capacity	: 20, 25, or 32 rounds
Magazine catch	: in bottom of pistol grip
Action	: recoil-action

I.M.I. Uzi

Cocking system	: cocking lever
Firing system	: full- and semi-automatic
Locking system	: inertia lock
Length	: unfolded: 65 cm (25.6"); folded: 47 cm (18.5")
Barrel length	: 26 cm (10.2")
Weight	: 3.5 kg (7.7 lb.)
Sight	: vertically adjustable front sight; laterally adjustable folding aperture sight
Safety	: grip safety with safety catch integrated into firing mode selector
Stock	: folding steel skeleton stock; synthetic pistol grip and hand grip

PARTICULARS
Matt black.

I.M.I. Uzi Carbine

SPECIFICATIONS

Caliber	: 9 mm Para of .45 ACP
Magazine	: detachable magazine
Cartridge capacity	: 9 mm: 25 rounds; .45: 16 rounds
Magazine catch	: in bottom of pistol grip
Action	: recoil-action
Cocking system	: cocking lever
Firing system	: semi-automatic
Locking system	: inertia lock
Length	: unfolded: 9 mm: 80 cm (31.5"); .45: 65 cm (25.6"); folded: 9 mm: 61 cm (24"); .45: 47 cm (18.5")
Barrel length	: 41 cm (16.1")
Weight	: 9 mm: 3.8 kg (8.4 lb.); .45: 3.5 kg (7.7 lb.)
Sight	: vertically adjustable front sight; laterally adjustable folding aperture sight 100 and 200 meters (328 and 656 ft
Safety	: grip safety with safety catch integrated into firing mode selector
Stock	: folding steel skeleton stock; synthetic pistol grip and hand grip

I.M.I. Uzi Carbine

I.M.I. Uzi Micro

I.M.I. Uzi Mini

PARTICULARS
Matt black; special model intended for regular police units.

I.M.I. Uzi Micro

SPECIFICATIONS
Caliber	: 9 mm Para
Magazine	: detachable magazine
Cartridge capacity	: 20 or 25 rounds
Magazine catch	: in bottom of pistol grip
Action	: recoil-action
Cocking system	: cocking lever
Firing system	: full- and semi-automatic
Locking system	: inertia lock
Length	: unfolded: 48.6 cm (19.1"); folded: 28.2 cm (11.1")
Barrel length	: 13.4 cm (5.3")
Weight	: 2.0 kg (4.4 lb.)
Sight	: vertically adjustable front sight; laterally adjustable folding aperture sight
Safety	: grip safety with safety catch integrated into firing mode selector
Stock	: folding steel skeleton stock; synthetic pistol grip and hand grip

PARTICULARS
Matt black; compensating slots have been cut into the barrel near the muzzle to reduce barrel jump during fully automatic firing.

I.M.I. Uzi Mini

SPECIFICATIONS
Caliber	: 9 mm Para
Magazine	: detachable magazine
Cartridge capacity	: 20 or 25 rounds
Magazine catch	: in bottom of pistol grip
Action	: recoil-action
Cocking system	: cocking lever
Firing system	: full- and semi-automatic
Locking system	: inertia lock
Length	: unfolded: 60 cm (23.6"); folded : 36 cm (14.2")
Barrel length	: 19.7 cm (7.8")
Weight	: 2.65 kg (5.8 lb.)
Sight	: vertically adjustable front sight; laterally adjustable folding aperture sight
Safety	: grip safety and safety catch integrated with firing mode selector
Stock	: folding steel skeleton stock; synthetic pistol grip and hand grip

PARTICULARS
Matt black; compensating slots have been cut into the barrel near the muzzle to reduce barrel jump during fully automatic firing. The illustration shows one of the latest Mini-Uzi models with a silencer and optical sight.

I.M.I. Uzi Mini

195

I.M.I. Uzi Pistol

SPECIFICATIONS

Caliber	: 9 mm Para
Magazine	: detachable magazine
Cartridge capacity	: 20 or 25 rounds
Magazine catch	: in bottom of pistol grip
Action	: recoil-action
Cocking system	: cocking lever
Firing system	: semi-automatic
Locking system	: inertia lock
Length	: 24 cm (9.4")
Barrel length	: 11.5 cm (4.5")
Weight	: 1.7 kg (3.7 lb.)
Sight	: vertically adjustable front sight; laterally adjustable folding aperture sight
Safety	: grip safety and safety catch integrated with firing mode selector
Stock	: synthetic pistol grip only

PARTICULARS

Matt black.

Imperator

De German Wischo Jagd- und Sportwaffen GmbH company is a commercial enterprise representing a large number of arms manufacturers in Europe. In addition, Wischo often commissions special models from various manufacturers which Wischo then markets itself. The Impera-

tor shotguns are produced for the company in Italy by Fabarm, among others. These guns are not standard Fabarm guns, but are manufactured to Wischo specifications.

Imperator Model SDASS Magnum

SPECIFICATIONS

Caliber	: 12/76 (3")
Magazine	: tubular magazine
Cartridge capacity	: 8 rounds
Magazine catch	: N/A
Action	: pump-action
Cocking system	: forearm
Firing system	: single round
Locking system	: rotating bolt head
Length	: 105 cm (41.3")
Barrel length	: 50 cm (19.7")
Weight	: 2.9 kg (6.4 lb.)
Sight	: bead
Safety	: push-button safety in rear of trigger guard
Stock	: hardwood, with pistol grip

PARTICULARS

Matt black protective coating.

Imperator Model SDASS Magnum

Imperator Model SDASS Police Combat-Special

SPECIFICATIONS

Caliber	: 12/76 (3")
Magazine	: tubular magazine
Cartridge capacity	: 6 rounds
Magazine catch	: N/A
Action	: pump-action
Cocking system	: forearm
Firing system	: single round
Locking system	: rotating bolt head
Length	: 90.8 cm (35.8")
Barrel length	: 36 cm (14.2")
Weight	: 2.7 kg (6.0 lb.)

Sight	: bead
Safety	: push-button safety in rear of trigger guard
Stock	: synthetic, with pistol grip

PARTICULARS

Matt black protective coating.

Imperator Model SDASS Police Magnum

SPECIFICATIONS

Caliber	: 12/76 (3")
Magazine	: tubular magazine
Cartridge capacity	: 8 rounds
Magazine catch	: N/A
Action	: pump-action
Cocking system	: forearm
Firing system	: single round
Locking system	: rotating bolt head
Length	: 105 cm (41.3")
Barrel length	: 50 cm (19.7")
Weight	: 3.1 kg (6.8 lb.)
Sight	: ventilated barrel rib and bead
Safety	: push-button safety in rear of trigger guard
Stock	: black synthetic, with pistol grip

PARTICULARS

Matt black protective coating.

Imperator Model SDASS Police Magnum

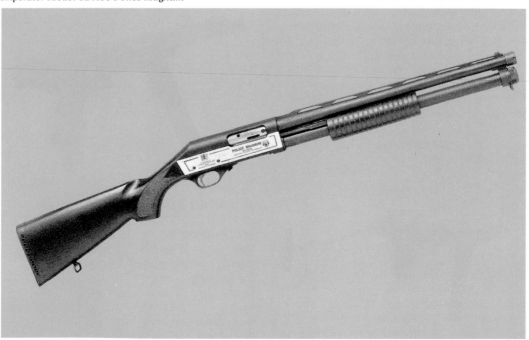

ITM Tool And Die

ITM Tool And Die, logo

PRODUCTION DESIGN & DEVELOPMENT PROTOTYPES
BUILD- DIES, FIXTURES, JIGS, TOOLING
GENERAL MACHINING AND PRECISION STAMPINGS

ITM Tool And Die
5416 Detroit Avenue
Cleveland, ohio 44102

JOHN MIHAITA
Owner

Phone (216) 631-3572
Fax (216) 631-1220

The American ITM Tool And Die Company is located in Cleveland, Ohio. The company specializes in research and development of prototypes for the arms industry. In addition, the company manufactures reloading dies for special calibers, various dies for industrial applications, and special tools. ITM is currently involved in the development of a series of sub-machine-guns. A number of these feature double cartridge feed systems and even double barrels. Development of prototypes is generally commissioned by arms manufacturers. In addition, ITM also conducts research on its own account and sells the prototypes to arms manufacturers. The weapons are being developed for use by military and police forces.

ITM Model 1 Dual Barrel (prototype)

SPECIFICATIONS

Caliber   : 9 mm Para
Magazine   : two detachable magazines
Cartridge capacity: to order

ITM Model 1 Dual-Barrel (prototype)

Magazine catch   : at rear of magazine slot
Action   : recoil-action
Cocking system   : two cocking levers
Firing system   : full- and semi-automatic
Locking system   : inertia lock
Length   : with unfolded stock: 76.2 cm (30"); folded: 48.3 cm (19")
Barrel length   : upper barrel: 25.4 cm (10"); lower barrel: 15.2 cm (6")
Weight   : 2.9 kg (6.5 lb.)
Sight   : adjustable rear sight and hooded front sight with low-visibility markings; special mounting for optical sights
Safety   : safety catch in front of trigger guard; automatic firing pin safety
Stock   : steel skeleton stock

PARTICULARS

Double-barreled sub-machine-gun; combined firing mode selector and barrel selector for upper barrel, lower barrel, or both. Special flash suppresser and recoil damper; separate cocking lever for each barrel system. Specially developed for barrage bursts, with the longer upper barrel used for precision fire. The weapon fires with the breech block closed. The theoretical rate of fire is 800 rounds per minute.

ITM Model 1 Dual-Barrel (prototype)

ITM Model 2 Dual Barrel (prototype)

SPECIFICATIONS

Caliber   : 9 mm Para
Magazine   : two detachable magazines
Cartridge capacity: to order
Magazine catch   : at rear of magazine slot
Action   : recoil-action
Cocking system   : two cocking levers
Firing system   : full- and semi-automatic

ITM Model 2 Dual-Barrel (prototype)

ITM Model 3 Dual-Barrel (prototype)

Locking system	: inertia lock
Length	: with unfolded stock: 76.2 cm (30"); folded: 48.3 cm (19")
Barrel length	: upper barrel: 32.4 cm (12.75"); lower barrel: 14.6 cm (5.75")
Weight	: 2.9 kg (6.5 lb.)
Sight	: adjustable rear sight and hooded front sight with low-visibility markings; special mounting for optical sights
Safety	: safety catch in front of trigger guard; automatic firing pin safety
Stock	: steel skeleton stock

PARTICULARS

Double-barreled sub-machine-gun; both barrels feature screw thread for special flash suppressers or silencers. Combined firing mode selector and barrel selector for upper barrel, lower barrel, or both. Special flash suppresser and recoil damper; separate cocking lever for each barrel system. Specially developed for barrage bursts, with the longer upper barrel used for precision fire. The weapon fires with the breech block closed. The theoretical rate of fire is 800 rounds per minute.

ITM Model 2 Dual-Barrel (prototype)

ITM Model 3 Dual Barrel (prototype)

SPECIFICATIONS

Caliber	: .308 Win. plus 9 mm Para
Magazine	: detachable magazine for 9 mm Para and cartridge drum for .308 Win.
Cartridge capacity	: to order
Magazine catch	: at rear of magazine slot
Action	: upper barrel: gas pressure; lower barrel: recoil-action
Cocking system	: two cocking levers
Firing system	: full- and semi-automatic
Locking system	: inertia lock
Length	: with unfolded stock: 91.4 cm (36"); folded: 68.6 cm (27")
Barrel length	: upper barrel .308 Win.: 40.6 cm (16"); lower barrel 9 mm Para: 20.3 cm (8")
Weight	: 4.4 kg (9.8 lb.)
Sight	: adjustable rear sight and hooded front sight with low-visibility markings; special mounting for optical sights
Safety	: safety catch in front of trigger guard; automatic firing pin safety
Stock	: steel skeleton stock

PARTICULARS

Double-barreled sub-machine-gun with two different calibers; both barrels feature special flash suppressers. Separate cocking levers for each barrel system.
Combined firing mode selector and barrel selector switch for upper barrel, lower barrel, or both barrels. Specially developed for barrage bursts, with the longer upper barrel used for precision fire. The weapon fires with the breech block closed. The theoretical rate of fire is 800 rounds per minute.

ITM Model 4 Dual Barrel (prototype)

SPECIFICATIONS

Caliber	: 9 mm Para
Magazine	: two detachable magazines
Cartridge capacity	: to order
Magazine catch	: at rear of magazine slot
Action	: recoil-action
Cocking system	: two cocking levers
Firing system	: full- and semi-automatic
Locking system	: inertia lock
Length	: with unfolded stock: 78.1 cm (30.75"); folded: 55.9 cm (22")
Barrel length	: top barrel: 31.1 cm (12.25"); lower barrel: 15.9 cm (6.25")
Weight	: 3.6 kg (8 lb.)
Sight	: adjustable rear sight and hooded front sight with low-visibility markings; special mounting for optical sights
Safety	: combined safety catch/firing mode selector and barrel selector switch for upper barrel, lower barrel, or both barrels
Stock	: steel skeleton stock

PARTICULARS

Double-barreled sub-machine-gun; both barrels feature special flash suppressers.

Separate cocking levers for each barrel system. Specially developed for barrage bursts, with the longer upper barrel used for precision fire.

The weapon fires with the breech block closed. The theoretical rate of fire is 800 rounds per minute.

ITM Model 5 (prototype)

SPECIFICATIONS

Caliber	: .308 Win.
Magazine	: detachable magazine of drum
Cartridge capacity	: 14 or 30 rounds; drum: 125 rounds
Magazine catch	: on right-hand side, above magazine slot

ITM Model 5 (prototype)

ITM Model 5 (prototype)

ITM Model 6 (prototype)

Action	: gas pressure
Cocking system	: cocking lever
Firing system	: full- and semi-automatic
Locking system	: rotating bolt head
Length	: with unfolded stock: 71.8 cm (28.25"); folded: 43.2 cm (17")
Barrel length	: 22.9 cm (9")
Weight	: 2.4 kg (5.4 lb.)
Sight	: adjustable rear sight and hooded front sight with low-visibility markings; special mounting for optical sights
Safety	: combined safety catch/firing mode selector
Stock	: steel skeleton stock

PARTICULARS

Large-caliber sub-machine-gun; barrel with special flash suppresser and recoil damper. The weapon fires with closed breech lock. The theoretical rate of fire is 600 rounds per minute.

ITM Model 6 (prototype)

SPECIFICATIONS

Caliber	: 9 mm Para

Magazine	: detachable magazine
Cartridge capacity	: to order
Magazine catch	: on right-hand side, behind magazine slot
Action	: recoil action
Cocking system	: cocking lever
Firing system	: full- and semi-automatic
Locking system	: inertia lock
Length	: with unfolded stock: 60 cm (23.5"); folded: 38.1 cm (15")
Barrel length	: 16.5 cm (6.5")
Weight	: 2.3 kg (5 lb.)
Sight	: adjustable rear sight and hooded front sight with low-visibility markings; special mounting for optical sights
Safety	: combined safety catch/firing mode selector
Stock	: steel skeleton stock

PARTICULARS

Threaded barrel for special flash suppresser or silencer.
The weapon fires with closed breech block. The theoretical rate of fire is 600 rounds per minute.

ITM Model 6 (prototype)

Johnson

The semi-automatic Johnson rifle was developed by Melvin Johnson, an officer of the Marine Corps Reserve. Several prototypes were constructed between 1937 and 1939 by the Marlin and Taft-Pierce armament factories. In 1938 and 1939 these were tested at Fort Benning and on the famous Aberdeen Proving Ground.

At the same time the M1 Garand was being tested, for which the top brass of the US Army expressed its preference. The Johnson was therefore not adopted as the standard army rifle. Despite this Johnson decided to produce the weapon bearing the designation M1941. This was done by the Johnson Automatics Manufacturing Company at Cranston, Rhode Island. Because production of the Garand rifle was not yet fully on stream in 1941 Johnson was able to sell several thousand M1941s to the US Marine Corps for their O.S.S. units.

Through intermediaries in the US government, Johnson also entered into a contract at the end of 1940 with the Dutch government in exile in London. The M1941 was intended for the Royal Dutch Indies Army. The supply of these weapons ceased abruptly when the Dutch Indies, the present-day Indonesian Republic, was occupied by Japanese troops in 1942. The Johnson M1941 uses the .30-06 caliber Springfield cartridge – although several

Johnson M1941

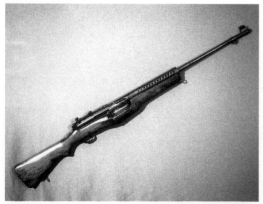

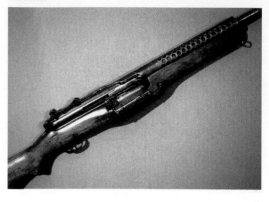

hundreds were produced for Chile for the 7 x 57 mm Mauser cartridge. The US Marines used the weapon extensively in their operations in the Far East and Europe until beyond 1945. The action is unusual for service rifles in that the recoil-action drives the barrel back after a round is fired, unlocking a rotating bolt head from the receiver.

This is therefore not gas pressure operation. The circular internal magazine of the Johnson is the most intriguing part of the weapon but some examples were made with a straight detachable magazine. The total production of the M1941 is estimated at about 70,000.

Johnson M1941

SPECIFICATIONS

Caliber	: .30-06 Springf.
Magazine	: internal magazine
Cartridge capacity	: 10 rounds
Magazine catch	: N/A
Action	: recoil-action
Cocking system	: cocking lever
Firing system	: semi-automatic
Locking system	: 8-lug rotating bolt head
Length	: 115.6 cm (45.5")
Barrel length	: 55.8 cm (22")
Weight	: 4.3 kg (9.5 lb.)
Sight	: aperture sight
Safety	: safety catch in front of trigger guard
Stock	: wooden stock with pressed steel hand grip

PARTICULARS
The round internal magazine can be loaded with 5-round clips. Production was halted in 1945.

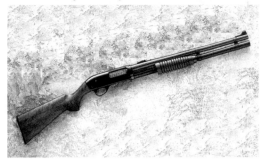

K k

KBI

KBI Inc. from Harrisburg, Pennsylvania are the importers for the USA and Canada of Armscor rifles and the semi-automatic AK-47 manufactured by the Hungarian FEG company. In addition, KBI import the original Russian Dragunov sniper rifle. The Dragunov is supplied with a complete and original set of accessories, including the PSO-4X optical sight, a sight pouch, four detachable magazines, a cartridge bag, a maintenance set, and an original bayonet. The official designation of this rifle is Snayperskaya Vintovka Dragunova (SVD).

The weapon was developed by Jewgeni Fjodorowits Dragonov and was introduced in the Russian Army in 1963. Shortly afterwards the rifle also became available to the other Warsaw Pact countries. The weapon was to replace the obsolete Mosin-Nagant M1891/30 sniper rifle dating from the Second World War. The system is a derivation from the famous Kalashnikov AK-47 rifle. The Dragunov is intended to be used with a telescopic sight, but it also has a normal tangent rear sight. The Dragunov is also manufactured in China and exported by the Chinese

Norinco company under the NDM-86 designation. Several other countries, most of them former Warsaw Pact countries, produce this sniper rifle under license. The riot guns of the Philippine Armscor company are of good quality. The Model M30 SAS shotgun is based on the Regiment's riot gun used by the British Special Air Services. In addition, Armscor produce models of the Colt M16 and the AK-47 for .22 LR.

KBI/Armscor Special Purpose Model M-30 DG

SPECIFICATIONS

Caliber	: 12/76 (3")
Magazine	: tubular magazine
Cartridge capacity	: 7 rounds
Magazine catch	: N/A.
Action	: pump-action
Cocking system	: forearm
Firing system	: single round
Locking system	: bolt lugs
Length	: 99.7 cm (39.25")
Barrel length	: 50.8 cm (20"); cylindrical choke
Weight	: 3.4 kg (7.5 lb.)
Sight	: adjustable rear sight
Safety	: push-button on front of trigger guard
Stock	: hardwood stock and forearm

PARTICULARS

Blued housing, tubular magazine and barrel; adjustable sight specially adapted for firing slugs.

KBI/Armscor Riotgun Model M-30 R6

SPECIFICATIONS

Caliber	: 12/76 (3")
Magazine	: tubular magazine

KBI, logo

KBI/Armscor Riotgun Model M-30 R6

Cartridge capacity: 5 rounds
Magazine catch : N/A
Action   : pump-action
Cocking system : forearm
Firing system   : single round
Locking system : bolt lugs
Length   : 95.9 cm (37.75")
Barrel length   : 47 cm (18.5"); cylindrical choke
Weight   : 3.2 kg (7 lb.)
Sight   : bead
Safety   : push-button catch on front of trigger guard
Stock   : hardwood stock and forearm

PARTICULARS
Blued housing, tubular magazine and barrel. The Model M-30 R8 riot gun (top) and the model M-30 R6 (bottom) are shown.

KBI/Armscor Riotgun Model M-30 R8

SPECIFICATIONS
Caliber   : 12/76 (3")
Magazine   : tubular magazine
Cartridge capacity: 7 rounds
Magazine catch   : N/A
Action   : pump-action

KBI/Armscor Riotgun Model M-30 R8

Cocking system : forearm
Firing system   : single round
Locking system : bolt lugs
Length   : 99.7 cm (39.25")
Barrel length   : 50.8 cm (20"); cylindrical choke
Weight   : 3.3 kg (7.2 lb.)
Sight   : bead
Safety   : push-button on front of trigger guard
Stock   : hardwood stock and forearm

PARTICULARS
Blued housing, tubular magazine and barrel.

KBI/Armscor Special Purpose Model M-30 SAS

SPECIFICATIONS
Caliber   : 12/76 (3")
Magazine   : tubular magazine
Cartridge capacity: 7 rounds + 4 rounds in Speedfeed stock
                    magazine
Magazine catch   : N/A
Action   : pump-action
Cocking system   : forearm
Firing system   : single round
Locking system   : bolt lugs
Length   : 99.7 cm (39.25")
Barrel length   : 50.8 cm (20"); cylindrical choke
Weight   : 3.4 kg (7.5 lb.)
Sight   : bead
Safety   : push-button on front of trigger guard
Stock   : synthetic stock and forearm

PARTICULARS
Matt black Parkerized; special Speedfeed tubular magazine in stock for 4 rounds. The model is based on the British S.A.S. riot gun.

KBI/Armscor Special Purpose Model M-30 SAS

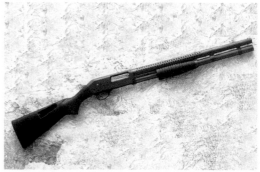

KBI/Tula Dragunov Model SVD

SPECIFICATIONS

Caliber	: 7.62 x 54R
Magazine	: detachable magazine
Cartridge capacity	: 10 rounds
Magazine catch	: behind magazine slot
Action	: gas pressure
Cocking system	: cocking lever
Firing system	: semi-automatic
Locking system	: rotating bolt head
Length	: 122.6 cm (48.25")
Barrel length	: 68.6 cm (27")
Weight	: 3.5 kg (7.8 lb.)
Sight	: adjustable tangent rear sight; special optical sight (PSO) with illuminated crosshairs and infrared detector
Safety	: safety catch on right-hand side of housing
Stock	: laminated hardwood skeleton stock with pistol grip

PARTICULARS

Matt black coating; detachable cheek piece.

Kel-Tec

In 1995 the American Kel-Tec CNC Industries Inc. company introduced the P-11, a 9 mm Para pistol with a double-

Kel-Tec, logo

action trigger system. This 400 gram handgun is the lightest and smallest 9 mm Para pistol ever designed. The weapon, which measures only 14 cm in length, was entirely designed by computer for plain-clothes police detectives or as a back-up gun for police and army personnel. A few years later, Kel-Tec developed a second compact weapon, the folding Sub-9 carbine, using the 9 mm caliber Para (Luger) cartridge. This weapon has a steel barrel, receiver housing and tube stock, but for the remainder uses the impact-resistant DuPont ST-800 synthetic and aircraft-grade aluminum, 7075-T6. An interesting feature is that the double-row 9 mm Para caliber detachable magazines of most makes of pistol can be used in this weapon. The folding aperture sight is not adjustable, but the front sight is.

Kel-Tec Sub-9 carbine

SPECIFICATIONS

Caliber	: 9 mm Para
Magazine	: detachable magazine
Cartridge capacity	: 10 to 33 rounds
Magazine catch	: ambidextrous, behind trigger guard

offices in Fichtenberg in Bavaria, Germany. This German gunsmith is one of the few custom rifle makers in Europe. The company has developed two special rifle compensators that act as recoil dampers. The Keppeler rifles offer a high degree of precision. Groups of three hits with a diameter of 70 mm at 300 meters (2.75" at 984 ft)using factory ammunition (.338 Lapua Magnum) are no exception. In 1995, Keppeler developed a special sniper rifle with a so-called bullpup stock. One of the features of this repeating bolt rifle is that the detachable magazine is angled downwards on the left-hand side.

Keppeler KS III Bullpup Sniper

SPECIFICATIONS

Caliber	: .308 Win., .300 Win.Mag., .338 Lapua Mag.
Cartridge capacity	: 3 or 5 rounds
Magazine catch	: N/A
Action	: bolt-action
Cocking system	: bolt lever
Firing system	: single round
Locking system	: 7-lug bolt
Length	: 110 cm (43.3")
Barrel length	: 65 cm (25.6"), incl. muzzle damper
Weight	: 5.0 kg (11.0 lb.), excl. optical sight
Sight	: none; special optical sight mounting
Safety	: safety catch on left-hand side of receiver housing, behind pistol grip, drop safety
Stock	: special skeleton stock

Action	: recoil-action
Cocking system	: cocking lever
Firing system	: semi-automatic
Locking system	: inertia lock
Length	: 76.2 cm (30")
Barrel length	: 40.9 cm (16.1")
Weight	: 2.1 kg (4.6 lb.)
Sight	: folding aperture sight; hooded front sight is adjustable
Safety	: safety catch on left-hand side of receiver housing, above pistol grip: blocks lever, hammer, and trigger bar
Stock	: steel tube stock with synthetic stock sleeve and forearm

PARTICULARS
Can use double-row detachable magazines of various makes of pistol (Smith & Wesson, Glock, Beretta). Folded, the carbine has a length of only 40.4 cm (15.9").

Keppeler

The company of Keppeler & Fritz was founded by Dieter Keppeler and has its

Keppeler KS III Bullpup Sniper

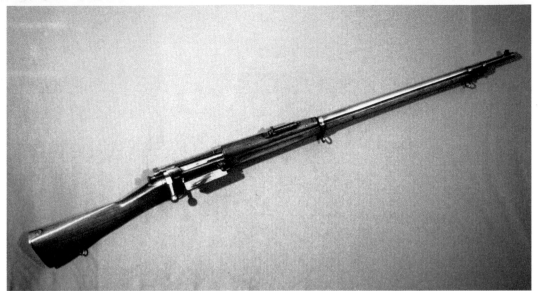

PARTICULARS
Matt blued; a bipod can be fitted to the underside of the forearm.

Krag-Jorgensen

The Krag-Jorgensen rifle was developed about 1885 by Ole Krag and Erik Jorgensen. Krag was a captain in the Norwegian army, and Jorgensen an armament engineer at the Norwegian state arsenal. In 1889, the rifle was introduced in the Danish army, using the 8 x 58R caliber. The United States purchased the weapon in 1892 with a slightly modified loading gate on the right-hand side of the weapon. The gate on the first model was hinged to open forwards.
The American version – and the model also later supplied to the Norwegian army – have the gate hinged at the lower edge, allowing it to open vertically. The advantage of this arrangement being that the rounds were less prone to drop from the weapon before the gate could be closed after loading. The US version, using the .30-40R caliber, was manufactured under license by the Springfield Armory at Springfield, Massachusetts, during 1894-

1897. The Krag-Jorgensen rifle shown is a Norwegian army model, chambered for 6.5 x 55 mm.
A large number of this basic model were manufactured as standard rifle, various carbine models, and two types of sniper rifle.

Krag-Jorgensen M1889/1894

SPECIFICATIONS

Caliber	: 6.5 x 55 mm
Magazine	: blind magazine
Cartridge capacity	: 5 rounds
Magazine catch	: N/A
Action	: bolt-action
Cocking system	: bolt lever
Firing system	: single round
Locking system	: single lug on front of bolt and slot in receiver for bolt lever
Length	: 127 cm (50")
Barrel length	: 76 cm (30")
Weight	: 4.1 kg (9 lb.)
Sight	: tangent rear sight
Safety	: wing-type catch on rear of bolt
Stock	: wooden stock and forearm

PARTICULARS
Based on the M1889 Krag-Jorgensen rifle. Manufactured for Denmark in 8 x 58R caliber, and in the USA by Springfield in .30-40R caliber.

Krico

Krico is the brand name of the German company, A. Kriegeskorte GmbH. The company has its offices at Fürth-Stadeln, near Nuremberg in Bavaria.

The company has a long history, trailing back to the year 1878, when Robert Kriegeskorte founded the Junghans & Kriegeskorte company. At the time, the company was located at Esslingen am Zollberg, starting out as wholesalers of gunpowder, dynamite, ammunition, and firearms.

In 1918, the founder's son, Max Kriegeskorte, took over the company. After the First World War, arms production and trade were curtailed, which is why, during the 1918 to 1928 period, Kriegeskorte also manufactured bicycle frames. At the end of the Second World War, the company ran into trouble when the production of arms was prohibited by the Allies. So Kriegeskorte switched to the

Krico, logo

production of household appliances. It wasn't until 1950 that the company received permission for the production of air rifles, and a year later, for smallbore rifles.

In 1954 the manufacture of hunting rifles in .22 Hornet and .222 Remington calibers, in the system-400, was taken up. In 1963 the system-600 and system-700 were developed for heavier calibers.

Krico Model 600-Sniper

SPECIFICATIONS

Caliber	: .222 Rem., .223 Rem., .22-250 Rem., .243 Win., .308 Win.
Magazine	: detachable magazine
Cartridge capacity	: 3-4 or separate 5-rounds detachable magazine
Magazine catch	: right-hand centre of magazine slot
Repeating system	: bolt-action
Firing system	: single round
Locking system	: 2-lug bolt
Length	: 116 cm (45.7")
Barrel length	: 60 cm (23.6")
Weight	: 5 kg (11.0 lb.) incl. optical sight
Sight	: Schmidt + Bender special sniper scope: 1.5-6 x 42 or 2.5-10 x 56 or 3-12 x 56
Safety	: safety catch on right-hand side of receiver
Stock	: walnut, special sniper stock with adjustable cheek piece

PARTICULARS

Barrel and receiver shot-blasted matt black, various trigger systems: German Setter (150-200 g), crisp trigger system (1000 g), match trigger (adjustable: 500-800 g); barrel with flash suppresser.

LAR Grizzly 50 Big Bore Competitor Rifle

Lar

LAR Grizzly 50 Big Bore Competitor Rifle

The American company of L.A.R. Manufacturing Inc., from West Jordan in the
state of Utah, was founded in 1968 and
was primarily a supplier of components to
other arms manufacturers. Among other
things, the company produced tripods for
various types of machine-gun for the US
armed forces, and parts for the M-16 army
rifle.

The company became famous for its Grizzly Magnum pistols chambered for .44
Magnum, .45 Winchester Magnum, and
even .50 Magnum (Action Express). Some
years ago, the increasing interest in heavy
long-range rifles using the .50 BMG
(Browning machine-gun) caliber made
LAR decide to market such a weapon, the
Big Bore Competitor. The US Army
initially took a great interest in this type of
rifle, since it required a sniper rifle for
ranges of 3000 yards and over for use in
the Gulf War.

Later, demand in the civilian sector also
boomed. In the America's, match shooting
with this type of weapon is not exceptional.

LAR, logo

SPECIFICATIONS

Caliber	: .50 BMG
Magazine	: none
Cartridge capacity	: single round
Magazine catch	: N/A
Action	: bolt-action
Cocking system	: bolt lever
Firing system	: single round
Locking system	: 2 heavy bolt lugs
Length	: 115.6 cm (45.5"), incl. muzzle brake
Barrel length	: 91.4 cm (36")
Weight	: 13.8 kg (30.4 lb.)
Sight	: none; suitable for sight mounting
Safety	: ambidextrous safety catch on pistol grip
Stock	: steel with rubber butt

PARTICULARS

Matt black phosphate finish; bipod. Effective range 3000 meters (3280 yd). The
large weight (mass) of the weapon and the
special muzzle damper substantially
reduce the heavy recoil.

Lee-Enfield

The name Enfield derives from the British
state arsenal at Enfield Lock along the
river Lea. The arsenal was established in
1804 for the assembly of Brown Bess flintlock muskets for the British infantry. The
components for these weapons were
mostly being manufactured in small
private workshops in Birmingham and
London.

In 1840, George Lovell was appointed
Government Inspector of Small Arms at
the arsenal. He reorganized the arsenal
into a large arms factory. In 1852 the

British government decided to replace the various types of flintlock and percussion rifles in use by the army with a new weapon. Several arms manufacturers were invited to develop prototypes. Following extensive testing, a new rifle was selected, the Rifle Musket Pattern 1853. The weapon was also known as the Enfield 3-groove on account of the three lands and grooves of the barrel rifling. The production was assigned to Enfield. The British army had been wanting a breech-loading rifle for some years. In 1867 it was decided to convert the existing Pattern 1853 rifle to breech loading. For this purpose, the weapon was fitted with a tilting bolt based on the American Snider system. This converted weapon was designated Enfield Snider.

In 1869 a special commission of the War Office decided to introduce another type of army rifle, the Martini-Henry. This weapon features the vertically sliding block invented by the Swiss designer, Friedrich von Martini. The barrel of the weapon was developed by Alexander Henry from Edinburgh. In 1871 the rifle was issued to the British army and navy. In 1888, the Enfield works took up production of a bolt-action rifle with a Lee magazine.

The weapon was issued to the British troops in 1889 as the Magazine Rifle Mark 1. A barrel redesign two years later caused the name to be changed to Lee-Metford. When the rifling changed in 1895, the weapon was renamed to Lee-Enfield. Based on the experience gained with the weapon in South Africa in the fight against the Boers, the weapon was extensively modified. The new rifle resulting from this operation (1902), was called the Short Magazine Lee-Enfield or SMLE, and today is known simply as the No. 1 rifle. In 1907 a new type of SMLE rifle was introduced in the British army, based on the No. 1 rifle.

This weapon is known as the Lee-Enfield Mark III. It is heavier than the No. 1 and has a magazine catch that enables the magazine follower to be blocked, turning the rifle into a single-shot weapon in which each round has to be loaded manually. In 1910 Enfield developed a new army rifle using the experimental .276 caliber. After the usual testing, the rifle was to be taking into production in 1914, but the outbreak of the First World War prevented this. The design was manufactured for Britain in the United States using the tried and trusted .303 British caliber. This rifle is known as the Pattern 1914 Enfield Rifle, sometimes called the No. 3 Rifle or P14.

At the time, the SMLE was still being manufactured at Enfield. During the 1914 to 1918 period, over two million SMLE rifles were produced for the front. For the British army, the weapon was manufactured by Winchester, Remington and Eddystone chambered for the .303 British ammunition.

The US version, using the .30-06 caliber, was issued to the US troops as the US M1917, P17 for short. After the war, Enfield developed two more types of SMLE rifles, the Mark V and the Mark VI, but these models were never produced in large numbers. In 1926 the name of the No. 1 Mark III rifle was officially changed to Rifle No. 1, Mark III. Also, the name of another type of rifle, the No. 1, Mark VI, was changed to No. 4, Mark I. In this rifle, the follower interrupter was dispensed with. At the outbreak of the Second World War a new rifle, the No. 4 Rifle, was introduced.

This weapon was not manufactured by Enfield, but by various other British arms factories, such as BSA of Birmingham, Fazackerley in Lancashire, and Maltby in Yorkshire. This was because Enfield were fully occupied with the production of the Bren machine-gun, the Sten sub-machine-gun, and the .38 Enfield revolver. The Allies decided to have the No. 4 rifle manufactured in the United States by Savage Arms, and in Canada at Long Branch.

For production reasons, this type differs slightly from the English model, which is why it is designated the No. 4 Rifle, Mark I*. In 1942 the first sniper rifle was introduced under the name No. 4 Rifle Mark 1 (T). The 'T' stands for Telescopic. The No. 4 rifle featured a triple magnification optical sight, originally developed for the Bren gun. This optical sight was designated the

Lee-Enfield No. 1, Mark I (SMLE)

Lee-Enfield No. 1, Mark III (SMLE)

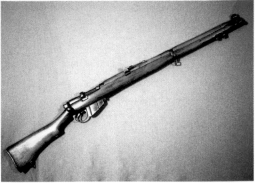

No. 32, Mark 1, succeeded in 1943 by the No. 32, Mark 2, and replaced in 1944 by the No. 32, Mark 3 with improved adjustment and a wider field of view. In 1943 a shortened version of the Lee-Enfield No. 4, Mark I was introduced as the No. 5 Mk I, better known as the Jungle carbine. This weapon was manufactured mainly by BSA and Fazackerley. In 1970 the last sniper version based on the Lee-Enfield rifle was produced.

This is the L42 A1, caliber 7.62 x 51 mm NATO. This weapon was used primarily by the British SAS in Northern Ireland and during the 1982 Falkland War.

Lee-Enfield No. 1, Mark I (SMLE)

SPECIFICATIONS

Caliber	: .303 British
Magazine	: detachable magazine
Cartridge capacity	: 10 rounds
Magazine catch	: on front of magazine
Action	: bolt-action
Cocking system	: bolt lever
Firing system	: single round
Locking system	: bolt lugs at the rear of the bolt
Length	: 113 cm (44.5")
Barrel length	: 64 cm (25.19")
Weight	: 3.7 kg (8.12 lb.)
Sight	: tangent rear sight
Safety	: wing-type catch on rear of bolt
Stock	: wooden stock and continuous forearm

PARTICULARS

Special magazine catch to block magazine follower, for manual loading of rounds.

Lee-Enfield No. 1, Mark III (SMLE)

SPECIFICATIONS

Caliber	: .303 British
Magazine	: detachable magazine
Cartridge capacity	: 10 rounds
Magazine catch	: on front of magazine
Action	: bolt-action
Cocking system	: bolt lever
Firing system	: single round
Locking system	: bolt lugs at the rear of the bolt
Length	: 113 cm (44.5")
Barrel length	: 64 cm (25.19")
Weight	: 3.9 kg (8.62 lb.)
Sight	: tangent rear sight
Safety	: wing-type catch on rear of bolt
Stock	: wooden stock and continuous forearm

PARTICULARS

Special magazine catch to block magazine follower, for manual loading of rounds. The weapon has a socket on the receiver for cartridge clips.

Lee-Enfield No. 4, Mark I (SMLE)

SPECIFICATIONS

Caliber	: .303 British
Magazine	: detachable magazine
Cartridge capacity	: 10 rounds
Magazine catch	: on front of magazine
Action	: bolt-action
Cocking system	: bolt lever
Firing system	: single round
Locking system	: bolt lugs at the rear of the bolt
Length	: 113 cm (44.5")
Barrel length	: 64 cm (25.2")
Weight	: 4 kg (8.8 lb.)
Sight	: flip-up sight

Lee-Enfield No. 4, Mark I (SMLE)

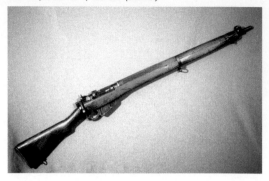

Safety	: wing-type catch on rear of bolt
Stock	: wooden stock and continuous forearm

PARTICULARS

The weapon has a socket on the receiver for cartridge clips. The barrel features a bayonet lug.

Lee-Enfield Pattern 14 Rifle P14

SPECIFICATIONS

Caliber	: .303 British
Magazine	: blind magazine
Cartridge capacity:	5 rounds
Magazine catch	: N/A
Action	: bolt-action
Cocking system	: bolt lever
Firing system	: single round
Locking system	: bolt lugs at the rear of the bolt
Length	: 117.5 cm (46.25")
Barrel length	: 66 cm (26")
Weight	: 4.4 kg (9.62 lb.)
Sight	: aperture sight
Safety	: wing-type catch on rear of bolt
Stock	: wooden stock and continuous forearm

Lee-Enfield Pattern 14 Rifle P14

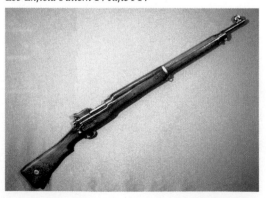

PARTICULARS

Manufactured in the United States during the First World War. The US version is the US M1917 (P17), caliber .30-06 Springfield.

Lee-Enfield No. 5 Mk1 Jungle carbine

SPECIFICATIONS

Caliber	: .303 British
Magazine	: detachable magazine
Cartridge capacity:	10 rounds
Magazine catch	: on front of magazine
Action	: bolt-action
Cocking system	: bolt lever
Firing system	: single round
Locking system	: bolt lugs at the rear of the bolt
Length	: 100.3 cm (39.5")
Barrel length	: 47.5 cm (18.7")
Weight	: 3.2 kg (7.15 lb.)
Sight	: aperture sight
Safety	: wing-type catch on rear of bolt
Stock	: wooden stock

PARTICULARS

Carbine model of the No. 4 Mark I rifle.

Lee-Enfield Bren Gun Light machine-gun Mark 2

SPECIFICATIONS

Caliber	: .303 British
Magazine	: detachable magazine
Cartridge capacity:	30-round detachable magazine or 100-round drum

Lee-Enfield No. 5 Mk1 Jungle carbine

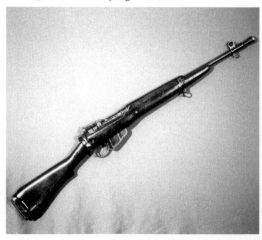

Lee-Enfield Brengun Light Machine Gun Mark 2

Lee-Enfield Stengun Mark II

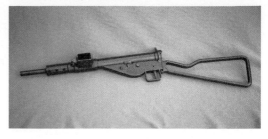

Magazine catch	: on front of magazine slot
Action	: gas pressure
Cocking system	: cocking lever
Firing system	: full- and semi-automatic
Locking system	: vertically sliding block (upwards)
Length	: 115.8 cm (45.6")
Barrel length	: 63.5 cm (25")
Weight	: 8.8 kg (19.3 lb.)
Sight	: tangent rear sight
Safety	: sliding catch on left-hand side, doubles as firing mode selector
Stock	: wooden stock

PARTICULARS

Produced in England and Canada. Gas pressure adjustment underneath gas block with four positions. The weapon has a carrying handle, also used for quick barrel changes.

Lee-Enfield Stengun Mark II

SPECIFICATIONS

Caliber	: 9 mm Para
Magazine	: detachable magazine
Cartridge capacity	: 32 rounds
Magazine catch	: push-button on side of magazine housing
Action	: recoil
Cocking system	: cocking lever
Firing system	: semi- and fully automatic
Locking system	: inertia lock
Length	: 76.2 cm (30")
Barrel length	: 19.7 cm (7.75")
Weight	: 3 kg (6.6 lb.)
Sight	: simple rear sight
Safety	: cocking lever can be locked in recess of breech block housing
Stock	: detachable steel skeleton stock

PARTICULARS

Developed by R.V. Shepperd and H.J. Turpin. The letters S and T were combined with the first part of the name Enfield to form the word Sten.
It was produced by BSA, Royal Ordnance, and in Canada.

Lee-Enfield Stengun Mark V

SPECIFICATIONS

Caliber	: 9 mm Para
Magazine	: detachable magazine
Cartridge capacity	: 32 rounds
Magazine catch	: push-button on side of magazine housing
Action	: recoil
Cocking system	: cocking lever
Firing system	: semi- and fully automatic
Locking system	: inertia lock
Length	: 76.2 cm (30")
Barrel length	: 19.8 cm (7.8")
Weight	: 3.9 kg (8.5 lb.)
Sight	: simple rearsight and winged front sight
Safety	: cocking lever can be locked in recess of breech block housing
Stock	: wooden stock, pistol grip and extra pistol grip

PARTICULARS

Developed by R.V. Shepperd and H.J. Turpin. The letters S and T were combined with the first part of the name Enfield to

Lee-Enfield Stengun Mark V

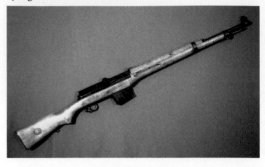

form the word Sten. The Mark V was developed in 1944 and remained in service until 1953.

Lee-Enfield L42 A1 Sniper

SPECIFICATIONS

Caliber : 7.62 x 51 mm
Magazine : detachable magazine
Cartridge capacity: 10 rounds
Magazine catch : in front of magazine slot
Action : bolt-action
Cocking system : bolt lever
Firing system : single round
Locking system : bolt lugs at the rear of the bolt
Length : 118 cm (46.5")
Barrel length : 69.8 (27.5")
Weight : 5.7 kg (12.6 lb.)
Sight : optical sight
Safety : wing-type catch on rear of bolt
Stock : wooden stock with cheek piece

PARTICULARS
Sniper rifle, based on the No. 4 Mark I, came into service in 1970.

Ljungmann

The Swedish Ljungmann AG42 rifle was designed in 1941 by Erik Eklund using the Ljungmann gas pressure system. The diverted gas pressure does not act on a piston and piston rod, but acts directly on the breech lock to cause the repeating action.
At the time it was a new system. Later adopted for use in the French Mas 1949 and AR-10, and Stoner's AR15/M16 rifles. A prototype was presented to the Swedish army as early as 1942. In practice, the rifle proved sensitive to dirt and gunpowder

residue, so a modified version, the AG42B, was developed and introduced in the Swedish army in 1953. The modifications included a stainless steel gas tube and a modified trigger system. In Denmark, the weapon was produced for a short time by Madsen. However, the Danish army showed no interest, so production there was halted. A derived model was manufactured in Egypt under the designation Hakim using the 8 x 57 mm Mauser caliber.

Ljungmann Model AG42B

SPECIFICATIONS

Caliber : 6.5 x 55 mm
Magazine : detachable magazine
Cartridge capacity: 10 rounds
Magazine catch : to rear of magazine slot
Action : gas pressure
Cocking system : cocking lever
Firing system : semi-automatic
Locking system : rotating bolt head
Length : 121.5 cm (47.8")
Barrel length : 62.3 cm (24.5")
Weight : 4.7 kg (10.4 lb.)
Sight : tangent rear sight
Safety : on rear of receiver
Stock : wooden stock and forearm

PARTICULARS
Exceptional design for its time. Special flash suppresser.
Features a rubber buffer on the right-hand side near the ejection port to assist ejection.

MagTech

The Brazilian armament and ammunition factory Companhia Brasileira de Cartuchos (CBC) is located in Sao Paulo. Using the MagTech trade name, the company manufactures pump-action shotguns and smallbore rifles.

In 1926 the Italian immigrant family Matarazzo founded the Companhia Brasileira Cartucheria, producing mainly shot cartridges for the home market. In a few decades, the company grew into a large concern exporting ammunition to a large number of countries. The American Remington Arms Company and the British ICI (Imperial Chemical Industries) concern owned CBC during the 1936 to 1979 period.

In 1979 the company was taken over by the Arbi & Imbel group, two large industrial companies in Brazil with operations in tourism, steel production, and the manufacture of arms and ammunition. The company name was changed to Companhia Brasileira de Cartuchos (CBC).

A subsidiary, the S.A. Marvin, which has its offices at Nova Iguacu near Rio the Janeiro, produces the brass cartridge cases for CBC ammunition. In 1991 and 1992 the company saw some extensive reorga-

nizations. Under the leadership of famous German ammunition specialist Charles von Helle, and with the help of a number of German laboratories, the entire ammunition production was modernized. MagTech do a lot of product development and have several 400 metro firing ranges for testing ammunition and weapons. The company exports about 80% of its production of ammunition and weapons to countries all over the world.

MagTech MT 586.2P

SPECIFICATIONS

Caliber	: 12/76 (3")
Magazine	: tubular magazine
Cartridge capacity	: 8 rounds
Magazine catch	: N/A
Action	: pump-action
Cocking system	: forearm
Firing system	: single round
Locking system	: vertically sliding block
Length	: 99.7 cm (39.25")
Barrel length	: 48.3 cm (19")
Weight	: 3.3 kg (7.3 lb.)
Sight	: bead
Safety	: push-button in rear of trigger guard
Stock	: Brazilian hardwood, with pistol grip

PARTICULARS

Chrome molybdenum barrels, blued. The Model 586.2P (top) and Model 586.2PG (bottom) are shown.

MagTech MT 586.2PG

SPECIFICATIONS

Caliber	: 12/76 (3")
Magazine	: tubular magazine
Cartridge capacity	: 8 rounds
Magazine catch	: N/A
Action	: pump-action

Magtech, logo

Magtech MT 586.2P

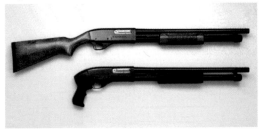

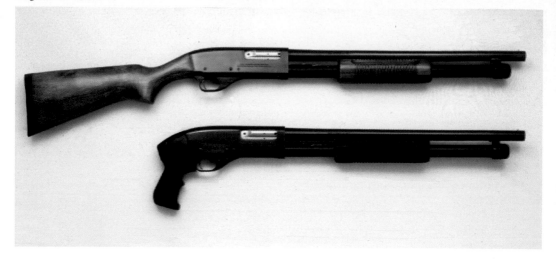

Cocking system	: forearm
Firing system	: single round
Locking system	: vertically sliding block
Length	: 74.3 cm (29.25")
Barrel length	: 48.3 cm (19")
Weight	: 3.0 kg (6.6 lb.)
Sight	: bead
Safety	: push-button in rear of trigger guard
Stock	: with synthetic pistol grip only

PARTICULARS
Chromium molybdenum barrels, blued. The Model 586.2P (top) and Model 586.2PG (bottom) are shown.

MAS/FAMAS

Most of the French armament industry is concentrated in three industrial areas lending the arms factories their names. In alphabetical order, they are:
- MAB Manufacture d'Armes de Bayonne;
- MAC Manufacture d'Armes de Chatellerault;
- MAS Manufacture d'Armes de Saint Etienne.

Of these, MAS is the best known because it has produced the greatest number of armament types. The MAS M1936 rifle has a modified Mauser blind magazine. The interesting thing about this is that the locking lugs are located at the rear of the bolt. Also, the rifle has no safety system. The MAS M1936/51 is a rifle with a special device for firing rifle grenades. In addition to a folding grenade sight, the weapon also features an adjustment screw for various grenade models. The MAS M1949 is a semi-automatic rifle operating on the gas pressure principle. The gas pressure does not act through a piston and link rod, but acts directly on the breech block.

The recent rifle model of the French army, the FAMAS, was developed during the seventies of the twentieth century as a successor to the MAS 1949. The FAMAS uses the so-called bullpup design. The repeating mechanism uses the Kiraly delayed recoil system. The recoil force of the fired round is received by a bolt lever that locks to the receiver housing. As the lever tilts, the breech block is unlocked and pushed backwards. The flash suppresser is suitable for attaching rifle grenades.

The nickname of this weapon, a combination of a rifle and carbine, is 'le Clarion' (the trumpet). Most of the old French army rifles from before the Second World War use the 8 mm Lebel caliber. After the war, the later models were manufactured to use the former French standard caliber, 7.5 x 54 mm. The FAMAS uses the standard NATO 5.56 x 45 mm or .223 Remington caliber.

MAS/Chatellerault Model 1924 M29

SPECIFICATIONS
Caliber : 7.5 x 54 mm
Magazine : detachable magazine
Cartridge capacity: 25 rounds
Magazine catch : to rear of magazine slot (on top of housing)
Action : gas pressure
Cocking system : cocking lever
Firing system : semi- and fully automatic
Locking system : vertically sliding block
Length : 108.2 cm (42.6")
Barrel length : 50 cm (19.7")
Weight : 11.1 kg (25.5 lb.)
Sight : tangent rear sight
Safety : rotary catch on trigger guard, above triggers
Stock : wooden stock

PARTICULARS
Folding bipod. Trigger system with two triggers: the front trigger is for semi-automatic fire, and the rear trigger for fully automatic fire.
The machine-gun is similar in appearance to the Browning Automatic Rifle (BAR).

MAS Model 1936

SPECIFICATIONS
Caliber : 7.5 x 54 mm M29
Magazine : blind magazine
Cartridge capacity: 5 rounds
Magazine catch : N/A
Action : bolt-action
Cocking system : bolt lever
Firing system : single round
Locking system : bolt lugs
Length : 102 cm (40.1")
Barrel length : 57 cm (22.6")

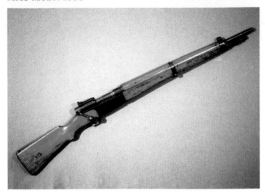

Weight : 3.8 kg (8.3 lb.)
Sight : tangent rear sight
Safety : none
Stock : wooden stock

PARTICULARS
A French army rifle supplied to the French troops from 1936 into the fifties of the twentieth century.

MAS Model 1936/51

SPECIFICATIONS
Caliber : 7.5 x 54 mm M29
Magazine : blind magazine
Cartridge capacity: 5 rounds
Magazine catch : N/A
Action : bolt-action
Cocking system : bolt lever
Firing system : single round
Locking system : bolt lugs
Length : 102 cm (40.1")
Barrel length : 57 cm (22.6")
Weight : 3.8 kg (8.3 lb.)
Sight : tangent rear sight

MAS Model 1936/51

217

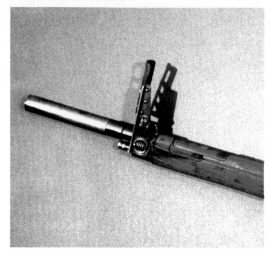

Safety   : none
Stock   : wooden stock

PARTICULARS
Successor to the French M1936 army rifle with a device for launching rifle grenades and with a special folding grenade sight.

MAS Model 1938 sub-machine-gun

MAS Model 1938 Sub-machine-gun

SPECIFICATIONS

Caliber   : 7.65 mm Long
Magazine   : detachable magazine
Cartridge capacity : 32 rounds
Magazine catch   : push-button on left-hand side of magazine housing
Action   : recoil
Cocking system   : cocking lever on right-hand side of receiver housing
Firing system   : fully automatic
Locking system   : inertia lock
Length   : 63 cm (24.8")
Barrel length   : 22.4 cm (8.8")
Weight   : 2.9 kg (6.3 lb.)
Sight   : flip-up sight
Safety   : trigger folds forward so it cannot be pressed
Stock   : wooden stock containing the main spring

PARTICULARS
Breech block angles slightly upwards relative to barrel. Wide ring on left-hand side of receiver housing as carrying sling swivel. This is a simplistic design.

MAS Model 1949

SPECIFICATIONS

Caliber   : 7.5 x 54 mm M29
Magazine   : detachable magazine
Cartridge capacity : 10 rounds
Magazine catch   : on right-hand side of magazine housing
Action   : gas pressure
Cocking system   : cocking lever
Firing system   : semi-automatic
Locking system   : vertically sliding block
Length   : 101 cm (39.8")
Barrel length   : 52.1 cm (20.5")
Weight   : 3.9 kg (8.6 lb.)

MAS Model 1949

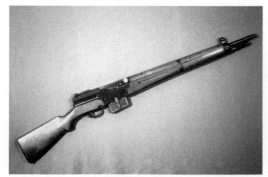

Sight	: tangent rear sight
Safety	: push-button at front of trigger guard
Stock	: wooden stock, forearm and hand grip

PARTICULARS
Direct gas pressure action on breech block. Some models feature a circular sling ring swivel on the right-hand side of the barrel band.
The weapon has a synthetic sleeve on the cocking lever.

FAMAS

SPECIFICATIONS

Caliber	: 5.56 x 45 mm NATO (.223 Rem.)
Magazine	: detachable magazine
Cartridge capacity	: 25 rounds
Magazine catch	: in front of magazine housing
Action	: gas pressure
Cocking system	: cocking lever
Firing system	: semi-automatic, fully automatic, and 3-shot burst
Locking system	: drop/lever bolt (Kiraly system)
Length	: 75.7 cm (29.8")
Barrel length	: 48.8 cm (19.2")

FAMAS

FAMAS

Weight	: 3.6 kg (7.96 lb.)
Sight	: adjustable aperture sight in carrying handle
Safety	: on front of trigger guard
Stock	: synthetic bullpup stock

PARTICULARS
Quick conversion for left-handed users. Model FAMAS F1 has rifle grenade rings around the forward part of the barrel and a folding bipod. The G1 is shown below as carbine version with an enlarged trigger guard.

Mauser

The founder of the famous Mauser arms factory, Peter Paul Mauser, was born in 1838 in Oderndorf on the Neckar in the German federal state of Würtenberg. His father, Franz Andreas Mauser, worked as a master rifle maker at the town's state arsenal. In 1859 Peter Paul Mauser was drafted for national service and detached to the artillery. His first invention was a breech-loading cannon, which did not meet with any interest from the military, however.
In 1865 he developed his first bolt-action rifle. The bolt of this rifle had a spring-loaded firing pin that was driven from the bolt by means of the trigger and sear. This proved a major improvement over other designs with a fixed firing pin which often resulted in the accidental firing of a round before the weapon had been fully locked. Based on his prototype, Paul Mauser received financial support to developed equipment and materials for the government. This is how the Mauser company

MAUSER

was born. Paul's brother Wilhelm was attracted by the commercial activities. At the time, neither Germany nor the bordering countries had any need for a new army rifle, which was a problem. In 1866 the Mauser brothers met an agent of the Remington Arms Company, Samuel Norris, who saw a future for the Mauser design. The rifles were to be produced in the arms factories at Liege in Belgium and in the United States.

This led to the Mauser-Norris rifle, which was introduced in 1867. Norris hoped to be able to sell the weapon to the French army, which wanted to replace the Chassepot rifle, but France preferred a weapon from within its own borders, and the Remington management were no longer prepared to support the project. In 1871 the rifle was selected by the Prussian army and introduced to the armed forces under the designation M71.

The rifle fired a black powder cartridge of 11.15 x 60R caliber. In 1873 the Oderndorf state arsenal was sold to Mauser & Co., providing them with a production facility. The rifle was also produced under license at Erfurt, Spandau, Amberg, Danzig, and by Steyr in Austria. Wilhelm Mauser died in 1882, after which the company was turned into the Waffenfabrik Mauser AG. In the same year a new M71 type was developed with a tubular magazine for eight rounds, the M71/84, which was followed by a model M87 in 1887 in 9.5 mm caliber for the Turkish army.

In 1888 the Gewehr 88 or Kommissionsgewehr was produced for the German army in 7.92 mm caliber because the army command were dissatisfied with the tubular magazine M71 rifle. In 1889 the Belgian army decided to switch to the Mauser rifle, which was manufactured under license by the FN factories in 7.65 Mauser caliber. The Spanish army also wanted this weapon, but in caliber 7 mm

(7 x 57 mm). This proved to be such an outstanding weapon for its time that it caused the Americans quite a bit of trouble during the Spanish-American war of 1898. The US Army decided to commission Springfield Armory to develop a similar rifle, the Springfield M1903. This weapon turned out to be so similar to the Mauser design that the US government was forced to pay Mauser a patent compensation of $200,000. In 1889 the German army decided to introduce the Model 1898 rifle developed by Mauser as the Gewehr 98, using the 7.92 Mauser caliber. Shorter versions of this rifle were subsequently named Kar-98a in 1904, Kar-98b (after the First World War), and Kar-98k in 1935. All in all, over 200 different versions are known to exist, apart from the many variants of hunting rifle in various calibers from .22 Long Rifle up to 9.3 x 57 mm. The Mauser 98 rifle will not be discussed in detail in this book. Good books on the subject are Mauser Military Rifles of the World by R.W.D. Ball, Sniper Variations of the German K98K Rifle by R.D. Law, and Mauser Carbine 98K by R.D. Law.

In 1914 Paul Mauser died, and in 1922 the name of the company was changed to Mauser Werke AG. After the Second World War, when the weapon production ban imposed by the allied forces had been lifted, the company restarted under the name Mauser Werke Oderndorf Waffensysteme GmbH.

Mauser Commissiegewehr Model 1888

SPECIFICATIONS

Caliber	: 8 x 57 I (.318" ball)
Magazine	: blind magazine
Cartridge capacity:	5 rounds (Mannlicher clip)
Magazine catch	: N/A
Action	: bolt-action
Cocking system	: bolt lever
Firing system	: single round
Locking system	: 2-lug bolt
Length	: 124 cm (48.9")
Barrel length	: 74 cm (29.1")
Weight	: 3.9 kg (8.6 lb.)
Sight	: tangent rear sight
Safety	: wing-type safety catch on rear of bolt
Stock	: walnut

Mauser Commissie rifle Model 1888

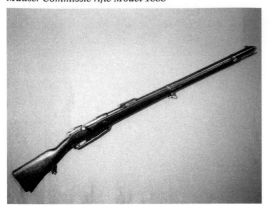

Mauser Model K98

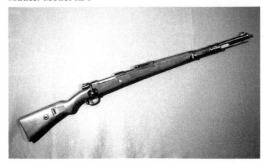

commemorate the 100th anniversary of the Mauser 98 system. A total of 1998 rifles of this series were manufactured.

PARTICULARS
Blued barrel and receiver. No wooden hand grip, but barrel with metal protective tube, running from receiver to muzzle.

Mauser Model Gewehr 98

SPECIFICATIONS

Caliber	: 8 x 57 IS
Magazine	: blind magazine
Cartridge capacity	: 5 rounds
Magazine catch	: N/A
Action	: bolt-action
Cocking system	: bolt lever
Firing system	: single round
Locking system	: 2-lug bolt
Length	: 125 cm (49.2")
Barrel length	: 74 cm (29.1")
Weight	: 4.1 kg (9 lb.)
Sight	: tangent rear sight (400-2000 meters/1312 ft–2187 yd)
Safety	: wing-type safety catch on rear of bolt
Stock	: walnut

PARTICULARS
Blued barrel and receiver. The illustration shows a special limited model issued to

Mauser Model Gewehr 98

Mauser Model K98

SPECIFICATIONS

Caliber	: 8 x 57 IS
Magazine	: blind magazine
Cartridge capacity	: 5 rounds
Magazine catch	: N/A
Action	: bolt-action
Cocking system	: bolt lever
Firing system	: single round
Locking system	: 2-lug bolt
Length	: 112 cm (44.1")
Barrel length	: 61 cm (24")
Weight	: 3.8 kg (8.4 lb.)
Sight	: tangent rear sight
Safety	: wing-type safety catch on rear of bolt
Stock	: walnut

PARTICULARS
Blued barrel and receiver. The illustration shows a detail of a cutaway Mauser K98 instruction model.

Mauser Model K98 (instructiemodel)

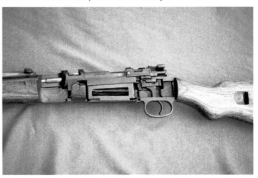

Mauser Model 86SR (Sniper Rifle)

SPECIFICATIONS

Caliber	: .308 Win.
Magazine	: detachable magazine
Cartridge capacity	: 9 rounds
Magazine catch	: right-hand side of magazine slot
Action	: bolt-action
Cocking system	: bolt lever
Firing system	: single round
Locking system	: 2-lug bolt
Length	: 127 cm (50")
Barrel length	: 75 cm (29.5"), incl. flash suppresser
Weight	: 6.2 kg (13.7 lb.)
Sight	: none; special sight mounting
Safety	: wing-type catch to rear of bolt
Stock	: matt black laminate stock with thumb hole and pistol grip, adjustable cheek and butt.

PARTICULARS

Mounting rail in forearm for bipod.

Mauser Model SR 93 Sniper

SPECIFICATIONS

Caliber	: .300 Win. Mag.
Magazine	: blind magazine
Cartridge capacity	: 5 rounds
Magazine catch	: N/A
Action	: bolt-action
Cocking system	: bolt lever
Firing system	: single round
Locking system	: 2-lug bolt
Length	: 123 cm (48.4")
Barrel length	: 60 cm (23.6") incl. muzzle damper
Weight	: 6.3 kg (13.9 lb.)
Sight	: none; special sight mounting

Mauser Model SR 93 Sniper

Safety	: ambidextrous safety catch above trigger
Stock	: special skeleton stock of magnesium and aluminium; bolt lever can be changed to right-hand side.

PARTICULARS

Integrated bipod; adjustable cheek and butt. Special sniper rifle for ranges up to 800 meters (874 yd).

Mauser Model SR 94 Professional

SPECIFICATIONS

Caliber	: .308 Win. of .300 Win. Mag.
Magazine	: blind magazine
Cartridge capacity	: 5 of 3 rounds (.300 WM)
Magazine catch	: N/A

Mauser Model SR 94 Professional

Action	: bolt-action
Cocking system	: bolt lever
Firing system	: single round
Locking system	: 6-lug bolt
Length	: 115.8 of 120.8 cm (45.6 of 47.6") incl. muzzle damper
Barrel length	: 68 of 73 cm (26.8 of 28.7") incl. muzzle damper
Weight	: 4.5 kg (9.9 lb.) without optical sight
Sight	: none; special sight mounting
Safety	: safety catch on left-hand side behind bolt lever
Stock	: laminate stock with rail in forearm for bipod or hand support; adjustable cheek and butt.

PARTICULARS
Matt black barrel and receiver.

Mauser Model SR 94 Sniper

SPECIFICATIONS

Caliber	: .308 Win.
Magazine	: blind magazine
Cartridge capacity:	4 rounds
Magazine catch	: N/A
Action	: bolt-action
Cocking system	: bolt lever
Firing system	: single round
Locking system	: 6-lug bolt
Length	: 115 cm (45.3")
Barrel length	: 60 cm (23.6")
Weight	: 4.5 kg (9.9 lb.)
Sight	: none; special sight mounting
Safety	: safety catch on left-hand side behind bolt lever
Stock	: synthetic stock with rail in forearm for bipod or hand support

PARTICULARS
Matt black barrel and receiver.

Mauser Model 96 Varmint

SPECIFICATIONS

Caliber	: .308 Win., .300 Win. Mag. (en .243 Win.)

Mauser Model SR 94 Sniper

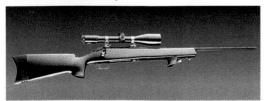

Mauser Model 96 Varmint

Magazine	: detachable magazine
Cartridge capacity:	.308: 3 of 5; .300: 2 or 4 rounds
Magazine catch	: lower left-hand side, near magazine
Action	: bolt-action
Cocking system	: bolt lever
Firing system	: single round
Locking system	: 16-lug bolt
Length	: 115 cm (45.3")
Barrel length	: 65 cm (25.6")
Weight	: 3.4 kg (7.5 lb.) without optical sight
Sight	: none; special sight mounting
Safety	: sliding catch on stock neck
Stock	: black synthetic stock

PARTICULARS
Matt black barrel and receiver. Straight backwards bolt repeating action with rotating bolt head. The weapon is also in use as a police sniper rifle.

Mauser Model SR 96

SPECIFICATIONS

Caliber	: .308 Win. of .300 Win. Mag.
Magazine	: detachable magazine
Cartridge capacity:	.308: 3 of 5; .300: 2 or 4 rounds
Magazine catch	: lower left-hand side, near magazine
Action	: bolt-action
Cocking system	: bolt lever
Firing system	: single round
Locking system	: 16-lug bolt
Length	: 113 of 118 cm (44.5 of 46.5")
Barrel length	: 60 or 65 cm (23.6 of 25.6")
Weight	: 3.8 kg (8.4 lb.) without optical sight
Sight	: none; special sight mounting

Mauser Model SR 96

Mauser Model 97

Safety   : sliding catch on grip back
Stock   : laminate stock with rail in forearm for bipod or
                  hand support; adjustable cheek and butt.

PARTICULARS
Matt black barrel and receiver. Straight backwards bolt repeating action with rotating bolt head.

Mauser Model 97

SPECIFICATIONS
Caliber   : .308 Win., .300 Win. Mag. (and various
                    hunting calibers)
Magazine   : detachable magazine
Cartridge capacity: 4 rounds
Magazine catch   : lower left-hand side in magazine
Action   : bolt-action
Cocking system   : bolt lever
Firing system   : single round
Locking system   : 16-lug bolt
Length   : 112 cm (44.1")
Barrel length   : 61 cm (24")
Weight   : 3.3 kg (7.3 lb.) without optical sight
Sight   : rear and front sight; special sight
                    mounting

Mauser Model SR 97 Sniper

Safety   : sliding catch on stock neck
Stock   : walnut stock

PARTICULARS
Matt black barrel and receiver. Straight backwards bolt repeating action with rotating bolt head. Also in use as a police sniper rifle.

The top illustration shows a weapon with a Mauser hook-in sight mounting. The safety catch doubles as cocking lever after previously engaging the safety.

Mauser Model SR 97 Sniper

SPECIFICATIONS
Caliber   : .300 Win. Mag.
Magazine   : blind magazine
Cartridge capacity: 5 rounds
Magazine catch   : N/A
Action   : bolt-action
Cocking system   : bolt lever
Firing system   : single round
Locking system   : 2-lug bolt
Length   : 123 cm (48.4")
Barrel length   : 60 cm (23.6") incl. muzzle brake
Weight   : 7.2 kg (15.9 lb.
Sight   : none; special sight mounting
Safety   : ambidextrous safety catch above trigger
Stock   : special skeleton stock of magnesium and
                    aluminium; bolt lever can be changed to right-
                    hand side

PARTICULARS
Bipod; adjustable cheek and butt. Special sniper rifle for ranges up to 800 meters (874 yd).

Mitchell Arms Inc.

In 1984, John Mitchell founded the Mitchell Arms company. Previously, he had been the manager of the High Standard armament factory, which went bankrupt in early 1984. Mitchell Arms has its offices in Santa Ana, California. In its early days, the company focused on military-style smallbore rifles, including the Colt M16, the Kalashnikov AK-47, and the French MAS assault rifle. Mitchell also manufactured replicas of the Colt Single Action Army (Peacemaker), calibers .44 Magnum and .45 Long Colt. In addition, replica were imported of various large-caliber black powder Colt and Remington revolvers, obtained from the famous Italian arms factory, Uberti.

Mitchell manufacture a number of carbine models that resemble sub-machine-guns. These weapons were previously manufactured by the American Feather company as AT-22 and AT-9. Since 1994 the company also manufactures single-barreled shotguns. This is a range of pump-action riot guns for police and army service.

Mitchell Guardian Angel LW-9 Lightweight Rifle

SPECIFICATIONS

Caliber	: 9 mm Para
Magazine	: detachable magazine
Cartridge capacity	: 25 rounds
Magazine catch	: on front of magazine
Action	: semi-automatic
Cocking system	: cocking lever
Firing system	: semi-automatic
Locking system	: inertia lock
Length	: 88.6 cm (34.9") (extended wire stock)
Barrel length	: 43.2 cm (17")
Weight	: 2.3 kg (5 lb.)
Sight	: military aperture sight and ringed front sight
Safety	: safety catch on front of trigger guard
Stock	: telescopic wire stock or black synthetic stock

PARTICULARS
Matt black protective coating.

Mitchell High Standard Model 9108

SPECIFICATIONS

Caliber	: 12/76 (3")
Magazine	: tubular magazine
Cartridge capacity	: 7 rounds
Magazine catch	: N/A
Action	: pump-action
Cocking system	: forearm
Firing system	: single round
Locking system	: vertically sliding block

Mitchell Guardian Angel LW-9 Lightweight Rifle

Length	: 110 cm (43.3")
Barrel length	: 61 cm (24")
Weight	: 3.4 kg (7.5 lb.)
Sight	: bead
Safety	: push-button safety in rear of trigger guard
Stock	: hardwood, with pistol grip

PARTICULARS
Steel housing; the stock is also available with a Speedstock system for 2 x 2 extra rounds in the back of the stock.

Mosin-Nagant

Sergei Ivanovich Mosin was a Russian artillery officer who worked as an armament engineer at the imperial arsenal at Tula. Around 1885 he took part in the research for a new army rifle to equip the Tsar's army. Prior to this, the army was still using the single-shot Berdan rifle, but it was realized that this weapon was hopelessly outdated.

The first tests took place sometime around 1890. In addition to a single-shot rifle design submitted by Mosin himself, entries by Belgian armament manufacturers Emil and Leon Nagant were also competing for this large order. Eventually, a compromise was reached, a Mosin rifle with a 5-round Nagant magazine system. However, the new rifle, which was first issued to troops in 1891, did not go by the name of its designers.

The official designation was Trehlinejnaja Vintovka Obrasca 1891 Goda. The name also referred to the new caliber, 3-line, or .30 (7.62 x 54R). The Mosin-Nagant name did not come into use until much later.

Strangely enough, some confusion exists about the name, as the name is also found in literature as Moisin-Nagant. At first, the Russian industry was unable to produce the weapon in any large numbers, and so the first batch of more than 500,000 rifles was manufactured by the French arms factory, Manufacture d'Armes the Chatellerault (MAC).

The Russian factories did not get into their stride until 1893, after which they produced over 1.4 million of these rifles in three years time. Round about 1900 the entire Russian army had been equipped with the new rifle. The rifle was extensively tested in the war against Japan. In 1914, at the start of the First World War, Serbia was also supplied with 120,000 M1891 rifles by the Russians. In 1930 the rifle underwent a facelift. First, the bolt was modified to simplify production. Also, a new type of tangent rear sight was fitted, and the front sight was fitted with a protective ring.

This weapon is designated M1891/30 or M1891/1930. The rifle was also produced in a few carbine models with a shorter barrel length of approx. 51 cm (20 in). In 1944 a carbine was developed that was based on an older model, the M1944. The carbine has a long folding spike bayonet. After the Second World War the bolt-action rifles were successively replaced by automatic rifles like the Tokarev and Simonov SKS, followed by the legendary AK-47.

Mosin-Nagant M1891

SPECIFICATIONS
Caliber	: 7.62 x 54R
Magazine	: blind magazine

Mosin-Nagant M1891

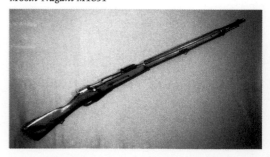

Cartridge capacity: 5 rounds
Magazine catch : N/A
Action : bolt-action
Cocking system : bolt lever
Firing system : single round
Locking system : bolt lugs
Length : 130.3 cm (51.3")
Barrel length : 80.2 cm (31.6")
Weight : 4.4 kg (9.7 lb.)
Sight : simple tangent rear sight
Safety : firing pin cocking knob can be locked by
pulling out and rotating a quarter turn
Stock : wood

PARTICULARS

During the bolt-action, the follower in the magazine is blocked by a special lever. This releases only the top cartridge for loading and holds back the remaining rounds.
This prevents the underside of the bolt from scraping along the topmost round in the magazine. A cleaning rod is stored under the barrel.

Mosin-Nagant M1891/30

SPECIFICATIONS

Caliber : 7.62 x 54R
Magazine : blind magazine
Cartridge capacity: 5 rounds

Mosin-Nagant M1891/30

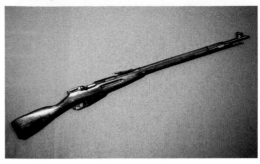

Magazine catch : N/A
Action : bolt-action
Cocking system : bolt lever
Firing system : single round
Locking system : bolt lugs
Length : 123 cm (48.4")
Barrel length : 73 cm (28.75")
Weight : 4 kg (8.8 lb.)
Sight : tangent rear sight and ringed front
sight
Safety : firing pin cocking knob can be locked by
pulling out and rotating a quarter turn
Stock : wood

PARTICULARS

During the bolt-action, the follower in the magazine is blocked by a special lever. This releases only the top cartridge for

Mosin-Nagant M1944

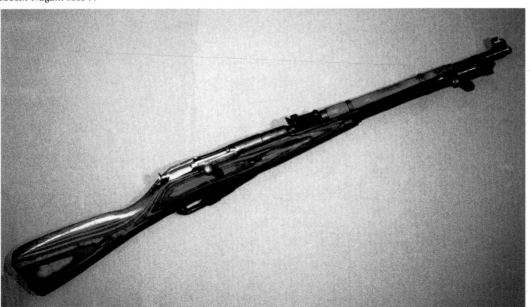

loading and holds back the remaining rounds. This prevents the underside of the bolt from scraping along the topmost round in the magazine.

A cleaning rod is stored under the barrel.

Mosin-Nagant M1944

SPECIFICATIONS

Caliber	: 7.62 x 54R
Magazine	: blind magazine
Cartridge capacity	: 5 rounds
Magazine catch	: N/A
Action	: bolt-action
Cocking system	: bolt lever
Firing system	: single round
Locking system	: bolt lugs
Length	: 102 cm (40.1") with folded bayonet
Barrel length	: 51.8 cm (20.4")
Weight	: 3.9 kg (8.6 lb.)
Sight	: tangent rear sight and ringed front sight
Safety	: firing pin cocking knob can be locked by pulling out and rotating a quarter turn
Stock	: wood

PARTICULARS

Folding bayonet which attaches behind the tangent rear sight mount.

Mosin-Nagant M1944

Mossberg

Mossberg, the American arms manufacturer from North Haven, Connecticut, has been in business for over 75 years. The company has introduced many innova-

Mossberg, logo

tions that were later copied by other manufacturers. The company offers a number of basic types, with a number of different models of each being available for various purposes. In addition to a large number of hunting models, the company also supplies shotguns for military use (riot guns) to the US Army. The Mossberg weapons were the only ones that could meet the strict military requirements. Mossberg also offer a number of specific models for police and other government use.

A number of these can be fitted with a special stock featuring the Speedlock system, in which special spring-loaded tubular magazines containing two extra rounds each are fitted to either side of the stock.

In 1996 Mossberg took over the Advanced Ordnance Corporation. This company produces components and special tools for the arms, automotive, and aviation industries. Also in 1996, a joint venture was started by Mossberg and Israel Military Industries.

This new company, Uzi America, has been established for the production of Jericho pistols (called Eagle in North America), Uzi sub-machine-guns, and the Galil rifles range for sale in the Americas. The Uzi and Galil weapons are supplied mainly to governments

Mossberg Model 500 Home Security

SPECIFICATIONS

Caliber	: 20/76 (3")
Magazine	: tubular magazine
Cartridge capacity	: 8 rounds
Magazine catch	: N/A
Action	: pump-action

Mossberg Model 500 Home Security

Cocking system	: forearm
Firing system	: single round
Locking system	: vertically sliding block
Length	: 118 cm (46.5")
Barrel length	: 53 cm (21")
Weight	: 3.2 kg (7 lb.)
Sight	: bead
Safety	: sliding catch on top of housing
Stock	: matt black synthetic

PARTICULARS
Matt black housing and barrel.

Mossberg Model 500 Mariner

SPECIFICATIONS

Caliber	: 12/76 (3")
Magazine	: tubular magazine
Cartridge capacity	: 6 rounds
Magazine catch	: N/A
Action	: pump-action
Cocking system	: forearm
Firing system	: single round
Locking system	: vertically sliding block

Mossberg Model 500 Mariner

Length	: 112 cm (44")
Barrel length	: 47 cm (18.5")
Weight	: 3.2 kg (7 lb.)
Sight	: bead or adjustable 'Ghost Ring' rear sight and bead
Safety	: sliding catch on top of housing
Stock	: black synthetic stock

PARTICULARS
Matt nickel coating.

Mossberg Model 500 Persuader

SPECIFICATIONS

Caliber	: 12/76 (3")
Magazine	: tubular magazine
Cartridge capacity	: 6 rounds
Magazine catch	: N/A
Action	: pump-action
Cocking system	: forearm
Firing system	: single round
Locking system	: vertically sliding block
Length	: 112 cm (44")
Barrel length	: 47 cm (18.5")
Weight	: 3.2 kg (7 lb.)

Mossberg Model 500 Persuader

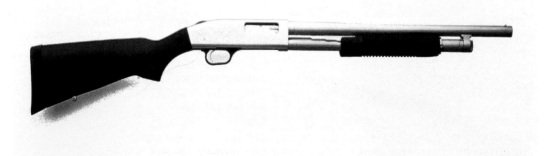

Sight	: adjustable 'Ghost Ring' rear sight and bead
Safety	: sliding catch on top of housing
Stock	: matt black synthetic

PARTICULARS

Matt black housing and barrel.

Mossberg Model 500 USA Mil-Spec

SPECIFICATIONS

Caliber	: 12/76 (3")
Magazine	: tubular magazine
Cartridge capacity	: 6 rounds
Magazine catch	: N/A
Action	: pump-action
Cocking system	: forearm
Firing system	: single round
Locking system	: vertically sliding block
Length	: 107 cm (42")
Barrel length	: 51 cm (20")
Weight	: 3.3 kg (7.25 lb.)
Sight	: bead
Safety	: sliding catch on top of housing
Stock	: matt green synthetic

Mossberg Model 500 USA Mil-Spec

PARTICULARS

Supplied with sling.

Mossberg Model 500 Viking

SPECIFICATIONS

Caliber	: 12/76 (3")
Magazine	: tubular magazine
Cartridge capacity	: 5 rounds
Magazine catch	: N/A
Action	: pump-action
Cocking system	: forearm
Firing system	: single round
Locking system	: vertically sliding block
Length	: 112 cm (44")
Barrel length	: 61 cm (24")
Weight	: 3.2 kg (7.1 lb.)
Sight	: 1.5-4.5 Tasco optical sight
Safety	: sliding catch on top of housing
Stock	: matt green synthetic

PARTICULARS

Matt black coating on housing and barrel; special slug barrel with rifling; supplied in a synthetic case.

Mossberg Model 590 Mariner

SPECIFICATIONS

Caliber	: 12/76 (3")
Magazine	: tubular magazine
Cartridge capacity	: 9 rounds
Magazine catch	: N/A
Action	: pump-action
Cocking system	: forearm
Firing system	: single round
Locking system	: vertically sliding block
Length	: 112 cm (44")

Barrel length	: 51 cm (20")
Weight	: 3.2 kg (7 lb.)
Sight	: bead or with adjustable 'Ghost Ring' rear sight and bead
Safety	: sliding catch on top of housing
Stock	: matt black stock

PARTICULARS
Matt nickel coating on housing, tubular magazine, and barrel.

Mossberg Model 590 Persuader

SPECIFICATIONS

Caliber	: 12/76 (3")
Magazine	: tubular magazine
Cartridge capacity:	9 rounds
Magazine catch	: N/A

Action	: pump-action
Cocking system	: forearm
Firing system	: single round
Locking system	: vertically sliding block
Length	: 114 cm (45")
Barrel length	: 47 cm (20")
Weight	: 3.3 kg (7.3 lb.)
Sight	: adjustable 'Ghost Ring' rear sight and bead
Safety	: sliding catch on top of housing
Stock	: matt black synthetic stock and forearm

PARTICULARS
Matt black housing, tubular magazine, and barrel.
The weapon has a Speedlock system on each side of the stock, with two extra rounds on either side.

Mossberg Model 590 Persuader

Mossberg Model 695 Slug Gun

Mossberg Model 695 Slug Gun

SPECIFICATIONS

Caliber : 12/76 (3")
Magazine : detachable magazine
Cartridge capacity: 2 or more rounds
Magazine catch : on front of magazine
Action : bolt-action
Cocking system : bolt lever
Firing system : single round
Locking system : bolt lugs
Length : 108 cm (42.5")
Barrel length : 56 cm (22") (rifled barrel with compensator holes)
Weight : 3.3 kg (7.2 lb.)
Sight : rear sight and bead, Weaver style optical sight mount on top of the teceiver is included

Safety : rotating safety ring on rear of bolt
Stock : matt black synthetic, with pistol grip

PARTICULARS
Synthetic case included; specially designed for precision fire using high-impact missiles up to 100 meters (328 ft).

Mossberg Model 9200 Pursuader

SPECIFICATIONS

Caliber : 12/76 (3")
Magazine : tubular magazine
Cartridge capacity: 5 rounds
Magazine catch : N/A
Action : semi-automatic, gas pressure
Cocking system : cocking lever
Firing system : semi-automatic
Locking system : vertically sliding block
Length : 112 cm (44")
Barrel length : 47 cm (18.5")
Weight : 3.2 kg (7 lb.)
Sight : bead
Safety : sliding catch on top of housing
Stock : matt black synthetic

PARTICULARS
Blued housing, matt black barrel.

PGM Ultimate Ratio Commando I

PGM

PGM, logo

The French PGM Precision company specializes in the field of high-precision sniper and anti-sniper rifles. The weapons are manufactured for calibers .308 Win. and .50 BMG (Browning machine-gun). PGM supply not only to French army and navy units, but also to numerous other countries. These rifles are considered to be among the top of the range match weapons for military purposes.

The Ultimate Ratio Intervention is currently being tested by the French police. All rifles chambered for .308 Win. (7.62 x 51 mm) are suitable for quick-fitting a silenced barrel without affecting the point of impact, and all components of the rifles are interchangeable.

PGM Ultimate Ratio Commando I

SPECIFICATIONS

Caliber	: 7.62 x 51 mm, or to order
Magazine	: detachable magazine
Cartridge capacity	: 5 rounds
Magazine catch	: underneath trigger guard
Action	: bolt-action
Cocking system	: bolt lever
Firing system	: single round
Locking system	: 3-lug bolt with gas pressure valves
Length	: 103 cm (40.6")
Barrel length	: 447 or 55 cm (incl. muzzle brake) (18.5 or 21.6"), fluted barrel
Weight	: 5.5 kg (12.1 lb.)

Sight	: none; various sight mountings: universal, Weaver, or Stanag
Safety	: safety catch on left-hand side of receiver
Stock	: skeleton stock with adjustable cheek and butt.

PARTICULARS

Receiver made of special aircraft-grade aluminum; adjustable and folding bipod. Special match trigger system. Metal parts matt black.

PGM Ultimate Ratio Commando II

SPECIFICATIONS

Caliber	: 7.62 x 51 mm, or to order
Magazine	: detachable magazine
Cartridge capacity	: 5 rounds
Magazine catch	: underneath trigger guard
Action	: bolt-action
Cocking system	: bolt lever
Firing system	: single round
Locking system	: 3-lug bolt with gas pressure valves
Length	: 102 cm (40.2"); folded: 74 cm (29.1")
Barrel length	: 47 cm (incl. muzzle damper) (18.5"), fluted barrel
Weight	: 5.5 kg (12.1 lb.)

PGM Ultimate Ratio Commando II

Sight	: none; various sight mountings: universal, Weaver, or Stanag
Safety	: safety catch on left-hand side of receiver
Stock	: folding skeleton stock with adjustable cheek and butt.

PARTICULARS

Receiver made of special aircraft-grade aluminum; adjustable and folding bipod. Special match trigger system. Metal parts matt black.

PGM Ultimate Ratio Hecate II

SPECIFICATIONS

Caliber	: .50 BMG
Magazine	: detachable magazine
Cartridge capacity	: 7 rounds
Magazine catch	: behind magazine housing
Action	: bolt-action
Cocking system	: bolt lever
Firing system	: single round
Locking system	: 3-lug bolt with gas pressure valves
Length	: 138 cm (54.3"); folded: 114 cm (44.9")
Barrel length	: 70 cm (incl. muzzle brake and recoil damper) (27.6")
Weight	: 13.5 kg (29.8 lb.)
Sight	: none; various sight mountings: universal, Weaver, or Stanag
Safety	: safety catch on right-hand side of receiver
Stock	: removable skeleton stock with adjustable cheek and butt.

PARTICULARS

Steel receiver and housing of special aircraft-grade aluminum; adjustable and folding bipod.
Folding carrying handle. Special match trigger system. Metal parts matt black. The rifle has an effective range of 1500 meters (1640 yd).

PGM Ultimate Ratio Intervention

SPECIFICATIONS

Caliber	: 7.62 x 51 mm, or to order
Magazine	: detachable magazine
Cartridge capacity	: 5 rounds
Magazine catch	: underneath trigger guard
Action	: bolt-action
Cocking system	: bolt lever
Firing system	: single round
Locking system	: 3-lug bolt with gas pressure valves
Length	: 103 cm (40.6")
Barrel length	: 47 or 60 cm (incl. muzzle damper) (18.5 or 23.6"); fluted
Weight	: 5.5 kg (12.1 lb.)
Sight	: none; various sight mountings: universal, Weaver, or Stanag
Safety	: safety catch on left-hand side of receiver
Stock	: skeleton stock with adjustable cheek and butt.

PARTICULARS

Receiver made of special aircraft-grade aluminum; barrel exchangeable with silenced barrel without affecting the point of impact; adjustable and folding bipod. Special match trigger system. Metal parts matt black.

PGM Suppressor

Remington

The Remington Arms Company was established in 1816 by father and son Remington under the name of E. Remington & Son. The company was located in Ilion, New York state. When a second son joined the business in 1844, the name was changed to E. Remington & Sons. The current name dates from 1888, following a takeover by businessmen Hartley and Graham. In 1902 a merger followed with the ammunition manufacturer, Union Cartridge Company.

These days Remington is part of the DuPont concern and has its offices at Bridgeport, Connecticut. During the early years, Remington gained fame with its Army Model 1863 black powder revolver. In that same year, the company introduced a breech-loading rifle with a rolling block bolt. This was based on the 1863 patents taken out by Leonard Geiger and Joseph Rider. The US government awarded Remington a contract for the supply 14,999 Rolling Block carbines chambered for .56-50 rimfire cartridges, followed by an order for 5000 rifles chambered for .46 rimfire. This rifle was also supplied to Sweden, among other countries. Remington was not particularly successful in the USA because large government contracts were mainly granted to the state-owned Springfield Armory. Remington did however manage to get in

Remington, logo

on the act as suppliers of components. For this reason, the company has focused on the civilian market. During World War I, Remington was contracted by the US government for the production of the Model 1917 Enfield army rifle. In the course of the Second World War, Remington manufactured large quantities of the Colt Model 1911-A1 .45 ACP pistol for the US forces.

It wasn't until 1966 that Remington really succeeded in re-entering the military market. During army tests for a new sniper rifle the army selected the Remington Model 700 as the best weapon, and the Sniper Rifle M40 was adopted by the US Marines. The result was that many police units also purchased this sniper rifle. Remington has marketed the model 700 in many different versions. In 1995 the range included 29 different models, from .17 Remington caliber in the Model Seven Lightweight up to .458 Winchester Magnum in the Model 700 Safari. The action, or receiver and bolt, of the Model 700 is used by many custom rifle makers all over the world as the basis for their own creations. Even the very heavy rifles by A-Square chambered for the .500 A-Square cartridge feature the Remington 700 bolt system, which goes some way to show the quality of the system. Since the introduction of this model, the weapon features the Williams adjustable rear sight (most of the photographs of Remington weapons were kindly provided by the Remington Arms Company).

Remington Model 11-87 Police

SPECIFICATIONS

Caliber	: 12/76 (3")
Magazine	: tubular magazine
Cartridge capacity	: 7 rounds
Magazine catch	: N/A
Action	: gas pressure
Cocking system	: cocking lever
Firing system	: semi-automatic
Locking system	: vertically sliding block
Length	: 98.5 cm (38.8")
Barrel length	: 45.7 cm (18")
Weight	: 3.5 kg (7.7 lb.)
Sight	: aperture sight and ringed front sight (Ghost ring)

Remington Model 11-87 SPS

SPECIFICATIONS

Caliber	: 12/76 (3")
Magazine	: tubular magazine
Cartridge capacity	: 7 rounds
Magazine catch	: N/A
Action	: gas pressure
Cocking system	: cocking lever
Firing system	: semi-automatic
Locking system	: vertically sliding block
Length	: 104 cm (41")
Barrel length	: 53.3 cm (21")
Weight	: 3.6 kg (8 lb.)
Sight	: adjustable rear sight and sight mount
Safety	: push-button in rear of trigger guard
Stock	: matt black synthetic stock and forearm

Safety	: push-button in rear of trigger guard
Stock	: matt black synthetic stock

PARTICULARS

Housing and barrel matt black phosphate finish.

Remington Model 11-87 SP Magnum

SPECIFICATIONS

Caliber	: 12/76 (3")
Magazine	: tubular magazine
Cartridge capacity	: 7 rounds
Magazine catch	: N/A
Action	: gas pressure
Cocking system	: cocking lever
Firing system	: semi-automatic
Locking system	: vertically sliding block
Length	: 104 cm (41")
Barrel length	: 53.3 cm (21")
Weight	: 3.6 kg (8 lb.)
Sight	: adjustable rearsight and sight mount
Safety	: push-button in rear of trigger guard
Stock	: walnut stock and forearm

PARTICULARS

Housing and barrel matt blued. With choke tube for slugs.

Remington Model 11-87 SP Magnum

PARTICULARS

Housing and barrel matt black phosphate finish. Rifled barrel for slugs.

Remington Model 40-XB KS

SPECIFICATIONS

Caliber	: .223 Rem. of .308 Win.
Magazine	: blind magazine (.223 Rem.) or detachable magazine (.308 Win.)
Cartridge capacity	: 5 rounds (.223 Rem.) or 4 rounds (.308 Win.)
Magazine catch	: right-hand side on underside of magazine slot

Remington Model 40-XB KS

Action	: bolt-action
Cocking system	: bolt lever
Firing system	: single round
Locking system	: 2-lug bolt
Length	: 118 cm (46.6")
Barrel length	: 69.2 cm (27.25")
Weight	: 4.6 kg (10.25 lb.)
Sight	: none; receiver drilled and tapped for sight mount
Safety	: safety catch on right-hand side behind bolt lever
Stock	: Kevlar synthetic stock

PARTICULARS
Stainless steel; free floating barrel.

Remington Model 700 Police

SPECIFICATIONS

Caliber	: .223 Rem. of .308 Win.
Magazine	: blind magazine (.223 Rem.) or detachable magazine (.308 Win.)
Cartridge capacity	: 5 rounds (.223 Rem.) or 4 rounds (.308 Win.)
Magazine catch	: right-hand side on underside of magazine slot
Action	: bolt-action
Cocking system	: bolt lever
Firing system	: single round
Locking system	: 2-lug bolt
Length	: 115 cm (45.3")
Barrel length	: 66 cm (26")
Weight	: 4.1 kg (9 lb.)
Sight	: none; receiver drilled and tapped for sight mount
Safety	: safety catch on right-hand side behind bolt lever
Stock	: Kevlar synthetic stock

PARTICULARS
Matt black; free floating barrel. This sniper rifle is also available in a short version with a 50.8 cm (20") barrel, but only for the .308 Win. caliber.

Remington Model 700 Police

Remington Model 700 Sendero

Remington Model 700 Sendero

SPECIFICATIONS

Caliber	: 7 mm Rem. Magn. or .300 Win. Mag..
Magazine	: blind magazine
Cartridge capacity	: 3 rounds
Magazine catch	: right-hand side on underside of magazine slot
Action	: bolt-action
Cocking system	: bolt lever
Firing system	: single round
Locking system	: 2-lug bolt
Length	: 118 cm (46.5")
Barrel length	: 66 cm (26")
Weight	: 4.1 kg (9 lb.)
Sight	: none; receiver drilled and tapped for sight mount
Safety	: safety catch on right-hand side behind bolt lever
Stock	: Kevlar synthetic stock

PARTICULARS
Matt black; heavy free floating barrel.

Remington Model 700 TWS-DM Police

SPECIFICATIONS

Caliber	: .308 Win. or .300 Win.Mag.
Magazine	: detachable magazine
Cartridge capacity	: 4 rounds
Magazine catch	: right-hand side on underside of magazine slot
Action	: bolt-action
Cocking system	: bolt lever

Remington Model 700 TWS-DM Police

Firing system	: single round
Locking system	: 2-lug bolt
Length	: 112 cm (44.1")
Barrel length	: 66 cm (26")
Weight	: 4.8 kg (10.5 lb.)
Sight	: Leupold Vari-X III 3.5 x 10
Safety	: safety catch on right-hand side behind bolt lever
Stock	: synthetic Kevlar stock

PARTICULARS

Matt black; free floating barrel; Harris bipod. TWS-DM stands for Tactical Weapon System-Detachable Magazine. This Tactical Weapon System rifle is supplied with a Michaels Quick-Adjust rifle sling, and comes in a Pelican rifle case.

Remington Model 700 VS

Remington Model 700 VS

SPECIFICATIONS

Caliber	: .223 Rem., .243 Win., .308 Win.
Magazine	: blind magazine
Cartridge capacity	: 5 or 4 rounds
Magazine catch	: right-hand side on underside of magazine slot
Action	: bolt-action
Cocking system	: bolt lever
Firing system	: single round
Locking system	: 2-lug bolt
Length	: 116.2 cm (45.75")
Barrel length	: 66 cm (26")
Weight	: 4.1 kg (9 lb.)
Sight	: none; receiver drilled and tapped for sight mount
Safety	: safety catch on right-hand side behind bolt lever
Stock	: Kevlar synthetic stock

PARTICULARS

Matt black; heavy free floating barrel.

Remington Model Seven Custom KS

Remington Model Seven Custom KS

SPECIFICATIONS

Caliber	: .223 Rem., .308 Win.
Magazine	: blind magazine
Cartridge capacity	: 5 or 4 rounds
Magazine catch	: right-hand side on underside of magazine slot for magazine base plate
Action	: bolt-action
Cocking system	: bolt lever
Firing system	: single round
Locking system	: 2-lug bolt
Length	: 99.7 cm (39.25")
Barrel length	: 50.8 cm (20")
Weight	: 2.8 kg (6.25 lb.)
Sight	: without or with rear sight; receiver drilled and tapped for sight mount
Safety	: safety catch on right-hand side behind bolt lever
Stock	: Kevlar synthetic stock

PARTICULARS

Matt black; heavy free floating barrel, often used in combination with laser sight as multipurpose tactical weapon.

Remington Model 870 Express Super Magnum

SPECIFICATIONS

Caliber	: 12/76 (3")

Remington Model 870 Express Super Magnum

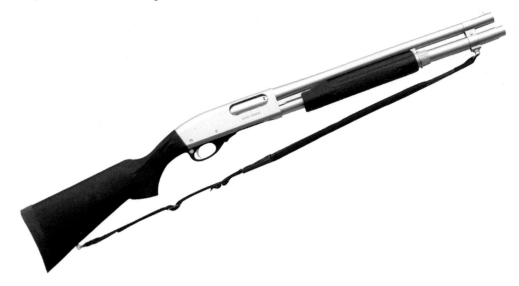

Magazine	: tubular magazine
Cartridge capacity	: 5 rounds
Magazine catch	: N/A
Action	: pump-action
Cocking system	: forearm
Firing system	: single round
Locking system	: vertically sliding block
Length	: 102.9 cm (40.5")
Barrel length	: 50.8 cm (20")
Weight	: 3.6 kg (8 lb.)
Sight	: adjustable rear sight and mounting rail
Safety	: push-button in rear of trigger guard
Stock	: walnut stock and forearm

PARTICULARS

Housing and barrel matt black phosphate finish. Cylindrical barrel for sabots, slugs, and buckshot.

Remington Model 870 HD Home Defense

SPECIFICATIONS

Caliber	: 12/76 (3")
Magazine	: tubular magazine
Cartridge capacity	: 5 rounds
Magazine catch	: N/A
Action	: pump-action
Cocking system	: forearm
Firing system	: single round
Locking system	: vertically sliding block
Length	: 98.5 cm (38.8")
Barrel length	: 45.7 cm (18")
Weight	: 3.4 kg (7.5 lb.)

Sight	: bead
Safety	: push-button in rear of trigger guard
Stock	: matt black synthetic stock

PARTICULARS

Receiver housing and barrel matt black phosphated finish.

Remington Model 870 Marine Magnum

SPECIFICATIONS

Caliber	: 12/76 (3")
Magazine	: tubular magazine
Cartridge capacity	: 7 rounds
Magazine catch	: N/A
Action	: pump-action
Cocking system	: forearm
Firing system	: single round
Locking system	: vertically sliding block
Length	: 98.5 cm (38.8")
Barrel length	: 45.7 cm (18")

Remington Model 870 HD Home Defense

Weight   : 3.4 kg (7.5 lb.)
Sight   : bead
Safety   : push-button in rear of trigger guard
Stock   : matt black synthetic stock

PARTICULARS
Receiver housing, barrel and tubular magazine nickel-plated.

Remington Model 870 Police

SPECIFICATIONS
Caliber   : 12/76 (3")
Magazine   : tubular magazine
Cartridge capacity: 5 rounds
Magazine catch   : N/A
Action   : pump-action
Cocking system   : forearm
Firing system   : single round
Locking system   : vertically sliding block
Length   : 98.5 or 103.6 cm (38.8 or 40.8")
Barrel length   : 45.7 or 50.8 cm (18 or 20")
Weight   : 3.4 or 3.5 kg (7.5 or 7.7 lb.)
Sight   : Williams rear sight or bead only
Safety   : push-button in rear of trigger guard
Stock   : hardwood stock or matt black synthetic stock

PARTICULARS
Receiver housing and barrel matt black phosphated finish.

Remington Model 870 Police Special

SPECIFICATIONS
Caliber   : 12/76 (3")
Magazine   : tubular magazine
Cartridge capacity: 5 rounds
Magazine catch   : N/A
Action   : pump-action
Cocking system   : forearm
Firing system   : single round

Remington Model 870 Police

Remington Model 870 Police Special

Locking system   : vertically sliding block
Length   : 98.5 cm (38.8")
Barrel length   : 45.7 cm (18")
Weight   : 3.4 kg (7.5 lb.)
Sight   : aperture rear sight and ringed bead
                    (Ghost ring)
Safety   : push-button catch in rear of trigger guard
Stock   : matt black synthetic stock

PARTICULARS
Receiver housing and barrel matt black phosphated finish.

Robar

Robar, logo

Robar Companies Inc. was established by Robert A. Barrkman, a passionate hunter and competition shooter. The company is located in Phoenix, Arizona. Robar developed from a custom-shop in which existing rifle models were converted to precision instruments to customers' individual specifications.
In addition, Robar produces a series of models of their own, based on the Remington Model 700 BDL receiver and bolt, to which exclusive stainless steel and fluted Robar match barrels are fitted. In addition, the hardware is fitted with McMillan fiberglass stocks and a modified

Robar Elite

Action	: pump-action
Cocking system	: forearm
Firing system	: single round
Locking system	: vertically sliding block
Length	: 98.5 cm (38.8")
Barrel length	: 45.7 cm (18")
Weight	: 3.4 of 3.5 kg (7.5 of 7.7 lb.)
Sight	: Ghost ring
Safety	: large push-button in rear of trigger guard
Stock	: matt black synthetic stock and forearm

PARTICULARS

Receiver housing and barrel with matt black NP3 coating.

Custom police model based on the Remington Model 870.

trigger system. This rifle has a guaranteed accuracy of a 3-round group within half an inch at 100 yards. The sniper rifles are mostly supplied to military and police units.

For some years now, Robar has been manufacturing long-range sniper rifles chambered for .50 BMG for army use, which feature a receiver and bolt system developed within the company itself. Robar also carries out other work on weapons, such as bluing or nickel-plating steel weapons, blackening stainless steel (anti-reflection measure for sniper rifles), and Parkerized finish.

The latter is a chemical process in which a coating of manganese or zinc phosphate is applied to the steel surface of the weapon as a protective measure against corrosion. Blued weapons are treated by means of a process developed by Robar, the so-called Roguard-finish. During this treatment, a rock-hard polymer coating is chemically applied to the metal. NP3 is a new steel surface treatment process developed by Robar in which a coating consisting of a combination of polytetrafluorethylene synthetic and nickel is applied to the weapon.

Robar Elite

SPECIFICATIONS

Caliber	: 12/76 (3")
Magazine	: tubular magazine
Cartridge capacity: 5 rounds	
Magazine catch	: N/A

Robar QR2 (Quick Reaction) sniper rifle

SPECIFICATIONS

Caliber	: any caliber
Magazine	: detachable magazine
Cartridge capacity	: to order, depending on caliber
Magazine catch	: in front end of trigger guard
Action	: bolt-action
Cocking system	: bolt lever
Firing system	: single round
Locking system	: 2-lug bolt (Remington 700 or Ruger M77)
Length	: 111.8 cm (44"), or to order
Barrel length	: 61 cm (24"), or to order
Weight	: 3.2 to 4.1 kg (7 to 9 lb.)
Sight	: none; sight mount to order
Safety	: safety catch on right-hand side behind bolt lever
Stock	: black, grey, or camouflage McMillan fibreglass stock with pistol grip

PARTICULARS

Matt black with NP3-laag; free floating fluted bench rest barrel; Harris bipod. Guaranteed precision of a 3-shot group of 13 mm (0.51") at 100 yards.

Robar QR2 (Quick Reaction) sniper rifle

ROBQ2

Robar RC-50

SPECIFICATIONS

Caliber	: .50 BMG
Magazine	: detachable magazine
Cartridge capacity	: 5 rounds
Magazine catch	: in front end of trigger guard
Action	: bolt-action
Cocking system	: bolt lever
Firing system	: single round
Locking system	: bolt lugs
Length	: 139.7 cm (55")
Barrel length	: 73.7 cm (29")

ROB50-2

Robar RC-50

Weight	: 11.3 kg (25 lb.)
Sight	: Weaver style sight mount
Safety	: safety catch on right-hand side behind bolt lever
Stock	: Mcmillan fibreglass stock with pistol grip and bipod, or McMillan folding stock for airborne or vehicle transport.

PARTICULARS

Heavy Robar bipod; chromium molybdenum barrel with special muzzle damper. Matt black NP3 coating.

This sniper rifle has been specially designed for military units at ranges between 1000 and 2000 meters (1093 and 2187 yd).

Robar SR60 Sniper rifle

Robar SR90 Sniper rifle

Robar SR60 Sniper rifle

SPECIFICATIONS

Caliber	: .308 Win., .300 Win. Mag. or to order
Magazine	: detachable magazine
Cartridge capacity: 5 or 4 rounds.	
Magazine catch	: in front end of trigger guard
Action	: bolt-action
Cocking system	: bolt lever
Firing system	: single round
Locking system	: 2-lug bolt (Remington 700-BDL)
Length	: 111.8 cm (44")
Barrel length	: 61 cm (24")
Weight	: 4.3 kg (9.4 lb.)
Sight	: sight mount to order
Safety	: safety catch on right-hand side behind bolt lever
Stock	: black, grey, or camouflage McMillan fibreglass stock with pistol grip in RMC-M40A1 rifle style.

PARTICULARS

Matt black with NP3 coating; stainless steel fluted match barrel; special bipod. This sniper rifle has been designed for police units. The rifle shown features the Leupold 3.5 x 10 Police optical sight. It has a guaranteed 3-shot group of 13 mm (0.51") at 100 yards.

Robar SR90 Sniper rifle

SPECIFICATIONS

Caliber	: .308 Win., .300 Win. Mag., or to order
Magazine	: detachable magazine
Cartridge capacity: 5 or 4 rounds resp.	
Magazine catch	: catch in front end of trigger guard
Action	: bolt-action
Cocking system	: bolt lever
Firing system	: single round
Locking system	: 2-lug bolt (Remington 700-BDL)
Length	: 111.8 cm (44")
Barrel length	: 61 cm (24")

Weight	: 4.7 kg (10.4 lb.)
Sight	: sight mount to order
Safety	: safety catch on right-hand side behind bolt lever
Stock	: black, grey or camouflage McMillan fibreglass stock with pistol grip, adjustable cheek and butt.

PARTICULARS

Matt black with NP3 coating; fluted stainless steel match barrel; special bipod. This sniper rifle was used by special units during the Gulf War.

Robar Thunder Ranch Precision Rifle

SPECIFICATIONS

Caliber	: any caliber
Magazine	: detachable magazine
Cartridge capacity: depends on caliber	

SR90-2

243

Robar Thunder Ranch Precision Rifle

Robar Thunder Ranch Precision Rifle

Magazine catch	: in front end of trigger guard
Action	: bolt-action
Cocking system	: bolt lever
Firing system	: single round
Locking system	: 2-lug bolt (Remington 700-BDL)
Length	: 102 or 112 cm (40 or 44")
Barrel length	: 51 or 61 cm (20 or 24")
Weight	: approx. 3.9 kg (8.5 lb.)
Sight	: sight mount to order
Safety	: safety catch on right-hand side behind bolt lever
Stock	: McMillan fibreglass stock with pistol grip; matt black, grey, or in various camouflage colours: Desert, Urban, Tiger of Woodland (shown)

PARTICULARS

Matt black with NP3 coating; Harris or special Robar bipod; free floating fluted stainless steel match barrel. The weapon has a guaranteed 3-shot group of 13 mm (0.51") at 100 yards.

Ross

The Canadian Ross rifle was developed in 1886 by Sir Charles Ross. It is an army rifle with a bolt that moves straight backwards. The rotation lock of the bolt used a separate lug that runs in a helical recess in the receiver. In 1902 the weapon was officially introduced with the Royal Northwest Mounted Police. During the 1900 to 1912 period, the Ross rifle was tested in England during military trials on various occasions, but it was rejected for army use. Nonetheless, the Canadian army decided to introduce the weapon in 1914. However, complaints by the troops came pouring in. The weapon proved prone to failure during the 1914-1918 trench war. The Canadian soldiers preferred the Lee-Enfield, and the Ross was abandoned in large numbers on the Flemish/French battle fields. In 1917 the US government ordered 20,000 Ross Mark III rifles, but the weapon was never introduced on any scale.

Ross Mark III

SPECIFICATIONS

Caliber	: .303 Br.
Magazine	: blind magazine
Cartridge capacity	: 5 rounds by clip
Magazine catch	: N/A
Action	: bolt-action
Cocking system	: bolt lever
Firing system	: single round
Locking system	: rotating bolt head
Length	: 128.5 cm (50.6")
Barrel length	: 76.5 cm (30.2")
Weight	: 4.5 kg (9.8 lb.)
Sight	: aperture sight
Safety	: wing-type catch near bolt lever
Stock	: walnut

PARTICULARS

Various types: Mark I: no detachable magazines; follower in magazine lockable for single-cartridge loading. Mark II (also called Model 1905): redesigned sights. Mark III (or Model 1910): detachable magazines.

Rottweil/Dynamit Nobel

In 1865, the company Alfred Nobel & Co. company was founded by the well-known chemist of that name. Initially, the

Ross Mark III

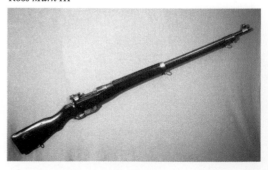

Dynamit Nobel

Magazine catch	: N/A
Action	: pump-action
Cocking system	: forearm
Firing system	: single round
Locking system	: rotating bolt head
Length	: 106 cm (41.7")
Barrel length	: 50 cm (19.7")
Weight	: 3.0 kg (6.6 lb.)
Sight	: bead
Safety	: push-button on front of trigger guard
Stock	: walnut

company specialized in the manufacture of dynamite, which Nobel had developed. In later years, other product groups were added to the company, such as ammunition, synthetics, and arms. In 1931 the company merged with RWS, the Rheinisch-Westfälischen Sprengstoff-Fabriken.

Under this brand name, the concern manufactures a wide range of rifle and shotgun ammunition. The Rottweil brand is named after the town in the Black Forest where shotgun cartridges were manufactured for Dynamit Nobel. Another part of the company is Geco (Genschow & Co), which used to produce pistol and revolver ammunition. These days Dynamit Nobel is a multinational company with more than 13,000 employees and many subsidiaries.

Rottweil Pump PSG/8

SPECIFICATIONS

Caliber	: 12/76 (3")
Magazine	: tubular magazine
Cartridge capacity: 7 rounds	

Rottweil Pump PSG/8

PARTICULARS
Matt black protective coating; steel barrel, light metal housing.

Ruger

Ruger, logo

STURM, RUGER & Company, INC.

In 1948, William Batterman Ruger and Alexander M. Sturm founded Sturm, Ruger & Company Inc. Together they rented a shed in Southport, Connecticut. Ruger had gained the necessary experience at what was then the Springfield Armory state arsenal, and at the Auto-Ordnance arms factory, the makers of the Thompson sub-machine-gun or Tommy-Gun. The first product of the small company was a small-bore pistol introduced in 1949. When Alexander Sturm was killed in an aircraft accident, William (Bill) Ruger continued the business on his own. During the period up to 1959 Ruger produced a large number of revolver models. It wasn't until 1959 that he introduced his first rifle design, a semi-automatic carbine chambered for .44 Magnum cartridges. The growth of the company necessitated the expansion of the works. In 1964 new factory premises were built in Newport, New Hampshire.

Production of the Ruger No. 1 single-shot rifle started in 1967. Until that time, single-shot rifles were rather looked down upon. The market offered mainly cheap hinged barrel weapons for small game hunting. Ruger himself had a great liking for heavy single-shot rifles from English manufacturers, such as those made by Alexander Henry, and he thought that a similar concept would be suitable for the North American market.

The well-known stock maker, Leonard Brownell, was engaged to design a graceful stock for this rifle type, and he was also made technical manager of the Newport factory. The No. 1 rifle became a great success. A subsequent rifle model was introduced in 1968 under the name Model 77. This was a bolt repeating rifle, the stock of which was designed by Brownell. It was a traditional rifle, rather unusual for that time. In 1974 he designed an automatic carbine, the Mini-14, chambered for .223 Rem, which in 1975 was succeeded by a semi-automatic civilian version. At first sight the Mini-14 looks like a cross between the M1 Garand rifle and the Winchester .30-M1 carbine. The M77 rifle was succeeded in early 1992 by the M77-Mark II rifle.

Compare with the M77, the Mark II has undergone a number of modifications, such as an improved extractor that grips the cartridge case as soon as it is pulled from the magazine by the bolt. Also, the receiver of the Mark II is made from stainless steel. For government services, Ruger has developed a series of automatic Mini-14 carbines, the MP-9 sub-machine-gun, the Police Carbine chambered for 9 mm Para or .40 S&W, and the M77 VLE MKII sniper rifle.

Ruger AC556 Automatic Carbine

SPECIFICATIONS

Caliber	: .223 Rem.
Magazine	: detachable magazine
Cartridge capacity:	20 or 30 rounds
Magazine catch	: in front of magazine slot
Action	: gas pressure
Cocking system	: cocking lever
Firing system	: fully automatic, 3-shot burst, and semi-automatic

Ruger AC556 Automatic Carbine

Locking system	: rotating bolt
Length	: 98 cm (38.6")
Barrel length	: 47 cm (18.5")
Weight	: 3.1 kg (6.87 lb.)
Sight	: adjustable aperture sight
Safety	: catch in front end of trigger guard (Garand type)
Stock	: fixed hardwood stock and hand grip

PARTICULARS
Matt black phosphate finish; firing mode selector on right-hand rear of receiver.

Ruger AC556F Automatic Carbine

SPECIFICATIONS

Caliber	: .223 Rem.
Magazine	: detachable magazine
Cartridge capacity:	20 or 30 rounds
Magazine catch	: in front of magazine slot
Action	: gas pressure
Cocking system	: cocking lever
Firing system	: fully automatic, 3-shot burst, and semi-automatic
Locking system	: rotating bolt
Length	: 82 cm (32.3"), or 55 cm (21.7") with folded stock
Barrel length	: 29 cm (11.5") incl. flash suppresser
Weight	: 3.3 kg (7.2 lb.)

Ruger AC556F Automatic Carbine

Sight	: adjustable aperture sight
Safety	: catch in front end of trigger guard (Garand type)
Stock	: fixed hardwood stock with steel folding stock. Synthetix pistol grip and hand grip.

PARTICULARS

Matt finish stainless steel; firing mode selector on right-hand rear of receiver.

Ruger AC556K Automatic Carbine

SPECIFICATIONS

Caliber	: .223 Rem.
Magazine	: detachable magazine
Cartridge capacity	: 20 or 30 rounds
Magazine catch	: in front of magazine slot
Action	: gas pressure
Cocking system	: cocking lever
Firing system	: fully automatic, 3-shot burst, and semi-automatic
Locking system	: rotating bolt
Length	: 82 cm (32.3"), or 55 cm (21.7") with folded stock
Barrel length	: 29 cm (11.5") incl. flash suppresser
Weight	: 3.3 kg (7.2 lb.)
Sight	: adjustable aperture sight
Safety	: catch in front end of trigger guard (Garand type)
Stock	: fixed hardwood stock with steel folding stock. Synthetic pistol grip and hand grip.

PARTICULARS

Matt black phosphate finish; firing mode selector on right-hand rear of receiver.

Ruger AC556K Automatic Carbine

Ruger Mini-14/5R Ranch Rifle

Ruger Mini-14/5R Ranch Rifle

SPECIFICATIONS

Caliber	: .223 Rem.
Magazine	: detachable magazine
Cartridge capacity	: 5, 20 or 30 rounds
Magazine catch	: in front of magazine slot
Action	: gas pressure
Cocking system	: cocking lever
Firing system	: semi-automatic
Locking system	: rotating bolt
Length	: 94.3 cm (37.13")
Barrel length	: 47 cm (18.5")
Weight	: 3.0 kg (6.6 lb.)
Sight	: aperture sight and sight mount
Safety	: catch in front end of trigger guard (Garand type)
Stock	: hardwood stock

PARTICULARS

Blued steel; synthetic hand grip.

Ruger Mini-14/5R Ranch Rifle Stainless

SPECIFICATIONS

Caliber	: .223 Rem.
Magazine	: detachable magazine
Cartridge capacity	: 5, 20 or 30 rounds
Magazine catch	: in front of magazine slot
Action	: gas pressure
Cocking system	: cocking lever
Firing system	: semi-automatic
Locking system	: rotating bolt head
Length	: 94.3 cm (37.13")
Barrel length	: 47 cm (18.5")
Weight	: 3.0 kg (6.6 lb.)
Sight	: aperture sight and sight mount
Safety	: catch in front end of trigger guard (Garand type)
Stock	: hardwood stock

Ruger Mini-14/5R Ranch Rifle Stainless

Ruger Mini-14/20GB Government

PARTICULARS
Matt finish stainless steel; synthetic hand grip

Ruger Mini-14/20GB Government

SPECIFICATIONS

Caliber	: .223 Rem.
Magazine	: detachable magazine
Cartridge capacity	: 5, 20 or 30 rounds
Magazine catch	: in front of magazine slot
Action	: gas pressure
Cocking system	: cocking lever
Firing system	: semi-automatic
Locking system	: rotating bolt head
Length	: 98 cm (38.75")
Barrel length	: 47 cm (18.5") incl. flash suppressor
Weight	: 3.1 kg (6.8 lb.)
Sight	: aperture sight and sight mount
Safety	: catch in front end of trigger guard (Garand type)
Stock	: hardwood stock

PARTICULARS
Blued or stainless steel; synthetic hand grip; winged front sight with bayonet lug halfway along the barrel.

Ruger Mini-14/20GB Government Automatic Carbine

SPECIFICATIONS

Caliber	: .223 Rem.
Magazine	: detachable magazine
Cartridge capacity	: 5, 20 or 30 rounds
Magazine catch	: in front of magazine slot
Action	: gas pressure
Cocking system	: cocking lever
Firing system	: semi-automatic, fully automatic, and three-shot burst
Locking system	: rotating bolt
Length	: 98 cm (38.75")
Barrel length	: 47 cm (18.5") incl. flash suppressor
Weight	: 3.1 kg (6.8 lb.)

Sight	: aperture sight and sight mount
Safety	: catch in front end of trigger guard (Garand type)
Stock	: hardwood stock or steel folding stock

PARTICULARS
Blued or stainless steel; synthetic hand grip; winged front sight with bayonet lug halfway along the barrel.

Ruger Mini-Thirty

SPECIFICATIONS

Caliber	: 7.62 x 39 mm
Magazine	: detachable magazine
Cartridge capacity	: 5 rounds
Magazine catch	: in front of magazine slot
Action	: gas pressure
Cocking system	: cocking lever
Firing system	: semi-automatic
Locking system	: rotating bolt
Length	: 94.3 cm (37.13")
Barrel length	: 47 cm (18.5")
Weight	: 3.1 kg (6.9 lb.)
Sight	: aperture sight and sight mount
Safety	: catch in front end of trigger guard (Garand type)
Stock	: hardwood stock, black synthetic hand grip

PARTICULARS
Blued finish.

Ruger Mini-14/20GB Government Automatic Carbine

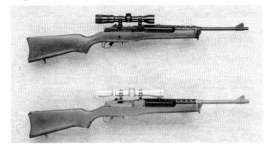

Ruger Mini-Thirty Stainless

SPECIFICATIONS

Caliber	: 7.62 x 39 mm
Magazine	: detachable magazine
Cartridge capacity	: 5 rounds
Magazine catch	: in front of magazine slot
Action	: gas pressure
Cocking system	: cocking lever
Firing system	: semi-automatic
Locking system	: rotating bolt
Length	: 94.3 cm (37.13")
Barrel length	: 47 cm (18.5")
Weight	: 3.1 kg (6.9 lb.)
Sight	: aperture sight and sight mount
Safety	: catch in front end of trigger guard (Garand type)
Stock	: hardwood stock, black synthetic hand grip

PARTICULARS

Matt-finish stainless steel. The illustration shows the Mini-Thirty (top) and the Mini-Thirty Stainless (bottom).

Ruger MP-9 sub-machine-gun

SPECIFICATIONS

Caliber	: 9 mm Para
Magazine	: detachable magazine
Cartridge capacity	: 32 rounds
Magazine catch	: in underside of pistol grip
Cocking system	: cocking lever
Firing system	: full- and semi-automatic
Locking system	: inertia lock
Length	: 37.6 cm (14.8") and 55.6 cm (21.9") with unfolded stock

Ruger MP-9 sub-machine-gun

Ruger MP-9 sub-machine-gun

Ruger M77 Mark II Police Sniper

Barrel length : 17.3 cm (6.8")
Weight : 3 kg (5.9 lb.)
Sight : aperture and front sight adjustable, standard optical sight mount
Safety : firing mode selector catch; locks trigger, interruptor and firing pin
Stock : steel/synthetic folding stock

PARTICULARS
Matt black phosphate finish; aperture sight horizontally adjustable, front sight vertically adjustable. Rate of fire is 550-650 rounds per minute.

Ruger M77 Mark II Police Sniper

SPECIFICATIONS
Caliber : .308 Win. of naar keuze
Magazine : blind magazine
Cartridge capacity: 4 rounds
Magazine catch : N/A; base plate removable
Cocking system : bolt lever
Firing system : single round
Locking system : 2-lug bolt
Length : 118.4 cm (46-5/8")
Barrel length : 66 cm (26")
Weight : 4.4 kg (9 lb.)
Sight : none; optical sight rings included
Safety : safety catch behind bolt lever
Stock : laminated American hardwood

PARTICULARS
Free floating barrel; adjustable trigger pull; extra accessories: Harris bipod, Leupold 3.5-10 x 42 optical sight.

Ruger Police Carbine

SPECIFICATIONS
Caliber : 9 mm Para or .40 S&W
Magazine : detachable magazine

Cartridge capacity: 10 rounds (.40 S&W); 10 or 15 rounds (9 mm Para)
Magazine catch : front of magazine
Action : recoil
Cocking system : cocking lever
Firing system : semi-automatic
Locking system : inertia lock
Length : 88.3 cm (34.75")
Barrel length : 41.3 cm (16.25")
Weight : 2.8 kg (6.4 lb.)
Sight : adjustable rear sight; receiver drilled and tapped for sight mount
Safety : push-button in rear of trigger guard
Stock : black synthetic stock

PARTICULARS
Optional torch clamp around barrel; the Ruger pistol magazines can be used in the carbine.

Ruger Police Carbine

Steyr SPP-Police sub-machine-gun

Steyr AUG

S s

Sako

Immediately after World War I, the Finnish Sako arms factory was established as a workshop for repairing and modifying the military rifles of the time. Many of these weapons were adapted for hunting. The Sako factory is located at Riihimäki, in the south of Finland.

The company, like many in the industry, suffered much from the depression during the thirties of the twentieth century. In the Second World War the company almost folded, and in 1946 it had to be virtually reconstructed from scratch.

During that period, the conversion of military rifles into hunting and competition weapons was the mainstay of its business. In the early fifties of the twentieth century the company developed a range of hunting and precision rifles based on three different receivers and bolts: the short bolt, designated S491, the medium bolt or M591, and the long and magnum bolt, or L691.

In addition, in the late eighties of the twentieth century, a sniper rifle was designed with an unusual type of bolt, the TRG series. This rifle is also available in a hunting version. Sako also produce separate receivers with bolts, as many custom rifle makers use the Sako action as the basis for

Sako, logo

their own products. Sako also offers a military line, with automatic rifles derived from the AK-47 rifle, such as the Sako RK-95, chambered for .223 Rem. or 7.62 x 39 mm. One part of the Sako concern is the ammunition factory, which produces cartridges from .22 Hornet up to .375 H&H Magnum.

The ammunition features specially developed bullets with fanciful names like Hammerhead, Powerhead and Speedhead. In addition, the factory produces a complete range of ammunition for handguns, including a special police round, the 9 mm Para KPO.

Sako RK-95

SPECIFICATIONS

Caliber	: .223 Rem., .308 Win. or 7.62 x 39 mm
Magazine	: detachable magazine
Cartridge capacity	: 30 rounds
Magazine catch	: on front of trigger guard
Action	: gas pressure
Cocking system	: cocking lever
Firing system	: full- or semi-automatic
Locking system	: rotating bolt head
Sight	: flip-up sight for 150 and 300 meters (492 and 984 ft); special mounting for the optical sight and night sight
Safety	: combined safety catch and firing mode selector on right-hand side of housing
Stock	: folding steel skeleton stock

PARTICULARS

Matt black coating; separate lug for rifle grenades or bayonet in accordance with NATO specifications; a special M203 grenade launcher can be mounted under the forearm.

Sako TRG-21 / TRG-41 Sniper

SPECIFICATIONS

Caliber	: .308 Win. (TRG-21) or .338 Lapua Mag. (TRG-41)
Magazine	: detachable magazine
Cartridge capacity	: 10 rounds (TRG-21) or 5 rounds (TRG-41)
Magazine catch	: on front of magazine
Action	: bolt-action
Cocking system	: bolt lever
Firing system	: single round
Locking system	: triangular bolt head
Length	: 115 or 120 cm (45.25 or 47.25")
Barrel length	: 66 or 69 cm (26 or 27.2")
Weight	: 4.7 or 5.1 kg (10.25 or 11.2 lb.) (excl. optical sight)
Sight	: none; special mount for optical sight or night sight
Safety	: safety catch in trigger guard, load indicator on rear of bolt
Stock	: aluminium forearm, synthetic stock with pistol grip, adjustable cheek and butt.

PARTICULARS

Folding bipod; adjustable match trigger from 1 to 2.5 kg (2 to 5 lb.); special flash suppressers and silencers.

Sako TRG-21 / TRG-41 Sniper

Savage

Savage, logo

In 1996, Savage Arms Inc. in Westfield, Massachusetts, celebrated its 133rd anniversary. The company was founded by Arthur William Savage. Up to 1960 the company's main claim to fame was its range of lever-action repeating rifles. Since then, Savage have developed a range of bolt-action rifles. The logo, the head of a Red Indian, dates back to the early twentieth century. In 1901, Savage decided to meet the requests from Cheyenne Indians to supply them with weapons for hunting in their Wyoming reservation. In exchange, the native Americans were prepared to promote Savage rifles at western shows which were popular at the time. In 1920 Savage introduced the Model 1920 Hi-Power, for .250-3000 and .300 Savage. This latter caliber was developed especially for Savage by Charles Newton. At some time around 1930, Nick Brewer, a young gun designer, came to work for a subsidiary of Savage, the Stevens Arms & Tool Company. He designed a number of different rifle models, including the successful Model 110 rifle, which was introduced in 1958. During the Second World War manufacture of sporting guns almost halted. In those years, Savage mainly produced Browning machine guns. After the war, Savage converted large numbers of German Mauser rifles into competition and hunting rifles. The result of this was a growing interest in bolt-action rifles. Over the years, a number of modifications to the Model 110 were introduced, particularly during the period after 1966 by engineer Bob Greenleaf. This resulted in a range of new types, although still based on the old M-110 model. For army and police units, Savage manufactures two types of sniper rifles for the medium range, the Model 110FP Tactical and the Model 111FXP, with and without detachable magazine.

Savage Model 110FP Tactical Sniper

SPECIFICATIONS

Caliber	: .308 Win., .30-06 Springf., .300 Win. Mag.
Magazine	: blind magazine
Cartridge capacity	: 4 rounds; 3 in .300 Win. Mag.
Magazine catch	: N/A
Action	: bolt-action
Cocking system	: bolt lever
Firing system	: single round
Locking system	: 2 lugs
Length	: 116 cm (45.5")
Barrel length	: 61 cm (24")
Weight	: 3.9 kg (8.5 lb.)
Sight	: none
Safety	: catch on right-hand side, in front of bolt lever
Stock	: black synthetic stock with pistol grip

PARTICULARS
Matt black coating; bolt features titanium coating; free floating barrel on bronze bed; receiver is drilled and tapped for sight mount. The rifle is also available in a left-handed version.

Savage Model 111 FXP3/FCXP3 Sniper

SPECIFICATIONS

Caliber	: .308 Win., .30-06 Springf., .300 Win. Mag. or .338 Win. Mag.
Magazine	: blind (FXP3) or detachable magazine (FCXP3)
Cartridge capacity	: 4 rounds; 3 in magnum

Savage Model 111 FXP3/FCXP3 Sniper

Magazine catch	: FXP3: none; FCXP3: mid left-hand side, below bolt
Action	: bolt-action
Cocking system	: bolt lever
Firing system	: single round
Locking system	: 2 lugs
Length	: 111 cm (43.5")
Barrel length	: 56 cm (22")
Weight	: 3.3 kg (7.25 lb.)
Sight	: none
Safety	: safety catch on right-hand side, in front of bolt lever
Stock	: black synthetic stock with pistol grip

PARTICULARS
Matt black coating; receiver is drilled and tapped for sight mount. The rifle is also available in a left-handed version.

Saxonia

Saxonia, logo

De German Saxonia arms factory, originally called the Wiesaer Gerätefabrik, has its offices in Schwarzenberg, in the former German Democratic Republic. Before the unification of Germany, the company mainly produced the Russian assault rifles, AK-47 and AK-74, under license. After the fall of the Berlin Wall, the company was privatized by the Treuhand organization, after which the name was changed to Saxonia Sport- und Jagdwaffen GmbH. The first weapon to be produced by the new company was the Pöhlberg rifle, introduced in 1993. A year later Saxonia marketed the Pöhlberg Sniper, followed in 1995 by the SM96 sniper rifle. The active company introduced the .50 BMG Sniper, or Big-Valve, in 1997.

Saxonia Hail

SPECIFICATIONS

Caliber	: 7.62 x 39 mm
Magazine	: detachable magazine
Cartridge capacity:	5 rounds (see particulars)
Magazine catch	: in front of trigger guard
Action	: gas pressure
Cocking system	: cocking lever
Firing system	: semi-automatic
Locking system	: 2-lug rotating bolt head lock
Length	: 88 cm (34.65")
Barrel length	: 41.5 cm (16.3")
Weight	: 3.8 kg (8.4 lb.)
Sight	: tangent rear sight up to 300 metres (984 ft)
Safety	: slide catch on right-hand side of housing, locks trigger
Stock	: matt black or silver aluminium stock with wooden inlays, or completely black

PARTICULARS

Optional sight mount and optical sight; AK type magazines can also be used.

Saxonia Semi-Pump

SPECIFICATIONS

Caliber	: 12/76
Magazine	: tubular magazine
Cartridge capacity:	15 rounds
Magazine catch	: N/A; loading slot: underside
Action	: gas pressure or pump-action
Cocking system	: pump-action
Firing system	: semi-automatic or single round
Locking system	: bolt lugs
Length	: 107, 117 or 127 cm (42, 46 or 50")
Barrel length	: 51, 61 or 71 cm (20, 24 or 28")
Weight	: 3.5 to 3.7 kg (7.7 to 8.2 lb.)
Sight	: rear and front sight
Safety	: push-button in rear of trigger guard
Stock	: synthetic stock and forearm/hand grip

PARTICULARS

Changeable from semi-auto to pump-action; barrel with muzzle flash suppresser; large bolt catch lever on left-hand side on housing; matt black housing and barrel.

Saxonia Semi-Pump Nickel

SPECIFICATIONS

Caliber	: 12/76
Magazine	: tubular magazine
Cartridge capacity:	15 rounds
Magazine catch	: N/A; loading slot: underside
Action	: gas pressure or pump-action
Cocking system	: pump-action
Firing system	: semi-automatic or single round
Locking system	: bolt lugs
Length	: 107, 117 of 127 cm (42, 46 of 50")
Barrel length	: 51, 61 or 71 cm (20, 24 of 28")
Weight	: 3.1 to 3.5 kg (6.8 to 7.7 lb.)
Sight	: rear and front sight
Safety	: push-button in rear of trigger guard
Stock	: synthetic stock and forearm/hand grip

PARTICULARS

Changeable from semi-auto to pump-action; barrel with muzzle flash suppresser; large bolt catch lever on left-hand side of housing.
Housing and barrel nickel-plated with matt finish.

Saxonia Semi-Pump Nickel

Scattergun Technologies

The American company of Scattergun Technologies Inc. from Nashville, Tennessee, has been manufacturing highly practical shotguns for over ten years, based on different Remington shotgun models.

The guns are in fact riot guns, intended for use by police and other government services. Most Scattergun models feature a Trak-Lock sight, which is an aperture sight with tritium low-visibility markings. One exception is the Rebuild Model. Scattergun will renovate your old Remington 870 shotgun, during which process all worn parts are replaced, and the barrel is re-chambered for 12 bore, 3 inch shot cartridges. A Flexitab follower is built in to prevent loading problems. Also, the sight is adapted, new springs are fitted, and the old rifle receives a new synthetic stock and forearm.

In addition, a new type of safety catch is fitted, and the entire rifle is given a special matt black synthetic coating. Finally, the trigger system is upgraded and adapted. Apart from complete rifles, Scattergun also sell various parts and accessories, including tubular magazine extenders, synthetic forearms with torch clamps, slings and swivels, various types of stocks, and special rifle bags.

Scattergun Border Patrol Model

SPECIFICATIONS

Caliber	: 12/76 (3")
Magazine	: tubular magazine
Cartridge capacity:	7 rounds
Magazine catch	: N/A
Action	: pump-action
Cocking system	: forearm
Firing system	: single round
Locking system	: vertically sliding block
Length	: 97 cm (38.25")

Scattergun Border Patrol Model

Scattergun Border Patrol Short Model

Scattergun Compact Model

Barrel length   : 45.7 cm (18"); cylindrical choke
Weight   : 3.6 kg (8 lb.)
Sight   : adjustable Track-Lock aperture sight
Safety   : special enlarged Jumbo safety catch in rear of
                   trigger guard
Stock   : matt black synthetic stock and forearm; special
                   shock-absorbing butt

PARTICULARS
Matt black coating on housing, tubular
magazine and barrel.
Based on the Remington Model 870
Magnum shotgun. Supplied with a special
Tactical sling.

Scattergun Border Patrol Short Model

SPECIFICATIONS
Caliber   : 12/76 (3")
Magazine   : tubular magazine
Cartridge capacity: 6 rounds
Magazine catch   : N/A
Action   : pump-action
Cocking system   : forearm
Firing system   : single round
Locking system   : vertically sliding block
Length   : 87 cm (34.25")
Barrel length   : 35.6 cm (14"); cylindrical choke
Weight   : 3.5 kg (7.75 lb.)
Sight   : adjustable Track-Lock aperture sight
Safety   : special enlarged Jumbo safety catch in rear of
                   trigger guard
Stock   : matt black synthetic stock and forearm; special
                   shock-absorbing butt

PARTICULARS
Matt black coating on housing, tubular
magazine and barrel.
Based on the Remington Model 870
Magnum shotgun. Supplied with a special
Tactical sling.

Scattergun Compact Model

SPECIFICATIONS
Caliber   : 12/76 (3")
Magazine   : tubular magazine
Cartridge capacity: 5 rounds
Magazine catch   : N/A
Action   : pump-action
Cocking system   : forearm
Firing system   : single round
Locking system   : vertically sliding block
Length   : 83 cm (32.75")
Barrel length   : 31.8 cm (12.5"); 1/2 choke (modified)
Weight   : 3.3 kg (7.25 lb.)
Sight   : adjustable Track-Lock aperture sight
Safety   : special enlarged Jumbo safety catch in rear of
                   trigger guard
Stock   : matt black synthetic stock and forearm; special
                   shock-absorbing butt

PARTICULARS
Matt black coating on housing, tubular
magazine and barrel.
Based on the Remington Model 870
Magnum shotgun. Supplied with a special
Tactical sling.

Scattergun Entry Model

SPECIFICATIONS
Caliber   : 12/76 (3")
Magazine   : tubular magazine
Cartridge capacity: 5 rounds
Magazine catch   : N/A
Action   : pump-action
Cocking system   : forearm
Firing system   : single round
Locking system   : vertically sliding block
Length   : 83 cm (32.75")
Barrel length   : 31.8 cm (12.5"); 1/2 choke (modified)
Weight   : 3.7 kg (8.25 lb.)

Scattergun Entry Model

Sight	: adjustable Track-Lock aperture sight
Safety	: special enlarged Jumbo safety catch in rear of trigger guard
Stock	: matt black synthetic stock and forearm; special shock-absorbing butt

PARTICULARS

Matt black coating on housing, tubular magazine and barrel. Forearm with built-in torch clamp and special fast-loading lever.
The left-hand side of the housing features a magazine for 6 extra rounds. Based on the Remington Model 870 Magnum shotgun. The gun is supplied with a special Tactical sling.

Scattergun Expert Model

SPECIFICATIONS

Caliber	: 12/76 (3")
Magazine	: tubular magazine
Cartridge capacity	: 7 rounds
Magazine catch	: N/A
Action	: pump-action
Cocking system	: forearm
Firing system	: single round
Locking system	: vertically sliding block
Length	: 95 cm (37.25")

Scattergun Expert Model

Barrel length	: 45.7 cm (18"); 1/2 choke (modified)
Weight	: 3.9 kg (8.5 lb.)
Sight	: adjustable Track-Lock aperture sight
Safety	: special enlarged Jumbo safety catch in rear of trigger guard
Stock	: matt black synthetic stock and forearm; special shock-absorbing butt

PARTICULARS

Special NP3 nickel-Teflon coating on housing, tubular magazine and barrel. Forearm with built-in torch clamp. Based on the Remington Model 870 Magnum shotgun.
The left-hand side of the housing features a magazine for 6 extra rounds. The gun is supplied with a special Tactical sling.

Scattergun F.B.I. Model

SPECIFICATIONS

Caliber	: 12/76 (3")
Magazine	: tubular magazine
Cartridge capacity	: 5 rounds
Magazine catch	: N/A
Action	: pump-action
Cocking system	: forearm
Firing system	: single round
Locking system	: vertically sliding block
Length	: 97 cm (38.25")
Barrel length	: 45.7 cm (18"); cylindrical choke
Weight	: 3.9 kg (8.5 lb.)
Sight	: adjustable Track-Lock aperture sight
Safety	: special enlarged Jumbo safety catch in rear of trigger guard
Stock	: matt black synthetic stock and forearm; special shock-absorbing butt

PARTICULARS

Matt black coating on housing, tubular magazine and barrel. Forearm with built-

Scattergun F.B.I. Model

Scattergun K-9 Model

in torch clamp. Based on the Remington Model 870 Magnum shotgun. The left-hand side of the housing features a magazine for 6 extra rounds.
The gun is supplied with a special Tactical sling

Scattergun K-9 Model

SPECIFICATIONS

Caliber	: 12/76 (3")
Magazine	: tubular magazine
Cartridge capacity	: 7 rounds
Magazine catch	: N/A
Action	: gas pressure
Cocking system	: cocking lever
Firing system	: semi-automatic
Locking system	: vertically sliding block
Length	: 98 cm (38.5")
Barrel length	: 45.7 cm (18"); cylindrical choke
Weight	: 3.9 kg (8.5 lb.)
Sight	: adjustable Track-Lock aperture sight
Safety	: special enlarged Jumbo safety catch in rear of trigger guard
Stock	: matt black synthetic stock and forearm; special shock-absorbing butt

PARTICULARS

Matt black coating on housing, tubular magazine and barrel. Based on the Remington Model 11-87 Magnum semi-automatic shotgun. The left-hand side of the housing features a magazine for 6 extra rounds. The gun is supplied with a special Tactical sling.

Scattergun Louis Awerbuck Signature Model

SPECIFICATIONS

Caliber	: 12/76 (3")
Magazine	: tubular magazine

Cartridge capacity	: 5 rounds
Magazine catch	: N/A
Action	: pump-action
Cocking system	: forearm
Firing system	: single round
Locking system	: vertically sliding block
Length	: 97 cm (38.25")
Barrel length	: 45.7 cm (18"); 1/2 choke (modified)
Weight	: 3.7 kg (8.25 lb.)
Sight	: adjustable Track-Lock aperture sight
Safety	: special enlarged Jumbo safety catch in rear of trigger guard
Stock	: Stock and forearm of beech; special shock-absorbing butt and special shock absorber built into stock.

PARTICULARS

Matt black coating on housing, tubular magazine and barrel. Based on the Remington Model 870 Magnum shotgun. The left-hand side of the housing features a magazine for 6 extra rounds.
The gun is supplied with a special Tactical sling.

Scattergun Patrol Model

SPECIFICATIONS

Caliber	: 12/76 (3")
Magazine	: tubular magazine
Cartridge capacity	: 5 rounds
Magazine catch	: N/A
Action	: pump-action
Cocking system	: forearm
Firing system	: single round
Locking system	: vertically sliding block
Length	: 97 cm (38.25")
Barrel length	: 45.7 cm (18"); cylindrical choke
Weight	: 3.4 kg (7.5 lb.)
Sight	: adjustable Track-Lock aperture sight
Safety	: special enlarged Jumbo safety catch in rear of trigger guard

Scattergun Louis Awerbuck Signature Model

Stock	: matt black synthetic stock and forearm; special shock-absorbing butt

PARTICULARS

Matt black coating on housing, tubular magazine and barrel. Based on the Remington Model 870 Magnum shotgun. The gun is supplied with a special Tactical sling.

Scattergun Professional Model

SPECIFICATIONS

Caliber	: 12/76 (3")
Magazine	: tubular magazine
Cartridge capacity	: 6 rounds
Magazine catch	: N/A

Action	: pump-action
Cocking system	: forearm
Firing system	: single round
Locking system	: vertically sliding block
Length	: 87 cm (34.25")
Barrel length	: 35.6 cm (14"); cylindrical choke
Weight	: 3.7 kg (8.25 lb.)
Sight	: adjustable Track-Lock aperture sight
Safety	: special enlarged Jumbo safety catch in rear of trigger guard
Stock	: matt black synthetic stock and forearm; special shock-absorbing butt

PARTICULARS

Matt black coating on housing, tubular magazine and barrel. Forearm with built-in torch clamp. Based on the Remington

Scattergun Rebuild Remington 870 Model

Model 870 Magnum shotgun. The left-hand side of the housing features a magazine for 6 extra rounds.
The gun is supplied with a special Tactical sling.

Scattergun Rebuild Remington 870 Model

Scattergun Standard Model

SPECIFICATIONS

Caliber	: 12/76 (3")
Magazine	: tubular magazine
Cartridge capacity	: 2 to 7 rounds
Magazine catch	: N/A
Action	: pump-action
Cocking system	: forearm
Firing system	: single round
Locking system	: vertically sliding block
Length	: 97 cm (38.25")
Barrel length	: 31.8 to 45.7 cm (12.5 to 18")
Weight	: 3.3 to 4.1 kg (7.25 to 9 lb.)
Sight	: adjustable Track-Lock aperture sight
Safety	: special enlarged Jumbo safety catch in rear of trigger guard
Stock	: matt black synthetic stock and forearm; special shock-absorbing butt

PARTICULARS

Matt black coating on housing, tubular magazine and barrel. Renovated Remington Model 870 shotgun. Accessories fitted to order.

Scattergun Standard Model

SPECIFICATIONS

Caliber	: 12/76 (3")
Magazine	: tubular magazine
Cartridge capacity	: 7 rounds
Magazine catch	: N/A
Action	: pump-action
Cocking system	: forearm
Firing system	: single round
Locking system	: vertically sliding block
Length	: 97 cm (38.25")
Barrel length	: 45.7 cm (18"); cylindrical choke
Weight	: 4.1 kg (9 lb.)
Sight	: adjustable Track-Lock aperture sight
Safety	: special enlarged Jumbo safety catch in rear of trigger guard
Stock	: matt black synthetic stock and forearm; special shock-absorbing butt

PARTICULARS

Matt black coating on housing, tubular magazine and barrel. Forearm with built-in torch clamp. Based on the Remington Model 870 Magnum shotgun. The left-hand side of the housing features a magazine for 6 extra rounds.
The gun is supplied with a special Tactical sling.

Scattergun SWAT Model

SPECIFICATIONS

Caliber	: 12/76 (3")
Magazine	: tubular magazine
Cartridge capacity	: 6 rounds
Magazine catch	: N/A
Action	: gas pressure
Cocking system	: cocking lever
Firing system	: semi-automatic
Locking system	: vertically sliding block
Length	: 88 cm (34.5")
Barrel length	: 35.6 cm (14"); cylindrical choke
Weight	: 3.97 kg (8.75 lb.)
Sight	: adjustable Track-Lock aperture sight
Safety	: special enlarged Jumbo safety catch in rear of trigger guard
Stock	: matt black synthetic stock and forearm; special shock-absorbing butt

Scattergun SWAT Model

PARTICULARS

Matt black coating on housing, tubular magazine and barrel. Special torch clamp around front of barrel. The left-hand side of the housing features a magazine for 6 extra rounds.

Based on the Remington Model 11-87 Magnum semi-automatic shotgun. The gun is supplied with a special Tactical sling.

Scattergun Urban Sniper Model

SPECIFICATIONS

Caliber	: 12/76 (3")
Magazine	: tubular magazine
Cartridge capacity	: 7 rounds
Magazine catch	: N/A
Action	: gas pressure
Cocking system	: cocking lever
Firing system	: semi-automatic
Locking system	: vertically sliding block
Length	: 98 cm (38.5")
Barrel length	: 45.7 cm (18"); rifled barrel
Weight	: 4.3 kg (9.5 lb.)
Sight	: adjustable Track-Lock aperture sight
Safety	: special enlarged Jumbo safety catch in rear of trigger guard
Stock	: matt black Monte Carlo synthetic stock and forearm; special shock-absorbing butt

PARTICULARS

Matt black coating on housing, tubular magazine and barrel. Special slug barrel with lands and grooves.

Fitted with a 2.75 x optical sight and adjustable bipod. The left-hand side of the housing features a magazine for 6 extra rounds. Based on the Remington Model 11-87 Magnum semi-automatic shotgun. The gun is supplied with a special Tactical sling.

Scattergun Urban Sniper Model

Schmidt-Rubin

The Swiss army received its first Schmidt-Rubin rifle in 1889. The gun had been developed by colonel and arms expert, Rudolf Schmidt, who also ran the national arms factory at Bern. The special 7.5 x 55 mm caliber was the brainchild of colonel-major Eduard Rubin, who worked at the Thuner ammunition factory. The Model 1889 Schmidt-Rubin rifle had an unusual bolt-action for the time, moving straight backwards instead of using a rotating motion with bolt lugs.

The cocking lever rotates the bolt, which causes the lugs on the bolt to engage recesses in the receiver. It is generally assumed that this bolt system was preferred in order to steer clear of existing patent rights. The first rifle model of 1889 had bolt lugs at the rear of a rotating bolt head sleeve. In the next type of rifle, the model 1911, these lugs had been moved to the front of the bolt sleeve. The last type, model 1931, had two bolt lugs at the front of the bolt. All models feature the distinctive ring at the rear of the bolt. This is a safety catch which doubles as a means of re-cocking the firing pin.

The operation of the Schmidt-Rubin rifles is as follows. The bolt lever is connected to a bolt rod which has a lug that moves in a helical slot in the bolt sleeve; by pulling the bolt lever straight backwards, the lug slides through the slot, causing the bolt sleeve to rotate through a full turn; this disengages the bolt lugs on the sleeve from their respective recesses in the receiver, thus unlocking the gun. The locking of the weapon takes place in reverse order. The rifles were produced by the well-known Schweizerische Industrie Gesellschaft (SIG) and the Eidgenossische Waffenfabrik Berne.

The Schmidt-Rubin rifles weren't replaced until 1957, when the semi-automatic rifle model 57 by SIG was introduced. This weapon also features the distinctive Schmidt-Rubin bolt lever and a similar

locking system. Most Schmidt-Rubin rifles carry a logo on the receiver bridge showing a large Swiss cross in a shield.

Schmidt-Rubin Rifle Model 1911

SPECIFICATIONS

Caliber	: 7.5 x 55 mm
Magazine	: detachable magazine
Cartridge capacity: 6 rounds	
Magazine catch	: on right-hand side of magazine slot
Action	: bolt-action
Cocking system	: cocking lever
Firing system	: single round
Locking system	: bolt lugs
Length	: 131 cm (51.6")
Barrel length	: 78 cm (30.7")
Weight	: 4.6 kg (10.15 lb.)
Sight	: tangent rear sight
Safety	: rotating ring on rear of bolt
Stock	: walnut

PARTICULARS
Rotating safety doubles as cocking ring for firing pin. Bolt lugs on front of rotating bolt head sleeve. Brown Bakelite cocking knob.

Schmidt-Rubin M31 (K31) carbine

SPECIFICATIONS

Caliber	: 7.5 x 55 mm
Magazine	: detachable magazine
Cartridge capacity: 6 rounds	
Magazine catch	: on right-hand side of magazine slot
Action	: bolt-action
Cocking system	: cocking lever
Firing system	: single round
Locking system	: bolt lugs
Length	: 110.5 cm (43.5")
Barrel length	: 65.5 cm (25.7")
Weight	: 4.0 kg (8.8 lb.)
Sight	: tangent rear sight
Safety	: rotating ring on rear of bolt
Stock	: walnut

PARTICULARS
Rotating safety doubles as cocking ring for firing pin.
Bolt lugs on front of bolt. Aluminum cocking knob.

Schmidt-Rubin K31/42 Sniper carbine

SPECIFICATIONS

Caliber	: 7.5 x 55 mm
Magazine	: detachable magazine
Cartridge capacity: 6 rounds	
Magazine catch	: on right-hand side of magazine slot
Action	: bolt-action
Cocking system	: cocking lever
Firing system	: single round
Locking system	: bolt lugs
Length	: 110.5 cm (43.5")
Barrel length	: 65.5 cm (25.7")
Weight	: 4.2 kg (9.25 lb.)
Sight	: tangent rear sight; 1.8 x optical sight
Safety	: rotating ring on rear of bolt
Stock	: walnut

PARTICULARS
Rotating safety doubles as cocking ring for

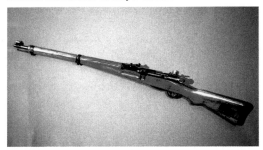

Detail of a Schmidt-Rubin K31/42

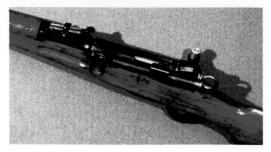

firing pin. Bolt lugs on front of bolt. Aluminum cocking knob. Small optical sight to the left-hand side of receiver and periscopic lens.

The K31/43 sniper carbine featured a similar 2.8 x optical sight.

SIG

The precursor of SIG, the Schweizerische Industrie Gesellschaft, was the Schweizerische Wagons Fabrik, which was founded in 1853 by Heinrich Moser, a watch maker, Friedrich Peyer im Hof, a politician, and Conrad Neher-Stokar, a Swiss army officer. Initially, the company constructed railway coaches, but in 1860 it took up the manufacture of arms, at the request of the Swiss army. In 1865 the armament factory was a separate company under the direct management of Friedrich Vetterli, who was responsible for the development of a military rifle, the Vetterli Model 1869. Shortly afterwards, the company was renamed to Schweizerische Industriegesellschaft, Neuhausen am Rheinfall, SIG for short. The company has since developed numerous types of weapons. From 1908 to 1911 SIG produced the first semi-automatic gas pressure operated rifle, the so-called Mondragon carbine, from a design of the Mexican general, Manuel Mondragon. In

1920 large quantities of Bergmann sub-machine-guns were manufactured and exported to Japan, Finland, and China, among other countries. In 1927 the first SIG machine-gun was introduced under the name KE-7, and supplied to the armies of Chili, China, Columbia, Finland, and Peru.

In 1938 SIG were faced with an export ban. Weapons could only be exported with a government license, a situation which continues to this day in the whole of Europe. During the Second World War, in which Swiss remained neutral, large quantities of weapons were produced for the Swiss army, including the MP41 sub-machine-gun, followed by the 44, 45, 46, and 48 types.

In 1947 the company received a Swiss army commission to design a semi-automatic pistol, which was adopted by the army as the model SP-47/8. This was later altered to become the SIG P210, aimed primarily at the civilian market. In the mid-fifties of the twentieth century, SIG were asked by the government to develop and manufacture an automatic rifle.

The result was the Sturmgewehr 57, 700,000 of which have been supplied to the Swiss army alone. In 1971 SIG took over the Hämmerli sports gun company, and in 1974 the German weapon manufacturers, Sauer & Sohn, based in Eckenforde, were incorporated. The latter cooperation culminated in the manufacture of a complete range of pistols, the SIG-Sauers. In 1984 a new rifle was developed by SIG, resulting in a complete family of guns, the SG 550/551.

SIG MP44

SPECIFICATIONS

Caliber	: 9 mm Para
Magazine	: detachable magazine
Cartridge capacity	: 40 rounds
Magazine catch	: on left-hand side of housing
Action	: recoil
Cocking system	: cocking lever
Firing system	: semi- and fully automatic
Locking system	: inertia lock
Length	: 83 cm (32.7")
Barrel length	: 30 cm (11.8")
Weight	: 3.95 kg (8.7 lb.)

Sight   : adjustable aperture sight
Safety   : catch on left-hand side of housing
Stock   : hardwood stock, steel forearm

PARTICULARS
Blued matt black.

SIG SG 540

SPECIFICATIONS
Caliber   : .223 Rem.
Magazine   : detachable magazine
Cartridge capacity : 20 or 30 rounds
Magazine catch   : in front of trigger guard
Action   : gas pressure (adjustable)
Cocking system   : cocking lever
Firing system   : semi- and fully automatic, and 3-round bursts
Locking system   : rotating bolt head
Length   : 95 cm (37.4")
Barrel length   : 46 cm (18.1") (excl. flash suppresser)
Weight   : 3.5 kg (7.7 lb.)
Sight   : adjustable aperture sight; special SIG sight
                     mount
Safety   : combined safety catch/firing mode selector
Stock   : synthetic stock, pistol grip and hand grip

PARTICULARS
Matt black phosphate finish; bolt catch
lever on left-hand side above trigger guard;
folding trigger guard; pressure point trigger
for semi-automatic precision fire; cleaning

SIG SG 540

set in pistol grip. Adjustable gas pressure
settings for normal use, rifle grenades and
dirty weapon; folding bipod.

SIG SG 540 Short

SPECIFICATIONS
Caliber   : .223 Rem.
Magazine   : detachable magazine
Cartridge capacity : 20 or 30 rounds
Magazine catch   : in front of trigger guard
Action   : gas pressure (adjustable)
Cocking system   : cocking lever
Firing system   : semi- and fully automatic, and 3-round bursts
Locking system   : rotating bolt head
Length   : unfolded stock: 95 cm (37.4");
                     folded stock 72 cm (28.3")
Barrel length   : 46 cm (18.1") (excl. flash suppresser)
Weight   : 3.6 kg (7.9 lb.)
Sight   : adjustable aperture sight; special SIG sight
                     mount
Safety   : combined safety catch/firing mode selector
Stock   : steel skeleton stock, synthetic pistol grip and
                     hand grip

PARTICULARS
Matt black phosphate finish; bolt catch
lever on left-hand side above trigger guard;
folding trigger guard; pressure point trigger for semi-automatic precision fire;
cleaning set in pistol grip.

Adjustable gas pressure settings for
normal use, rifle grenades, and dirty
weapon; folding bipod.

SIG SG 541

SPECIFICATIONS
Caliber   : .223 Rem. of .308 Win.
Magazine   : detachable magazine
Cartridge capacity : 20 or 30 rounds
Magazine catch   : in front of trigger guard

SIG SG 540 Short

SIG SG 541

Action	: gas pressure (adjustable)
Cocking system	: cocking lever
Firing system	: semi- and fully automatic and 3-round bursts
Locking system	: rotating bolt head
Length	: 100 cm (39.4")
Barrel length	: 46.5 cm (18.3")
Weight	: 4.0 kg (8.9 lb.)
Sight	: adjustable aperture sight; special sight mount
Safety	: ambidextrous combined safety catch/firing mode selector
Stock	: synthetic folding stock, pistol grip and ventilated hand grip

PARTICULARS

Matt black phosphate finish; folding bipod; combined flash suppresser and grenade launcher. Adjustable gas pressure settings for normal use, rifle grenades, and dirty weapon.

The illustration shows the SG 541 rifle (bottom) and the shortened version (top).

SIG SG 542

SPECIFICATIONS

Caliber	: .308 Win.
Magazine	: detachable magazine
Cartridge capacity	: 20 or 30 rounds
Magazine catch	: in front of trigger guard
Action	: gas pressure (adjustable)
Cocking system	: cocking lever
Firing system	: semi- and fully automatic and 3-round bursts
Locking system	: rotating bolt head
Length	: 100.2 cm (39.4")
Barrel length	: 46.5 cm (18.3") (excl. flash suppresser

SIG SG 542

Weight	: 3.8 kg (8.3 lb.)
Sight	: adjustable aperture sight; special SIG sight mount
Safety	: combined safety catch/firing mode selector
Stock	: synthetic stock, pistol grip and hand grip

PARTICULARS

Matt black phosphate finish; bolt catch lever on left-hand side above trigger guard; folding trigger guard; pressure point trigger for semi-automatic precision fire; cleaning set in pistol grip.

Adjustable gas pressure settings for normal use, rifle grenades, and dirty weapon; folding bipod.

SIG SG 543

SPECIFICATIONS

Caliber	: .223 Rem.
Magazine	: detachable magazine
Cartridge capacity	: 20 or 30 rounds
Magazine catch	: in front of trigger guard
Action	: gas pressure (adjustable)
Cocking system	: cocking lever
Firing system	: semi- and fully automatic and 3-round bursts
Locking system	: rotating bolt head
Length	: unfolded stock: 80.5 cm (31.7"); folded stock: 57 cm (22.4")
Barrel length	: 30 cm (11.8") (excl. flash suppresser

SIG SG 543

Weight	: 2.95 kg (6.5 lb.)
Sight	: adjustable aperture sight
Safety	: combined safety catch/firing mode selector
Stock	: steel skeleton stock, synthetic pistol grip and hand grip

PARTICULARS

Matt black phosphate finish; bolt catch lever on left-hand side above trigger guard; folding trigger guard; pressure point trigger for semi-automatic precision fire; cleaning set in pistol grip.
Adjustable gas pressure settings for normal use, rifle grenades, and dirty weapon.

SIG SG 550 Sniper

SPECIFICATIONS

Caliber	: .223 Rem.
Magazine	: losse detachable magazine
Cartridge capacity	: 20 or 30 rounds
Magazine catch	: to front of trigger guard
Action	: gas pressure
Cocking system	: cocking lever
Firing system	: semi-automatic on gas pressure
Locking system	: rotating bolt head
Length	: 108 cm (42.5")
Barrel length	: 61 cm (24")

Weight	: 7.02 kg (15.5 lb.)
Sight	: optical sight
Safety	: ambidextrous safety catch above pistol grip
Stock	: synthetic folding stock with adjustable cheek and butt; synthetic pistol grip with palm rest and synthetic hand grip with folding bipod

PARTICULARS

Matt black phosphate finish steel. Interconnectable magazines.

SIG SG 550 SP

SPECIFICATIONS

Caliber	: .223 Rem.
Magazine	: detachable magazine
Cartridge capacity	: 20 or 30 rounds
Magazine catch	: to front of trigger guard
Action	: gas pressure (adjustable)
Cocking system	: cocking lever
Firing system	: fully automatic, 3-shot burst and semi-automatic
Locking system	: rotating bolt head
Length	: with unfolded stock: 99.8 cm (39.3"); folded: 77.2 cm (30.4")
Barrel length	: 52.8 cm (20.8")
Weight	: 4.1 kg (9 lb.)
Sight	: adjustable aperture sight and/or sight mount

SIG SG 550 SP

Safety	: ambidextrous safety catch above pistol grip; doubles as firing mode selector
Stock	: synthetic folding stock and hand grip

PARTICULARS

Matt black phosphate finish; with folding bipod, inter-connectable magazines, and bayonet lug.
Features adjustable gas pressure settings for normal use, rifle grenades, and dirty weapon..

SIG SG 550 - Stg P90

SPECIFICATIONS

Caliber	: .223 Rem.
Magazine	: detachable magazine
Cartridge capacity	: 20 or 30 rounds
Magazine catch	: to front of trigger guard
Action	: gas pressure (adjustable)
Cocking system	: cocking lever
Firing system	: semi-automatic
Locking system	: rotating bolt head
Length	: with unfolded stock: 99.8 cm (39.3"); folded: 77.2 cm (30.4")
Barrel length	: 45 cm (17.7")
Weight	: 4.1 kg (9 lb.)

SIG SG 550 - Stg P90

Sight	: adjustable aperture sight and/or sight mount
Safety	: ambidextrous safety catch above pistol grip; doubles as firing mode selector
Stock	: synthetic folding stock and hand grip

PARTICULARS

Matt black phosphate finish; with folding bipod, inter-connectable magazines, and bayonet lug.
Features adjustable gas pressure settings for normal use, rifle grenades, and dirty weapon.

SIG SG 551-LB (Long Barrel)

SPECIFICATIONS

Caliber	: .223 Rem.
Magazine	: detachable magazine
Cartridge capacity	: 20- or 30-rounds
Magazine catch	: in front of trigger guard
Action	: gas pressure (adjustable)
Cocking system	: cocking lever
Firing system	: automatic, semi-automatic and 3-shot burst
Locking system	: rotating bolt head
Length	: 100 cm (39.4")
Barrel length	: 53 cm (20.9")
Weight	: 4 kg 8.8 lb.)
Sight	: adjustable aperture sight; suitable for sight mount
Safety	: ambidextrous safety catch above pistol grip; doubles as firing mode selector for semi-automatic, 3-round burst, or fully automatic
Stock	: black synthetic folding stock and hand grip

PARTICULARS

Matt black phosphate finish; inter-connectable magazines.
Features adjustable gas pressure settings for normal use, rifle grenades, and dirty weapon.

SIG SG 551-LB (Long Barrel)

SIG SG 551/552-SP Commando

SIG SG 551/552-SP Commando

SPECIFICATIONS

Caliber : .223 Rem.
Magazine : losse detachable magazine
Cartridge capacity: 20- or 30-rounds
Magazine catch : in front of trigger guard
Action : gas pressure (adjustable)
Cocking system : cocking lever
Firing system : fully automatic, 3-shot burst and semi-automatic
Locking system : rotating bolt head
Length : with unfolded stock: 82.6 cm (32.5"); folded: 60 cm (23.6")
Barrel length : 40.6 cm (16")
Weight : 3.5 kg (7.7 lb.)

SIG SG 551-1P

Sight : adjustable aperture sight or sight mount
Safety : ambidextrous safety catch above pistol grip; doubles as firing mode selector
Stock : black synthetic folding stock with large rubber cheek and synthetic hand grip

PARTICULARS

Sub-machine-gun chambered for .223 Rem. Inter-connectable magazines; special flash suppresser for use with night sight.

Features adjustable gas pressure settings for normal use, rifle grenades, and dirty weapon.

SIG SG 551-1P

SPECIFICATIONS

Caliber : .223 Rem.
Magazine : detachable magazine
Cartridge capacity: 20- or 30-rounds
Magazine catch : in front of trigger guard
Action : gas pressure (adjustable)
Cocking system : cocking lever
Firing system : automatic, semi-automatic and 3-shot burst
Locking system : rotating bolt head
Length : 82.8 cm (32.6")
Barrel length : 35 cm (13.8")
Weight : 3.4 kg (7.5 lb.)
Sight : adjustable aperture sight or sight mount

| Safety | : ambidextrous safety catch above pistol grip; doubles as firing mode selector for semi-automatic, 3-round burst or fully automatic |
| Stock | : synthetic folding stock with large soft rubber cheek and synthetic hand grip |

PARTICULARS

Matt black phosphate finish. Inter-connectable magazines.
Features adjustable gas pressure settings for normal use, rifle grenades, and dirty weapon.

SIG SG 551-SWAT (Special Weapons And Tactics) carbine

SPECIFICATIONS

Caliber	: .223 Rem.
Magazine	: detachable magazine
Cartridge capacity: 20- or 30-rounds
Magazine catch	: in front of trigger guard
Action	: gas pressure (adjustable)
Cocking system	: cocking lever
Firing system	: fully automatic, semi-automatic and 3-shot burst
Locking system	: rotating bolt head
Length	: 100 cm (39.4")
Barrel length	: 53 cm (20.9")
Weight	: 4 kg (8.8 lb.)
Sight	: adjustable aperture sight; suitable for sight mounting with Hensoldt 6 x 42 BL optical sight, Trijicon ACOG combat sight, or a night/optical sight
Safety	: ambidextrous safety catch above pistol grip; doubles as firing mode selector for semi-automatic, 3-round burst, or fully automatic
Stock	: black synthetic folding stock and hand grip

PARTICULARS

Matt black phosphate finish. Folding

SIG SG 551-SWAT (Special Weapons And Tactics)

SIG SG 551-SWAT (Special Weapons And Tactics)

stock with rubber cheek. Gas block with bayonet lug; special mount below hand grip for MagLite torch or laser pointer. Adjustable gas pressure settings for normal use, rifle grenades, and dirty weapon. Inter-connectable magazines.

SIG SSG 2000 Sniper

SPECIFICATIONS

Caliber	: .308 Win. or 7.5 x 55 mm Swiss
Magazine	: detachable magazine
Cartridge capacity: 5 rounds
Magazine catch	: in front of trigger guard
Action	: bolt-action
Cocking system	: bolt lever
Firing system	: single round
Locking system	: 6-lug bolt
Length	: 121 cm (47.6")
Barrel length	: 61 cm (24")
Weight	: 6.6 kg (14.6 lb.)
Sight	: Zeiss Diatal ZA 8x56 of S&B 1.5-6x42 optical sight
Safety	: on right-hand side behind bolt lever, indicator pin in rear of bolt
Stock	: walnut stock with thumb hole, adjustable cheek and butt.

SIG SSG 2000 Sniper

SIG SSG 3000 Sniper

PARTICULARS
Matt black phosphate finish; special flash suppresser; special adjustable bipod.

SIG SSG 3000 Sniper

SPECIFICATIONS

Caliber	: .308 Win.
Magazine	: detachable magazine
Cartridge capacity	: 5 rounds
Magazine catch	: in front of trigger guard
Action	: bolt-action
Cocking system	: bolt lever
Firing system	: single round
Locking system	: 6-lug bolt
Length	: 118 cm (46.5")
Barrel length	: 61 cm (without flash suppresser) (24")
Weight	: 6.2 kg (13.7 lb.)
Sight	: mounting rail with 1.5-6 x 42 BL Hensoldt optical sight
Safety	: safety catch above bolt rod, firing catch in front of trigger; indicator pin in rear of bolt
Stock	: black laminated wooden stock with adjustable cheek and butt and pistol grip

PARTICULARS
Matt black phosphate finish; forearm with bipod.

Sommer + Ockenfuss

The short Bullpup Sniper by Sommer + Ockenfuss is manufactured by German rifle makers Keppeler & Fritz. The repeating system resembles a pump-action, in that the pistol grip must be pulled

Sommer + Ockenfuss, logo

backwards and then pushed forwards. The bolt is extremely short, only 4.5 cm(1.77") in length. It operates almost like a vertically sliding block, and has three large bolt lugs in front of each other. The rifle features a special Lothar-Walther barrel with a combined flash suppresser and recoil damper. The underside of the forearm contains a special rail for mounting various accessories, including a folding bipod.

The pistol grip has a grip safety, which locks the trigger. If the pistol grip repeating action is used without depressing the grip safety, the bolt locks after 1 cm and drops downwards, out of reach of the primer.

Sommer + Ockenfuss Shorty

SPECIFICATIONS

Caliber	: 6 mm BR, .308 Win., .300 Win. Mag. or other caliber to order
Magazine	: detachable magazine in rear of stock
Cartridge capacity	: 5 or 10 rounds
Magazine catch	: on right-hand lower side near magazine slot
Repeating system	: pump-action by pulling back pistol grip
Firing system	: single round
Locking system	: 3-lug bolt
Length	: 85 cm (33.5")
Barrel length	: 65 cm (25.6")
Weight	: 4.1 kg (9.5 lb.)

Repeating action

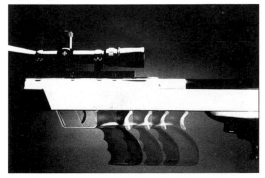

Sommer + Ockenfuss Shorty

Sight	: mounting rail with optical sight rings
Safety	: grip safety with trigger and bolt locking
Stock	: synthetic bullpup stock

PARTICULARS
Matt black blasted barrel with fluting, flash suppresser and recoil damper; adjustable match trigger.

Springfield Armory

Springfield Armory, logo

The Springfield Armory name is linked with the original Springfield Armory factory, the US Government Arsenal, located in Massachusetts since 1777. Rifles dating from that period include the Springfield Model 1873 Trapdoor Rifle, and the Springfield Model M1903. In 1968, the company was disbanded by the Secretary of Defense, Robert S. MacNamarra. Three years later, a Texas businessman bought the rights to the Springfield name. The patent rights connected with the name ceased to apply. The new Springfield did not survive and disappeared in 1974. Some years afterwards, the remains of the company were purchased by Robert Reese, an experienced arms wholesaler. He saw a commercial future for the old company and moved it to Geneso, Illinois. Together with his three sons, he went to work to initially produce a large series of the M1A,

a civilian version of the US M14 army rifle. The current Springfield range comprises a range of pistols based on the Colt Government, the M1A National Match .308 Win. rifle, the M6 Scout Survival carbine (a twin-barreled carbine chambered for .22 Long Rifle and .410 shot cartridges), the famous M1 Garand rifle .30-06 (also available in calibers .308 Win. and .270 Win), a Beretta BM-59 army .308 Win. rifle built under license, and the SAR-48, a copy of the FN-FAL chambered for the .308 Win. cartridge. A number of these weapons are not manufactured by Springfield themselves, but are imported from, among others, the Brazilian Imbel arms factory at Itajuba. Examples include the Colt M1911-A1 pistol, and the SAR-48 rifle. In November 1992, Springfield Armory had to cease its operations due to financial difficulties, but the company did not suffer bankruptcy. A new start was made with a downsized company under the name Springfield Inc. Strangely enough, one of the causes of the company's problems was its great success. The company had grown too fast, particularly as a result of its range of special pistols, which generated worldwide demand. Another cause was the miserable failure of a number of costly projects. Examples include the Linkless 10 mm pistol that did not materialize, and the Omega Project. The Omega pistols, produced by Peters Stahl in Germany, were introduced on the North American market by Springfield, but the scheme came to nothing. The third cause were the enormous losses resulting from the SASS conversion project. This project consisted of a single-shot conversion set for the Colt 1911 pistol that enabled it to fire rifle

Springfield Krag-Jorgensen Model 1896

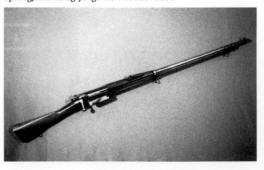

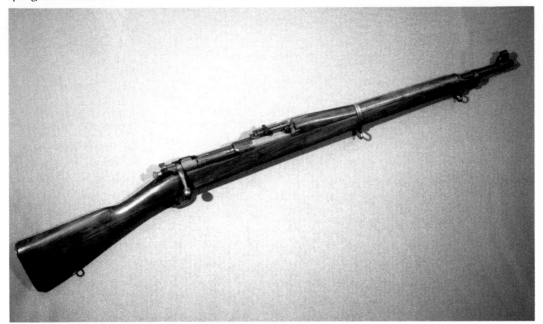

rounds. In addition, the company had suffered financial damage with the IMI project. Springfield had made an agreement with the Israeli IMI company to sell the Uzi sub-machine-gun and the Uzi semi-automatic carbine in North America. However, the introduction of the Federal Assault Rifle Ban made the import and sale of these weapons illegal in the USA By now Springfield have managed to overcome the difficulties, and are thriving as never before.

Springfield Krag-Jorgensen Model 1896

SPECIFICATIONS

Caliber	: .30-40 Krag
Magazine	: inwendig magazine
Cartridge capacity	: 5 rounds
Magazine catch	: N/A: loading port on right-hand side of receiver
Action	: bolt-action
Cocking system	: bolt lever
Firing system	: single round
Locking system	: bolt lugs
Length	: 124.7 cm (49.1")
Barrel length	: 76.2 cm (30")
Weight	: 4.1 kg (8.9 lb.)
Sight	: tangent rear sight
Safety	: catch in top of bolt
Stock	: wooden stock

PARTICULARS

Adopted by the US armed forces in 1896. Springfield manufactured about 62,000 of these rifles. Versions include the M1896 Cadet Rifle and M1896 carbine. Succeeded in 1898 by the Model 1898 rifle. This weapon featured only a few modifications compared with the Model 1896.

Springfield Model 1903

SPECIFICATIONS

Caliber	: .30-06 Spr.
Magazine	: blind magazine
Cartridge capacity	: 5 rounds
Magazine catch	: N/A
Action	: bolt-action
Cocking system	: bolt lever
Firing system	: single round
Locking system	: bolt lugs
Length	: 109.7 cm (43.2")
Barrel length	: 61 cm (24")
Weight	: 3.9 kg (8.68 lb.)
Sight	: tangent rear sight
Safety	: wing-type catch on rear of bolt
Stock	: wooden stock and forearm

PARTICULARS

Produced by Springfield, Rock Island

Arsenal, Remington, and Smith-Corona from 1903 to 1943. The different models are M1903A1: with a semi-pistol grip; M1903A2: the rifle system without the stock, as an artillery training weapon; M1903A3: the tangent rear sight has been replaced by an adjustable aperture sight; M1903A4: sniper model with optical sight and without iron sights; M1903 Mark 1: a model featuring the Pedersen system, making the weapon capable of semi-automatic fire.

Springfield Model M1917 (P17) Enfield

SPECIFICATIONS

Caliber   : .30-06 Spr.
Magazine   : blind magazine
Cartridge capacity: 5 rounds
Magazine catch   : N/A
Action   : bolt-action
Cocking system   : bolt lever
Firing system   : single round
Locking system   : bolt lugs
Length   : 117.5 cm (46.25")
Barrel length   : 66 cm (26")
Weight   : 4.4 kg (9.6 lb.)
Sight   : adjustable aperture sight
Safety   : wing-type catch on rear of bolt
Stock   : wooden stock and forearm

PARTICULARS

American version of the Enfield Pattern 1914 or P14 rifle chambered for .30-06 Springfield ammo. During the Second World War, large quantities of these rifles were converted to use the 8 x 57 mm Mauser cartridge and supplied to Nationalist China.

Springfield Model M1917 (P17) Enfield

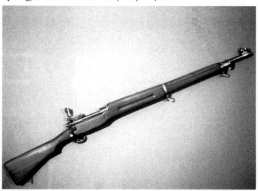

Springfield Garand M1A-T26

Springfield Garand M1A-T26

SPECIFICATIONS

Caliber   : .30-06
Magazine   : blind magazine
Cartridge capacity: 8 rounds
Magazine catch   : N/A
Action   : gas pressure
Cocking system   : cocking lever
Firing system   : semi-automatic
Locking system   : rotating bolt head
Length   : 93.3 cm (37.6")
Barrel length   : 45.7 cm (18")
Weight   : 3.85 kg (8.5 lb.)
Sight   : military aperture sight
Safety   : catch in front end of trigger guard
Stock   : wood

PARTICULARS

Shortened version of the standard M1 Garand, made in 1945 for the US armed forces in the Indian Ocean.

Springfield Garand M1D Sniper

SPECIFICATIONS

Caliber   : .30-06
Magazine   : blind magazine
Cartridge capacity: 8 rounds
Magazine catch   : N/A
Action   : gas pressure
Cocking system   : cocking lever
Firing system   : semi-automatic
Locking system   : rotating bolt head
Length   : 110.7 cm (43.6")
Barrel length   : 61 cm (24")
Weight   : 5.3 kg (11.75 lb.), incl. optical sight
Sight   : military aperture sight, 2.2 x Lyman M84 optical sight

Springfield Garand M1D Sniper

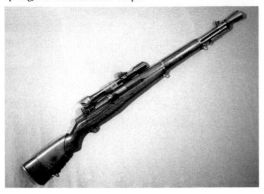

Safety   : catch in front end of trigger guard
Stock   : wood

PARTICULARS
Initially designated M1E8 rifle. Issued in 1944 to the armed forced under the name .30 M1D sniper rifle.

The M1D sniper saw service in Korea and Vietnam. The weapon remained in use with the US Army until early 1995.

Springfield M14 / .30 T44E4

SPECIFICATIONS
Caliber   : .308 Win.
Magazine   : detachable magazine
Cartridge capacity: 20-rounds
Magazine catch   : to rear of magazine slot
Action   : gas pressure
Cocking system   : cocking lever
Firing system   : semi- and fully automatic
Locking system   : rotating bolt head
Length   : 112 cm (44.1")

Springfield M14 / .30 T44E4

Barrel length   : 55.9 cm (22")
Weight   : 3.9 kg (8.7 lb.)
Sight   : adjustable aperture sight
Safety   : safety catch in front end of trigger guard
Stock   : wooden stock and hand grip

PARTICULARS
Matt black. Firing mode selector for semi- and fully automatic fire on right-hand side of receiver, above trigger guard. An adapter for cartridge clips is fitted in front of the aperture sight.

Springfield M1A Basic

SPECIFICATIONS
Caliber   : .308 Win.
Magazine   : detachable magazine
Cartridge capacity: 5-, 10- or 20-rounds
Magazine catch   : to rear of magazine slot
Action   : gas pressure
Cocking system   : cocking lever
Firing system   : semi-automatic
Locking system   : rotating bolt head
Length   : 112.6 cm (44 1/3")
Barrel length   : 55.9 cm (22")
Weight   : 4.1 kg (9 lb.)
Sight   : military aperture sight
Safety   : safety catch in front end of trigger guard
Stock   : synthetic stock and hand grip

PARTICULARS
Matt black. An adapter for cartridge clips is fitted in front of the aperture sight.

Springfield M1A-A1 Bush Rifle

SPECIFICATIONS
Caliber   : .308 Win.
Magazine   : detachable magazine
Cartridge capacity: 5, 10 or 20 rounds
Magazine catch   : to rear of magazine slot
Action   : gas pressure

Springfield M1A Basic

Springfield M1A-A1 Bush Rifle

Cocking system	: cocking lever
Firing system	: semi-automatic
Locking system	: rotating bolt head
Length	: 102.9 cm (40.5")
Barrel length	: 45.7 cm (18")
Weight	: 4.1 kg (9 lb.)
Sight	: military aperture sight
Safety	: safety catch in front end of trigger guard
Stock	: walnut, with brown synthetic hand grip

PARTICULARS

Matt black phosphate finish. An adapter for cartridge clips is fitted in front of the aperture sight.

Springfield M1A Bush Rifle Fiberglass

SPECIFICATIONS

Caliber	: .308 Win.
Magazine	: detachable magazine
Cartridge capacity	: 5, 10 or 20 rounds
Magazine catch	: to rear of magazine slot
Action	: gas pressure
Cocking system	: cocking lever
Firing system	: semi-automatic
Locking system	: rotating bolt head
Length	: 102.9 cm (40.5")
Barrel length	: 45.7 cm (18")
Weight	: 4.0 kg (8.9 lb.)
Sight	: military aperture sight

Springfield M1A Bush Rifle Fiberglass

Safety	: safety catch in front end of trigger guard
Stock	: black fibreglass stock, with black synthetic hand grip

PARTICULARS

Matt black phosphate finish. An adapter for cartridge clips is fitted in front of the aperture sight.

The illustration shows the M1A Bush Rifle Fiberglass (top) and the version with wooden stock (bottom).

Springfield M1A National Match

SPECIFICATIONS

Caliber	: .308 Win.
Magazine	: detachable magazine
Cartridge capacity	: 5-, 10- or 20-rounds
Magazine catch	: to rear of magazine slot
Action	: gas pressure
Cocking system	: cocking lever
Firing system	: semi-automatic
Locking system	: rotating bolt head
Length	: 112.6 cm (44 1/3")
Barrel length	: 55.9 cm (22")
Weight	: 4.9 kg (10.8 lb.)
Sight	: adjustable aperture sight
Safety	: safety catch in front end of trigger guard
Stock	: walnut stock with synthetic hand grip

PARTICULARS

Matt black. An adapter for cartridge clips is fitted in front of the aperture sight.

Springfield M1A-A1 Scout

SPECIFICATIONS

Caliber	: .308 Win.
Magazine	: detachable magazine
Cartridge capacity	: 5, 10 or 20 rounds
Magazine catch	: to rear of magazine slot
Action	: gas pressure

Springfield M1A National Match

Cocking system	: cocking lever
Firing system	: semi-automatic
Locking system	: rotating bolt head
Length	: 102.9 cm (40.5")
Barrel length	: 45.7 cm (18")
Weight	: 4.1 kg (9 lb.)
Sight	: military aperture sight
Safety	: safety catch in front end of trigger guard
Stock	: black fibreglass stock, with black synthetic hand grip

PARTICULARS

Matt black phosphate finish. The hand grip has an opening with mounting rail for an optical sight.
Barrel with combined flash suppresser and recoil damper. An adapter for cartridge clips is fitted in front of the aperture sight.

Springfield M1A Super Match

SPECIFICATIONS

Caliber	: .308 Win.
Magazine	: detachable magazine
Cartridge capacity	: 5-, 10- or 20-rounds
Magazine catch	: to rear of magazine slot
Action	: gas pressure
Cocking system	: cocking lever
Firing system	: semi-automatic
Locking system	: rotating bolt head
Length	: 112.6 cm (44 1/3")
Barrel length	: 55.9 cm (22")

Springfield M1A Super Match

Weight	: 5.1 kg (11.2 lb.)
Sight	: adjustable aperture sight
Safety	: safety catch in front end of trigger guard
Stock	: walnut stock with synthetic hand grip

PARTICULARS

Matt black. Also available as the Supermatch model with a Douglas Premium, Hart of Kreiger barrel. An adapter for cartridge clips is fitted in front of the aperture sight.

Springfield M1A/M-21 Tactical Model

SPECIFICATIONS

Caliber	: .308 Win.
Magazine	: detachable magazine
Cartridge capacity	: 5-, 10- or 20-rounds
Magazine catch	: to rear of magazine slot
Action	: gas pressure
Cocking system	: cocking lever

Firing system	: semi-automatic
Locking system	: rotating bolt head
Length	: 111.8 cm (44")
Barrel length	: 55.9 cm (22")
Weight	: 5.3 kg (11.6 lb.)
Sight	: military aperture sight and optical sight
Safety	: safety catch in front end of trigger guard
Stock	: walnut stock with synthetic hand grip

Length	: 81.3 cm (32")
Barrel length	: 46.4 cm (18.25")
Weight	: 1.8 kg (4 lb.)
Sight	: flip-up sight; suitable for sight mount
Stock	: steel skeleton stock with storage space for extra ammunition

PARTICULARS

Matt black; special Douglas Premium barrel.
This long-range rifle is fitted with a bipod, a special sight mount and an optical sight with range finder. An adapter for cartridge clips is fitted in front of the aperture sight.

PARTICULARS

Matt black or matt finish stainless steel. Derived from the US Air Force M6 Survival rifle.
Manufactured for Springfield by the Czech CZ arms factory. The M6 Scout in stainless steel is shown.

Springfield M6 Scout & Scout Stainless

SPECIFICATIONS

Caliber	: .22 LR of .22 Hornet and .410 shot barrel
Magazine	: N/A
Cartridge capacity	: single round
Magazine catch	: N/A
Action	: self-cocking hinged frame
Cocking system	: self-cocking hinged frame
Firing system	: single round
Locking system	: bolt on top of barrel block

Springfield SAR-4800 rifle

SPECIFICATIONS

Caliber	: .308 Win. of .223 Rem.
Magazine	: detachable magazine
Cartridge capacity	: 20-rounds
Magazine catch	: to rear of magazine slot
Action	: adjustable gas pressure
Cocking system	: cocking lever
Firing system	: semi-automatic
Locking system	: breech lock with bolt lugs
Length	: 308: 110 cm (43.3"); 223: 97.2 cm (38.25")
Barrel length	: 308: 53.3 cm (21"); 223: 45.7 cm (18")
Weight	: 308: 5.0 kg (11.1 lb.); 223: 4.8 kg (10.5 lb.)

Springfield M6 Scout & Scout Stainless

Springfield SAR-4800 rifle

Sight	: military aperture sight
Safety	: safety catch on left-hand side of housing
Stock	: synthetic stock with pistol grip and metal hand grip

PARTICULARS
Derived from the FN-FAL; manufactured for Springfield in Brazil under license to the Fabrique Nationale (FN) in Belgium.

Springfield SAR-8 rifle

SPECIFICATIONS
Caliber	: .308 Win.
Magazine	: detachable magazine
Cartridge capacity	: 20-rounds
Magazine catch	: on right-hand side of magazine slot
Action	: gas pressure
Cocking system	: cocking lever
Firing system	: semi-automatic
Locking system	: roller lock (Heckler & Koch system)
Length	: 102.6 cm (40.38")
Barrel length	: 45.7 cm (18")
Weight	: 4.8 kg (10.6 lb.)
Sight	: military aperture sight and hooded front sight
Safety	: safety catch on right-hand side of housing
Stock	: synthetic stock with pistol grip and hand grip

PARTICULARS
Matt black; manufactured for Springfield in Brazil under license to Heckler & Koch (Heckler & Koch G-3/HK-91).

Springfield SAR-8 Counter Sniper

SPECIFICATIONS
Caliber	: .308 Win.
Magazine	: detachable magazine
Cartridge capacity	: 20-rounds

Springfield SAR-8 rifle

Springfield SAR-8 Counter Sniper

Magazine catch	: to right-hand side of magazine slot
Action	: gas pressure
Cocking system	: cocking lever
Firing system	: semi-automatic
Locking system	: roller lock (Heckler & Koch system)
Length	: 117.5 cm (46.25")
Barrel length	: 58.4 cm (23")
Weight	: 6.6 kg (14.5 lb.)
Sight	: none; special sight mount
Safety	: safety catch on right-hand side of housing
Stock	: synthetic skeleton stock with pistol grip and free floating aluminium hand grip; adjustable cheek and butt.

PARTICULARS
Matt black; a special folding bipod is manufactured for Springfield in Brazil under license to Heckler & Koch.

Steyr

Steyr, logo

The history of the Steyr concern starts in 1831 with the birth of Josef Werndl in the Austrian town of Steyr. His father, Leopold Werndl, was the owner of an armament factory that manufactured rifle parts for the Vienna arms industry. Following an apprenticeship in Vienna and Prague, Josef entered his father's company. He was unable to reconcile himself with the conservative production techniques being used, and quite literally took off. In 1849 he entered service with the army. On the basis of his work experience he was employed in a rifle factory in Vienna, where he became familiar with modern American machines for mass production. In 1852 Josef left for the German industrial area in Thuringia, where he worked in various arms factories until he went from there to North-America. In America he worked for Remington and Colt at Hartford. Full of ideas he returned to Austria in late 1853 and started an arms workshop in the town of Wehrgraben. In 1864 Josef, together with his brother Franz, founded Josef und Franz Werndl & Comp. in their home town, Steyr. In 1866 Werndl tried to persuade the Minister of War to equip the army with a Werndl-Holub breech-loading rifle. After extensive army trials, Werndl received an order for 100,000 rifles of the Rifle Model 1867.

The Steyr works were expanded, and a subsidiary was established in Budapest. As a result of all the expansion, company liquidity suffered. Werndl decided to reinforce the financial position of the company by issuing stock certificates, and for this purpose the company was changed into the Österreichische Waffenfabriks-Gesellschaft, with its offices in Vienna. In 1873 Werndl received an order from the Royal Prussian army for the manufacture of no less than 500,000 Mauser rifles Model 1871. After that, Werndl was inundated with government contracts from France, Persia, Rumania, Greece, China, and Chili.

In 1882 the tide changed. By now, every European army had been supplied with breech-loading rifles, so no large order followed. Faced with a crisis, Werndl decided to use the available production capacity for the manufacture of other products. Examples include dynamos, electric motors, and light bulbs. In 1884 Steyr was the first European town with electric street lighting. In 1885 a new breech-loading rifle with a magazine for 5 rounds using the Mannlicher system was taken into production, for which an immediate order for 87,000 was received. Josef Werndl died from pneumonia in 1899. The company

Steyr M1886 rifle

continued under a four-headed management until 1896, when Otto Schönauer took over. By then the company had grown into a large concern with several factories and some 10,000 employees. Around the turn of the nineteenth and twentieth centuries the company manufactured several products, including bicycles. In 1919, motorcars and lorries were made.

After the Second World War, Steyr had a very tough time, and it wasn't until 1950 that the Allies granted permission to restart the production of firearms. From then on, the company produced mainly hunting rifles under the name of Mannlicher-Schönauer. The company then changed into Steyr-Daimler-Puch AG, and in 1987 the arms production was accommodated in a separate subsidiary, Steyr-Mannlicher AG. The modern Steyr concern now produces hunting and competition rifles, such as the Steyr-Mannlicher guns, but also military weapons, such as sniper rifles and the advanced Steyr AUG (Armee Universal Gewehr) rifle. The company is currently engaged in the development of an ACR (Advanced Combat Rifle) for trials in the United States.

Steyr M1886 rifle

SPECIFICATIONS

Caliber	: 8 x 50R mm
Magazine	: blind magazine
Cartridge capacity	: 5 rounds
Magazine catch	: N/A
Action	: bolt-action
Cocking system	: bolt lever
Firing system	: single round
Locking system	: bolt lugs
Length	: 128 cm (50.38")

Barrel length	: 76.5 cm (30.1")
Weight	: 4.4 kg (9.7 lb.)
Sight	: tangent rear sight
Safety	: catch on rear of bolt
Stock	: wooden stock and forearm

Steyr M1895 rifle

PARTICULARS

Derived from the first M1885 army rifle. The tangent rear sight indicates the distance in paces (75 cm/29.5"). The magazine was loaded with a cartridge clip that dropped from the bottom of the magazine when the last round was fired.

Safety	: catch on rear of bolt
Stock	: wooden stock and forearm

Steyr M1895 rifle

SPECIFICATIONS

Caliber	: 8 x 56R mm
Magazine	: blind magazine
Cartridge capacity	: 5 rounds
Magazine catch	: N/A
Action	: bolt-action
Cocking system	: bolt lever
Firing system	: single round
Locking system	: bolt lugs
Length	: 127 cm (50")
Barrel length	: 76.5 cm (30.1")
Weight	: 3.8 kg (8.3 lb.)
Sight	: tangent rear sight

PARTICULARS

Introduced in the Austrian-Hungarian army in 1895 to replace the M1886 rifle. Introduced in the Bulgarian army in 1897. The magazine was loaded with a cartridge clip that dropped from the bottom of the magazine when the last round was fired.

Steyr M1895/96 carbine

SPECIFICATIONS

Caliber	: 8 x 56R mm
Magazine	: blind magazine

Steyr M1895/96 carbine

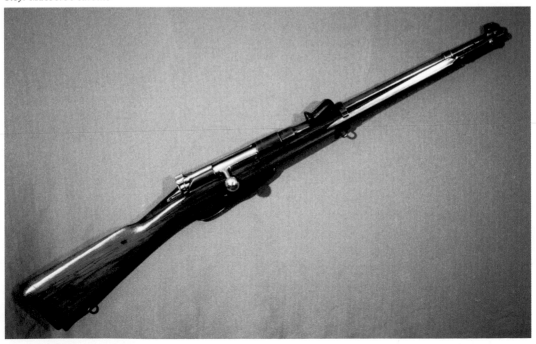

Detail of the Steyr M1895/96 carbine

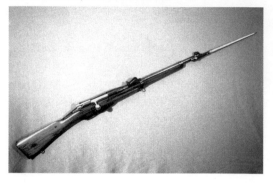

Cartridge capacity: 5 rounds
Magazine catch   : N/A
Action   : bolt-action
Cocking system   : bolt lever
Firing system   : single round
Locking system   : bolt lugs
Length   : 100.3 cm (39.5")
Barrel length   : 49.9 cm (19.65")
Weight   : 3.4 kg (7.5 lb.)
Sight   : tangent rear sight
Safety   : catch on rear of bolt
Stock   : wooden stock and forearm

PARTICULARS

Derived from the M1895 rifle. Designed as a cavalry carbine with a folding bayonet. The magazine was loaded with a cartridge clip that dropped from the bottom of the magazine when the last round was fired.

Steyr AUG A1

SPECIFICATIONS

Caliber   : .223 Rem.
Magazine   : detachable magazine

Steyr AUG A1

Cartridge capacity: 30 or 40 rounds
Magazine catch   : push-button in stock
Action   : gas pressure
Cocking system   : cocking lever
Firing system   : full- and semi-automatic
Locking system   : 8-lug rotating bolt head
Length   : 63, 69, 79 or 89 cm (24.8, 27.2, 31.1 or 35")
Barrel length   : 35, 40, 50 or 61 cm (13.8, 16, 20 or 24")
Weight   : 3.1, 3.3, 3.6 or 3.9 kg (6.8, 7.3, 7.9 of 8.6 lb.)
Sight   : optical sight with 1.5 times magnification
Safety   : push-button behind trigger
Stock   : synthetic bullpup stock with extra grip

PARTICULARS

Aluminum receiver; can be converted for left-handed use. Trigger doubles as firing mode selector: light pressure results in semi-automatic action, and full depression produces an automatic burst. The Steyr AUG is shown with the 35, 40 and 50 cm (13.8, 16, 20") barrels.

Steyr AUG A2

SPECIFICATIONS

Caliber   : .223 Rem.
Magazine   : detachable magazine
Cartridge capacity: 30 or 40 rounds
Magazine catch   : push-button in stock
Action   : gas pressure
Cocking system   : cocking lever
Firing system   : full- and semi-automatic
Locking system   : 8-lug rotating bolt head
Length   : 71.5, 80 or 90.7 cm (28.1, 31.5 or 35.7")

Steyr AUG A2

Barrel length	: 40.6, 50.8 or 61 cm (16, 20 or 24")
Weight	: 3.8, 4.0 or 5.0 kg (8.4, 8.8 or 11 lb.)
Sight	: removable optical sight, 1.5 times magnification
Safety	: push-button safety behind trigger
Stock	: synthetic bullpup stock with extra grip

PARTICULARS

Aluminum receiver; can be converted for left-handed use. Trigger doubles as firing mode selector: light pressure results in semi-automatic action, and full depression produces an automatic burst. Differences compared with the AUG A1: optical sight and mount are removable. The optical sight features mounting points for night sight; upper adjusting knob of optical sight

protected by an extra projection. Folding cocking lever.

Steyr AUG-Police

SPECIFICATIONS

Caliber	: 9 mm Para
Magazine	: detachable magazine
Cartridge capacity	: 32 rounds
Magazine catch	: to rear of magazine slot
Action	: recoil
Cocking system	: cocking lever
Firing system	: semi-automatic
Locking system	: inertia lock
Length	: 66.5 cm (26.2")
Barrel length	: 42 cm (16.5")
Weight	: 3.3 kg (8.6 lb.)
Sight	: optical sight, 1.5 times magnification
Safety	: push-button behind trigger
Stock	: synthetic bullpup stock with extra grip

PARTICULARS

Aluminium receiver; can be converted for left-handed use.

Steyr AUG Sniper

SPECIFICATIONS

Caliber	: .223 Rem.
Magazine	: detachable magazine

Steyr AUG Sniper

Cartridge capacity: 30 or 40 rounds
Magazine catch : push-button in stock
Action : gas pressure
Cocking system : cocking lever
Firing system : full- and semi-automatic
Locking system : 8-lug rotating bolt head
Length : 89 cm (35")
Barrel length : 61 cm (24")
Weight : 3.9 kg (8.6 lb.)
Sight : mount for optical sight
Safety : push-button behind trigger
Stock : synthetic bullpup stock with extra grip

PARTICULARS
Folding bipod; can be converted for left-handed use.
Trigger doubles as firing mode selector: light pressure results in semi-automatic action, and full depression produces an automatic burst.

Steyr AUG Standard

SPECIFICATIONS
Caliber : .223 Rem.
Magazine : detachable magazine
Cartridge capacity: 30 or 40 rounds
Magazine catch : push-button in stock

Steyr AUG Standard

Action : gas pressure
Cocking system : cocking lever
Firing system : full- and semi-automatic
Locking system : 8-lug rotating bolt head
Length : 79 cm (31.1")
Barrel length : 50.8 cm (20")
Weight : 3.6 kg (8 lb.)
Sight : laterally adjustable military aperture sight in carrying handle; vertically adjustable shrouded front sight
Safety : push-button behind trigger
Stock : synthetic bullpup stock with extra grip

PARTICULARS
Aluminum receiver; can be converted for left-handed use.
Trigger doubles as firing mode selector: light pressure results in semi-automatic action, and full depression produces an automatic burst.

Steyr-Mannlicher Model M-Professional

SPECIFICATIONS
Caliber : .308 Win., .30-06 Springf., .243 Win.
Magazine : detachable magazine
Cartridge capacity: 5 rounds
Magazine catch : bottom of detachable magazine
Action : bolt-action
Cocking system : bolt lever
Firing system : single round
Locking system : 6 lugs at rear of bolt
Length : 110 cm (43.3")
Barrel length : 60 cm (23.6")
Weight : 3.3 kg (7.3 lb.)
Sight : laterally adjustable rear sight; receiver drilled and tapped for sight mount
Safety : safety catch on right-hand side of receiver, behind bolt lever
Stock : brown or green synthetic stock with angled stock comb

Steyr-Mannlicher Model M-Professional

Steyr-Mannlicher Model Police SSG-PI Counter Sniper

Steyr-Mannlicher Model Police SSG-PII

PARTICULARS

Stecher trigger system (rear trigger acts as accelerator for extra light trigger pull).

Steyr-Mannlicher Model Police SSG-PI Counter Sniper Rifle

SPECIFICATIONS

Caliber	: .308 Win.
Magazine	: rotating detachable magazine
Cartridge capacity: 5 rounds	
Magazine catch	: ambidextrous in bottom of magazine
Action	: bolt-action
Cocking system	: bolt lever
Firing system	: single round
Locking system	: 6 lugs at rear of bolt
Length	: 113 cm (44.5")
Barrel length	: 65 cm (25.6")
Weight	: 4.1 kg (9 lb.)
Sight	: iron sights; Hensoldt 10 x 42
Safety	: safety catch on right-hand side of receiver, behind bolt lever; loading indicator in rear of bolt
Stock	: black synthetic stock with pistol grip

PARTICULARS

Mounting rail for hand stop or Parker-Hale folding bipod under forearm.

The illustration shows the Steyr Police SSG-PI (top) and the Steyr Police SSG-PII (with double set trigger).

Steyr-Mannlicher Model Police SSG-PII

SPECIFICATIONS

Caliber	: .308 Win.
Magazine	: rotating detachable magazine
Cartridge capacity: 5 rounds	

Magazine catch	: ambidextrous in bottom of magazine
Action	: bolt-action
Cocking system	: bolt lever
Firing system	: single round
Locking system	: 6 lugs at rear of bolt
Length	: 113 cm (44.5")
Barrel length	: 65 cm (25.6")
Weight	: 4.3 kg (9.6 lb.)
Sight	: none; Hensoldt 10 x 42 optical sight
Safety	: safety catch on right-hand side of receiver, behind bolt lever; loading indicator in rear of bolt
Stock	: black synthetic stock with pistol grip

PARTICULARS

Mounting rail for hand stop or Parker-Hale folding bipod under forearm.

The illustration shows the Steyr Police SSG-PI (top) and the Steyr Police SSG-PII (with double set trigger).

Steyr-Mannlicher Model Police SSG-PIV SD

SPECIFICATIONS

Caliber	: .308 Win.
Magazine	: rotating detachable magazine

Steyr-Mannlicher Model Police SSG-PIV SD

Cartridge capacity: 5 rounds
Magazine catch : ambidextrous in bottom of magazine
Action : bolt-action
Cocking system : bolt lever
Firing system : single round
Locking system : 6 lugs at rear of bolt
Length : 100.3 cm (39.5")
Barrel length : 40.7 cm (16"), excl. flash suppresser
Weight : 3.8 kg (8.6 lb.)
Sight : none; Hensoldt 10 x 42 optical sight
Safety : safety catch on right-hand side of receiver,
          behind bolt lever; loading indicator in rear of
          bolt
Stock : black synthetic stock with pistol grip

PARTICULARS
Mounting rail for hand stop or Parker-Hale folding bipod under forearm. The screw-on flash suppresser is removable to make way for the silencer.

Steyr Scout carbine

SPECIFICATIONS
Caliber : .308 Win.
Magazine : detachable magazine
Cartridge capacity: 5- or 10-rounds
Magazine catch : ambidextrous in bottom of magazine
Action : bolt-action
Cocking system : bolt lever

Steyr Scout carbine

Firing system	: single round
Locking system	: 2-lug bolt
Length	: 100.5 cm (39.6")
Barrel length	: 48.5 cm (19")
Weight	: 3.14 kg (6.9 lb.)
Sight	: Picatinny mounting rail with special 2.5 x 28 Leupold M8 Scout optical sight
Safety	: safety catch in stock throat with three positions: fire; locked trigger, and locked trigger and bolt
Stock	: Zytel synthetic stock and pistol grip

PARTICULARS

Stock with integrated folding bipod in forearm; the stock has storage space for an extra 5- or 10-round detachable magazine; length of butt adjustable. Developed in cooperation with American arms expert Jeff Cooper.

Steyr SPP-Police carbine

SPECIFICATIONS

Caliber	: 9 mm Para
Magazine	: detachable magazine
Cartridge capacity	: 15- or 30-rounds
Magazine catch	: ambidextrous in bottom of magazine
Action	: recoil
Cocking system	: cocking lever on rear of housing
Firing system	: semi-automatic
Locking system	: rotating barrel
Length	: 59.8 cm (23.5")
Barrel length	: 13 cm (5.9")
Weight	: 1.75 kg (3.85 lb.)
Sight	: laterally adjustable micrometre sight; vertically adjustable front sight
Safety	: push-button above trigger guard, automatic sear lock
Stock	: synthetic skeleton stock, pistol grip and extra front grip

Steyr SPP-Police carbine

PARTICULARS
Special bolt-action: barrel rotates instead of breech. Also available as a pistol model, without shoulder stock.
Threaded muzzle to take the flash suppresser or the silencer.

Stoner/Knight

Stoner/Knight, logo

The American Knight's Manufacturing Company was founded by C. Reed Knight and has its offices in Vero Beach, Florida. Knight started out cultivating oranges, and ran a small arms factory as a hobby. This soon got out of hand, since a payroll of 70 employees can hardly qualify as a hobby any longer. Knight contacted the well-known arms designer Eugene Stoner. Stoner is famous for designing a number of well-known weapons, including the AR-10, the Stoner-63, and in particular the AR-15/M-16 army rifle. The Stoner SR-25 rifle is in fact a derivative of the AR-10 design.
Stoner designed this advanced army rifle in 1954, when he was in the employment of the ArmaLite Division, a subsidiary of the Fairchild Aircraft Company. This rifle was the precursor of the AR-15 rifle. Contrary to the AR-15, the AR-10 did not generate any interest from the military. The rifle was produced in small numbers in the Netherlands at the Nederlandse Artillerie Inrichtingen works. None of the NATO partners showed the slightest interest in the gun. America opted for the AR-15/M-16 concept chambered for the .223 Remington cartridge. In Europe, one of the preferred weapons was the FN-FAL chambered for 7.62 x 51 mm NATO (i.e. .308 Winchester). The AR-10 rifles produced in

the Netherlands were sold to Portugal, the Sudan, and Burma. Reed Knight himself was interested in another design by Stoner, the Stoner-63, a semi-automatic rifle chambered for the .308 Win. cartridge. In the United States, the Pentagon had already opted the AR-15 concept, so the Stoner-63 was not to be selected. Only a small special unit of the US Navy, the Navy Seals, use this weapon in a fully automatic version.

The Stoner SR-25 (Sniper-Rifle) is a mix between the AR-10, the AR-15, and the Stoner-63. Many of its components are interchangeable with the components of the AR-15 rifle. The special cold-hammered barrel of the SR-25 comes from Remington, who use the barrel themselves for their military M24 sniper rifle. This barrel has 5R lands and grooves, i.e. the lands and grooves do not have sharp edges, but have been slightly rounded according to a new concept. This system improves accuracy and extends the service life of the barrel. For this reason, the accuracy of the SR-25 is guaranteed to produce a 5-shot group of 1 inch (25 mm/0.98") at 100 meters (328 ft), which is a spectacular performance for a semi-automatic rifle. Experience by competition marksmen has shown the SR-25 rifle capable of even better performance.

Stoner AR-10

SPECIFICATIONS

Caliber	: .308 Win.
Magazine	: detachable magazine
Cartridge capacity	: 5- or 20-rounds
Magazine catch	: on right-hand side of housing
Action	: gas pressure
Cocking system	: cocking lever

Stoner AR-10

Firing system	: semi- and fully automatic
Locking system	: rotating bolt head
Length	: 105 cm (41.3")
Barrel length	: 50.8 cm (20")
Weight	: 3.1 kg (6.85 lb.)
Sight	: adjustable aperture sight and front sight, precursor of later AR-15/M16 sight
Safety	: rotary catch on left-hand side of housing; doubles as fire selector
Stock	: black synthetic stock and pistol grip

PARTICULARS

Matt black phosphate finish; folding bipod. Various development models. Dutch production at the Artillerie Inrichtingen (AI) ceased in 1961. Nowadays a version of the AR-10 is again being manufactured by ArmaLite. The illustration shows an early model of the AI-AR-10 (serial number 000046), an (AI) AR-10 model used as a light machine-gun, and the carbine model of the (AI) AR-10.

Stoner LMG

SPECIFICATIONS

Caliber	: .223 Rem
Magazine	: detachable magazine
Cartridge capacity	: box magazine with 200 rounds or cartridge belt

Stoner AR-10 LMG

Stoner AR-10

Stoner AR-10 carbine

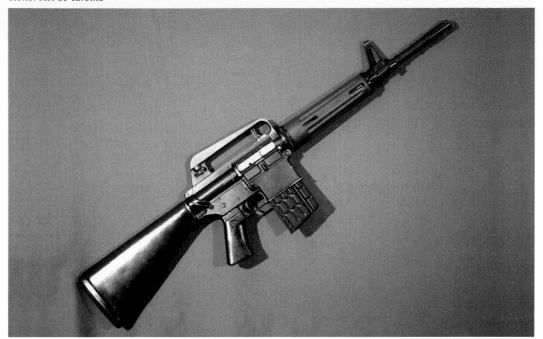

Stoner LMG

Stoner Model 63A1/XM207 LMG

Magazine catch	: left-hand side of housing
Action	: gas pressure
Cocking system	: cocking lever
Firing system	: fully automatic
Locking system	: rotating bolt head
Length	: 82.5 cm with extending stock (32.5"); without: 66 cm (26")
Barrel length	: 39.6 cm (15.6")
Weight	: 7.3 kg (16.1 lb.) incl. full box magazine
Sight	: folding aperture sight; special RIS sight mount
Safety	: ambidextrous rotary safety catch on housing
Stock	: black extending stock, pistol and forearm

PARTICULARS

Matt black phosphate finish; bipod; RIS hand grip for 3-sided mounting of acces- sories. This light machine-gun was devel- oped especially by Eugene Stoner during the last years of his life.

Stoner Model 63A1/XM207 LMG

SPECIFICATIONS

Caliber	: .223 Rem.
Magazine	: box magazine
Cartridge capacity	: 100-round box magazine
Magazine catch	: on right-hand side of housing
Action	: gas pressure
Cocking system	: cocking lever
Firing system	: fully automatic
Locking system	: rotating bolt head
Length	: 102.2 cm (40.25")
Barrel length	: 50.8 cm (20")
Weight	: 5.7 kg (12.5 lb.)

Stoner Model 63A1/XM207 LMG

Sight	: adjustable aperture sight and front sight
Safety	: rotary safety catch on left-hand side of housing
Stock	: black synthetic stock and pistol grip

PARTICULARS

Matt black phosphate finish; folding bipod. Various development models. Manufactured in 1965 under license by the Dutch arms and ammunition factory 'de Kruithoorn'. The weapon has also been manufactured as an assault rifle, Model 63/XM22 (see below).

Stoner SR-15

SPECIFICATIONS

Caliber	: .223 Rem.

Stoner SR-15

Magazine	: detachable magazine
Cartridge capacity	: 5-, 10- or 20-rounds
Magazine catch	: on right-hand side of housing
Action	: gas pressure
Cocking system	: cocking lever
Firing system	: semi-automatic
Locking system	: rotating bolt head
Length	: SR-15 M4: 86 cm, or SR-15 M5/Match: 96.5 cm (34 of 38")
Barrel length	: 40.6 or 50.8 cm (16 or 20")
Weight	: SR-15 M4: 3.1 kg (6.8 lb.); SR-15 M5: 3.4 kg (7.6 lb.), or SR-15 Match: 3.6 kg (7.9 lb.)
Sight	: folding aperture sight; special RIS sight mount and accessory rail
Safety	: rotary safety catch on left-hand side of housing
Stock	: black synthetic stock or extendable skeleton stock; pistol grip

PARTICULARS

Matt black phosphate finish; Harris bipod; SR-15 is available as Match rifle, M5 standard rifle, and M4 carbine.

Stoner SR-25 Carbine

SPECIFICATIONS

Caliber	: .308 Win.
Magazine	: detachable magazine
Cartridge capacity	: 5-, 10- or 20-rounds
Magazine catch	: on right-hand side of housing

Stoner SR-25 Carbine

Action	: gas pressure
Cocking system	: cocking lever
Firing system	: semi-automatic
Locking system	: rotating bolt head
Length	: 91 cm (35.75")
Barrel length	: 40.6 cm (16")
Weight	: 3.5 kg (7.75 lb.)
Sight	: none; special sight mount rail
Safety	: rotary safety catch on left-hand side of housing
Stock	: black synthetic stock and pistol grip

PARTICULARS
Matt black phosphate finish; Harris bipod. The illustration shows the SR-25 Carbine (top) and the SR-25 match (bottom).

Stoner SR-25 Match

SPECIFICATIONS

Caliber	: .308 Win.
Magazine	: detachable magazine
Cartridge capacity	: 5-, 10- or 20-rounds
Magazine catch	: on right-hand side of housing
Action	: gas pressure

Stoner SR-25 Match

Stoner SR-50 Sniper

Cocking system	: cocking lever
Firing system	: semi-automatic
Locking system	: rotating bolt head
Length	: 111 cm (43.5")
Barrel length	: 61 cm (24")
Weight	: 4.9 kg (10.75 lb.)
Sight	: none; special sight mounting rail
Safety	: safety rotary catch on left-hand side of housing
Stock	: black synthetic stock and pistol grip

PARTICULARS
Matt black phosphate finish; Harris bipod; free floating Remington match barrel. The weapon is also available as the SR-25 Lightweight Match with a weight of 4.3 kg (9.5 lb.).

Stoner SR-50 Sniper

SPECIFICATIONS

Caliber	: .50 BMG
Magazine	: detachable magazine
Cartridge capacity	: 5 or 10-rounds
Magazine catch	: on right-hand side of housing
Action	: gas pressure
Cocking system	: cocking lever
Firing system	: semi-automatic
Locking system	: rotating bolt head
Length	: 148.6 cm (58.5")
Barrel length	: 102 cm (40")
Weight	: 14.1 kg (31 lb.)
Sight	: none; special sight mounting rail
Safety	: rotary safety catch on left-hand side of housing
Stock	: black synthetic stock and pistol grip

PARTICULARS
Matt black phosphate finish; bipod. The weapon was developed as a long-range sniper rifle for use by special army units.

Uu - Vv

Unique

Unique, logo

Unique is the brand name of the French MAPF (Manufacture d'Armes des Pyrenees Francaises) arms factory. The company is located in the town of Hendaye, where the Pyrenees meet the Bay of Biscay. MAPF produce a range of interesting rifles with barrels that can be exchanged for shooting different calibers.

The match rifles, like the smallbore T-2000 and the T-3000 in various large calibers, are of high quality. The company also produces the famous Unique DES-69 competition pistol and the I.S. (International Silhouette) pistol. In addition, Unique manufacture the F.11, the smallbore model of the well-known French FAMAS army rifle.

The TGC Varmint Match rifle is in use with many French police units as a sniper rifle.

Unique TGC sniper

SPECIFICATIONS

Caliber	: .300 Savage, .300 Win.Mag., .308 Win., .30-06 Springf.
Magazine	: detachable magazine
Cartridge capacity	: 3 or 5 rounds
Magazine catch	: on right-hand side of detachable magazine
Action	: bolt-action
Cócking system	: bolt lever
Firing system	: single round
Locking system	: 3-lug bolt
Length	: 104 cm (41")
Barrel length	: 51.5 cm (20.3")
Weight	: 5.5 kg (12.1 lb.)
Sight	: none; sight mounting rail
Safety	: safety catch on right-hand side behind bolt lever
Stock	: walnut stock with adjustable cheek and pistol grip

PARTICULARS

Special bipod with hand stop in guide rail below forearm. Used as a sniper rifle by French police units.

The rifle has a replaceable barrel for fast conversion to other calibers. The gun is also available in a left-handed version.

Voere

De Austrian Voere company has been producing arms since 1951, but its history goes back longer than that. In 1940, a company was founded in the town of Kufstein by the Krieghoff company of Suhl, in the south of Germany. The company produced equipment for the German army. After the Second World

War, it switched to the production of other types of goods, such as office and school furniture, and light machinery. The name of the company was changed to Tiroler Maschinenbau und Holzindustriegesellschaft. Shortly afterwards, the company took up the manufacture of drilling and grinding equipment. In 1951 part of the production capacity was switched to the manufacture of arms. The first product was an air rifle known as the Tyrol LG-51.

In addition, the name of the company was changed to Tiroler Sportwaffenfabrik und Apparatebau GmbH. In 1964 the company hit serious financial trouble, and bankruptcy seemed unavoidable. However, in 1965 the factory was taken over by the German metal-processing company, Voerein Vöhrenbach. The name was changed to Tiroler Jagd- und Sportwaffenfabrik Voere, and again in 1988 to Voere-Kufsteiner Gerätebau und Handelsgesellschaft mbH.

The first model from that period was a semi-automatic smallbore rifle, the model 0014, followed by the model 1014 in a military look. Some years later, the models 2114 and 2115 followed. These were semi-automatic smallbore rifles that could be switched to single-shot use. A number of models were developed for hunting use based on the well-known Mauser 98 rifle. These were the Voere 2150, 2155, and 2165. In 1992 a large-caliber semi-automatic rifle was introduced. The model 2185 was designed by the well-known gun designer Sirkis.

Voere achieved its greatest triumph in the area of gun design in 1991 with the introduction of the VEC-91 rifle. VEC is short for Voere Electronic Caseless. The rifle is a bolt-action rifle of classic appearance, but its inner workings are revolutionary. The gun fires caseless 5.7 x 26 mm caliber

Voere, logo

VOERE
Jagd- und Sportgewehre

Voere Model 2185 Match

ammunition, officially designated 5.7 x 26 UCC. The addition UCC stands for Usel Caseless Cartridge. The cartridge was designed by Austrian inventor Hubert Usel. It consists of a compressed powder body with a primer and a bullet pressed into the powder body. The cartridge is fired electronically. One version of the model 2185 rifle is in use by police units as a sniper rifle.

Voere Model 2185 Match

SPECIFICATIONS

Caliber	: .30-06 Springf., .308 Win.
Magazine	: detachable magazine
Cartridge capacity:	5 rounds
Magazine catch	: in rear of magazine slot
Action	: gas pressure
Cocking system	: cocking lever
Firing system	: semi-automatic
Locking system	: 3-lug rotating bolt head
Length	: 115 cm (45.3")
Barrel length	: 51 cm (20.1")
Weight	: 5 kg (11.0 lb.)
Sight	: adjustable sight and shrouded front sight; receiver drilled and tapped for sight mounting
Safety	: safety catch in front end of trigger guard
Stock	: laminate stock with pistol grip

PARTICULARS

Sniper model of the Voere Model 2185 Match. Rifle can be fitted with a folding bipod. The stock features an adjustable cheek and butt.

Walther

During the inter-war years, the German Walther company manufactured not only excellent competitive firearms, but also military ordnance, for instance the Bergmann MP34/1 sub-machine-gun. Theodor Bergmann was a gun engineer who often cooperated with a well-known gun designer, Hugo Schmeisser. The latter had previously developed sub-machine-guns for Bergmann, such as the Bergmann MP18/I and the MP28/II. Since Schmeisser had entered into a cooperation with Haenel, another German arms factory, the MP34/I was developed by one of Bergmann's brothers. In 1932 a number of prototypes were manufactured in Denmark at Schultz & Larsen. The weapons were manufactured under license by Walther in Zella Mehlis. The German army showed no interest in the gun. Only a few thousands of these sub-machine-guns were produced for the German police and for a small export order for Bolivia. In 1935 Bergmann modified the gun, naming the new model the Bergmann MP35/I. Several thousands of these were sold to Denmark, Sweden, and Ethiopia. In 1940 the German SS adopted the weapon, which was manufactured for them under license by Junker

Walther, logo

& Ruh. Also in 1940, a rifle was developed as part of a German army research program, the rifle 41(W), the W standing for Walther. This semi-automatic weapon was gas-pressure operated. The gas pressure was diverted by means of a curious hood contraption around the muzzle. During the period up to 1943 thousands of rifles were produced for use at the Eastern front.

In 1943 the weapon was succeeded by the G43 rifle, which was produced both by Walther and other factories, such as the Gustloff Werke and the Berliner-Lübecker Maschinenfabrik. The G43 (G for gewehr) had a more orthodox mechanism for diverting gas from the barrel, still in use today. The gun also featured a detachable magazine. This gun saw much use as a sniper rifle.

After the Second World War the Czech army adopted the gun for sniper use. In 1982 Walther developed a new type of sniper rifle, the semi-automatic WA-2000, chambered for .300 Win. Mag., .308 Win. and 7.5 x 55 mm (Swiss). For the time, the rifle was very expensive. The 1984 Walther price list offers the gun for DM 9,885.-, excluding optical sight, assembly and bipod. The futuristic-looking weapon suffered from a number of teething troubles, and was never given a fair chance. As far as known it is no longer being produced by Walther.

Walther G41(W)

SPECIFICATIONS
Caliber   : 8 x 57 mm Mauser

Walther G41(W)

Magazine   : blind magazine
Cartridge capacity: 10 rounds
Magazine catch : none
Action   : gas pressure
Cocking system : cocking lever
Firing system   : semi-automatic
Locking system : bolt lugs
Length   : 113 cm (44.5")
Barrel length   : 54.5 cm (21.5")
Weight   : 5.0 kg (11 lb.)
Sight   : tangent rear sight
Safety   : safety catch on rear of receiver
Stock   : wooden stock

PARTICULARS
Muzzle hood for diverting gas pressure to operate the repeating action. The magazine had to be loaded from above through the receiver.

Walther G43

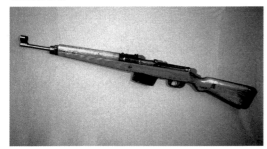

Walther G43

SPECIFICATIONS
Caliber   : 8 x 57 mm Mauser
Magazine   : detachable magazine
Cartridge capacity: 10 rounds
Magazine catch : on right-hand side of housing
Action   : gas pressure
Cocking system : cocking lever
Firing system   : semi-automatic
Locking system : bolt lugs
Length   : 111.7 cm (44")
Barrel length   : 55.8 cm (22")
Weight   : 4.3 kg (9.6 lb.)
Sight   : tangent rear sight and sight mount on right-hand side of receiver
Safety   : catch on rear of receiver
Stock   : wooden stock and hand grip

PARTICULARS
Gas tap halfway along the barrel. The weapon was also produced as a carbine

Walther Bergmann MP34

under the designation Kar43 with a total length of 106 cm (41.7").

Walther Bergmann MP34

SPECIFICATIONS
Caliber   : 9 mm Para
Magazine   : detachable magazine
Cartridge capacity: 24 or 32 rounds
Magazine catch : right-hand side, near magazine slot
Action   : recoil
Cocking system : bolt lever
Firing system   : auto- en semi-automatic
Locking system : inertia lock
Length   : 84 cm (33.1")
Barrel length   : 19.6 cm (7.8")
Weight   : 4.0 kg (8.9 lb.)
Sight   : adjustable tangent rear sight
Safety   : on left-hand side of the receiver, below rear sight
Stock   : wooden stock

PARTICULARS
Double trigger mechanism: press top part for semi-automatic fire, and bottom part for fully automatic fire.
The gun has a barrel with a combined compensator and flash suppresser.

Walther WA-2000 Sniper

SPECIFICATIONS
Caliber   : .300 Win.Mag., .308 win. of 7,5 x 55 mm
Magazine   : detachable magazine
Cartridge capacity: 6 rounds
Magazine catch : to rear of magazine slot, in stock
Action   : gas pressure
Cocking system : ambidextrous cocking lever
Firing system   : semi-automatic
Locking system : rotating bolt head with 7 bolt lugs

Length	: 90.5 cm (35.6")
Barrel length	: 65 cm (25.6")
Weight	: 7.9 kg (17.4 lb.), incl. optical sight
Sight	: optical sight with mount: Schmidt & Bender 2.5-10x56 or to order
Safety	: on left-hand side of housing, above trigger guard
Stock	: synthetic, wood and light metal bullpup stock

PARTICULARS

Modular construction; fast barrel and bolt exchange for the various calibers using barrel nut above pistol grip.

Detachable magazine is located in the stock behind the pistol grip. Adjustable cheek and butt. The gun has a fluted barrel.

Winchester

In 1855 Horace Smith, Daniel B. Wesson, and C.C. Palmer founded the Volcanic Repeating Arms Company, One of the stockholders was Oliver F. Winchester, a clothing manufacturer from New Haven, Connecticut. At the time, the company

Winchester, logo

produced the Volcanic lever-action rifle. In 1857 Oliver Winchester became the majority stockholder, and the company name was changed to New Haven Arms Company. In 1860, B. Tyler Henry, the company's designer, filed a patent for a gun that would later be called the Henry rifle.

In 1866 the company name was changed to Winchester Repeating Arms Company. The first rifle by the new company was the Winchester Model 1866. This weapon became so popular that, in spite of the advent of later models, some 171,000 were made up to 1899. In 1873 Winchester marketed an improved model lever-action rifle, the Model 1873. The production of this rifle continued up to 1920 and totaled about 19,500. The next rifle was the Model 1876, of which almost 64,000 were manufactured. Later types include the Model 1886, and in particular the famous Model 1894, more than 3 million of which were made. The successor of this type, the Model 1895, is still being manufactured by Winchester.

In addition to the lever-action rifles Winchester produced shotguns and bolt-action rifles for hunting. The first Winchester bolt-action rifle was the Model 1883, based on a patent taken out by Benjamin B. Hotchkiss, and it was produced up to 1889. A subsequent model bolt-action rifle was the Lee Straight Pull Model dating from 1895, which Winchester produced for the US Navy. This model was also manufactured in a sporting version and sold as the Lee Sporting Model. Winchester also operated in the field of semi-automatic weapons. In 1903 the first Model 1903 Self-Loading Rifle was introduced, using a .22 rimfire cartridge.

In 1905 a heavier semi-automatic rifle was introduced, the Model 1905, using the .35 Winchester SL and .32 Winchester SL (SL: Self-Loading) cartridges. This type was the first to feature a detachable magazine. In 1907 the improved Model 1907 was introduced, using the .351 Win.-SL cartridge. It was produced until 1957. This model was succeeded in 1910 by a new model, the M1910-SL, which used the .401 Win.-SL cartridge. During the First World War Winchester mainly produced the Enfield Pattern 14 army rifle chambered for the .303 British cartridge, under contract to the British government. The company produced about 246,000 of these rifles.

From 1917 to 1918 Winchester converted part of its machinery for the production of the US Rifle Model 1917, caliber .30-06 Springfield. At the start of the Second World War, Winchester developed the famous .30-M1 carbine, of which the company itself produced some 818,000. This carbine was manufactured under license right up to the end of the war by many different arms factories, including Inland, Underwood, Quality Hardware & Machine Corp., Rock-Ola, Saginaw, Irwin-Pedersen, National Postal Meters, Standard Products, and IBM. The total war production of this carbine numbers over six million. A highly detailed report on the development and production of this gun can be found in the book War Baby by the American author, Larry L. Ruth. Winchester was also closely involved in the manufacture of the M1-Garand army rifle.

Winchester/Browning Automatic Rifle (BAR)

SPECIFICATIONS

Caliber	: .30-06 Springf.
Magazine	: detachable magazine
Cartridge capacity:	20 rounds
Magazine catch	: in front end of trigger guard
Action	: gas pressure
Cocking system	: cocking lever
Firing system	: semi- and fully automatic
Locking system	: vertically sliding block

Winchester Browning Automatic Rifle (BAR)

Winchester Browning Automatic Rifle (BAR)

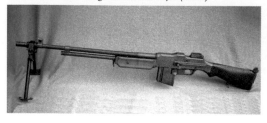

Winchester .30-M1 carbine

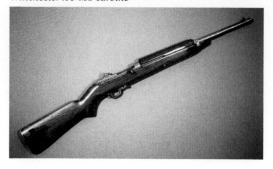

Length	: 121.4 cm (47.8")
Barrel length	: 61 cm (24")
Weight	: 8.8 kg (19.4 lb.)
Sight	: eye piece tangent rear sight
Safety	: safety catch, combined with firing mode selector
Stock	: wooden stock or black synthetic

PARTICULARS

Light machine-gun, manufactured by Winchester, Colt and Marlin-Rockwell. The illustration shows the model M1922 with cooling fins around the barrel. Next to it is the model M1918A1 with a wooden pistol grip.

Winchester .30-M1 carbine

SPECIFICATIONS

Caliber	: .30-M1 Carbine
Magazine	: detachable magazine
Cartridge capacity:	5-, 15- or 30-rounds
Magazine catch	: right-hand front on trigger guard
Action	: gas pressure
Cocking system	: cocking lever
Locking system	: 2-lug rotating bolt

Winchester .30-M1 carbine

Length	: 90.5 cm (35.65")
Barrel length	: 45.8 cm (18")
Weight	: 2.5 kg (5.45 lb.)
Sight	: adjustable military aperture sight
Safety	: safety rotary catch on right-hand front of trigger guard
Stock	: walnut stock and hand grip

PARTICULARS

The model M1A1 had a folding steel tube stock.

The illustration shows one of the first models with a push-button safety catch in

Winchester .30-M1A1 carbine

the trigger guard and a flip-up sight. Below it is the .30-M1A1 with a steel folding stock as paratrooper model.

Winchester .30-M2 carbine

SPECIFICATIONS

Caliber	: .30-M1 Carbine
Magazine	: detachable magazine
Cartridge capacity:	5-, 15- or 30-rounds
Magazine catch	: right-hand front on trigger guard
Action	: gas pressure
Cocking system	: cocking lever
Locking system	: 2-lug rotating bolt
Length	: 90.5 cm (35.65")
Barrel length	: 45.8 cm (18")
Weight	: 2.5 kg (5.45 lb.)
Sight	: adjustable military aperture sight
Safety	: rotary safety catch on front right-hand side of trigger guard
Stock	: walnut stock and hand grip

PARTICULARS

This is a detailed view, clearly showing the switch for automatic or semi-automatic fire.

Winchester .30-M2 carbine

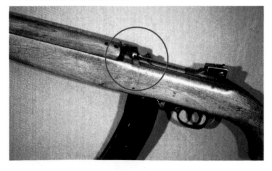

The M3 carbine featured various sight mount systems for use with infrared optical sights, the so-called Snooper scopes.

Winchester Model 70

SPECIFICATIONS

Caliber	: all common calibers, including: .308 Win., .30-06 Springf., .300 Win. Mag.
Magazine	: blind magazine
Cartridge capacity:	5 rounds
Magazine catch	: N/A
Action	: bolt-action
Cocking system	: bolt lever
Firing system	: single round
Locking system	: 2-lug bolt (Mauser system)
Length	: 113.7 to 118.8 cm (44.75 to 46.75")
Barrel length	: 61 to 66 cm (24 to 26")
Weight	: 3.3 to 4.9 kg (7.25 to 11 lb.)
Sight	: none, prepared for sight mount
Safety	: safety catch on right-hand rear side of bolt
Stock	: wooden of synthetic stock

PARTICULARS

Stainless steel of mat-finish blued. The rifle shown features the Boss compensator.

This rifle is much used as a basis for various sniper rifles.

Winchester Model 1300 Defender

SPECIFICATIONS

Caliber	: 12/76 (3")
Magazine	: tubular magazine
Cartridge capacity:	7 rounds; 8 rounds in 12/70 (2.75")
Magazine catch	: N/A
Action	: pump-action
Cocking system	: forearm

Winchester Model 1300 Defender

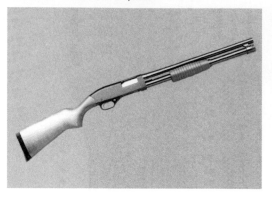

Winchester Model 1300 Short Defender Synthetic

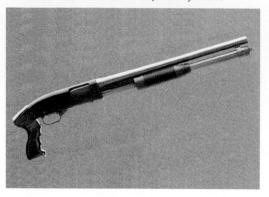

Firing system	: single round
Locking system	: rotating bolt head
Length	: 98 cm (38 5/8")
Barrel length	: 45.7 cm (18")
Weight	: 2.9 kg (6.5 lb.)
Sight	: bead
Safety	: push-button on front of trigger guard
Stock	: hardwood stock and forearm, with pistol grip

PARTICULARS

Blued barrel and tubular magazine; matt black housing

Winchester Model 1300 Defender Synthethic

SPECIFICATIONS

Caliber	: 12/76 (3")
Magazine	: tubular magazine
Cartridge capacity: 7 rounds; 8 rounds in 12/70 (2.75")	
Magazine catch	: N/A
Action	: pump-action
Cocking system	: forearm
Firing system	: single round

Winchester Model 1300 Defender Synthethic

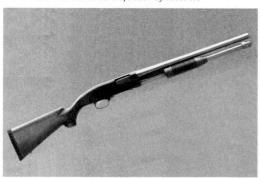

Locking system	: rotating bolt head
Length	: 98 cm (38 5/8")
Barrel length	: 45.7 cm (18")
Weight	: 2.8 kg (6.25 lb.)
Sight	: bead
Safety	: push-button on front of trigger guard
Stock	: synthetic stock and forearm, with pistol grip

PARTICULARS

Matt grey coating on barrel and tubular magazine; matt black housing.

Winchester Model 1300 Short Defender Synthetic

SPECIFICATIONS

Caliber	: 12/76 (3")
Magazine	: tubular magazine
Cartridge capacity: 6 rounds; 7 rounds in 12/70 (2.75")	
Magazine catch	: N/A
Action	: pump-action
Cocking system	: forearm
Firing system	: single round
Locking system	: rotating bolt head
Length	: 73 cm (28 5/8")
Barrel length	: 45.7 cm (18")
Weight	: 2.6 kg (5.75 lb.)
Sight	: bead
Safety	: push-button catch on front of trigger guard
Stock	: synthetic pistol grip and forearm

PARTICULARS

Matt gray coating on barrel and tubular magazine; matt black housing.

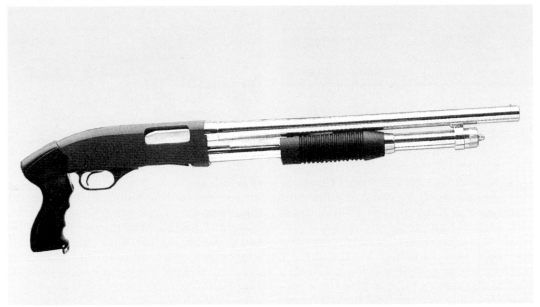

Winchester Model 1300 Stainless Marine

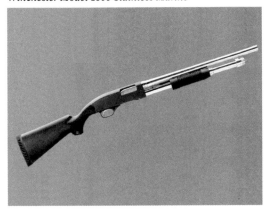

Winchester Model 1300 Short Stainless Marine

SPECIFICATIONS

Caliber	: 12/76 (3")
Magazine	: tubular magazine
Cartridge capacity	: 6 rounds; 7 rounds in 12/70 (2.75")
Magazine catch	: N/A
Action	: pump-action
Cocking system	: forearm
Firing system	: single round
Locking system	: rotating bolt head
Length	: 73 cm (28 5/8")
Barrel length	: 45.7 cm (18")
Weight	: 2.6 kg (5.75 lb.)

Sight	: bead
Safety	: push-button on front of trigger guard
Stock	: synthetic pistol grip and forearm

PARTICULARS

Stainless steel barrel and tubular magazine; matt black housing.

Winchester Model 1300 Stainless Marine

SPECIFICATIONS

Caliber	: 12/76 (3")
Magazine	: tubular magazine
Cartridge capacity	: 6 rounds; 7 rounds in 12/70 (2.75")
Magazine catch	: N/A
Action	: pump-action
Cocking system	: forearm
Firing system	: single round
Locking system	: rotating bolt head
Length	: 98 cm (38 5/8")
Barrel length	: 45.7 cm (18")
Weight	: 3.1 kg (6.75 lb.)
Sight	: bead
Safety	: push-button on front of trigger guard
Stock	: synthetic stock and forearm, with pistol grip

PARTICULARS

Stainless steel barrel and tubular magazine. Specially designed for use in damp areas or on ships.

Z z

Z-M Weapons

De Z-M Weapons company from Bernard-ston, Massachusetts produces rifles and carbines based on the AR-15 rifle type. The owner and designer, Allan Zitta, builds these weapons, the only remaining standard part of which is the AR-15 receiver housing. Zitta introduced funda-mental changes to the gas pressure oper-ated repeating system. The breech block was the only part to be left untouched. The sight mount consists of various Weaver rails for mounting optical sights on top of the housing, and in front of the hand grip for mounting an aiming light or laser. The company also engages in the design and production of special silencers, compen-sators and accessories for pistols and rifles.

Z-M LR300 M/L (Military & Law)

SPECIFICATIONS

Caliber	: .223 Rem.
Magazine	: detachable magazine or double drum magazine
Cartridge capacity:	10, 20, 30 or 180 rounds
Magazine catch	: push-button in right-hand side of housing
Action	: gas pressure
Cocking system	: cocking lever
Firing system	: semi- and fully automatic
Locking system	: rotating bolt head
Length	: with unfolded stock: 78.7 cm (31"); folded: 54.6 cm (21.5")
Barrel length	: 29.2 cm (11.5")
Weight	: 3.2 kg (7 lb.)
Sight	: aperture sight and front sight with Trijicon low-visibility markings; Weaver mounting rails
Safety	: combined rotary safety catch/firing mode selector on left-hand side of housing
Stock	: steel folding stock with synthetic pistol grip and hand grip with separate pistol grip

PARTICULARS

Fitted with folding bipod. Reduced recoil thanks to improved gas pressure system. Standard AR-15/M16 magazines can be used. Short barrel with special flash suppresser. The illustration shows a detailed view of the double drum maga-zine.

Z-M LR300 SA

SPECIFICATIONS

Caliber	: .223 Rem.
Magazine	: detachable magazine
Cartridge capacity:	10, 20 or 30 rounds
Magazine catch	: push-button in right-hand side of housing
Action	: gas pressure
Cocking system	: cocking lever
Firing system	: semi-automatic
Locking system	: rotating bolt head

Z-M Weapons, logo

Length : with unfolded stock: 91.4 cm (36");
folded: 66.7 cm (26.25")

Barrel length : 41.3 cm (16.25")

Weight : 3.3 kg (7.2 lb.)

Sight : aperture sight and front sight with Trijicon
low-visibility markings; Weaver mounting
rails

Safety : rotary catch on left-hand side of housing

Stock : steel folding stock with synthetic pistol grip
and hand grip

Z-M LR300 SA

PARTICULARS

Fitted with folding bipod. Reduced recoil
thanks to improved gas pressure system.
The standard AR-15/M16 magazines can
be used.

Steyr AUG Police 9 mm Para

CZ 2000 Assault Rifle Short

Index

SIG SSG 3000 Sniper

SIG SG550 Sniper

Information on the Internet

- Armament Technology:
  www.armament.com

- Benelli shotguns:
  www.benelli.it/english

- Beretta: www.beretta.it

- Blaser: www.blaser.de

- Browning Arms Company:
  www.browning.com

- Colt M16, etc.:
  www.moreammo.com

- CZ/Ceska Zbrojovka:
  www.czub.cz

- Dakota Arms:
  www.dakotaarms.com

- Firearm links:
  www.gunhoo.com

- Heckler & Koch:
  www.moreammo.com

- Lazzeroni Arms:
  www.lazzeroni.com

- Mauser:
  www.mauser-werke.de

- Mossberg shotguns:
  www.mossberg.com

- North American Int.Techn.
  (M16-.45ACP): www.nait.com

- Pauza snipers:
  www.specialoperations.com

- Remington Arms:
  www.Remington.com

- Riotguns:
  www.scattergun.com

- Ruger (Sturm & Ruger):
  www.ruger-firearms.com

- Russian firearms:
  www.izhmash.ru

- Russian firearms:
  www.mehzavod.ru

- Scattergun Technologies Inc.:
  www.scattergun.com

- Sig-Sauer:
  www.sigarms.com

- Snipers:
  www.cybersniper.com

- Snipers:
  www.snipercountry.com

- Sniperstore-USA:
  www.sniper-store.com

- Soldiers of Fortune:
  www.sofmag.com

- Steyr AUG:
  www.moreammo.com

- Verney-Carron:
  www.verney-carron.com

- Vihtavuori:
  www.vihtavuori.fi

- Winchester/U.S. Repeating Arms:
  www.winchester.com

- US Marine Corps:
  www.usmc.mil

- Z-M sniper:
  www.shooters.com/zmweapons

SIG SG551-1P carbine

Acknowledgements

I should like to extend my special gratitude to arms dealer, Verschoor, 's-Gravendeel; to Mr. R.H.G. Koster of the Milring Company, Amsterdam; and Mr. J. Winters of the antique arms shop 'De Donderbus', Rotterdam.
Thanks are due to the following persons and companies, listed in alphabetical order, for their cooperation.
Without them, this book might not have been written, or would at least have been less comprehensive.

- Accuracy International, P.o. box 81, Portsmouth, Hampshire, PO3 5SJ (GB)

- AKAH: Albrecht Kind GmbH & Co., P.o. box 310283, D-51617 Gummersbach (D)

- Armalite Inc./Eagle Arms, P.o. box 486, Coal Valley, IL 61240 (USA)

- Armament Technology, 3045 Robie Street, Suite 113, Halifax N.S. B3K 4P6 (CAN)

- Armscorp USA, 4424 John Avenue, Baltimore, MD 21227-1558 (USA)

- Auto-Ordnance Corp., West Hurley, NY 12491 (USA)

- Baikal/Izhevsky Mekhanichesky Zavod, Promishlennaya 8, Izhevsk, USSR-426063 (Rus)

- Benelli Armi SA, Via della Stazione 50, I-61029 Urbino (I)

- Beretta, Via Pietro Beretta 18, I-25063 Gardone V.T. (Brescia) (I)

- Blaser Jagdwaffen GmbH, Ziegelstadel 1, D-88316 Isny im Allgäu (D)

- Brown Precision Inc., P.O. Box 270W, Los Molinos CA 96055 (USA)

- Browning Inc. One Browning Place, Morgan, Utah 84050 (USA)

- Browning S.A., Parc Industriel des Hauts Sarts, B-4040 Herstal (B)

- Burris Company, P.o. Box 1747, Greeley, CO 80631 (USA)

- Bushmaster Firearms Co., 999 Roosevelt Trail, P.O. Box 1479, Windham, ME 04062 (USA)

- Calico Light Weapon Systems, 405 East 19th Street, Bakersfield, CA 93305 (USA)

- Chevalier Public Relations, One Centerpointe Drive, Suite 300, Lake oswego OR 97035 (USA)

- Colt's Manufacturing Company Inc., P.O. Box 1868, Hartford CT 06144-1868 (USA)

- CZ-Ceska Zbrojovka A.s., 688 27 Uhersky Brod Czech Republic

- Dakota Arms Inc., HC 55, Box 326, Sturgis SD 57785 (USA)

- DAW, 12400 Blue Ridge Blvd, Grandview, MO 64030 (USA)

- D & L Sports Inc., P.O. Box 651, Gillette, WY 82717 (USA)

- Antique firearms: De Donderbus, Oostzeedijk Beneden 231a, 3061 VW Rotterdam (NL)

- DEVTEK-Diemaco, 1036 Wilson Avenue, Kitchener, Ontario N2C 1J3 (CAN)

- DPMS (Defense Procurement Manufacturing Services Inc.), 13983 Industry Avenue, Becker MN 55308 (USA)

- Dynamit Nobel, Kaiserstrasse 1, D-53840 Troisdorf (D)

- Erma Werke GmbH, Johann Ziegler Strasse 13-15, D-85221 Dachau (D)

- Fabarm S.p.A. , Via Averolda 31, I-25039 Travagliato, Brescia (I)

- Fegarmy, Soroksari ut 158, 1095 Budapest, H-1440 Budapest PF6 (H)

- FN-Herstal, Parc Industriel des Hauts Sarts, B-4040 Herstal (B)

- Franchi Spa, Via del Serpente 12, I-25131 Brescia (I)

- Frankonia Jagd, D-97064 Würzburg (D)

- Gibbs Rifle Company Inc., Cannon Hill Industrial Park, Poute 2, Box 214, Hoffmann Road, Martinsburg, WV 25401 (USA)

- GOL/Gottfried Prechtl, Mierendorffstrasse 26, D-69469 Weinheim (D)

- Harrington & Richardson 1871 Inc., 60 Industrial Rowe, Gardner MA 01440-2832 (USA)

- Harris Gunworks, 3840 N. 28th Avenue, Phoenix, AZ-85017 (USA)

- Heckler & Koch GmbH, Postbus 1329, D-78722 Oberndorf/Neckar (D)

- Heckler & Koch Inc., 21480 Pacific Blvd., Sterling, VA 20166-8903 (USA)

- Hege/Zeughaus GmbH, Zeughausgasse 2, D-88662 Überlingen (D)

- Hellenic Arms Industry SA, 160 Kifissias Avenue, GR-11525 Athene (GR)

- Helmut Hofmann GmbH, Postfach 60, D-97634 Mellrichstadt (D)

- Hesse Arms, 1126 70th Street East, Inver Grove Heights, MN 55077-2416 (USA)

- IMI/Israel Industries Ltd, P.O. Box 1044, Ramat Hasharon 47100, Israel

- ITM Tool And Die, 5416 Detroit Avenue, Cleveland, OH 44102 (USA)

- KBI Inc./Armscor, P.O. Box 6625, Harrisburg PA 17112 (USA)

- Kel-Tec CNC Industries Inc. P.O. Box 3427, Cocoa, FL-32924 (USA)

- Keppeler & Fritz GmbH, Aspachweg 4, D-74427 Fichtenberg (D)

- Eduard Kettner, Mathias-Brüggen Strasse 80, D-50827 Köln (D)

- Knight's Manuf. Comp./Stoner, 7750 9th Street S.W., Vero Beach, FL 32968 (USA)

- Krico-Kriegeskorte GmbH, Nürnbergerstrasse 6, D-90602 Pyrbaum (D)

- L.A.R. Mfg. Inc., 4133 West farm Road, West Jordan, UT 84088 (USA)

- Leupold & Stevens Inc., P.O. Box 688, beaverton, OR 97075 (USA)

- MagTech/CBC, Av. Humberto de Campos 3220, Ribeirao Pires, SP Brazil

- Mauser-Werke, Postfach 1349, D-78722 Oberndorf a.N. (D)

- Milring, R.H.G. Koster, Geerdinkhof 672, NL-1103 RN Amsterdam (NL)

- Mitchell Arms Inc., 3400 W. MacArthur Blvd. #1, Santa Ana, CA 92704 (USA)

- O.F. Mossberg & Sons Inc., 7 Grasso Avenue, P.O. Box 497, North Haven, CT 06473 (USA)

- New England Firearms, 60 Industrial Rowe, Gardner MA 01440-2832 (USA)

- Nikon Inc., 1300 Walt Whitman Road, Melville, NY 11747-3064 (USA)

- PGM Precision, P.O. Box 29, 74334 Poisy Cedex (F)

- Redfield Inc., 5800 E. Jewell Avenue, Denver, CO 80227 (USA)

- Remington Arms Company Inc., 870 Remington Drive, P.O. Box 700, Madison, NC 27025-0700 (USA)

- Robar Co., 21438 N. 7th Avenue, Suite B, Phoenix, AZ 85027 (USA)

- Rottweil/Dynamit Nobel, Kaiserstrasse 1, D-53840 Troisdorf (D)

- Ruger / Sturm, Ruger & Company Inc, Lacey Place Southport, CT 06490 (USA)

- Sako Ltd., P.O. Box 149, 11101 Riihimaki (FINL)

- Sauer & Sohn GmbH, Sauerstrasse 2-6, D-24340 Eckenforde (D)

- Savage Arms Inc., 100 Springdale Road, Westfield MA 01085 (USA)

- Saxonia GmbH, Am Schwarzwasser 1, 08340 Schwarzenberg (D)

- Scattergun Technologies Inc., 620 8th Avenue South, Nashville, TN 37203 (USA)

- Schmidt & Bender GmbH, Am Grossacker 42, D-35444 Biebertal (D)

- SIG Schweizerische Industrie Gesellschaft, CH-8212 Nauhausen am Rheinfall (CH)

- Sommer + Ockenfuss, Postbus 1329, D-72258 Baiersbronn (D)

- Springfield Armory, 420 West Main Street, geneso, IL 61254 (USA)

- Steyr-Daimler-Puch AG, Mannlicherstrasse 1, A-4400 Steyr (A)

- Stoeger Industries, 5 Mansard Court, Wayne, NJ 07470 (USA)

- Stoner/Knight's Manuf. Comp., 7750 9th Street S.W., Vero Beach, FL 32968 (USA)

- Sturm, Ruger & Company Inc, Lacey Place Southport, CT 06490 (USA)

- Modern military firearms: Technisch Bureau H.A. Muller, Postbus 219, 6800 AE Arnhem

- Unique/Manufacture d'Armes des Pyrenees Francaises, 10 Rue des Allees, F-64700 Hendaye (F)

- Valmet Co./Tourula Works, P.O. Box 60, Jyvaskyla, SF-40101 (Finland)

- Verney-Carron, Bvld Thiers 54, Boite Postale 72, F-42002 St.-Etienne (F)

- Verschoor Wapenhandel, Schenkeldijk 9, 3295 EC 's-Gravendeel (NL)

- Voere GmbH, Untere Sparchen 56, A-6333 Kufstein (A)

- Walther Sportwaffen, P.O. Box 4325, D-89033 Ulm (D)

- Weatherby, 3100 El Camino Real, Atascadero, CA 93422 (USA)

- Winchester/U.S. Repeating Arms Company Inc., 275 Winchester Ave., Morgan, Utah 84050-9333 (USA)

- Wischo Jagd- und Sportwaffen GmbH & Co. KG, Dresdener Strasse 30, D-91058 Erlangen (D)

- Antonio Zoli Fabbrica d'Armi, Via Zanardelli 39, I-25063 Gardone V.T. (Brescia) (I)

- and others, who are unintentially not mentiond.

A special thank you too to my wife, Annelies Hartink, for her invaluable work editing the text and for her endless patience with me in addition to her devotion to our family that enabled me to continue writing in peace.